The Law of Third Sector Organizations in Europe

Antonio Fici
Editor

The Law of Third Sector Organizations in Europe

Foundations, Trends and Prospects

Fondazione TERZJUS ETS

bancaetica

fondazione finanzaetica

AIRC

Springer

G. Giappichelli Editore

Editor
Antonio Fici
Department of History, Cultural Heritage,
Education and Society
University of Rome Tor Vergata
Rome, Italy

ISBN 978-3-031-41743-6 ISBN 978-3-031-41744-3 (eBook)
https://doi.org/10.1007/978-3-031-41744-3

This Springer imprint is published by the registered company Springer Nature Switzerland AG
The registered company address is: Gewerbestrasse 11, 6330 Cham, Switzerland

Paper in this product is recyclable.

Foreword

The subject of this volume—the law of the third sector organizations in Europe—is particularly topical and relevant today. In 2022, when the Terzjus Foundation—at the initiative of its scientific director professor Antonio Fici—first conceived the idea of this work, the relevance that an analysis of the legislation on third sector organizations could have with regard to the orientation of the policies of the European Union was not really clear.

Up until that point, the Foundation had primarily focused its efforts on the preparation of a report on the situation and evolution of the law of the third sector in Italy, taking the important legislative reform introduced in 2017 as its starting point. That met with and, indeed, continues to meet with the original mission of Terzjus: to be a centre for the study, research, monitoring and proposal of policies regarding the law in the third sector, providing a service to the typical stakeholders (associations, foundations, social enterprises and cooperatives), as well as supporting the positive evolution of the practices of the public administrations, and, finally, contributing to the positive evolution of the relevant legislation.

The original structure which led to the creation of the Terzjus Foundation—which is composed of networks of Italian third sector organizations, large philanthropic foundations, public bodies and professional associations, with the support of a highly skilled Scientific Committee—has enabled the Foundation to draw from a wealth of academic, professional and operational knowledge as it carries out its research.

The positive response given to the Terzjus report on Italian third sector law has encouraged the Foundation to set its sights on the European level, which is also a perspective that is clearly specified in its own statutes.

This gave rise to the idea of devising a study to analyse ten different cases of legislation on third sector organizations at national level and three transversal contributions dedicated to a comparison of the 10 national cases and overview of European legislation; a comparison with the experience in the United States; and, finally, a deep dive into the barriers and incentives for the development of European philanthropy, written by the secretary general of Terzjus Gabriele Sepio.

The preparation of this work coincided with the adoption, in December 2021, of an "Action plan for the social economy", which was introduced by the EU at the initiative of Commissioner Nicolas Schmit and, more recently, with the European Commission's proposal of a recommendation which aims to ensure that the Member States both develop and implement social economy policies designed to favour inclusion, employment and social innovation.

In this context, a comparative study of what is happening in the major EU countries can only help to develop a better and more up-to-date identification of the actors which make up the diverse world of the third sector and of the social economy, in order to promote both its reinforcement and development within a Union framework that is less fragmented and more efficient.

Furthermore, it is quite clear that the adoption of an "Action plan for the social economy", as well as a recommendation, which presumably will be approved in November 2023 by the European Council of the EU Heads of State and of Government, constitutes important new elements in this area, as well as a turning point in Community policies which, thus far, had never fully recognized the importance and the specific nature of the social economy as a "third pillar" of our territorial, national and European communities.

Whilst hoping that this volume proves to be a useful tool in this context, it only remains for me to thank all of those who have contributed to this volume: the scientific director of Terzjus, Antonio Fici, for having conceived the idea and coordinating the work; the Banca Etica and the Fondazione Finanza Etica who have sponsored the initiative, thus enabling its realization; Fondazione AIRC for further funding; and, finally, Springer, the publisher, who, together with Giappichelli, kindly accepted our proposal to publish the volume.

The third sector is on the verge of a new era, and with this research work, the Terzjus Foundation has tried to contribute to the development of principles, orientations and policies so that it may become a key element in the lives of the citizens of Europe.

Terzjus Foundation, Rome, Italy
July 2023

Luigi Bobba

Preface

This book deals with third sector organizations from a comparative legal perspective, and as such it is the first of its kind. This is mainly due to the fact that third sector organizations are a relatively new category of organizations. It was first conceptualized in the United States in the 1970s but was almost immediately confused with the more generic category of non-profit organizations. This fact has not contributed to the development of the third sector. Non-profit organizations are characterized by a solely negative element, the non-profit purpose or profit non-distribution constraint. In contrast, third sector organizations are qualified in positive terms by the pursuit of a "social" or "worthy" purpose, which implies the performance of public benefit or general interest activities without a profit aim. This book helps the reader to gain a clear understanding of the difference between simple non-profit organizations and third sector organizations, thereby contributing to the conceptual autonomy of the latter from the former, notably from a legal point of view.

Third sector organizations are recognized by law, with this exact denomination, only in one European country, namely in Italy, where a Code of the Third Sector was enacted in 2017. However, the comparative legal analysis conducted in this book shows that organizations equivalent to Italian third sector organizations are provided for and regulated in almost all the EU countries. In particular, the category of public benefit organizations has the largest number of traits in common with that of third sector organizations. The fact that in many European countries public benefit organizations are regulated in tax law has circumscribed the knowledge thereof to small circles of practitioners and scholars. Public benefit organizations have, moreover, been largely ignored in the institutional debate, also at the European Union level, where other sector labels, such as "social economy entities" or "social enterprises", have had more success. The situation seems now to be partially different. Just some weeks ago, the European Commission released a proposal for a recommendation on developing social economy framework conditions, accompanied by two staff working documents, one of which focuses on the public benefit status in the EU.

The above explains why this book comes at the right moment, precisely when economic, social and pandemic crises are leading national states and the European Union to provide greater visibility, better operational conditions and more sophisticated support measures in favour of organizations that may help public bodies to satisfy the needs of their citizens, communities and territories, which otherwise risk remaining unmet. Third sector organizations are allies of the State and merit even more attention than organizations oriented to making profits for distribution to their owners. This now also seems to be clearer at the European Union level, as shown by the increased consideration given by EU institutions to this topic.

Being the first of its kind, one of the main objectives of this book was to collect the diverse national experiences, make a first comparison between them, and lay the foundations for further legal research in this field. The variety of denominations, sources and features found at the national level meant that it was first of all necessary to identify and describe the relevant legal framework on third sector organizations. This may justify a tone that at times is descriptive. But the book enables readers to now know what they have to seek and compare if they have an interest in third sector law.

The editor of this book wishes to thank all of the people and organizations that have contributed to its realization. First of all, the distinguished colleagues who have accepted to participate in this collective experience, hopefully the first of a long series. Secondly, the Terzjus Foundation, an Italian third sector organization working on third sector law, of which I am honoured to serve as Scientific Director, for having promoted the research that led to this book, as well as the main sponsors of the initiative, Banca Etica and Fondazione Finanza Etica, for their financial support without which this book would probably not have seen the light of day. Thanks also to the AIRC Foundation for additional funding and to our publishers, Giappichelli and Springer, for the interest shown in this new area of law by accepting to publish this book. Our hope is that the book may somehow contribute to the further development of all third sector organizations in Europe and beyond.

Rome, Italy
July 2023

Antonio Fici

Contents

Part I
National Perspectives on the Law of Third Sector Organizations

Chapter 1
The Third Sector in Belgium

Henri Culot and Joanne Defer

Contents

Henri Culot is a professor of Economic Law at UCLouvain (orcid 0000-0002-3421-6542) and a member of the Brussels Bar.
Joanne Defer is a lawyer and a member of the Brussels Bar.

H. Culot (✉)
UCLouvain, CRIDES, Louvain-la-Neuve, Belgium
e-mail: henri.culot@uclouvain.be

J. Defer
Brussels Bar, Brussels, Belgium
e-mail: joanne.defer@priouxculot.com

A. Fici (ed.), *The Law of Third Sector Organizations in Europe*,
https://doi.org/10.1007/978-3-031-41744-3_1

Abstract The third sector has existed in Belgium for a long time, even if it is not generally referred to by this term. It has always found legal structures to develop its activities and to foster its prosperity. This chapter shows how, starting from a rigid distinction between companies and associations, structures more adapted to the social economy or third sector have gradually emerged. Most of the chapter is devoted to the consequences of the reforms of 2018 and 2019, which have reshaped the law of enterprises, companies and associations. There is now a wide range of structures that can host social economy activities. These can be non-profit associations, which may engage in any economic activity, companies, which need not be only devoted to the enrichment of their shareholders, or cooperative companies, which can receive an accreditation in recognition of their specificities.

1 Introduction

The term ‘third sector’ is not commonly used in Belgium, but the reality it refers to is not unknown. During the nineteenth century, society evolved to be organised into ‘pillars’ (catholic, liberal and socialist), each of which consisted of institutions and organisations such as political parties, youth movements, mutual health organisations, trade unions, banking and insurance cooperatives, education networks, etc. All of these interacted with both civil society and the public authority. Although this system has evolved over time and is now largely outdated, there are still traces of it and there is a significant presence of actors on the borderline between business, functional public service and non-profit organisations.

Despite its importance, this sector has not benefited from a uniform and coherent regulation. There are, of course, many regulations specific to each particular activity, which will not be discussed in this chapter. Apart from that, the initiatives taken to grant some form of recognition or status to this sector—whatever its exact limits or definition—have remained *ad hoc* and have tended to be the fruits of legislative accidents rather than the result of a coherent policy. Nor have they achieved widespread social recognition: they involve a small number of actors (compared to the number they could potentially include), they do not last long before being abrogated or fundamentally modified, and they are hardly known to the public at large.

In practice, the third sector therefore uses a range of legal structures spreading over associations and company law. Although numbers vary according to the sources, the non-profit association is clearly, by far, the most commonly chosen social form for enterprises of the social economy.[1]

After giving a historical overview to understand the current rules (actions Sects. 2 and 3), this contribution will present how non-profit legal persons (Sect. 4) and companies (Sect. 5) can be used in the social economy. We will then outline the specificities of the cooperative company (Sect. 6).

2 Historical Background

2.1 *Summa Divisio* Between Companies and Non-profit Associations Prior to 1995

For a long time, the Belgian legal system either provided for instruments that were exclusively geared towards profit-making, or for purely non-profit purposes thereby theoretically ruling out any possibility for them to actively participate in the economy. The accredited cooperative company has been a notable exception since 1962 (see Sect. 6.2 below).

In this respect, our legal system was traditionally based on a *summa divisio* between commercial companies (*société commerciale – handelsvennootschap*) and non-profit associations (*association sans but lucratif – vereniging zonder winstoogmerk*).[2] Commercial companies were governed by the Napoleonic Code de Commerce and then later by the Lois coordonnées 'sur les sociétés commerciales' [Coordinated Laws on Commercial Companies] of 1935 (hereinafter, "CLCC"). Non-profit associations were only granted legal personality after World War I, when their functioning was organized by the Law of 27 June 1921 'sur les associations sans but lucratif' [concerning non-profit associations].

The intention was to maintain a strict divide between the activities that could be exercised by companies and associations. As we shall see, this rigid *summa divisio* evolved over time towards a more flexible approach to the activities and purposes of these legal forms.

Under the Code de commerce and later the CLCC, commercial companies were profit oriented. Article 1 CLCC provided that the purpose of a commercial company was to engage in commercial transactions (*actes de commerce – daden van koophandel*).

[1] De Gols and Leurquin (2020). These authors also provide valuable statistics on the social economy in Belgium, regarding, for example the size of enterprises, the level of employment, the economic sectors in which they are active, etc.

[2] Gol (2021).

Commercial transactions were those listed by articles 2 to 3 of the Code of Commerce (Code de commerce—Wetboek van koophandel). They include the sale of merchandise, factories and manufacturers, banking, exchange and finance activities, and many more. Those operations were presumed to be conducted with the intention of making profits.[3] Agricultural activities, medical and para-medical professions, legal professions, such as lawyers and notaries, etc. were not considered as commercial activities. This comes from an older tradition when these activities were deemed honourable for the upper classes and the nobility, were classified as civil activities and were supposed to be carried out without an intention of making profits.[4]

Commercial activities could be carried out by individuals or by companies. In the latter case, the commercial company was intended to pursue a commercial activity that would generate profits to be shared between its shareholders.[5] The common intention of the shareholders to seek and share profits was the very essence of a commercial company.

Until the end of World War I, non-profit associations were neither legally recognised nor regulated. The underlying reason was the government's fear that associations such as trade-unions, professional corporations, religious congregations or political associations could become powerful,[6] as well as the related concern that they could, over time, build up large estates without ever paying inheritance tax.[7]

It took 90 years for the freedom of association enshrined in the Constitution since 1831 to be implemented with the Law of 27 June 1921 concerning non-profit associations. This law provided that non-profit associations were forbidden (i) to exercise a commercial or industrial activity and (ii) to provide their members with any material gain (article 1 of the Law of 27 June 1921). They were thus supposed to pursue a "disinterested purpose" (*but désintéressé – belangeloos doel*), conceived as a social mission of charitable, educational, cultural, folkloric, sanitary or other nature, excluding the enrichment of the members. Moreover, this goal was to be realised without engaging in commercial or industrial activities.[8]

The possibility for a non-profit association to engage in an ancillary commercial activity was nonetheless foreseen by the preparatory legislative work and commonly admitted in practice,[9] provided that it was necessary for the achievement of its disinterested purpose and that the generated profits were solely allocated to the enhancement of this purpose (and not to the members of the association). However,

[3] Coipel (2020).

[4] Simonart (2016).

[5] Tilquin and Fanard (2008).

[6] Bogaert (2019).

[7] For more details about the historical developments, see Coipel and Davagle (2017).

[8] For more details about this definition and the numerous controversies that it generated, see Coipel and Davagle (2017).

[9] t'Kint (2013).

the definitions of "necessary" and "ancillary" and their practical implications generated intense controversy in doctrine and case-law, as well as abuses in practice.[10]

Many non-profit associations carried out commercial activities (almost) without any limit. This was a consequence of a judgment of the Court of Cassation in the case known as the "the priest's swimming pool",[11] linking the definition of commercial transactions to the intention of making profit. A priest operated a swimming pool as part of the parish activities. The Court ruled that this activity could not be qualified as commercial (although any other public swimming pool would be) because the priest did not seek to make profits but rather to serve his community. More generally, the Court held that the activities enumerated by articles 2 to 3 of the Code of commerce were presumed to be carried out with an intention of making profits. However, their commercial nature could be refuted in a particular case if it was established that they were not carried out with an intention of making profits. Since non-profit associations did not intend to make profits, it was nearly impossible to establish the commercial nature of their activities.[12]

This judgment of the Court of Cassation has been criticized because it led to legal uncertainty and, according to some authors, to discrimination between (i) the private for-profit sector on one side, and (ii) the private non-profit sector as well as the public sector, on the other side.[13] With this binary theory, the rules applicable to commercial actors were inaccessible to the private non-profit sector (i.e. social economy initiatives adopting the non-profit association form), even though they carried out the same activities.

2.2 *Inadequate Legal Framework*

This legal landscape proved to be somewhat ill-suited to the actors of the social economy sector who aspired to pursue a socially driven economic activity without the intention to make and distribute profits.

Indeed, legal uncertainty prevailed regarding the activities that non-profit associations could engage in. Without being able to precisely determine the meaning of "ancillary", social economy initiatives adopting the non-profit association form and pursuing a commercial activity other than ancillary constantly faced the risk of judicial dissolution (article 18 of the Law of 27 June 1921), and their directors the risk of being held liable. Furthermore, non-profit associations typically had poorer access to bank loans.[14]

[10] Garroy (2021).

[11] Cass. (1973).

[12] Thirion (2010).

[13] Thirion (2010).

[14] Lemaitre (1996).

Moreover, insofar as the core purpose of a commercial company is to seek and share profits, it could not be validly constituted for other purposes (including social purposes), and it could not validly act selflessly (make donations, for example).[15] Legal acts without an appropriate consideration could be declared void.

Consequently, neither the commercial company nor the non-profit association form equipped the actors of the social economy sector with the adequate legal structure to smoothly implement such initiatives.[16] However, such structures were needed by many actors of major importance, such as schools and universities, hospitals, charities selling various goods and services, and the like.

The cooperative company offered an interesting but limited alternative. The recognition of this company form in Belgium is linked to the increasing importance devoted to social issues in the second half of the nineteenth century.

The cooperative company was designed to be a collaborative framework between workers and/or customers and itself.[17] It was based on the idea that it operates in the balanced interests of shareholders (who are sometimes also workers or customers) to satisfy their professional or private needs. At the time of their creation, the (public) limited liability company (*société anonyme – naamloze vennootschap*) was designed for capitalists engaging in substantial business activities, while the cooperative company served as its counterpart for the poor who pooled their efforts to survive. The modest investments supposedly involved justified a much lighter regulatory framework.

The cooperative company evolved over time and became a useful instrument for some social economy initiatives, but it did not encompass all its possible forms. It was designed to satisfy its shareholders'needs; it did not necessarily extend to the pursuit of a social mission and, above all, it remained a company with the mandatory goal of making profits for the benefit of the shareholders. In practice, the cooperative company form was often diverted from its original ideal because of the high degree of flexibility offered by its regime.[18] The cooperative company will be further discussed in Sect. 6.

2.3 The Introduction of the Social Purpose Company in 1995

To provide a legal status to entities wishing to engage in commercial transactions without making profits (or limited profits only), the Law of 13 April 1995 'modifiant les lois sur les sociétés commerciales, coordonnées le 30 novembre 1935' [amending the laws on commercial companies, coordinated on 30 November 1935] (MB 17 June

[15] Cass. (2005); Cf. François and Verheyden (2021).

[16] Demonty (1998).

[17] Culot and Tissot (2018).

[18] Corbisier (2021).

1995) introduced a new instrument to the Belgian legal landscape: the social purpose company (*société à finalité sociale – vennootschap met een sociaal oogmerk*).

The social purpose company was a legal status that could be adopted by any of the regular company forms governed by Belgian law. In other words, it was a social variant to the existing company forms.[19] It was also thought of as a label signalling the particular purpose of the company.

Like any commercial company, a social purpose company could engage in commercial transactions. However, contrary to an ordinary company, the social purpose company did not intend to (significantly) enrich its shareholders: they could seek limited profits or no profit at all.[20] Its articles of incorporation had to specify the following (article 164*bis* CLCC which became article 661 of the Companies'Code):

- The social purpose of the company must be precisely described in the articles of incorporation. They must explain how the activities of the company will realize this social purpose. The main goal of the company cannot be the enrichment of its shareholders.
- The shareholders seek no financial advantage or a limited financial advantage only.
- In case of a limited financial advantage, the maximum rate of distribution of the profits cannot exceed the interest rate established by a Royal Decree in execution of the Law of 20 July 1955. Since 1996, this interest rate has been fixed at 6%, meaning that a maximum of 6% of paid-up capital could be distributed as dividends every year (article 1, § 2, 5° of the Royal Decree of 8 January 1962 'fixant les conditions d'agrément des groupements nationaux de sociétés coopératives et des sociétés coopératives' [laying down the conditions for the accreditation of national groupings of cooperative companies and of cooperative companies], MB 19 January 1962). This was coupled with a special tax regime whereby, up to a limited nominal amount, the dividend paid by a social purpose company was not subject to withholding tax.
- The social purpose pursued by the social purpose company can be social, cultural, humanitarian, religious, educational, environmental, and more.[21]

It can be achieved in different ways. Generally, the social purpose is achieved through the activities of the company. For instance, a social purpose company can employ former prisoners to foster their rehabilitation. Others prefer to allocate their profits to the chosen social purpose, in particular by making donations.[22]

- The board of directors must draft a special report annually to describe (i) how the company ensures the achievement of its social purpose and (ii) how expenses are

---

[19] Mercier (2016).

[20] Tilquin and Fanard (2008).

[21] Lemaitre (1996).

[22] Demonty (1998).

allocated to achieve this purpose.[23] This is conceived as a means to prevent abuses.
- The terms according to which its employees can become shareholders 1 year after being recruited, and according to which they lose this quality 1 year after leaving the company. It is a specificity of the social purpose company to be obliged to allow for its workers to participate in its capital.[24]
- The limitation of the voting power at the general meeting of the shareholders. Democracy being a fundamental feature of the social economy, voting at the general meeting may be implemented either by following the "one person, one vote" principle or by granting one vote per share with a limit of 10% of the voting power.[25]
- An asset-lock clause was mandatory. In the event of liquidation, after all liabilities have been cleared and the shares have been repaid, liquidation proceeds must "be allocated in a way that comes as close as possible to the company's social purpose". This means that they cannot be allocated to the shareholders, which is coherent with the "no or limited profit" condition.

This set of conditions, especially the mandatory workers'participation, was often regarded as too constraining, in view of the meagre (fiscal, reputational, etc.) advantages linked to this special status. The social purpose company therefore proved to be less successful in practice than anticipated.[26] Statistics are not easy to find, but sources refer to approximately 1000 cooperative companies with a social purpose.[27]

The non-profit association form was, in most cases, more appealing because it was mandatory to be eligible for various sorts of public support.[28] Non-profit associations also benefit from a favourable tax regime, in so far as they do not carry out any commercial activity other than an ancillary activity (see Sect. 4.5.1).

Later reforms have somewhat softened the traditional *summa divisio* between companies and associations, but not necessarily entirely in the interests of the actors of the social economy sector. This essentially implied the application of the rules of company law to the non-profit associations, or at least to some of them. For instance, in 2014, rules governing the auditing of accounts were made applicable to the larger non-profit associations. Non-profit associations also became subject to the material jurisdiction of commercial courts (in lieu of the previously competent civil courts).[29]

[23] Demonty (1998).

[24] Coipel (2008).

[25] Coipel (2008).

[26] Aydogdu (2021).

[27] De Gols and Leurquin (2020). Companies that are not cooperatives could also have a social purpose, but cooperatives were by far the most common form of social purpose companies.

[28] Defourny and Nyssens (2008).

[29] Gol (2021).

3 Reforms of 2018–2019

Two new pieces of legislation have turned the existing legislative landscape upside down: the Law of 15 April 2018 'portant réforme du droit des entreprises' [reforming the law of enterprises] (MB 27 April 2018) and the Law of 23 March 2019 'introduisant le Code des sociétés et des associations et portant des dispositions diverses' [law introducing the Code of Companies and Associations and containing various provisions] (MB 4 April 2019).

3.1 Reform of Enterprise Law in 2018

Firstly, the Law of 15 April 2018 replaced the concept of "commerciality", and thus of a commercial company, with the concept of "enterprise" (article 254, al. 1 of the Law of 15 April 2018). As a consequence, the Code of Commerce was replaced by the Code of Economic Law (Code de droit économique Wetboek van economisch recht).[30]

The definition of the enterprise is a formal rather than a material one. In other words, entities fall under the definition of an enterprise for what they are, rather than for the activities in which they are engaged. Subject to specific exceptions, the enterprise encompasses the following organizations: (i) natural persons with a self-employed activity, (ii) all legal persons and (iii) all other organizations without a legal personality, except if they do not intend to distribute profits to their members or directors (article I.1, al. 1 of the Code of Economic Law).

The concept of enterprise is thus much broader than the concept of commercial actor. All non-profit organisations are enterprises if they have a legal personality.

One of the main objectives behind this paradigm shift was to scrap the distinction between commercial operations and non-commercial operations, which became more and more difficult to maintain, especially when faced with non-profit associations that carried out economic activities as their main activities.[31] It was necessary to reconcile the legal framework with this reality.[32] The distinction between commercial and non-commercial companies therefore disappeared.

A consequence of the adoption of the new concept of enterprise is that the rules that previously applied to commercial actors now apply to all enterprises. This was nonetheless not as ground-breaking as it may seem since, as stated previously, many rules of the commercial economy already applied to non-profit associations. Among the most important changes are:

30 Garroy (2021).

31 Culot (2020).

32 Bogaert (2019).

- The extension to non-profit associations of the freedom to undertake any economic activity,[33] as established by articles II.3 and II.4 of the Code of Economic Law: "Everyone is free to carry out the economic activity of their choice".
- The application of insolvency law to non-profit associations. While previously only commercial actors could be declared bankrupt, now all enterprises can face bankruptcy (articles I.22, 8° and XX.99 of the Code of Economic Law).
- The competence of the commercial courts (renamed enterprise courts) for all matters concerning non-profit associations, which was already partially the case since 2014.

The associative sector was generally not keen on the qualification of non-profit associations as enterprises.[34] Within the ordinary understanding of the concept, an enterprise is characterised by an intention to seek and share profits, thereby enriching its owners. It refers, at least symbolically, to the world of business and capitalism, of which many non-profit associations do not want to be a part.

This conceptual revolution has nonetheless brought new perspectives to the social economy sector. Non-profit associations provided actors of this sector with a more adequate instrument to combine a social mission with an economic activity. An outcome of this first reform was to highlight that, contrary to an ancient belief, not all enterprises seek and share profits.

3.2 Reform of Company and Association Law of 2019

Secondly, the Law of 23 March 2019 introduced the Code of Companies and Associations (Code des sociétés et des associations – Wetboek van vennootschappen en verenigingen) (hereinafter, the "CCA").

The CCA was adopted to replace the former Code of Companies of 1999 (Code des sociétés – Wetboek van vennootschappen), which itself replaced the aforementioned Coordinated Laws on Commercial Companies.

The main objectives of this reform were a "simplification, flexibilization, modernisation and international mobility" of Belgian company law in order to make it competitive and attract more business within the territory.[35]

The new code gathers in one *corpus* the rules applicable to companies and those applicable to non-profit associations (as well as foundations). It therefore also replaces the Law of 27 June 1921 governing non-profit associations.

Albeit not all-encompassing, the convergence between both sets of rules was strengthened, especially in "Book 2" laying down rules applicable to all legal

[33] Culot (2020).

[34] Culot (2020).

[35] Dieux (2019).

persons. Many mechanisms and solutions that were previously specific to companies now apply to non-profit associations as well. Without going into detail at this point, this includes rules concerning day-to-day management, directors'liability, conflicts of interests, liquidation procedure, etc.[36] This assimilation certainly makes the legal form of non-profit association more suitable than before to the pursuit of a socially driven economic activity.

Above all, the new code introduces a new (but only partially different) distinguishing criterion between companies and non-profit associations: the distribution or non-distribution of profits. This means that the prohibition on conducting commercial activities (a concept that had been repealed in 2018 anyway) is no longer a distinguishing feature of the non-profit association. The new definitions of the company and the non-profit association based on this criterion is further discussed in Sects. 4 and 5.

4 The Non-Profit Legal Persons as an Instrument of the Social Economy

4.1 Non-Profit Association

4.1.1 New Definition of the Non-Profit Association

As previously stated, the Law of 27 June 1921 forbade non-profit associations from (i) pursuing any commercial activity other than that considered to be ancillary and necessary to its disinterested goal and from (ii) distributing profits to its members or directors.

Article 1:2 CCA henceforth provides for a new definition of the non-profit association. It states that a non-profit association is driven by a disinterested goal in the pursuit of one or more specific activities.

There is no longer any restriction to the nature of the activities that can be carried out by a non-profit association. Read together with the previously mentioned articles II.3 and II.4 of the Code of Economic Law which proclaim the freedom to undertake any economic activity, this new definition is understood as permitting non-profit associations to carry out socially driven economic activities or any other economic activity. Consequently, non-profit associations are henceforth in principle allowed to seek profits in the pursuit of their economic activity, even if the interplay with other types of rules (subsidies, tax rules) makes this less easy in practice.[37]

However, the same provision states that a non-profit association may not distribute or procure any direct or indirect financial advantage to its founders, members, directors, or any other person, except in pursuit of its disinterested goal. Here lies the

[36] Gol (2021).

[37] Denef and Van Baelen (2020).

new distinguishing feature between companies and non-profit associations: while companies must seek and share profits, non-profit associations can seek profits but are prohibited from distributing them directly or indirectly, under penalty of nullity of the operation.

The preparatory work of the CCA reveals that prohibited distributions encompass any distribution or capital transfer from the non-profit association, which are comparable to a dividend payment in a company.[38]

Disguised distributions, that is, any transfer of assets or value outside of market conditions, are also prohibited. Indirect distributions are defined by article 1:4 CCA as operations of the non-profit association by which its assets decrease or its liabilities increase and for which it receives a compensation that it is patently too low or non-existent.

This prohibition is mitigated by the explicit authorization to provide services for free or at advantageous prices when this falls within the scope of the disinterested goal of the non-profit association. Those advantages must be delivered within the limits of a normal fulfilment of its specified activities (article 1:4, al. 2 CCA).

As was previously the case, Belgian law also recognizes the international non-profit association as an alternative form of association. It is defined as an association within the meaning of article 1:2 CCA which has a purpose of international utility (article 10:1 CCA). Its legal personality is granted by a royal decree.

The international non-profit association is governed according to the same principles as its 'domestic'counterpart, although the CCA grants a higher level of flexibility to the founders and members of an international non-profit association in modelling its articles of incorporation and its operating rules. An international non-profit association is recognised as an enterprise which can undertake the economic activity of its choice, provided that is does not distribute its profit to its members or directors, even indirectly.[39]

4.1.2 Convergence of the Rules Governing Non-Profit Associations with those Applicable to Companies

When referring to non-profit associations, the term "non-profit" is increasingly replaced by "social profit", in an effort to express their "economic weight and their legitimacy as 'enterprises'".[40]

The CCA has introduced rules—drawn from company law—which make non-profit associations better equipped to participate in the economy. The main objectives are to make them technically efficient and to provide third parties such as creditors with an adequate protection.[41]

---

[38] Projet de loi portant réforme du droit des entreprises, exposé des motifs, *Doc. parl.*, Ch. repr., sess. ord. 2017–2018, n° 54 2828/001, pp. 13–14.

[39] Navez and Deckers (2020)

[40] Nyssens and Huybrechts (2020).

[41] Garroy (2021).

The following evolutions are significant:

- Harmonisation of the rules governing the liability of directors in companies and non-profit associations. Under the former regime, directors of non-profit associations were liable for any error or negligence (even the slightest) committed in the performance of their duties, regardless of whether this affected the non-profit association itself or third parties.[42]

They are now subject to the same provision applicable to directors of companies, which clarifies that directors are only liable to the company or association for decisions, acts or conducts that patently exceed the margin within which prudent and diligent directors in the same circumstances can reasonably have a diverging opinion (article 2:56, al. 1 CCA). *Vis-à-vis* third parties and the non-profit association itself, directors are liable for any damage resulting from a violation of the CCA or of the articles of incorporation of the entity (article 2:56, al. 3 CCA).

The amount of damages to be paid by the directors is capped to an amount fixed between 125,000 EUR and 12 million EUR, depending on the legal person's annual turnover and the total of its balance sheet. The directors do not benefit from the cap in case of gross negligence or wilful misconduct, among other exceptions. This provides a more comfortable framework for directors of a non-profit association to carry out an economic activity, considering the inevitable risks of business.

- Adoption of conflict of interest rules for non-profit associations. The avoidance of conflicts of interest was previously solely guided by good governance principles and potentially by the articles of incorporation of the entity. No hard law rules provided for a mandatory procedure to be observed in such situations.[43]

The CCA now defines a conflict of interest in a non-profit association as a situation in which the board of directors is called upon to make a decision in relation to which a director, either directly or indirectly, has a conflicting interest of a patrimonial nature. The CCA provides for a thorough *modus operandi* modelled on the one applicable to companies. It ensures that the best interests of the non-profit association and its members are protected, notably by excluding the conflicted director from the decision-making process and by imposing publicity measures that prevent the operation from being carried out in secret (article 9:8 CCA).

- Creation of an "alarm bell" procedure for non-profit associations. Under article 2: 52 CCA (which applies to all legal persons), if serious and consistent matters are likely to jeopardise the continuity of the legal person, the board of directors shall deliberate on the measures that should be taken to ensure the continuity of the economic activity for a minimum of 12 months.

The rationale of this rule is to protect economic exchanges and relationships (especially creditors) by ensuring that financial difficulties are not left without an

[42] Simonart (2020).

[43] Coipel and Davagle (2017); Simonart (2020).

appropriate response. This also applies to non-profit associations which are now enterprises like any other and will presumably gain greater economic weight.

- Creation of an elaborate liquidation procedure applicable to non-profit associations. The Law of 27 June 1921 only provided for rather sketchy liquidation rules. This new procedure resembles that applicable to companies to ensure that non-profit associations do not opt for liquidation to avoid bankruptcy and paying back their creditors.[44]
- Extension of the definition of day-to-day management. Since the Law of 27 June 1921 did not provide for a definition of this concept, associations had to settle for the narrow definition established by the Court of Cassation according to which day-to-day management was limited to the daily needs of the association and the accomplishment of acts that are both urgent and of minor importance.[45]

The CCA now defines day-to-day management as acts and decisions which do not exceed the daily needs of the associations, or which do not justify the intervention of the board of directors because of their minor importance or urgent nature (article 9: 10, al. 2 CCA). Therefore, it is no longer a requirement that the acts to be accomplished be both urgent and of minor importance: they can be urgent, of minor importance or both.

This broader definition, which also applies to companies, provides managers with a higher degree of flexibility and freedom to efficiently pursue the non-profit association's economy activity.

Possibility to appoint a legal person as a director of a non-profit association. The legal person is represented by a permanent representative (articles 9:5, al. 1 et 2: 55 CCA).

Some elements of company law have nonetheless not been made applicable to non-profit associations:

- Companies and non-profit associations are still governed by two different paradigms. A company is characterised by an association of shareholders who make a contribution. In exchange for their investment, they receive shares in the company. By contrast, membership in a non-profit association is not conditional upon an investment and does not entail the right to hold shares in return.
- Founders of a company must prepare a financial plan in which they justify the amount of the initial contributions considering the planned activities for a minimum period of 2 years (articles 5:4, 6:5 and 7:3 CCA). The financial plan must notably include a description of the activities, a description of the sources of funding and a revenue and expense budget. In the event of bankruptcy within 3 years after the incorporation of the company, if the contributions were patently too low to sustain the planned activities for a period of at least 2 years, the

[44] Simonart (2020).

[45] Cass. (2009).

founders may be held liable for the company's commitments (articles 5:16, 6:17 and 7:18 CCA).

The obligation to prepare a financial plan and the liability of the founders do not exist in non-profit associations since founders do not make contributions.

- As the non-profit association does not issue shares in consideration for contributions, rules governing transfers of shares do not apply to them.
- Likewise, rules governing capital increases do not apply to non-profit associations since they do not have a capital.
- As previously stated, an "alarm bell" procedure is now provided for in cases where the continuity of the non-profit association is jeopardised. However, unlike companies, the board of director does not have to call a general meeting to discuss the measures to be adopted and therefore the board will not be held liable for damage suffered by a third party for not convening such a meeting (articles 5:153, 6:119 and 7:228 CCA).
- Rules regarding control, parent companies and subsidiaries that apply to companies do not apply to non-profit associations (articles 1:14 sq. CCA). This also results from the absence of shares in non-profit associations. The concept of ownership remains inexistent in the associative form and, consequently, the logic of corporate groups has not been transposed to non-profit associations, notwithstanding the acknowledged fact that some associations are controlled by others and that, therefore, groups of associations exist in much the same way as groups of companies.

Overall, recent legislative evolutions have tended to move towards a convergence of the rules applicable to companies and to non-profit associations. This should make them more suitable to pursue an economic activity and certainly constitutes a more favourable framework for the implementation of social economy initiatives.

4.1.3 The Concern to Preserve the Core Specificities and Values of the Associative Form

One could, however, question whether this assimilation goes too far. Aiming to preserve the core specificities and values of the associative sector, some authors place a value on fighting against fake non-profit associations, much the same way as they do against fake cooperative companies (see Sect. 6.2). Fake non-profit associations are those which use the legal form of a non-profit association with the intention to enrich their members.[46]

In this regard, the CCA provides for specific sanctions to ensure that non-profit associations remain faithful to their intrinsic characteristics[47]:

[46] Culot (2020).

[47] Coipel (2020).

- Nullity of a non-profit association if it is not incorporated to pursue a disinterested goal but is rather established for profit purposes (article 9:4, 4° and 5° CCA).
- Nullity of operations in breach of the disinterested goal pursued by the non-profit association (article 1:2 CCA).
- Judicial dissolution of the non-profit association may be requested if it does not allocate its profits to its disinterested goal or if it distributes or procures a direct or indirect financial advantage to its members or directors (article 2:113, 2° and 3° CCA).
- An asset-lock applies to non-profit associations. If they are liquidated, the proceeds may not be allocated directly or indirectly to the members or to the directors. The general meeting will decide on the allocation of the remaining assets, failing which the liquidator will have to transfer the assets to "an allocation that comes as close as possible to the purpose for which the association was established" (article 2:132 CCA).

Some authors contend that the aforementioned sanctions might not suffice to safeguard the ethics of the associative form and that specificities other than the pursuit of a disinterested goal and the prohibition of distributions should have been considered by the CCA.

According to Michel Coipel, the functioning of the non-profit association must reflect the primacy of its social mission. Abstaining from distributions and procuring financial advantages is not sufficient, the "lifestyle" of the non-profit association must also remain sober and conservative. Coipel specifically refers to "unnecessary and lavish expenditures" such as excessive remunerations, visits to restaurants, luxury cars or international travel, which are incompatible with the values of the associative sector.[48]

In this regard, he argues that the annual management reporting obligations for larger non-profit associations should have been tailored to the specificities of the associative form, rather than being identical to the obligations applicable to non-listed companies. The annual management report should demonstrate how expenditures (including remunerations) contribute to the realisation of the social mission pursued by the non-profit association.[49]

Similarly, as previously stated, conflict of interest rules applicable to companies have been entirely transposed to non-profit associations, without considering that patrimonial conflicts of interest are less likely to occur than in a company, while moral conflicts are more likely to emerge and should have been envisaged by the CCA.[50]

To sum up, while a convergence of the rules governing companies and non-profit associations is welcome to enable the latter to actively participate in the economy,

---

[48] Coipel (2020).

[49] Coipel (2020).

[50] Coipel and Davagle (2019).

this should not go so far as a complete assimilation disregarding the specificities of the associative form.

4.2 *Foundation*

A foundation displays the following features (article 1:3 CCA):

- It is a legal person without members;
- It is established by a legal act by one or more persons;
- Its assets are allocated to the pursuit of a disinterested purpose in the context of the exercise of one or more specific activities which constitute its object;
- Like an association, it may not distribute or procure, directly or indirectly, any financial advantage to its founders, directors or any other person, except for the disinterested purpose determined by its articles of incorporation.

A foundation can be recognised to be of "public utility" if "it seeks to carry out a mission of a philanthropic, philosophical, religious, scientific, artistic, educational or cultural nature" (article 11:1 CCA). Other foundations are called "private foundations".

The main difference between foundations and non-profit associations is that the foundation has no members and thus no general meeting. It is a pool of assets managed by a board of directors. A non-profit association must have at least two members, but they are not under the obligation to make a financial contribution.[51]

4.3 *Mutuals*

Mutuals (*mutualités – ziekenfondsen*) are regulated by the Law of 6 August 1990 'relative aux mutualités et aux unions nationales de mutualités' [on mutuals and national unions of mutuals] (MB 28 September 1990).

They are defined as associations of natural persons which, in a spirit of foresight, mutual assistance and solidarity, aim to promote physical, mental, and social well-being.[52]

In concrete terms, their missions are provided for by law and consist of, at least[53]:

- Participating in the execution of the compulsory health insurance. For instance, mutuals process refunds of their members' healthcare provider consultation

[51] Coipel and Davagle (2017).

[52] Article 2, §1 of the Law of 6 August 1990.

[53] Article 3, al. 1 of the Law of 6 August 1990.

certificates. As refunds are provided for by the public social security system, they are identical for all mutuals.

- Providing refunds for the prevention and treatment of illness and disability, as well as allowances for work incapacity and the promotion of physical, mental and social well-being (i.e. supplementary health insurance). For instance, mutuals can provide their members with allowances to (partially) compensate for their psychotherapy sessions or their membership in a sports club.
- In a general perspective, providing help, information, guidance, and assistance to promote physical, mental, and social well-being.

All natural persons must be affiliated to the mutual of their choice in order to benefit from refunds and allowances. To remain affiliated, it is compulsory to pay a subscription fee.

Similarly to a non-profit association, a mutual is composed of two organs: a board of directors and a general meeting.

The board of directors is elected by the assembly which is composed of all the natural persons who are members of the mutual. Among other things, the general meeting defines the content of the supplementary health insurance that the mutual offers to its members.[54]

All mutuals must be affiliated to a national union of mutuals (*unions nationales de mutualités – landsbonden van ziekenfondsen*) which is an association of at least two mutuals. There are five national unions of mutuals in Belgium, some of which are historically linked to a political or philosophical movement: Christian, neutral, socialist, liberal, and free.

One of the main missions of national unions of mutuals is to supervise the proper functioning of its affiliated mutuals.[55]

4.4 Accounting Rules Applicable to Non-Profit Legal Persons

Non-profit associations were formerly exempt from any accountancy obligation, and thus from the obligation to publish their annual accounts (contrarily to companies). This leniency was explained by the purely "disinterested" conception of their purpose and the prohibition to engage in commercial and industrial activities, that applied at the time. In addition, accounting obligations were thought to limit the freedom of association.[56]

However, non-profit associations did engage in commercial activities and some of them carried a large economic weight (see Sect. 2.1). Moreover, a few scandals

---

[54] Article 9, §1, 4° of the Law of 6 August 1990.

[55] Office de Contrôle des Mutualités (2022).

[56] Kilesse (2004).

erupted involving unscrupulous uses of non-profit associations'resources.[57] It was thus necessary to foster transparency and accountability in the sector of non-profit associations.

With this aim in mind, the Law of 2 May 2002 'sur les associations sans but lucratif, les associations internationales sans but lucratif et les foundations' [on non-profit associations, international non-profit associations and foundations] (MB 11 December 2002) introduced a new accounting framework for non-profit associations.

This framework subjected non-profit associations to different sets of rules depending on their size. In that respect, stricter and more constraining rules applied to larger non-profit associations whereas smaller non-profit associations were imposed less and more flexible rules. The objective was to establish accounting obligations that are proportionate to the economic weight of the non-profit association, as is also the case for companies.

The CCA has maintained this distinguishing criterion, which applies according to different categories:

1. "micro" non-profit associations or foundations are those that do not exceed more than one of the following criteria (articles 1:29 and 1:31 CCA):

   a. annual average of the number of employees: 10;
   b. annual turnover of € 700.000;
   c. total of the balance sheet of € 350.000.

Micro associations or foundations must keep accounts according to a micro-scheme, which is a simplified version of the classic accounting scheme for large associations and foundations (articles 3:47, §4 and 3:51, §4 CCA).

2. "small" non-profit associations or foundations are those that do not exceed more than one of the following criteria (articles 1:28 and 1:30 CCA):

   a. annual average of the number of employees: 50;
   b. annual turnover of € 9 million;
   c. total of the balance sheet of € 4.5 million.

Small associations or foundations must keep accounts according to a shortened scheme, which is a shortened version of the classic accounting scheme for large associations and foundations, however more elaborate than the micro-scheme applicable to micro associations and foundations (articles 3:47, §3 and 3:51, §3 CCA).

[57] Kilesse (2004).

3. A subcategory of small associations and foundations are eligible for an even simpler accounting method, essentially in the form of a cash accounting (articles 3:47, §2 and 3:51, §2 CCA and art. III.82, §2 of the Code of Economic Law). This subcategory includes the associations or foundations that do not exceed more than one of the following criteria:
   a. annual average of the number of employees: 5;
   b. annual income, excluding non-recurring revenue: € 334.500;
   c. total of assets: € 1.337.000;
   d. total of debts: € 1.337.000.
4. Non-profit associations that do not meet the criteria to be defined as "small" or "micro" are commonly referred to as "large" non-profit associations. They must comply with the full set of accounting obligations.

In sum, the accounting treatment of non-profit associations illustrates the recognition of their economic significance and thus, the necessity to monitor their accounts in the same way as any other economic actor. It also acknowledges their specificities and is designed to avoid overburdening the smaller actors, which would negatively impact on the vitality of associative life.

4.5 Tax Considerations Linked to Non-Profit Legal Persons

4.5.1 The Tax Regime Applicable to Non-Profit Legal Persons

The Belgian Income Tax Code of 1992 (Code des impôts sur les revenus – Wetboek van de inkomstenbelastingen) (hereinafter, the "ITC/92") distinguishes between tax on legal persons and corporate tax.[58]

Under the ITC/92, non-profit legal persons (which are tax residents of Belgium) are subject either to the tax on legal persons or to corporate tax, depending on whether they "are engaged in profit-making exploitation or operations" (article 220, 3° ITC/92). This has to be established *in concreto*, considering "the concrete factual and operational situation" of the non-profit legal person.[59]

If "profit-making exploitation or operations" can be identified, the non-profit legal person will be subject to corporate tax on all of its profits. Conversely, if it is established that its economic activities are not carried out with an intention of making profits, the non-profit legal person will be subject to tax on legal persons.

There are, however, some exceptions to this rule, where non-profit legal persons will not be subject to corporate tax but rather to the tax on legal persons even though they make profits:

---

[58] For a general presentation of the income tax regime of the social economy, see Garroy (2020).
[59] Ceci (2020).

- Non-profit associations and other legal persons which are exclusively or mainly active in "privileged fields". Each field is subject to its own admission method which can notably consist of an accreditation of the non-profit legal person.[60] A limitative list is provided by article 181 ITC/92. It includes, for example, the following areas: (i) the protection and development of the professional or interprofessional interests of their members, (ii) education, (iii) the organisation of fairs or exhibitions, (iv) assistance to families or the elderly and (v) the certification of financial securities.
- With regard to isolated operations or exceptional operations (article 182, 1° ITC/92).
- With regard to operations that consist in the investment of funds collected by the non-profit legal person in the course of its statutory mission (article 182, 2° ITC/92).
- Non-profit legal persons that carry out an ancillary economic activity with an intention of making profits and non-profit legal persons that seek profits but do not implement commercial or industrial methods[61] in their activities (article 182, 3° ITC/92).

The purpose of this rule, which existed prior to the reforms of 2018–2019, is to avoid unfair competition between economic actors: all those seeking to make profits using commercial or industrial methods should be taxed similarly.[62] The application of these rules does not strictly depend on the legal form, as they apply to associations and to other legal persons.

Nonetheless, this analysis clearly depends on subjective judgements, which can lead to legal uncertainty and, potentially, to a difference of treatment between non-profit legal persons.[63] Indeed, without delving into detail, the tax base, tax rates and collecting methods vary between the two, with tax on legal persons being generally more favourable than corporate tax. In a nutshell, those subject to the former usually benefit in practice from a tax-free regime.

4.5.2 Tax Reductions on Donations to Some Non-Profit Legal Persons

In order to incentivise donations to non-profit legal persons which pursue a social mission, a system of tax reductions is implemented by article 145/33 ITC/92.

This provision contains a list of non-profit legal persons that can receive donations admitted for tax reductions and it includes, among others, universities, social services centres, museums, cultural institutions and institutions which assist people or countries in need (e.g., war victims, protected children, individuals with

[60] Garroy and Gérard (2019).

[61] The analysis must consider the commercial or industrial methods implemented by similar enterprises in the same sector.

[62] Ceci (2020).

[63] Ceci (2020).

disabilities or illnesses, development cooperation). Some organisations are directly covered by the law, others require prior accreditation by the Minister of Finance. Interestingly, this advantageous tax regime benefits institutions which are either public or private, and which may take the form of non-profit associations without this status being systematically required.

Under this tax system, a tax reduction is granted annually to each taxpayer that has made admitted donations. The tax reduction is equal to 45% of the total amount of admitted donations. To be eligible for the tax reduction, the taxpayer should make one or more donations for an amount of at least € 40 per non-profit legal person and per year. The amount of the tax reduction cannot exceed 10% of the taxpayer's net income or 392.200 EUR.

5 The Company as an Instrument of the Social Economy

5.1 A New Approach to the Purposes of a Company

As previously stated, a company is traditionally profit oriented. The shareholders first and foremost seek to make and then share the profits generated by its economic activities. Former pieces of legislation governing company law limited the purposes of a company to the procurement of a financial advantage for its shareholders.

A decision of the Court of Cassation of 28 November 2013 states that the interest of the company is determined by the profit-making goal of its present and future shareholders.[64] This decision was received with mixed feelings. Some rejoiced at the idea that the goals of the company were to be envisaged in the long-term, as indicated by the reference to future shareholders. Others regretted that the interests of other stakeholders and non-financial interests were not even mentioned.

Companies could, of course, acquire the social purpose status. However, this came with plenty of strict conditions to be fulfilled (see Sect. 2.3 above). Consequently, very few companies opted for the social purpose legal form.

The reform of 2019 repealed the social purpose company in favour of a more flexible approach to the purposes a company can pursue.

Article 1:1 CCA now provides that *one of* the purposes of a company is to procure a direct or indirect financial advantage to its partners [shareholders]. Two conclusions can be drawn from this provision: (i) any company can henceforth set other purposes for itself, including social purposes, provided that distribution to the shareholders remains one the purposes, and (ii) the profit purpose of a company does not have to be its main purpose; any company can limit the financial advantages that it procures to its shareholders.

This text differs from the original text of the bill which did not include the possibility for companies to pursue purposes other than profit-making and

[64] Cass. (2013).

distribution. The rationale of the member of Parliament who submitted the amendment was to advocate for a "true liberalism".[65] He argued that the shareholders should be free to set other purposes that would condition the realisation of the profit purpose.[66]

His amendment was also motivated by political considerations. He trusted that it would encourage the founders to consider assigning purposes other than profit – especially social purposes – to their company.[67]

A second amendment submitted by the same member of Parliament, which was also adopted in the final text, consists in the obligation to specify those other purposes (if any) in the articles of incorporation of the company (articles 2:8, § 2, 11° and 2:5, § 1, al. 3 CCA).[68] The objective is to provide directors with legal protection when they make decisions that take non-profit interests into account. Conversely, directors may be liable if they neglect to pursue those other purposes.[69] The other purposes indicated in the articles of incorporation may be modified subject to a strict procedure and a special majority of 80% of the votes at the general meeting (articles 5:101, 6:86 and 7:154 CCA).

Notwithstanding the foregoing, the profit purpose remains the so-called "legal specificity" of a company: it was officially reaffirmed that the purpose of a company is to distribute at least some of the generated profits to its shareholders.[70] In this respect, leonine clauses (i.e. provisions which exclude one or more shareholders from participating in the profits) amount to a breach of the profit purpose of a company and are forbidden by company law (articles 4:2, 5:14, 6:15 and 7:16 CCA).

To a large extent, the CCA has introduced a greater flexibility to the purposes a company can pursue, while remaining a company. Subject to the conditions above, the purposes of a company are now highly customisable.

This is certainly more practical than the previous social purpose company which was subject to overly constraining rules.

[65] Projet de loi introduisant le Code des sociétés et des associations et portant des dispositions diverses, amendement n° 331 de M. de Lamotte, *Doc. parl.*, Ch. repr., sess. ord. 2017–2018, n° 54-3119/008, p. 190.

[66] Amendement n° 331 de M. de Lamotte, p. 190.

[67] François and Verheyden (2021).

[68] Projet de loi introduisant le Code des sociétés et des associations et portant des dispositions diverses, amendement n° 332 de M. de Lamotte, *Doc. parl.*, Ch. repr., sess. ord. 2017–2018, n° 54-3119/008, p. 192.

[69] François and Verheyden (2021).

[70] Amendement n° 331 de M. de Lamotte, p. 190.

5.2 *Should Companies and Non-Profit Associations Be Kept as Separate Legal Forms?*

Considering that companies may now pursue purposes other than profit, including social purposes, and associations are allowed to engage in any economic activity, one may wonder if it is relevant to maintain two distinct legal forms.

Dirk Van Gerven pleads in favour of a single legal form which could either seek profits or not seek profits at all and would generally pursue a mixed purpose.[71] He believes that it is unreasonable nowadays for companies to limit themselves to a profit purpose. According to him, all companies should reconcile their profit purpose with social purposes.

While social entrepreneurship must certainly be encouraged, completely discarding the associative form for a fully customisable company form would, however, assuredly fail to win over the associative sector. It is very much attached to the legal specificities of the non-profit association which serve as safeguards of its values and as a label clearly signalling to the general public the goal of the legal person. In this respect, the prohibition of distributions and asset-lock are considered as essential: the associative sector values holding on to a legal form which can never be used as a means to enrich its shareholders or members.

6 The Cooperative Company and Its Accreditation

6.1 *The Cooperative Ideal*

While the traditional company primarily serves the interests of its shareholders, the cooperative company is ideally designed as a grouping of people with a "double quality": besides being shareholders, they are also employees or customers, and the company serves to satisfy their professional or private needs.[72] The cooperative company aspires to be a collaborative framework between its workers and/or customers and itself.[73]

This collaborative framework can take different forms. For instance, the shareholders can, at the same time, also be workers of the cooperative.[74] The profits are then allocated to those shareholders-workers as a form of additional remuneration. The shareholders of the cooperative can also be its customers or clients. In this case, they have a privileged access to the goods or services supplied by the cooperative.

---

[71] Van Gerven (2020).

[72] Gollier et al. (2020).

[73] Culot and Tissot (2018).

[74] Delcorde and Bernaerts (2021).

Alternatively, the shareholders can be suppliers of the cooperative who join forces to market their products.[75]

This cooperative ideal also entails a democratic functioning, sometimes translated into a "one person, one vote" principle to mark the difference from other companies where power is proportional to the shareholders' (economic) contributions.

6.2 The Issue of "Fake Cooperatives" and Their Accreditation as a Solution

As previously stated, the inception of the cooperative form is linked to the increasing importance of social issues in the second half of the nineteenth century.

Surprisingly, the principles and values of the cooperative ideal were not embedded in the first pieces of legislation governing the cooperative company. It was conceived as a flexible company form, which was loosely regulated and hence provided its founders with broad organisational latitude.

Moreover, no precise definition of this company form was provided for by law.[76] It was simply stated that the cooperative company is composed of a variable number of shareholders and variable contributions.[77]

The perks of the cooperative form included: low minimum capital requirements (compared to the public limited liability company), the possibility of appointing a sole director, the possibility of issuing shares with multiple voting rights, the possibility to issue new shares or to cancel shares without amending the articles of incorporation thereby making it possible to increase the capital without resorting to a notary, etc..[78]

For the abovementioned reasons, the cooperative company was soon diverted from the original cooperative ideal.[79] It was used by entrepreneurs who were solely interested in the degree of latitude granted, rather than in the cooperative ideal. They were referred to as "fake cooperatives" because their founders adopted this company form for practical reasons, without aspiring to the cooperative values.[80] This was not illegal, however, as the cooperative ideal was not translated into mandatory rules of company law.

By contrast, "real cooperatives" pursued the cooperative ideal, at least in the mind and the public discourse of their shareholders. They wanted their "specialness" to be recognized and protected and found it difficult to accept the existence of fake cooperatives with which they shared the same company form but not the same

[75] Culot and Tissot (2018); Gollier et al. (2020).

[76] Culot and Tissot (2018).

[77] Delcorde and Bernaerts (2021).

[78] Culot and Tissot (2018).

[79] Corbisier (2021).

[80] Delcorde and Bernaerts (2021).

values. They highlighted the importance for third parties to be able to distinguish between real and fake cooperatives.

The accreditation was presented as a solution to this problem.[81] The Law of 20 July 1955 'portant institution d'un Conseil national de la Coopération' [establishing a National Cooperation Council] (MB 10 August 1955) provides for the accreditation of cooperative companies and lays down five cooperative principles which are further specified by a Royal Decree of 8 January 1962 'fixant les conditions d'agrément des groupements de sociétés coopératives et des sociétés coopératives' [laying down the conditions for the accreditation of groups of cooperative companies and cooperative companies] (MB 19 January 1962):

- Voluntary adhesion, meaning everyone must be allowed to take part in the company if fulfilling the (general) conditions laid down in the articles of association;
- Equality of voting power at the general meetings, or at least limitation of any shareholder's voting power, to prevent any particular shareholder from controlling the company;
- Appointment of directors and auditors by the general meeting;
- Moderate dividends, called "interest rate" and only granted to the owners of shares;
- A discount granted to the shareholders (article 5 of the Law of 20 July 1955) (see more on this below).

The administration of the Ministry of Economic Affairs verifies that these conditions are met by the cooperative company before the Minister grants the accreditation.

In practice, a few cooperative companies were granted the accreditation, but the system did not encounter great success. It is more or less unknown by the general public and did not solve the problem of fake cooperatives for many cooperatives who considered themselves to be "real" but still refused to abide by (at least one of) the conditions of the accreditation.

6.3 The Cooperative Company Under the CCA

6.3.1 Characteristics of the Cooperative Form

In a renewed effort to tackle fake cooperatives, the CCA henceforward specifies the "characteristic values" of the cooperative form in its definition, in order to make sure that such companies are driven by the cooperative ideal.[82]

At the same time, the rules applicable to the (private) limited liability company (*société à reponsabilité limitée/besloten vennootschap*) were significantly lightened.

[81] Bogaert (2021).

[82] Delcorde and Bernaerts (2021).

This company is now characterised by a high degree of flexibility, greater than the one enjoyed by the cooperative company in its previous or current format. Therefore, fake cooperatives are both forbidden to remain cooperatives (due to the new definition) and—given their reasons for choosing the cooperative form in the first place—strongly encouraged to become a limited liability company.

The main purpose of a cooperative company embodied in its definition is inspired by the European cooperative company (article 1, §3 of Council Regulation (EC) No 1435/2003 of 22 July 2003 on the Statute for a European Cooperative Society (SCE), OJ L 207 of 18 August 2003). The CCA defines this main purpose as "the satisfaction of the needs and/or the development of economic and/or social activities of the cooperative's shareholders or of interested third parties, notably by concluding agreements with them concerning the provision of goods or services or performance of work, as part of the activities carried out by the company". It adds that "the cooperative company may also have as its goal the intention to meet the needs of its shareholders or of its parent companies and their shareholders or of interested third parties whether or not through the intervention of subsidiaries. It may also have the aim of promoting their economic and/or social activities through participation in one or more other companies" (article 6:1, §1, CCA).

Pressured by the (very diverse) members of the cooperative world, the legislator opted for an overly broad definition so as not to affect the development of the cooperative sector (i.e. to accommodate the effective situation and circumstances of any vociferous cooperative considering itself as "real") (Malherbe et al. 2020). It thereby implicitly renounced affirming a strong specificity of the cooperative company. In particular, it is important to state that the main purpose of the company is to satisfy its shareholders'economic needs, but this specificity gets completely lost when one adds the needs of "third parties", because obviously the very nature of *any* economic activity is to satisfy *someone's* needs.

Furthermore, the CCA provides for a series of mandatory rules as a means to safeguard the cooperative ideal. The existence of these rules explains why the cooperative company is now less flexible than the limited liability company.

- The articles of incorporation must specify the cooperative purpose of the company and the values that it stands for (article 6:1, §4, CCA).[83]
- Considering the cooperative company is based on an idea of cooperation, it must be incorporated by at least three founders and it must have at least three shareholders at all times (article 6:3 and 6:126 CCA).
- Equality between the shareholders being one of the fundamental principles of the cooperative form, all shares issued by the company must grant the right to vote at the general meeting (articles 6:19 and 6:39 CCA). It makes sense to prohibit non-voting shares considering that cooperative companies aspire to bring individuals together for a common project. Every shareholder must therefore be able to contribute to its accomplishment. Shares granting multiple voting rights remain

[83] Gollier et al. (2020).

nonetheless allowed (article 6:41 CCA), meaning that some shareholders can be granted so many voting rights that the unitary voting right of others becomes meaningless.
- To accomplish their common project, shareholders should be able to know one another. Accordingly, only registered shares can be issued by a cooperative company (and not dematerialised shares) (article 6:19 CCA). Similarly, its shares cannot be admitted for trading on a regulated or unregulated market (article 6:1, §2 CCA).
- Notwithstanding any contrary provision in the articles of incorporation, the general meeting can exclude a shareholder for justified reasons (article 6:123, §1 CCA). The objective is to protect the cooperative company from shareholders who do not share its values, although exclusion can sometimes be used for less noble reasons.
- The cooperative ideal entails that shareholders must be able to join and leave the company easily and smoothly. The procedure for issuing new shares is therefore simplified compared to that applicable to other company forms insofar as it does not require an amendment of the cooperative company's articles of incorporation before a notary. Regarding the exit of a shareholder, the CCA provides for a mandatory right to leave the company (article 6:120 CCA). The company must then, in principle, reimburse the shareholder's contribution.

The CCA also provides for non-mandatory rules which aim to facilitate the implementation of the cooperative ideal in the functioning of the company. In this regard, to ensure that its shareholders share the same values, the articles of incorporation of the cooperative company can provide for specific admission criteria. The articles may also provide that any shareholder that ceases to meet these criteria will have to leave the company and will thus lose his shareholder status (article 6:54, 6:105 and 6:122 CCA).

6.3.2 Accreditation of the Cooperative Company

The possibility for a cooperative company to be accredited pursuant to the Law of 20 July 1955 (see Sect. 6.2) as a guarantee that it is driven by the cooperative ideal has been maintained notwithstanding the new safeguards introduced by the CCA. Indeed, this law provides for criteria that are stricter than the conditions laid down in the CCA.

The CCA provides that a cooperative may be accredited if its main purpose is to provide its shareholders with a social or financial advantage in order to satisfy their professional or private needs (article 8:4 CCA).

Moreover, its functioning and its articles of incorporation must comply with the cooperative principles enshrined in the Law of 20 July 1955. Those principles are specified by article 1 of the Royal Decree of 8 January 1962.

- Voluntary adhesion. The Royal Decree states that the adhesion of the shareholders must be voluntary. The cooperative must be open to all and can refuse the admission of shareholders or exclude shareholders solely if they do not comply or cease to comply with the criteria contained in its articles of incorporation, or in case they commit acts in breach of the interests of the company. In that case, the company must explain the reasons for its decision.

- Equality or limitation of voting power at the general meetings. The principle "one person, one vote", regardless of the number of shares held by each shareholder, must be applied when voting at the general meeting of shareholders. Nevertheless, the articles of incorporation may depart from this rule provided that one shareholder does not benefit from more than 10% of the voting power. In addition, shares of the same value categories must grant the same rights and obligations.
- Appointment of directors and auditors by the general meeting. They may also be appointed in the articles of incorporation, but in that case, the possibility and the terms for revoking them must be specified.

The Royal Decree states that directors are in principle not remunerated for their duties. However, if they are, their remuneration must be determined by the general meeting, and it cannot consist of a share of the profits of the company.

- Moderate "interest rate", limited to shares. A dividend can only be awarded to the owners of shares, and it may not exceed 6% of the nominal values of the shares.
- Discounts for shareholders. If the financial advantage granted by the cooperative company to its shareholders is a discount, it must be allocated in proportion to the number or value of operations between the company and the shareholder.

The Royal Decree provides that part of the annual resources of the cooperative company must be allocated to the information and training of its existing or potential shareholders, or of the general public.

As a means to prevent abuses, the board of directors must annually prepare a special report to describe how the cooperative company has fulfilled the conditions for accreditation.

Besides the recognition that they are 'real'cooperatives, accreditation is favourable for cooperative companies in terms of taxation (SPF/FOD Economie 2022).

6.3.3 Accreditation as a Social Enterprise

A cooperative company may receive an accreditation as a social enterprise, if its main purpose is to generate, in the general interest, a positive societal impact for human beings, the environment or society (article 8:5 CCA).

The accreditation of a cooperative company as a social enterprise replaces the previous status of social purpose company (see Sect. 2.3). There are less conditions to be fulfilled, but while previously the social purpose company status could be adopted by a company of any form, only a cooperative company may henceforth be accredited as a social enterprise.

To be accredited as a social enterprise, a cooperative company must fulfil the following conditions (article 8:5 CCA and article 6 of the Royal Decree of 28 June 2019 'fixant les conditions d'agrément comme entreprise agricole et comme entreprise sociale' [laying down the conditions for the accreditation as agricultural company and as social enterprise], MB 11 July 2019):

- Its articles of incorporation must specify its object, which must serve to generate a positive societal impact for human beings, the environment or society.
- Similarly to social purpose companies, financial advantages that are distributed to the shareholders cannot exceed the interest rate established in execution of the Law of 20 July 1955. The interest rate is currently set at 6% of the shareholders'contributions.
- An asset lock is imposed. A departing shareholder may not receive more than the nominal value of their contribution. In the event of liquidation of the company, after all liabilities have been cleared and the shares repaid, liquidation proceeds must be allocated as closely as possible to its goal[84] as a social enterprise. However, if the company continues to exist but stops (voluntarily or not) being accredited as a social enterprise, the asset lock provisions cease to apply. This is considered to be a major loophole in the legal regime that would require the adoption of a new law to be fixed.[85]
- Directors cannot be remunerated unless the general meeting decides to grant a limited compensation or limited attendance fees.
- No shareholder can hold more than 10% of the voting power at the general meeting.
- Dividends can only be paid to shareholders after setting an (unspecified) amount which the company retains to carry on the necessary or useful projects for the accomplishment of the company's object.

The board of directors annually drafts a special report to describe how the cooperative company has fulfilled the conditions for accreditation as a social enterprise, as well as the activities carried out and the means adopted by the company to achieve its object.

Ultimately, social economy actors who adopt the cooperative company form can choose between (i) no accreditation, (ii) accreditation (pursuant to the Law of 20 July 1955), (iii) accreditation as a social enterprise, or (iv) both the accreditation and the accreditation as a social enterprise.

Even without considering the flaws in the drafting of the legal texts,[86] this system of rules creates more confusion than clarity and hardly enables the general public to get a clear view of the cooperative landscape. It therefore fails to fulfil the objective of regrouping the social economy sector under a widely recognized label.

[84] While the legal text refers to the object, this should more accurately be read as a reference to the goal of the company (Cools 2021).

[85] Cools (2021).

[86] Simonart (2022).

7 Conclusion

This chapter gives a contrasting picture of the third sector in Belgium. There is an active, developed and prosperous third sector. There are also legal structures under Belgian law to accommodate these activities. The legal system even offers a wide choice of solutions, which should enable everyone to find one that is adapted to their needs or situation.

However, both the evolution of the rules over time and their current configuration show that the overall design is not sufficiently coherent. One reason is probably the incremental nature of the construction: once a structure is created and used by some, it becomes difficult to repeal it completely when a reform is made. Another reason is clearly the considerable influence of social economy actors on policy makers, which ultimately leads to reforms and amendments implementing many particular requests, even if this is detrimental to the coherence or readability of the overall system.

Nonetheless, from a pragmatic point of view, the system generally works to the satisfaction of the relevant actors. Some of them would like to see some specific improvements (several of which would, indeed, be desirable), but no significant force is arguing for a fundamental (new) reform of the associative and corporate structures. The experiments carried out in Belgium and the ideas developed there—even when they fail—can serve as inspiration for other countries.

References

Aydogdu R (2021) Économie solidaire en Belgique. In: Association Henri Capitant (ed) La solidarité. Bruylant, Bruxelles, pp 387–403

Bogaert D (2019) Les entités non lucratives et le Code des sociétés et des associations. JT:757–767

Bogaert D (2021) L'entreprise sociale: une promesse du monde d'après? JT:329–332

Ceci E (2020) Les conséquences fiscales pour les ASBL de l'autorisation d'exercer toute activité économique. In: Culot H (dir) Le nouveau régime des A(I)SBL. Larcier, Bruxelles, pp 167–189

Coipel M (2008) Les sociétés privées à responsabilité limitée. *Rép not* XII(4). Larcier, Bruxelles

Coipel M (2020) Le nouveau champ d'action de l'ASBL et l'importante distinction entre son but et son objet. In: Culot H (dir.) Le nouveau régime des A(I)SBL. Larcier, Bruxelles, pp 35–70

Coipel M, Davagle M (2017) Associations sans but lucratif. *Rép. not.*, XII(8). Larcier, Bruxelles

Coipel M, Davagle M (2019) L'association sans but lucratif. In: Navez E-J (dir) Le nouveau droit des sociétés et des associations. Larcier, Bruxelles, pp 173–228

Cools S (2021) t Amendement: Asset lock bij verlies van erkenning als sociale onderneming. RPS-TRV, pp 970–974

Corbisier I (2021) L'ASBL belge par rapport à ses voisines française et luxembourgeoise dans le contexte du développement de l'économie sociale sur le plan européen: quelles perspectives d'amélioration du cadre juridique? , JT, pp 484–494

Cour of Cassation (2009) 26 February 2009. ECLI:BE:CASS:2009:ARR.20090226.1. Pas 2009: 592, TRV 2009: 444, RPS 2010: 298, note Simonart V Le délégué à la gestion journalière, le chief executive officer et les administrateurs exécutifs

Court of Cassation (1973) 19 January 1973. RCJB 1974: 321, note Van Ryn J, Heenen J Esprit de lucre et droit commercial

Court of Cassation (2005) 30 September 2005. ECLI:BE:CASS:2005:ARR.20050930. RPS 2006: 57
Court of Cassation (2013) 28 November 2013. ECLI:BE:CASS:2013:ARR.20131128.2. RDC 2014: 854-865, RPS 2014: 41–63, JT 2013:597–600
Culot H (2020) La qualification des ASBL comme entreprises et ses conséquences. In: Culot H (dir) Le nouveau régime des A(I)SBL. Larcier, Bruxelles, pp 9–33
Culot H, Tissot N (2018) Le cadre juridique de la société coopérative et les perspectives d'avenir. In: Delcorde J-A (dir) La société coopérative: nouvelles évolutions. Larcier, Bruxelles, pp 11–45
De Gols M, Leurquin E (2020) Het gewicht van sociale ondernemingen in België in kaart gebracht. RPS-TRV, pp 803–814
Defourny J, Nyssens M (2008) Social enterprise in Europe: recent trends and developments. Soc Enterp J 4(3):202–228
Delcorde J-A, Bernaerts M (2021) La société coopérative dans le Code des sociétés et des associations: un instrument de l'économie durable? In: Tilquin T (dir) Les instruments de droit des sociétés et de droit financier de l'économie durable. Larcier, Bruxelles, pp 363–415
Demonty B (1998) Sociétés à finalité sociale. Rép not XII(2/10). Larcier, Bruxelles
Denef M, Van Baelen B (2020) Sociaal ondernemerschap in vergelijkend perspectief: juridische variaties van een ontluikende paradigmashift? RPS-TRV:942–956
Dieux X (2019) Le nouveau Code des sociétés (et des associations): une 'anonymisation' silencieuse. In: Pottier E (dir) Het Wetboek van vennootschappen en verenigingen: (r)evolutie? Le Code des sociétés et associations: (r)évolution? Larcier, Bruxelles, pp 1–25
François A, Verheyden M (2021) Ceci n'est pas une société? Premières réflexions relatives au but lucratif à l'aune du Code des sociétés et des associations. In: Jafferali R (dir) Entre tradition et pragmatisme. Larcier, Bruxelles, pp 1149–1178
Garroy S (2020) Entreprise sociale et fiscalité directe en Belgique. RPS-TRV, pp 922–941
Garroy S (2021) Évolution des rapports entre association sans but lucratif et marché en droit belge: chemin de la liberté ou marche funèbre? JT, pp 466–471
Garroy S, Gérard X (2019) L'impact du Code des sociétés et des associations sur le régime de fiscalisation des revenus des ASBL: lorsque l'un part et l'autre reste. In: Herve L, Richelle I (dir) Incidences fiscales de la réforme du droit des sociétés. Larcier, Bruxelles, p 242
Gol D (2021) Le secteur non marchand et le Code des sociétés et associations. JT, pp 472–483
Gollier JM, Hollebecq H, Jacobs L, Flament S (2020) Coöperaties: missiegedreven ondernemingen voor alle sectoren – La coopérative: une société à mission, ouverte à tous les métiers. RPS-TRV: 899–921
Kilesse A (2004) Le nouveau cadre comptable des petites et des grandes ASBL. RDC-TBH, pp 323–376
Lemaitre H-P (1996) Sociétés coopératives et sociétés à finalité sociale. JT, pp 293–298
Malherbe J, De Cordt Y, Lambrecht P, Malherbe P, Culot H (2020) Droit des sociétés, 5th edn. Larcier, Bruxelles
Mercier S (2016) Droit des sociétés. Larcier Business, Bruxelles
Navez E-J, Deckers V (2020) Le nouveau régime des AISBL. In: Culot H (dir) Le nouveau régime des A(I)SBL, Larcier, Bruxelles, pp. 111–151
Nyssens M, Huybrechts B (2020) Social enterprises and their ecosystems in Europe, Country Report, Belgium. Publications Office of the European Union, Luxembourg
Office de Contrôle des Mutualités (2022) Unions Nationales. https://www.ocm-cdz.be/fr/particuliers/organisation-du-secteur/unions-nationales. Accessed 16 September 2022
Simonart V (2016) Associations sans but lucratif, associations internationales sans but lucratif et fondations. Bruylant, Bruxelles
Simonart V (2020) Le nouveau régime des ASBL. In: Culot H (dir) Le nouveau régime des A(I)SBL. Larcier, Bruxelles, pp 71–110
Simonart V (2022) L'Amendement: Double agrément des sociétés coopératives ? RPS-TRV: 59–61

SPF/FOD Economie (2022) Les avantages liés à l'agrément des sociétés coopératives. https://economie.fgov.be/fr/themes/entreprises/creer-une-entreprise/demarches-pour-creer-une/formes-de-societes/societes-cooperatives/agrement/les-avantages-lies-lagrement
t'Kint P (2013) Le droit des ASBL, tome I. Larcier, Bruxelles
Thirion N (2010) Les activités économiques sont-elles solubles dans la piscine du curé? , RPS, pp 144–159
Tilquin T, Fanard B (2008) Les éléments essentiels de la société. In: DAL G-A (ed) Le droit des sociétés aujourd'hui: principes, évolutions et perspectives. Jeune Barreau, Bruxelles, pp 7–73
Van Gerven D (2020) Editoriaal: Wettelijk doel anno 2020, een stap naar de afschaffing van de vereniging zonder winstoogmerk. RPS-TRV, pp 227–228

Chapter 2
The Diversity of Third Sector Organisations in Denmark

Karsten Engsig Sørensen

Contents

Abstract Denmark does not have an overarching act regulating the third sector. The only act that targets the third sector is the Act on Registered Social Enterprises, and that act only targets a part of the sector, i.e. those conducting commercial activities. In addition to this act there are rules in tax law and other public benefit schemes whose intention is to benefit the sector and consequently help to promote the sector. Denmark offers a wide range of corporate forms that are used in the third sector. With one exception, all these corporate forms may be used for third sector activities as well as for activities falling outside the sector. The most popular corporate forms for the third sector are the associations and foundations and the features that make them suitable for the third sector are explained.

Karsten Engsig Sørensen is Professor, dr.jur. at the Department of Law at Aarhus University.

K. E. Sørensen (✉)
Aarhus University, Department of Law, Aarhus, Denmark
e-mail: kes@law.au.dk

A. Fici (ed.), *The Law of Third Sector Organizations in Europe*,
https://doi.org/10.1007/978-3-031-41744-3_2

1 Zooming in on the Organisations Used in the Third Sector

The term 'third sector' is not used as a legal term in Denmark and the term is also seldom used as a general term. If used, the term is often used interchangeably with terms like social economy or voluntary sector. For the purpose of this chapter, the term is defined as organisations that are privately held, and thus not controlled by the public, they must be self-governed, have a social purpose, and distribution of dividends etc. to shareholders, owners, members etc. must be limited.[1]

Several attempts have been made to estimate the size and importance of this sector in Denmark. This has been made difficult by the fact that not all organisations are registered in Denmark. The largest database is the Central Business Register (CBR)[2] which contains data on several different types of legal entities, but only those non-commercial organisations that employ persons, are registered for VAT, or receive public funding need to register. Thus, there is a number of organisations belonging to the third sector that are not registered.

A study published in 2006 used the definition of a non-profit organisation applied by the John Hopkins University Non-Profit Sector Project (and thus includes all non-profit organisations, including those who do not have a social purpose) and estimated that it included a total of 101,274 organisations. Most of these were associations (83,000), but 8000 were self-owned institutions and 6200 were foundations.[3] The report also concluded that more than half of the work performed in these organisations was performed by salaried workers, and the amount of salaried workers was the equivalent of 140,000 full time positions.[4] A report from 2018 estimating the number of full-time salaried employed workers in the third sector in Denmark in 2014 set the number at almost 133,000.[5] This report did not include any estimate of the number and types of organisations used.[6]

---

[1] The definition follows partly that used in the report of Enjolras et al. (2018), pp. 33–42. However, in the definition used by Enjolras et al. they include all organisations that are non-profit, i.e. that do not allow any distribution to shareholders etc., whether or not they have a social purpose. Their definition would therefore include all foundations and associations since these have no 'owners'and are therefore, by definition, non-profit.

[2] The register is called Centrale VirksomhedsRegister (abbreviated CVR) in Danish and is available at https://datacvr.virk.dk/data/.

[3] The rest, approximately 3000, were countrywide organisations. Here the organisational form is not specified but, in all probability, most of these are associations. See further Boje and Ibsen (2006), p. 229.

[4] See ibid., p. 209.

[5] See Enjolras et al. (2018), p. 76.

[6] But the study did include (some) cooperatives and mutuals, ibid., p. 26. It is mentioned that cooperatives and mutuals are mainly part of the social economy in Southern Europe, which could indicate that these organisations were not included in the examination of Denmark. But the report does not specify the number and types of organisations that belong to the third sector in Denmark.

In 2014, the government adopted the Act on Registered Social Enterprises, hereafter referred to as the RSE Act.[7] Registration under the new act is voluntary for those enterprises that fulfil the conditions set out in the act. These conditions will ensure that the registered social enterprises belong to the third sector as defined above and will ensure that the social enterprise has a substantial commercial activity. The conditions are outlined below in Sect. 4.

A search in the Central Business Register (CBR) on 23 July 2023 shows that 938 social enterprises were registered.[8] It must be remembered that social enterprises need not register and indeed, given that the advantages of registering are limited, see further below, it must be assumed that not all social enterprises have registered.[9]

The 938 social enterprises registered as such in December 2021 used the following forms of organisation:

- Voluntary associations: 675
- Private limited companies: 92 [10]
- Associations: 75
- Enterprise foundations: 35
- Foundations and other self-owned institutions: 16
- Other forms of organisations: 20
- Public limited companies: 8
- Institutions belonging to the church: 4
- Cooperatives (with and without limited liability): 4
- Partnerships: 4
- Other companies with limited liability: 2
- Association with limited liability: 2
- Foreign corporate form: 1[11]

This adds several new types of organisations to those used in the third sector in Denmark. In particular, it includes private and public companies, partnership and cooperatives which are the types of corporate form most often used for commercial activities in Denmark.

[7] See Act no. 711 from 25 June 2014.

[8] The search was made to cover those registered under the RSE Act and having the status as either 'normal'or 'active'.

[9] Thus, a survey of Danish social enterprises published in 2018 showed that in June 2017 there were 637 social enterprises, but only 264 of them were registered under the RSE Act. Of course, it may be that by December 2021 all of those existing in 2017 (and a few more) had registered, but it is more likely that the figure may mean that today less than half of social enterprises register. See the survey by Lund and Sørensen (2018), p. 41.

[10] This number includes five private limited companies of the type called Iværksætterselskab, which is a corporate form inspired by the German Unternehmergesellschaft, i.e., a private limited company with a low minimum capital. This corporate form is being phased out, as the Danish government decided that it was often misused; see further Hansen (2019), pp. 667–686.

[11] The company in question uses the abbreviation R/H, which is not an abbreviation known to the author.

To sum up, a range of different types of organisations are used for the third sector in Denmark. To find out whether an organisation belongs to the third sector or not, it will not be enough just to check its form, as there is no corporate form that may only be used for the third sector. The only way we know for sure that an organisation belongs to the third sector is either to check its articles of association or charter or check whether it is a registered social enterprise.

In Sect. 3 the types of organisations most widely used in the third sector will be highlighted and then in Sect. 4 the regulation of registered social enterprises will be explained. First, however, Sect. 2 will outline how tax law and public schemes may incentivise actors in the third sector to use certain organisational forms or incentivise them to modify the organisation to become part of the third sector.

2 Tax and Other Public Benefits

An incentive to use certain types of organisation in the third sector or an incentive to have a specific purpose may flow from either tax law, public funded schemes or public procurements.

2.1 Tax Law

Traditional corporate forms with commercial activities will be subject to tax on the profit they make, and therefore tax law will not incentivise them to enter the third sector.[12] But there are special tax regimes for associations and foundations that may have that effect.

Foundations will normally be taxed according to the Foundation Tax Act, Act no. 700 from 20 April 2021.[13] This implies that they will, for most purposes, be taxed as commercial companies, but there are a few special features. Here, only those differences which may have implications for the third sector will be highlighted. Thus, a foundation is allowed to deduct from its taxable income distributions to a purpose defined as "almenvelgørende eller på anden måde almennyttige formål", see §4(1) of the Foundation Tax Act. Foundations will also be allowed to deduct

[12] Cooperatives are subject to a special tax regime on their commercial activities, see the Corporate Tax Act, Act no. 251 from 22 February 2021, §§14–16A, if the cooperative fulfils the conditions listed in §(1)(3) of the Act.

[13] Smaller foundations which need not be covered by either the Foundation and Certain Association Act or the Enterprise Foundation Act because they do not fulfil the requirements regarding capital and/or activities (see below Sect. 3.2) will be taxed according to §1(1)(6) of the Corporate Tax Act, see below in the main text. Today, it is not possible to form foundations that do not fulfil the requirements of one of the two acts, but there are still some older foundations that fall outside the acts.

'internal'distributions that are allocations to expenses within the foundation if these expenses have an 'almenvelgørende/almennyttigt'purpose.[14] Thus, it is clear that the terms 'almenvelgørende' and 'almennyttige' are central for taxation of foundations. The Danish terms may be translated as a requirement to the effect that the organisation's purpose is either charitable for the general public or benefits the general public. The Danish tax authorities will require that the distributions (or allocations to expenses) benefit a wider group of persons or institutions. If the foundation has the purpose of benefitting the employees of a specific enterprise this will not be a wide enough group.[15] Next, the purpose should either be to benefit persons in this wider group who are in financial needs, or it should benefit social, cultural, environmental, scientific, humanitarian, educational, religious, national purposes or help combat sickness. Furthermore, distributions to sports or animal welfare organisations may fall within the terms. On the other hand, distributions to political or trade organisations will not be deductible.[16] Therefore, it is clear that foundations are encouraged to distribute to such charitable purposes, but they are also encouraged themselves to engage in such purposes, since internal investments in activities that have the charitable purpose listed will be deductible.

Associations, self-owned institutions and foundations will be taxed according to §1(1)(6) of the Corporate Tax Act, Act no. 251 from 22 February 2021 if they are not among the institutions covered by the Foundation Tax Act, see above.[17] Taxation according to §1(1)(6) of the Corporate Tax Act presupposes that there is an organisation with some capital and a firm structure that allows it to be a tax subject on its own.[18] They will not be subject to tax to the extent that they do not have any commercial activity or do not receive taxable income in the form of dividends, interest or royalties. They will also be allowed to deduct from their taxable income any distribution they make if the distribution is made according to the purpose set in the article of association and are benefitting an 'almennyttig/almenvelgørende' purpose, see §3(2) of the Corporate Tax Act.[19] It is not only distributions of this

[14]See Bolander et al. (2021), p. 937, and guidelines published by the tax authorities, Juridisk Vejledning, C.D.9.9.1.1, available at https://skat.dk/skat.aspx?oID=2047579&chk=217592. The foundation will also be able to deduct amounts that are not distributed but are reserved for later distribution to a purpose that is 'almenvelgørende/almennyttigt', see §4(3)-(9) of the Foundation Tax Act.

[15]See guidelines from the tax authorities available at https://skat.dk/skat.aspx?oID=2047581&chk=217592.

[16]For a discussion of these concepts, see Hansen (2016), pp. 54–61.

[17]As mentioned, the Foundation Tax Act covers most foundations, but also a select group of associations. These are associations organising workers (unions) or employers and trade associations. For the special tax rules applicable to the later types of associations see Bolander et al. (2021), pp. 940–942.

[18]For a discussion of the requirement for an entity to be covered by §1(1)(6) see Bolander et al. (2021), pp. 859–863.

[19]According to the tax authorities, deductions will normally require that the articles of association stipulate how the assets of the association should be allocated in the event of a liquidation, as it should be made clear that they should be used for an 'almenvelgørende/almennyttig' purpose, see

kind that may be deducted, but also amounts reserved for later distribution for such purposes, see §3(3) of the Corporate Tax Act.[20] The tax authorities note that the terms 'almenvelgørende/almennyttig' should be defined in a similar way as the terms used in §4 of the Foundation Tax Act, see above. Thus, associations that have a taxable income will be encouraged to distribute to such charitable purposes, but contrary to foundations, there will not be an incentive to allocate money for such purposes within the association.

Tax laws favour certain non-profit charitable organisations by allowing taxpayers to deduct donations to these organisation—within certain limits—on their tax return. However, to be approved for this regime there are several strict conditions that the organisation needs to fulfil. The first regime is found in §8A of the Danish Tax Assessment Act, Act no. 1735 from 17 August 2021. This provision allows for deduction of donations up to approximately the equivalence of EUR 3000 for each donator, if the receiving organisation according to its articles of association, charter or similar is dedicated to an 'almenvelgørende/almennyttig' purpose.[21] As we have seen, these terms are used elsewhere in the tax legislation, but here it is stipulated that it is required that funds are used to the benefit of a wide range of persons that add up to more than 35,000 persons. Also, it is a requirement that the organisation receives donations from more than 100 persons annually. The donation must at least be DKK 200 a year and the organisation must have a capital (or annual income) of more than DKK 150,000. Of greater interest for our purpose is the fact that there are also some requirements for the management of the organisations that seek approval under this scheme. Thus, if it is an association this must have a board of directors that is not self-supplementing, i.e., it should not be the board members themselves who decide who should fill vacancies. For foundations it is a requirement that it is either a foundation governed by one of the two acts on foundations, see below, or if that is not the case, it is a requirement that the foundation has at least one member that is independent from the founder.

The Tax Assessment Act §12 regulates the deduction of concurrent payments to certain charitable or religious organisations. A person may donate up to 15% of their income under such a scheme. It is a requirement that the organisation (which can be a foundation, association or self-owned institution) fulfils all the requirements listed above for donation under §8A. Furthermore, it is a requirement that the organisation in its articles of association or charter has as its purpose to support an 'almenvelgørende/almennyttig' purpose. In this context, this means that the organisation should either (1) benefit a humanitarian purpose that helps humans in distress,

---

the guidelines published in Juridisk Vejledning C.D.8.9.1.3.2, available at https://skat.dk/skat.aspx?oid=2049763.

[20] However, if the organisation has both income from commercial and non-commercial activities, any distribution (or reserve) will first be seen as coming from the non-commercial activities, and therefore tax deduction is only possible if more is distributed, see §3(3) of the Corporate Tax Act.

[21] The condition for falling within the rules are detailed in Ministerial Order no. 1656 of 29 December 2018.

(2) benefit science (3) benefit the protection of the natural environment or (4) be a religious organisation fulfilling certain requirements.[22]

This means that organisations may have an incentive to make a charitable use of its funds in order to qualify for approval under one of the two tax deduction schemes outlined. This applies to a range of different organisations (but not traditional commercial corporate types), but it requires that the articles of association or charter is amended to reflect the necessary charitable purpose and requirements regarding the management.

2.2 *Public Funded Schemes That May Favour the Third Sector*

There are different public funded schemes that may benefit the third sector.[23] Many of these schemes are temporary, but two of the more permanent schemes are outlined below.

One of these more permanent schemes is found in the Act on Public Information, Act no. 1115 of 31 August 2018. The act regulates how municipalities should support different activities related to general education and different activities for children. There are two categories of support and for both it is made possible for associations to apply for support given that certain conditions are fulfilled. For instance, associations that seek support for adult education must stipulate its purpose in its articles of association (the act does not specify the purpose), must have a board of a least five persons elected among the members of the association, must allow members to be elected to the board, have their head office in the municipality granting the support and, finally, have an activity that is 'almennyttig' and continuous.[24] This example therefore shows that the public scheme favours associations that fulfil some basic requirements including the fact that they are 'almennyttig' which will indicate that they belong to the third sector.

Another example is found in the Act on Free Schools and Private Schools, Act no. 1656 of 9 August 2021. This act allows for support for setting up schools, as the state pays part of the cost of teaching, and the rest will be paid by the parents of the children attending the school. To receive funding, a range of requirements must be complied with, and these includes some requirements as to how the school is organised. According to §5 of the Act, schools eligible for support must be self-owned institutions. The institution must adopt articles of association that regulate how the school is managed and how it can be liquidated. But the Act also stipulates

[22] See §§4 and 5 of Ministerial Order no. 1656 from 29 December 2018.

[23] See, for instance, the overview of schemes favouring social enterprises in the report prepared for the Commission, Hulgård and Chodorkoff (2019), pp. 57–59 (available at https://doi.org/10.2767/7).

[24] See §4(2) of the Act on Public Information.

some basic requirements on how the institution should be run. First, it must be independent and may only use its funds for its teaching activities, see §5(2). Its purpose may not deviate from the purpose set in the Act, and in the event that the institution is liquidated any funds remaining must be used for teaching activities as approved by the Ministry of Education. The articles of association must be published on the webpage of the school and, finally, it is stipulated that the institution must be managed by a board.[25]

2.3 *Public Procurement*

Public procurement may be of interest for the organisations in the third sector which are willing to engage in commercial activities. If the public is allowed in their procurements to favour organisations that are active in the third sector, this may make it attractive for organisations to move into that sector. Even though there are some opportunities for favouring social enterprises in procurements, it seems that these are seldom used in Denmark so far.

The Danish Public Procurement Act, Act no. 1564 of 15 December 2015, has implemented the rules benefitting certain social economic enterprises found in Directive 2014/24/24 on public procurement. According to Article 20 of the directive (§54 of the Danish Act), for most type of procurements it is possible to favour enterprises which operate sheltered workshops and economic operators whose main aim is the social and professional integration of disabled or disadvantaged persons or who employ at least 30% disabled or disadvantaged workers. For a range of specific types of services (listed in Annex XIV of the directive), it is possible to favour some social enterprises according to Article 77 of the Directive (§190 of the Danish Act). It is stressed in the Danish implementation that not all registered social enterprises will benefit from §190, but only those that fulfil the following conditions set out in Article 77(2) and §190 of the Danish Public Procurement Act.

For public procurements that are not covered by the EU procurement rules it is assumed that it will be easier to favour social enterprises. However, these will mostly be small-scale tenders.[26]

[25] Also, a number of persons are barred from being a member of the board, namely those associated with the persons or entity that rent property to the school, see §5(8) of the Act.

[26] It seems that this question has not drawn much attention in Danish law, most likely because there are very few (and less important) procurements that are not covered by the directives. However, given that there is a cross-border interest in such procurements, EUlaw still requires that the fundamental principles of non-discrimination, transparency and proportionality are observed. But still, it would be possible to favour social enterprises to some extent, see also the case law of the Court of Justice of the European Union, in particular Case C-113/13, Spezzino and Case C-70/95, Sodemare.

3 The Most Popular Forms of Organisations

In Denmark the freedom to contract means that a wide variety of type of entities may be formed. Often these organisations are not governed by any legislation or governed by a relatively flexible legislation and this allows many different types of organisations to engage in the third sector. This is also evident from the fact that so many different types have managed to register as a registered social enterprise, see Sect. 1 above.

It is not possible to go through all the types of organisations that may be used and consequently the following is only an overview of the most popular types.

3.1 *Associations*

Associations seem to be the most popular form of organisation in the third sector.[27] It is a corporate form that is very flexible and takes many forms. There is no legislation covering associations and they are regulated by principles developed through case law and legal doctrine. Associations may have economic activities, but most do not. The associations do not have owners or shareholders, but members. Members are not entitled to any profit from the association, which is why these are, by definition, non-profit organisations. In addition, the members are normally not entitled to any of its assets when the association is dissolved.[28] Members will normally not be liable for the obligations of the associations but will have to pay for membership according to the articles of association. The influence of members and the management of the association must be regulated in the articles of association. There will normally be a general meeting of members and an elected board, but it is not a requirement (although tax law, see below, and other public schemes may encourage their establishment).

For tax purposes it is important that the association be recognised by the tax authorities as a tax subject as otherwise its members risk that it be taxed as a partnership. For non-commercial associations[29] most of the following characteristics should be present: it is an independent organisation, with a non-commercial purpose,

[27] The survey published in 2004 of non-profit organisations in Denmark established that at the time there were more than 101,000 associations. Many of these are undoubtably small and far from all may belong to the third sector as their purpose may not be social. This is also indicated in the survey where it was calculated that 57% of the associations were engaged in cultural activities, sports and hobbies, and therefore most likely do not qualify as belonging to the third sector. However, 11% of the associations were engaged in politics, religion, environment and 9% were engaged in social and health related activities, see Boje and Ibsen (2006), pp. 228–229. It is likely that a large part of the two latter groups will belong to the third sector.

[28] See Hasselbalch (1997), pp. 69–71.

[29] Commercial associations need to register, see below, and once that happens, they are recognised by the tax authority.

with articles of association adopted at a meeting of the members, and have a management elected by the members.[30]

Associations do not need to register when they are formed unless they have a commercial activity.[31] They do, however, have to register in the CBR if they employ persons, have a VAT number, or receive public funding. A total of 118, 435 were registered in the CBR database by 23 July 2023, but the actual number of associations may be twice that.[32] We do not know precisely how many associations belong to the third sector, apart from the 636 that have registered as a social enterprise, see Sect. 1 above.

3.2 *Foundations*

Foundations have existed in Denmark for centuries, but foundations used for conducting enterprises appeared in the late nineteenth century.[33] Since 1984, foundations have been regulated by two acts; the Act on Foundations and certain Associations, Act no. 2020 of 11 December 2020 and the Act on Enterprise Foundations, Act no. 984 of 20 September 2019. The regulation found in the two acts has many similarities, but there are differences. The following will focus on the main features of the two acts.

To become a foundation, a number of requirements must be fulfilled. This includes, for enterprise foundations, a minimum capital of DKK 300,000, a requirement of a commercial activity which should raise an annual profit of at least DKK 250,000 and amount to more than 10% of the annual profit of the foundation. This commercial activity can be conducted in the foundation or in another entity controlled by the foundation. For other foundations the requirement is that they should have a minimum capital of one million DKK.[34]

A key element is that the foundation should be separated from the founder (and other major contributors to the foundation). To ensure this, there are additional requirements regarding the purpose of the foundation, its management, and finally asset locks that must be observed.

The charter of the foundation must specify its purpose (activity purpose) and state how it will distribute funds (distribution purpose).[35]

---

[30] For the full list of characteristics, see Werlauff (2019), pp. 176–177.

[31] For associations with a commercial activity and limited liability there is a duty to register with the Business Authority, see Act on Certain Commercial Enterprises, Act no. 249 of 1 February 2021.

[32] The survey of associations published in 2006 concluded that at that time only 45% of all associations were registered in the CBR, see Boje and Ibsen (2006), p. 172.

[33] See the historical account in the government report, 970/1982, p 23. One of the first enterprise foundations was the Carlsberg Foundation established in 1876.

[34] See §8 of the Act on Foundations and Certain Associations.

[35] See §27(1) of the Act on Enterprise Foundations and §6 of the Act on Foundations and Certain Associations.

The activity purpose for enterprise foundations needs to include the commercial activity pursued, but for other foundations there are few requirements. Thus, the purpose need not cover a social purpose.

The distribution purpose should either be to benefit certain persons, a specific sector, an activity, or a social purpose. Consequently, the founder(s) is(are) relatively free to formulate this purpose, except for two distinct restrictions set in the law. According to §28 of the Act on Enterprise Foundations and §7 of the Act on Foundations and certain Associations, if members of certain families are granted preference in distributions, it may only cover those persons living at the time the foundation is formed and one unborn generation. Distribution may not be made to the founder(s), any member of management of the foundation, nor its accountant. However, usual remuneration for the latter are allowed.[36] Consequently, a founder cannot favour themselves and only favour their family for a foreseeable time span. On the other hand, it is clear that the acts do not require that distribution is made to a social purpose, but as discussed above tax law may incentivise this.

Management of a foundation must normally consist of a board of at least three directors.[37] The board of directors should be appointed according to the rules set out in the charter of the enterprise foundation. Consequently, the founder(s) may choose different solutions, but there are some restrictions. The most important are:

- The founder(s) (and their close relatives) must not form the majority of the board.[38]
- To ensure the foundation's independence, it is required that at least one of the three board members should be independent of the founder(s) (and family). If there are more than three members of the board of an enterprise foundation, more than one member should be independent.[39]
- For enterprise foundations, the board members must not be appointed by the management of the company controlled by the foundation and, normally, the chair and vice-chair of the board must not be a director of the controlled company, see §37(4)-(5) of the Act on enterprise foundations.
- An indirect limitation may apply when the distribution purpose includes the member of a family or specific persons since no distribution must be made to

[36] See §87 of the Act on Enterprise Foundations and §31 of the Act on Foundations and Certain Associations.

[37] See §37(1) of the Act on Enterprise Foundations and §11 of the Act on Foundations and Certain Associations. Additionally, in enterprise foundations the board must contain representatives of the employees if the number of employees exceeds 35 persons, see § 64 of the Act on Enterprise Foundations.

[38] See §40 of the Act on Enterprise Foundations and §16 of the Act on Foundations and Certain Associations. If the foundation is formed by a business, the same applies to the person who directly or indirectly owns more than half the votes or shares in the company.

[39] This requirement is not found in the act but is taken from the definition of foundations by the Danish Business Authority, see Vejledning om Ledelsen i de erhvervsdrivende fonde, available at https://erhvervsstyrelsen.dk/vejledning-ledelsen-i-de-erhvervsdrivende-fonde.

anyone serving in management of the foundation. Therefore, persons entitled to distributions will have to forego distributions if they enter management.[40]

The first board is normally stipulated by the founder(s) (subject to approval by the foundation authority), but additional members are often appointed by the board itself or by outside persons, organisations, or public authorities. However, the charter may also set up a committee that may appoint up to half of the board members.

Even so, it appears that the board may not be fully independent of the founder in its composition. However, the independence of foundations is ensured by several additional requirements. First, the Act on Enterprise Foundations stresses that the board of directors has a duty to promote the interests and purpose of the foundation, see §38 of the Act on Enterprise Foundations.[41] Second, independence is ensured by the fact that only the foundation authority may dismiss a board member.[42] So the founder(s) holds no power over a board member once appointed.

The board has the overall responsibility of running the foundation, but it may appoint one or more managing director(s) to handle the day-to-day business.[43]

The board of directors is responsible for distributing funds. There is no duty to distribute a specific part of the annual profit as the board is allowed to make reasonable reserves for future needs.[44] However, if the capital of the foundation is clearly misbalanced with its distributions, the foundation authority may request or even require additional distributions to be made.[45] Furthermore, tax law encourages certain distributions, see Sect. 2.1 above.

It is only possible to make distributions according to the distribution purpose specified in the charter. This restriction applies to all distribution disregarding the form. As mentioned, no distribution to the founders and management is allowed

[40] See §87 of the Act on Enterprise Foundations and §31 of the Act on Foundations and Certain Associations.

[41] It is also made clear by the foundation authorities that the board must not take instructions from anyone outside the board, including, of course, the founder (and family), see Vejledning om Opmærksomhedspunkter for bestyrelsesmedlemmer i erhvervsdrivende fonde, available at https://erhvervsstyrelsen.dk/vejledning-opmaerksomhedspunkter-bestyrelsesmedlemmer-i-erhvervsdrivende-fonde.

[42] See §45 of the Act on Enterprise Foundations and §14 of the Act on Foundations and Certain Associations. Board members should resign if they become seriously ill, go bankrupt, or if they prove to be 'unworthy', see §44 and §13 of the two acts respectively. If they do not do so, they may be dismissed by the foundation authority.

[43] See §37 of the Act on Enterprise Foundations and §11(3) of the Act on Foundations and Certain Associations.

[44] See §77 of the Act on Enterprise Foundations and §29(2) of the Act on Foundations and Certain Associations.

[45] See § 9 of the Act on Enterprise Foundations and §30 of the Act on Foundations and Certain Associations.

(apart from remuneration), and it is stipulated that this prevents the foundation from offering any loan or providing security for loans to the founders and management.[46]

The remuneration of the board must not exceed what is customary given the amount of work and the financial position of the foundation.[47] The intention is to prevent excessive remuneration.

3.3 *Self-Owned Institutions*

The survey published in 2006 indicated that there were a high number of self-owned institutions (8000). Many of these will be controlled by the public, but 27% of these were private schools supported under the scheme mentioned in Sect. 2.2, and these are likely to belong to the third sector.[48]

The term 'self-owned institutions'may be rather unique to Denmark.[49] It is clear that this term also includes foundations, as foundations are self-owned. Even though self-owned institutions have many similarities with foundations, they may to some degree differ from foundations as these are defined in the two acts on foundations.[50] But even though they may to some extent differ from foundations, they will be governed by the rules found in the two acts on foundations, see above.[51]

3.4 *Private Limited Companies*

This company form is the limited liability company form most widely used in Denmark for for-profit activities. Even though profit is normally distributed among the shareholders in these companies, it is possible in the articles of association to modify this to allow the company to register as a social enterprise.[52] Although the activities of a private limited company are, by definition, commercial, there is

[46]See §87(2)–(3) of the Act on Enterprise Foundations and §31(2) of the Act on Foundations and Certain Associations.

[47]See §49 of the Act on Enterprise Foundations and §18 of the Act on Foundations and Certain Associations.

[48]See Boje and Ibsen (2006), p. 228.

[49]See Boje and Ibsen (2006), p. 97.

[50]For a more detailed account of this question see Feldthusen and Poulsen (2012), pp. 215–224 and the report published by the Danish Ministry of Finance in 2009 entitled Selvejende institutioner – styring, regulering og effektivitet (the report is available at https://fm.dk/udgivelser/2009/april/selvejende-institutioner-styring-regulering-og-effektivitet/).

[51]See §1(1) of the two acts.

[52]Sørensen and Neville (2014), p. 281. As discussed on page 286 of the article, a transition from normal profit allocation to an allocation benefiting other stakeholders or a social purpose will require a majority of 9/10 of the shareholders.

nothing to prevent the company from adopting an overall social purpose and thereby become part of the third sector.[53] It must be assumed that private limited companies only constitute a very small fraction of the third sector, but this company form does make up for a more substantial part of the registered social enterprises, see above Sect. 1.

The company form shares many features with private limited companies found in other continental European countries.

4 Registered Social Enterprises[54]

Even though it is only a fraction of the third sector entities that are registered as a social enterprise under the RSE Act, these are interesting because they are the only enterprises that clearly signal that they belong to the third sector.

To register, the enterprise must fulfil the following conditions, see §5 of the RSE Act:

- It must have a social purpose.
- It must be commercially operated.
- It must be independent from the public sector.
- It must act inclusively and responsibly in its activities, and.
- It must have a social approach to the management of its profits.

Each of the conditions will be briefly discussed.

The text of the act does not specify how to comply with the requirements for the *social purpose*, but some clarification can be found in the preparatory documents of the Act. First, it is stated that 'social purpose' is to be understood as a requirement that the undertaking has social, employment, health, environmental or cultural aims. The preparatory documents also indicate that a registered social enterprise could be working either *for* a specific target group or cause, or *with* a specific target group or cause. The first would be the case if an enterprise worked to improve the conditions for a group (*e.g.*, drug abusers) or cause (*e.g.* the environment) by, *e.g.*, making products that benefit drug abusers or the environment, by running the business in a special way, or by using part of the profit for the benefit of the target group or cause. To work with a group or cause could for example, involve employing or educating persons with a specific disability. The social purpose would normally be adopted in the articles of association or similar founding documents of the entity.

[53] It may be questioned whether the management may pursue the social purpose to the extent where it threatens the existence of the company and its business, see the discussion by Mollerup and Akbatani (2021), pp. 70–74. But even if that is the case, this evidently does not prevent the companies from committing to a social purpose.

[54] The following is based on the report I prepared for the IACL on the topic: The social enterprise: a new form of the business enterprise?

The condition that it is *commercially operated* should ensure that it is indeed an enterprise. This does not mean that the majority of the entity's income must derive from commercial activities, but it is required that the commercial activities should be a significant element. Thus, even though an enterprise receives public funding or donations from different sources it may still qualify for registration if it has profits generated by from commercial activities that amount to at least 10% of all profit raised. Normally, the fulfilment of this condition is documented by submitting the latest annual report, but if such a report is not available (for instance because the enterprise has been recently formed) a budget for the coming 3–5 years may be used.[55]

The condition that the enterprise should be *independent from the public* sector means that the public should not influence the management of the company. Thus, for instance, if the public appoints the majority of the management the conditions will not be fulfilled. If the enterprise receives a large part of its income from the public, it may also be controlled de facto by the public and therefore cannot register.[56]

The requirement to *act inclusively and responsibly* in its activities is interpreted as a requirement that the entity involves stakeholders as well as incorporates the social purpose in its business strategy and activities. In order to be registered, the entity should explain how it will be inclusive and responsible in its activities, and this description should be updated in the annual report, see below.

Finally, the requirement that the entity should use its *profits primarily for social purposes* indicates that it should only allow a limited dividend to the shareholders/ owners, see below. Instead, profits may be used either to reinvest in the social enterprise, invest in other registered social enterprises, or by donating the profit to other organisations which are committed to a social purpose, see §5(1)(5) of the RSE Act.

According to §6 of the RSE Act, it is up to the enterprise that apply for registration to document the fulfilment of the above conditions. The Danish Business Authority is responsible for registration and should ensure that the conditions are fulfilled upon registration.

Once registration has taken place the management of the social enterprise will be subject to a number of special duties, which includes applying an asset lock as well as reporting requirements.

The Act contains several provisions on the duties of the management. These duties are imposed on the central management body of the company. This term is well defined for the types of companies that are covered by the Danish Companies

[55] The Danish Business Authority has set out guidelines for the registration under the RSE Act, and these guidelines indicate how to document the different conditions, see Vejledning om Registrering som registeret socialøkonomisk virksomhed (8 August 2019) available at https://erhvervsstyrelsen.dk/vejledning-registrering-som-registreret-socialoekonomisk-virksomhed.

[56] See the guidelines, Vejledning om Registrering som registeret socialøkonomisk virksomhed (8 August 2019).

Act (i.e., mainly public and private limited companies),[57] but for other types of organisations with a different type of management structure it may prove more difficult to decide who constitutes the central management body. The RSE Act does not stipulate how management is composed, as this will be determined by the rules governing the corporate entity.

Firstly, the RSE Act emphasises that the central management body is responsible for the information submitted upon registration and for the subsequent annual reporting, see below. Next, there is an obligation to deregister an entity which no longer meets the conditions for registration, see §7 of the RSE Act. The effect of these provisions is that management is always under an obligation to pursue the social purpose adopted by the social enterprise.

There are no rules limiting the influence of the owners, members or shareholders of the entity. Their influence will be regulated by the rules applicable to the legal entity, and for companies covered by the Danish Companies Act, shareholders can decide on most issues related to running the company. However, if the shareholders in a registered social enterprise either adopt a decision that infringes its social purpose or decide to distribute a larger dividend than allowed under the Act, management no longer complies but must deregister.[58]

The act provides that owners, members or shareholders of a registered social enterprise should only be permitted to receive a total return corresponding to their original investment plus a reasonable annual return on the investment. This is clearly open to interpretation, but the act introduces two upper limits to indicate what constitutes a reasonable annual return, see §5(2) of the RSE Act.[59] Thus, the annual return can be no higher than 15% above the base rate, and no more than 35% of the annual profit may be paid out as dividend in a single year. If dividends are not paid in one year, the amount payable can be carried forward and be used in the distribution of profit in the following year. In addition to these requirements, the registered social enterprise also has to comply with the restrictions on the distribution of dividends found in the rules governing the entity.

To avoid the above-mentioned restrictions being circumvented, a number of additional restrictions are imposed on registered social enterprises. First of all, the cap set for distributions applies to any form of profit distribution. This includes loans

[57] According to §5(1) no. 4 of the Companies Act, for companies that only have one management organ—the executive directors—this will be the central management organ. For companies with a two-tier structure, the structure used by the company may differ. If it uses the traditional structure where the board of directors, while appointing the executive managers, will still be involved in making managerial decisions, the board of directors will be the central management organ. If the company uses the newer—German inspired—two-tier system with a supervisory board and an organ with executive managers, the latter will be the central management organ.

[58] After deregistration, the entity may act outside the social purpose (if the articles of association are changed), but there will still be asset locks in place which will prevent the distribution of large dividends, see below.

[59] As acknowledged in the *travaux préparatoires,* this solution is inspired by the solution adopted at the time for Community Interest Companies in the UK.

where the payment of interest is profit-dependent. Any capital reductions must observe the caps.

Secondly, management fees may not exceed what is customary given the nature and extent of work carried out and what may be regarded as reasonable in relation to the entity's social purposes, see §9 of the Act.[60] There is little guidance on determining what is customary and what are reasonable fees. The *travaux préparatoires* indicate that comparisons should be made with the fees paid in enterprises where the management undertakes a similar amount of work as that in the social enterprise. But it is also indicated that having a similar level of salary as in comparable enterprises may not be justified when the special social purpose is taken into account. Thus, a similar (high) fee may take money away from the social purpose. This indicates that management in social enterprises may have to accept lower salaries than those in other enterprises.[61]

The rules governing deregistration are also aimed at preventing circumvention, see below.

Finally, the registered social enterprise must make an annual report which, *inter alia*, ensures that stakeholders and the Danish Business Authority are able to keep an eye on the enterprise. The following should be reported, see §8:[62]

- The total fees, etc., paid to existing and former members of management, and any payments made to promoters of the registered social enterprise.
- Agreements entered into by the registered social enterprise with closely related parties.
- Cash holdings and other assets that are distributed or paid out of the company's assets.
- How the registered social enterprise has fulfilled its social purposes.
- The total dividends received by the owners/members/shareholders.

There is no requirement for the report to be audited. According to the travaux préparatoires, if a company chooses to include the information in its management report and the company is subject to auditing, this information will need to be audited together will the rest of the management report. However, since a company can just omit this information from its management report, it can easily avoid audit.

[60] It is not only the formal salary that should be within the boundaries set by the Act, but also any other type of fee, see also the reporting requirement in §8 outlined below. The same broad view on the regulation of fees is taken in the restrictions applicable in enterprise foundations where fees are restricted under §19, see Mikkelsen and Bunch (2009), p. 448.

[61] The Danish Business Authority has not issued any guidance on how this condition should be fulfilled. For enterprise foundations there is a requirement that fees for management should not be more than what is customary and reasonable given the financial position of the foundation. Here there is no indication that the distribution purpose of the foundation could affect the size of the fee.

[62] According to § 8(1) of the RSE Act, a registered entity must prepare an annual account according to the rules applied for class B, whether or not the entity is required to make such a report under the rules applicable to the entity.

The Danish Business Authority has the obligation to ensure that the requirements outlined above are complied with.[63] Whereas 10% of those who apply for registration are subject to control, there are only a few controls of those enterprises already registered. Consequently, the most common transgression of the rules is that the registered social enterprise does not submit the annual report as required under §8.[64] Usually, the sanction will be that the Danish Business Authority will deregister the enterprise, as the power to impose fines is seldom used.[65]

Potentially, other stakeholders could also supervise the registered social enterprise, for instance by requesting copies of the annual report. However, according to information received via telephone from the Danish Business Authority, hardly anyone asks for access to these reports. Stakeholders may use other tools for questioning the management about the activities of the social enterprise, since, for instance, shareholders and members may have the right to ask questions under the rules applicable to the entity.[66]

The enterprise is free to deregister at any time. Additionally, the management will have a duty to deregister if they conclude that the enterprise no longer fulfils the conditions (and this cannot be corrected). Finally, deregistration may be triggered by the Danish Business Authority. In case of a deregistration, the caps applicable during registration must still be observed for the profit made during the time the entity was operating under the scheme, see §10(3) of the RSE Act. For deregistered enterprises, this means that the profit accumulated during registration cannot be used for distributions exceeding the caps afterwards but must be used to serve the social purpose. Any profit accumulated before registration is not covered by these restrictions.

According to §17(4) any violation of the above restrictions after deregistration is punishable by fine. However, the act does not stipulate how the Danish Business Authority should enforce this. After deregistration the enterprise no longer needs to report on how it uses its profit and consequently, the Business Authority needs to do

---

[63] Foundations are also subject to supervision by the foundation authorities, but they will focus on the fulfilment of the requirement under the two laws applicable to enterprise foundations and other foundations.

[64] According to the evaluation conducted by the Danish Business Authority in 2018 (Evaluering af lov om registrerede socialøkonomiske virksomheder, December 2018, available at https://erhvervsstyrelsen.dk/evaluering-af-lov-om-registrerede-socialokonomiske-virksomheder) in 2016 only 21% of all registered social enterprises complied with § 8 and 32% partly complied. Consequently, just under half failed to comply.

[65] This information was made available to the authors during a telephone interview conducted on 29 September 2020 with one of the employees at the Danish Business Authority. The Business Authority has the power to impose a fine if a registered social enterprise does not manage its profits according to the restrictions imposed on them. There is no power to impose fines for enterprises that do not fulfil the reporting requirements under §8.

[66] For instance, in private and public limited companies any shareholder has the right to ask questions to the management, see the Danish Companies Act §102. In associations and foundations stakeholders will normally not have any formal right to ask questions to the management.

very outreaching work if they should detect violation of these rules. It seems the Danish Business Authority does not make any effort to enforce these rules.[67]

A social enterprise may also be liquidated, for instance through a bankruptcy. In the event there is any profit left after paying off creditors this profit should be used within the limits set by the rules requiring a social handling of the profit, see §10 (1) of the RSE Act.

5 Concluding Remarks

Denmark offers a wide range of corporate forms that are used in the third sector. With one exception all these corporate forms may be used for third sector activities as well as for activities falling outside the sector. The exception is the social enterprises registered under the RSE Act, but only a small fraction of the third sector organisations uses this opportunity for registration.

It is to be assumed that the third sector is substantial in Denmark but the precise number of organisations that are committed to this sector is not known, partly because not all organisations need to register and, even if they do register, it cannot be determined without individual examination of each organisation whether they belong to the sector or not.

Denmark does not have an overarching act regulating the third sector. The only act that targets the third sector is the RSE Act which only covers organisations that have a commercial activity. There are, however, rules in tax law and other benefit schemes that intend to benefit the sector and consequently help to promote the sector.

References

Boje TP, Ibsen B (2006) Frivillighed og nonprofit i Danmark. Socialforskningsinstituttet

Bolander J et al (2021) Lærebog om indkomstskat, 3rd edn. DJØF Publishing

Danish Business Authority (2018) Evaluering af lov om registrerede socialøkonomiske virksomheder. https://erhvervsstyrelsen.dk/evaluering-af-lov-om-registrerede-socialokonomiske-virksomheder

Danish Business Authority (2019) Vejledning om Registrering som registeret socialøkonomisk virksomhed. https://erhvervsstyrelsen.dk/vejledning-registrering-som-registreret-socialoekonomisk-virksomhed

Danish Business Authority Vejledning om Opmærksomhedspunkter for bestyrelsesmedlemmer i erhvervsdrivende fonde. https://erhvervsstyrelsen.dk/vejledning-opmaerksomhedspunkter-bestyrelsesmedlemmer-i-erhvervsdrivende-fonde

Danish Ministry of Finance (2009) Selvejende institutioner – styring, regulering og effektivitet. https://fm.dk/udgivelser/2009/april/selvejende-institutioner-styring-regulering-og-effektivitet/

[67] Again, this information was obtained during the interview with a representative from the Business Authority in September 2020.

Danish Tax Authority Juridisk Vejledning, C.D.9.9.1.1. https://skat.dk/skat.aspx?oID=2047579&chk=217592
Enjolras B, Salamon LM, Sivesind KH, Zimmer A (2018) The third sector as a renewable resource for Europe: concepts, impacts, challenges and opportunities. Palgrave Macmillan
Feldthusen RK, Poulsen M (2012) Selvejede institutioner – med focus på grundbetingelser og fonde. Juristen:215–224
Hansen HS (2016) Begreberne almennyttige og almenvelgørende formål i skatteretten. Revision og Regnskabsvæsen 2016(11):54–61
Hansen JL (2019) Companies without legal capital and the strange case of Denmark. Eur Comp Financ Law Rev 16:667–686
Hasselbalch O (1997) Foreningsret. DJØF Publishing
Hulgård L, Chodorkoff LM (2019) Social enterprises and their ecosystems in Europe: country report, Denmark, European Commission
Lund AB, Sørensen KI (2018) Komparative analyser af dansk socialøkonomi: Sorgfrit udkomme & timeligt velvære? Copenhagen Business School, CBS, p 41. Available at https://static1.squarespace.com/static/5b7c3a93266c073142e2df2f/t/5bb5f1abec212d48c3ac4dc6/1538650541842/Baggrundsrapport-SORGFRIT-UDKOMME-OG-TIMELIGT-VELV%C3%86REv2+Kapitel+1.pdf
Mikkelsen JH, Bunch L (2009) Erhvervsdrivende fonde – en lovkommentar. DJØF Publishing
Mollerup H, Akbatani YFB (2021) Benefit Corporation – en mulig selskabsform under dansk selskabsret? Revision og Regnskabsvæsen 2021, 2, pp. 70–74
Sørensen KE, Neville M (2014) Social enterprises: how should company law balance flexibility and credibility? Eur Bus Org Law Rev 15:267–308
Werlauff E (2019) Valg af selskabsform. Werlauff§Jura, III Edition

Chapter 3
French *Economie Sociale et Solidaire* in the Middle of the Ford

Véronique Magnier

Contents

Abstract The French law passed on 31 July 2014 instituted a new business segment: the social and solidarity economy. Sitting alongside the public sector that is often too overwhelmed to satisfy all needs and the private sector that is only interested in selfish satisfaction, the ESS has progressively gained in coherence and autonomy. However, French Law has not chosen to establish a fully-fledged third sector as shown by the presence of commercial companies amongst the organisations of the ESS. Therefore, only the future will tell which sector will win, bearing in mind that the ESS has inherent limits and competitors in the private sector. In the end, the solution could come from a supranational or even European legislative level.

Véronique Magnier is Professor of law at Paris-Saclay University.

V. Magnier (✉)
Paris-Saclay University, Department of Law, Paris, France
e-mail: Veronique.magnier@universite-paris-saclay.fr

A. Fici (ed.), *The Law of Third Sector Organizations in Europe*,
https://doi.org/10.1007/978-3-031-41744-3_3

1 Introduction

The *Economie sociale et solidaire* (thereafter ESS) has a long history and its roots go back to the nineteenth century in France, with the first workers associations, consumers or residents cooperatives and mutual aid entities. Two centuries later, the ESS has become a pioneer in the context of social innovation and is finding a growing audience among younger generations in search of meaning in their commitments, whether they be voluntary or professional. The capacity of social organisations to adapt in order to preserve their specificities in a socio-economic environment marked by profound transformations is proving to be one of their distinctive features.

Historically, this sector of the economy responds to economic, social and solidarity-based considerations; its aim is to make up for the shortcomings of other traditional schemes. These schemes are centred on the satisfaction of individual needs and respond to a logic that lacks a global and holistic vision of economic reality. The ESS form of economy favours the satisfaction of community of interests, whilst the private sector is still marked by the prevalence of selfish interests. Its dynamism and attractiveness are reflected in the figures. The weight of the ESS is significant: the ESS represents 10% of France's GDP and nearly 14% of private jobs in France. The sector employs 2.38 million people. The fertility of the ESS' field is due, above all, to the plurality of its actors, from associations and mutual insurance companies, also including private commercial organisations, overall representing more than 225,000 private legal entities. Therefore, by the diversity of their forms, the companies of the ESS are working to put people back at the centre of the economy and to respond to the major challenges facing society: combating illiteracy and high school dropout rates, supporting the autonomy of the elderly and people with disabilities, combating exclusion and unemployment, developing the circular economy, promoting the sharing economy to fight against the "digital divide."

This success and the importance of these struggles lead us to question the ESS' place in France: has it become, through its evolutions and transformations, a parallel economy better adapted to the modern challenges facing society than the private and public sectors?

A first indication is that the ESS sector has been favoured by the legislator who, in order to allow organisations in this sector to evolve with confidence in a stable and adapted framework, has recognized its existence through law n° 2014-856 of 31 July 2014 for the *Economie sociale et solidaire*[1] [thereafter law of 31 July 2014]. This law outlined the contours and prerogatives of the ESS. However, the ESS suffers from sociological shortcomings: less known than the private sector, the organisations of the ESS suffer from a lack of recognition. It is possible to attribute this shortcoming to the fact that their commitment is usually local and less well identified than the involvement of large companies with a national and even international dimension. If localism and the recognition deficit constitute the first sociological

[1] V. in Legifrance (https://www.legifrance.gouv.fr)

limits of the ESS, more fundamentally there are also economic shortcomings to be noted: operating at the crossroads of the private and public sectors, the ESS is still seeking its economic positioning. The situation once denounced by one of the fathers of the ESS, André Lipietz, remains relevant: "Paradoxically, the ESS entities have been fitted into the general mould of society 'with market'and represent the only alternative to the dominant logic of 'production for profit'. Therefore, it is necessary for those in charge of the ESS to have the capacity to have their original approach recognised and to ensure that it is effective".[2]

It seems particularly important to analyse the precise delimitation of the ESS' scope, and therefore of the status of the organisations that claim to be part of it, at a time when several societal developments are prompting questions about the specific identity of the organisations that make up the sector. The study will therefore focus on the identity of the ESS sector (1), then describe the status of the organisations that claim to be part of it (2), before considering the future prospects of this sector (3).

2 Identifying the ESS Sector

The ESS sector is based on common values, all founded on the concept of 'social utility'. In this respect, it should be considered as a coherent and autonomous whole. The ESS sector has acquired this coherence and autonomy over the course of French economic history. The most remarkable step was taken when, in addition to purely social values, the sector was enriched with a new value, that of solidarity, giving the sector its name: *Social and Solidarity Economy.*

In practice, however, this sector is neither coherent nor fully autonomous and the legislator has its share of responsibility for this given its refusal to recognise a new sector that it has refused to call, as in other countries, the "third sector". This was not the choice it made when it came to qualifying this sector in order to protect it. It did not choose to enshrine this concept of Anglo-Saxon origin, as if it were taking note that the organisations referring to this sector or claiming a label from the ESS were too varied, even disparate, to be part of a "third sector". Moreover, the legislation results in a certain hybridity between sectors, with the ESS sometimes leaning towards the private sector, as will be explained later.

This is why it is conceptually difficult to formalise the ESS as a complete economic model. To explain this French specificity, it is necessary to return to the history of this sector, which was built in France in stages, starting with a purely social economy and then opening up to the so-called 'solidarity economy' and thus succeeding in establishing itself as an inclusive "social and solidarity economy" (Sect. 2.1) without being able to make it a third sector in the strict sense of the term (Sect. 2.2).

---

[2]V. Lipietz (2001).

2.1 An Inclusive Sector

The ESS sector has a long history. Its economy is based on the concept of 'social utility',[3] which has the following criteria: open membership, equality, production of economic value, non-profit purpose, independence and solidarity.

The earliest organisations to distinguish themselves historically from the private and public sectors in order to prefigure the contours of this emerging sector, in what was still a predominantly rural France, were the associations with a social vocation and the agricultural cooperatives. Mutual societies then made their contribution at the end of the nineteenth century, in particular mutual aid organisations offering social protection systems at a time when the Welfare State was being rolled out across the country.[4] Gradually, a sector emerged that was distinct from the public sector and that also proclaimed its autonomy from the still dominant religious congregations. From that time onward, most of the actors claiming to be a part of the Social Economy sector were keen to preserve their independence and autonomy of action vis-à-vis the public authorities, but also vis-à-vis the power of the Church.

The twentieth century signalled the beginning of a new era, marked by the development of new expressions of solidarity, going beyond social assistance, towards people who were both members and actors of the organisation. Later, with the deep economic crisis leading to a sharp rise in unemployment, solidarity concerns gradually turned towards third party beneficiaries, outside the organisations, who were often too vulnerable to voluntarily join an organisation (the unemployed, the disabled…). This addressed the 'excluded'of society, living outside the traditional socio-economic circuits. This movement enabled the gradual transition from a purely social economy to a social and solidarity economy.

Conceptually,[5] this evolution makes it possible to identify a first period of development of the social economy *stricto sensu*, marked by what has been called "horizontal solidarity", favouring sharing and support *between* the "actor-members" ("explicit members") of the association or similar organisations. A second period followed, which sought to promote a form of "vertical solidarity", open to a category of 'beneficiaries-actors' ("implicit members" or "quasi-members") outside the organisation. It is mainly under the pressure of economic crises that organisations claiming this solidarity approach have developed, most often using the status of social economy enterprises in order to help the unemployed and, more generally, all those excluded from society.

The organisations in the field of the ESS have therefore structured themselves in relation to the functioning of the market, taking advantage of the opportunities that the latter offered or the failures that it experienced. Thus, periods of economic

[3] According to the regulation on European Social Entrepreneurship Funds (EuSEFs), 'Social impact'is described as a key characteristic of qualifying social enterprises and of investment funds targeting such entities.

[4] V. Laville (2016).

[5] V. Garabé et al. (2001), p. 280.

growth have favoured the development of a "horizontal solidarity", while periods of crisis, have tended to favour so-called "vertical solidarity".

Although the link between the two types of economy, social on the one hand and solidarity on the other, has not always been easy to formalise,[6] it appears that the solidarity action implemented is precisely aimed at enabling the most vulnerable to gradually recover their production-socialisation capacities,[7] thus promoting their reintegration into society. The concept of the solidarity economy is now fully recognized by public authorities and, compared to the social economy, it constitutes a particular modality. It is old in terms of its content and more recent in terms of the claim to its autonomy. Although the solidarity-based organisations, unlike the founding model of the social economy, mainly develop their projects according to the needs of non-member third parties,[8] the sector now forms a coherent and autonomous whole, distinct from other sectors.

However, since the ESS is, by its very nature, 'inclusive', it is constantly evolving and has its own 'dynamics'that are difficult to formalise. This dynamism is an integral part of this sector: it is even the consequence of particular conditions that presided over the emergence, structuring and existence of this sector. It can be seen above all as the result of a process whereby, from the end of the 1970s and 1980s in France, a group of cooperative, mutualist and associative organisations, although working in various fields of activity, gathered together and ultimately succeeded in constituting a fully-fledged institutional field that was recognized later on as such by the public authorities.

Today, each of these forms is still present, even when one of the two modalities dominates social relations, and the distinction is no longer conceptually difficult. However, the problem has moved to the other side of the spectrum. Recent legislation has, indeed, added to the complexity, even confusion, by allowing companies which, by their nature, are for profit organisations, to enter the field of the ESS. The inclusion of commercial companies in the ESS leads to a hybridization of this sector and, consequently, to the impossibility of recognising a 'third sector' as such.

---

[6] Laville (1995).

[7] In both cases, it is a question of remedying what can be called the 'weight of fate', even when this directly affects the integrity and autonomy of the individuals concerned. In other words, it is the initial 'handicaps'faced by these people that require a form of solidarity for them that can be described as 'vertical'. Furthermore, it can also be noted that a certain number of structures are characterised by the coexistence of these two forms of solidarity. This is the case, for example, of associations of parents of disabled children. See Boltanski and Thévenot (1991).

[8] V. Garabé et al. (2001).

2.2 A Hybrid Sector

The notion of "third sector",[9] of Anglo-Saxon origin, is a notion that often appears in debates on the ESS. It was developed, in particular, in France, by E. Archambault who addressed the crucial issue of what to do with any surpluses generated by ESS organisations as a result of their economic activity. While in associations, surpluses are always reinvested in the organisation, cooperatives and mutual companies have the possibility to "distribute them to their members or customers in the form of price discounts or reductions on subsequent membership fees".[10] The author then introduced a new division within the ESS itself, by removing the last two mentioned forms of organisations from the scope of the "third sector". Following *this summa divisio*, only associations and foundations could claim to be part of this sector. As foundations are very little developed in France, unlike the very important role they play in the Anglo-Saxon world, the field of the "third sector" would have been reduced to a very small portion in France.

Although this analysis was not followed up on,[11] it did show the desire of a majority of actors to exclude from the ESS sector any form of organisation with a vocation to distribute its surpluses to the members of the ESS organisation. However, the law of 31 July 2014 has done the opposite by letting commercial companies engage in the ESS, making it difficult, if not impossible, to establish a third sector in France. By continuing to have to satisfy the individual interests of its shareholders, commercial companies cannot fully satisfy the criteria of the ESS, even if they shares most of its values (v. *infra*). Worse, one could fear an infiltration, or even an instrumentalization, of the ESS by the private sector, causing the former to lose the autonomy that it took so long to acquire and that it continues to claim. The legislator's desire to create an ESS dynamic of its own finally prevailed, but without succeeding in creating a third sector as such.

3 ESS Organisations Statute

The law of 31 July 2014 recognises the ESS as a specific mode of enterprise. At the institutional level, it creates the French Chamber of the *Economie sociale et solidaire*, ESS France, and entrusts BPI France with the task of providing financing adapted to this sector. It also creates the status of *socially useful and solidarity*

---

[9] Lipietz (2001).

[10] Archambault (1996), p. 7.

[11] This analysis has been widely resisted, as the sharing of surpluses that cooperatives and mutuals may undertake can also be analysed as a form of regularisation required by the impossibility for these organisations to know their 'fair price' accurately throughout the year. It is therefore possible to include organisations such as associations, cooperatives, mutual societies and (in part) foundations in an autonomous third sector.

enterprise label (ESUS). It specifies the values common to all ESS organisations (Sect. 3.1) and draws up a restrictive list (Sect. 2.2).

3.1 Value-Based Community

The law on ESS affirms the desire to create an autonomous sector with its own values. These values meet the many objectives of the law: to better identify the contours of a contemporary, open and inclusive ESS; to recognise the ESS as a specific mode of enterprise; to strengthen local sustainable development policies; to consolidate the network, governance and financing tools of ESS actors, to provoke a "cooperative shock"; and to give back the power to act to employees. Its objectives are also ambitious. According to the law, the ESS must respond to economic, social, and even societal and environmental considerations, going against the traditional patterns of the private sector.

To achieve this, the law of 31 July 2014 sets out the founding criteria of the ESS, in terms of purpose, governance and financing. It enshrines the notion of social utility (Sect. 3.1.1), the obligation to adopt democratic management (Sect. 3.1.2) and the requirement not to pursue a profit-making purpose (Sect. 3.1.3).

3.1.1 A Social Purpose with Social Utility

The criterion of social utility is the basis for the status of the ESS organisation.

The ESS Act states that enterprises whose social purpose meets at least one of the following four conditions are considered to be socially useful:

1. Their objective is to provide, through their activity, support to people in vulnerable situations, either because of their economic or social situation, or because of their personal situation, and particularly their needs for social, medico-social or health support, or to contribute to the fight against their exclusion. These people may be employees, service users, clients, members or beneficiaries of the company;
2. They aim to contribute to the preservation and development of social cohesion or to the maintenance and strengthening of territorial cohesion;
3. They aim to contribute to education, particularly through popular education and the implementation of participation methods involving the beneficiaries of these activities in the territories concerned. They contribute to the reduction of social and cultural inequalities, particularly between men and women;
4. They aim to contribute to sustainable development, energy transition, promotion of culture or international solidarity, provided that their activity also contributes to producing an impact either by supporting vulnerable groups, or by maintaining and recreating territorial solidarity or by participating in education for citizenship.

These criteria are very broad and not cumulative. However, there is nothing to prevent an organisation from satisfying several criteria, provided that there is agreement on their social utility.[12]

3.1.2 Democratic Governance

The mode of governance is defined and organised by the statutes of the ESS organisation. It provides for information and participation of members, employees and stakeholders. This information should not be related to financial data only, but also to the company's accomplishments.

3.1.3 Entity's Limited Profit Motive

In principle, all ESS structures share a common characteristic: they should not be profit-oriented. Nonetheless, the issue of surpluses or profits in commercial companies arises. According to the provisions of the law passed 31 July 2014 applicable to commercial companies, the profits they generate must be mainly devoted to the objective of maintaining or developing the company's activity. Similarly, the mandatory reserves established may not be shared or distributed. However, the law provides for exceptions to these prohibitions, which must be provided for in the articles of association. Thus, by law, the general meeting may vote to incorporate sums taken from the reserves into the capital (which increases the value of the shares) or to distribute free shares. The law provides for limits to this incorporation.

The fulfilment of the three criteria of purpose, governance and limited profit-making allows entry into the ESS sector of enterprises with heterogeneous legal status whose purpose, organisation or functioning differ from the classical models.

3.2 Diversified Forms

Since its origin, the social economy sector has defined itself by reference to its statutes. This characteristic therefore constitutes a strong historical reality in terms of identity, which is irreversible, and which is therefore impossible to ignore completely. But this has not prevented the legislator from bringing a wide variety of organisations into the scope of the ESS law. The law proceeds by enumeration and creates the status of socially useful and solidarity enterprise (ESUS).

The five structures of the ESS are associations, foundations, non-profit mutual organisations, cooperatives and commercial companies with a social utility. While

[12] See. *infra*, Sect. 3.1.

the first category belongs to the ESS sector by nature, the others have to meet certain conditions in order to qualify.

The associations covered by the law of 31 July 2014 are those classically governed by the 1901 law, which established freedom of association. They therefore fall under the common law of associations and are an integral part of the ESS without needing to declare themselves as such. The law does not impose any administrative constraints on them. According to the law, they benefit from various advantages, including more secure and diversified funding.[13] Today, they represent 93.7% of all ESS entities.

Foundations of individuals, companies or those "sheltered" by another foundation are covered by the law of 31 July 2014. Very little developed in France, foundations represent only 0.3% of all ESS entities.

Mutual societies, as long as they are non-profit-oriented, are also part of the ESS sector. They have mainly developed in the field of health and insurance, one of the pillars of ESS. They embody it through their democratic governance and societal usefulness, as illustrated by their management of the health crisis, during which they all decided to pay back contributions to their members.

The common law co-operatives are composed of associate members who hold at least a share of the structure's capital. Entering the ESS sector, SCOPs[14] or SCICs[15] are companies under special law. They must meet the requirements of cooperatives in terms of governance based on the democratic principle of "one person, one vote". The nominal value of the share is fixed by the statutes. The capital constituted by the total of these shares is variable, which allows the free entry and exit of members. The law requires that surpluses be set aside at the end of each financial year: at least 57.5% of the result must be allocated to non-distributable reserves, and this rate must be increased to 100% by each annual general meeting, or by articles. The share of the result thus allocated to the reserves is deductible from company tax. These companies are subject to a five-year review to analyse the development of the cooperative project on the basis of, among other things, annual management reports. In addition, SCICs must have a specific purpose: their purpose is the production or supply of goods and services of collective interest that are of social utility. Thus, the protected interest is collective, whereby all the associates and stakeholders can come together around a common object by organising a multi-stakeholder dynamic (the social utility character). Rooted in a geographical territory, or within a professional community, or dedicated to a specific target public, the SCIC form can cover any type of activity that provides services to organisations or individuals, without restriction. Cooperatives of this type represents 5.2% of all ESS entities.

The law on ESS also created a new status, that of commercial companies of social utility: whilst holding commercial status, they respect the founding principles of

[13] Noguès (2014), p. 18.

[14] SCOP stands for '*Société coopérative participative ouvrière*'.

[15] SCIC stands for '*Société coopérative d'intérêt collectif*'.

ESS. Their purpose is social and should have priority over their economic objectives. ESS commercial companies make up only 0.2%.

It is in this plurality, which has already been noted as posing real problems of identity, that the social economy can find a particularly effective means of ensuring that the specificity of its model is recognised, that is affirmed and that its independence is maintained. Therefore, whatever their status, whether it be associative, cooperative, commercial or other, ESS enterprises can also apply for ESUS accreditation. This approval allows them to further enhance their social impact and to have access to private funding, particularly from solidarity-based employee savings. Political labels such as ESUS represent more than 700 structures and provide financial (BPI,[16] FISO[17]...) and fiscal advantages. There is also the LUCIE label and other labels exist, but these are developing outside of any regulation. They allow entities to obtain greater support and benefit from increased recognition. However, their award criteria must be strict in order to prevent companies from appropriating them for so-called "marketing"[18] purposes.

At the supranational level, the ESS is recognised by various public bodies, such as the European Union through its ESS Lab, or its Commission's expert group on social entrepreneurship. Private entities also take part in this economy, notably through labels such as the B-Label, which allows them to convey standards, claim quality and ultimately be recognised by consumers and users.

The means of funding available to organisations in the ESS sector are particularly numerous and diverse. They can be bank loans, public grants, solidarity-based savings,[19] crowdfunding and social impact bonds. Nonetheless, ESS entities lack funding, mainly because most investors do not have a good understanding of ESS business models. In addition, there is still a weak debt culture among some ESS organisations, such as associations, whilst this culture is more favourable to the private sector.[20] However, things are changing. The health crisis has allowed ESS actors to innovate, particularly with regards to health, environmental and climate issues.[21]

---

[16] BPI France is a public investment bank. It is a French organisation for the financing and development of companies resulting from the merger of Oséo, CDC Entreprises, FSI and FSI Régions.

[17] FISO is the BPI's Social Innovation Fund.

[18] V. Florian Moeslein.

[19] Solidarity savings represented 12.6 billion EUR of assets in 2018.

[20] According to Christophe Deconinck, Director of the fund 'Solidarity Investments', the development of ESS seems to be slowed down by reluctance, or even a lack of interest, on the part of the government, which does not make ESS a priority, but merely a possibility.

[21] Research carried out by the students of a Paris-Saclay legal clinic project showed that SSE actors have observed trends during the health crisis. According to Aurelie Jourdon, founder of OMEVA, the crisis has shown that enterprises are willing to integrate a social utility dimension within their activities. Cecile Leclair, Director General of Avise, has also stated that the health crisis has encouraged the development of an awareness of environmental and climate challenges. She has observed that consumers are more careful about what they are buying and are looking for higher ethical standards.

It can be noted that one of the major interests of ESS and the relevance of its model lies in the fact that this sector combines in a privileged way, and this sometimes happens within one and the same structure, activities of a very different nature, of a market and non-market-type. What makes the concept strong is also, paradoxically enough, one of its main sources of weakness. It is obvious that such internal diversity does occur without raising formidable identity problems. Today, several developments are leading to questions being raised about the future of this specific identity of the organisations making up the ESS sector.

4 Prospects for the ESS Sector

The perspectives aim to question both the intrinsic weaknesses of ESS (Sect. 4.1) and its positioning in relation to its competitors, in this case private sector organisations (Sect. 4.2).

4.1 Endogenous Concern Related to "Social Impact" Measures

While there is a consensus on the criterion of social utility and the values it embodies, there are many ways of approaching it. In order to present a certain degree of social utility, the organisation's activity is first defined by default: it must guarantee the coverage of needs that are not normally or sufficiently taken into account by the market. However, this approach has a number of limitations and raises a number of questions that have been widely debated, particularly within the National Council of the Associative Life (CNVA).[22]

A first important limitation is that social utility is defined here only by reference to the market, a rather restrictive conception. It neglects the fact that many associations, but this is true for other ESS organisations, also assume responsibility for interventions for which they prove to be better suited than the public authority. Since the beginning of the 1980s, controversies have regularly arisen, particularly concerning the "solidarity" aspect of the sector, around the possibility of awarding a "social utility" label to certain associations whose aims go beyond the interests of their members alone, in order to serve what the official texts call the "general interest". It goes without saying that the solidarity-based activities of the ESS sector attest to the relative failure of the State to take charge of, and protect, these collective interests.

[22]The CNVA (Conseil National de la Vie Associative) is a department attached to the Prime Minister, responsible for studying and monitoring all issues relating to associative life, giving its opinion on draft legislative or regulatory texts submitted to it and proposing useful measures for the development of associative life.

There is also the question of the link between social utility and the evaluation of economic value, another ESS criterion. There is indeed a productive dimension of social and solidarity economy organisations. ESS enterprises produce market and non-market economic or social added value. This duality is a productive characteristic shared by organisations in this sector.[23] The output of ESS enterprises cannot be understood only in terms of the implemented production function. Beyond the goods produced and/or services rendered, which correspond to the purpose of the organisation, the way it operates can generate a series of effects with a real social value that is very specific to the ESS organisations. This specificity results primarily from the range of social links generated due to the great plurality of actors involved in an ESS organisation: members, elected administrators, third party beneficiaries, stakeholders, directors and employees.[24]

It is because this parallel structure produces a lot of wealth that the question of measuring its social impact is essential.[25]

Certainly, qualifying as a 'social enterprise' implies going beyond classical notions of performance, putting forward the social impact as a new criterion that should have at least two distinctive features: it should take account of longer-term effects and the impacts created by the activities should concern stakeholders at large (not only shareholders). Hence, it would offer an alternative way of measuring performance, other than the mere output of financial returns, requiring new metrics to evaluate the kind of 'transformation' generated by the activities on people and the environment.

But this measure raises at least three types of questions that are being addressed by the GECES.[26]

---

[23] Thus, the fact that the sector receives subsidies, and therefore the calculation of net value added requires the deduction of these subsidies, is not a particularity, nor does it represent the existence of joint production. Such situations are quite common in other economic sectors.

[24] Boltanski and Thévenot (1991) have highlighted this greater "wealth" of social economy enterprises compared to traditional enterprises, based on specific examples concerning the Crédit Mutuel de Bretagne (CMB). Thus, in the examination of credit applications, where traditional banks operate on the basis of the two usual "logics" of profit-making enterprises: the "industrial" (technicality, professionalism) and "commercial" (conquest of markets, competitiveness) logics, the studies carried out revealed the intervention of two other logics within the CMB: the "domestic" (proximity to people) and "civic" (well-being of the community as a whole).

[25] According to Denis Stokkink, President of the ThinkTank Pour la solidarité européenne, it is "extremely important to calculate this social indicator and to formulate social impact indicators that should be ex-ante and monitored throughout the life of the structure" (Interview with Denis Stokkink, President of the ThinkTank Pour la solidarité européenne, carried out by the students of the Legal Clinic Paris Saclay, as part of the ESS Workshop, on 23 February 2021.

[26] The GECES, the EU Commission Expert Group set up in October 2012 to agree upon a European methodology which could be applied across the European social economy, does not contradict this when it defines social impact as the "*reflection of social effects, such as long and short term measures, adjusted for effects obtained by others (alternative attribution), effects that would have occurred anyway (deadweight effect), negative consequences (displacement) and effects that decline over time (decrease)*".

First and foremost, whether social impact should be measured remains, in itself, debatable. There are pros and cons. Even the "cons" are divided between those for whom the 'social'dimension is impossible to quantify, and those who say it is not even relevant to do so, mainly for ethical ones.

Another limit regarding measurement is due to the multidimensional nature of social organisations. As previously observed, social organisations do not form a harmonised sector in France and there are many ways to be "social", including those embraced by commercial companies. This means it is hard to establish a set of common standards for such different forms.

Finally, measuring social impact is the subject of a dilemma: either it requires outsourcing the measurement to a third party, and this is costly (mainly for organisations whose main goal is not to make profit); or it relies on self-assessment, but this choice entails the risk of 'impact washing'. Because using the right metrics is not easy, self-assessment requires a long-learning process, or may be exposed to a number of biases.

There is still a lack of relevant standards, a lack of reliability, of harmonised standards, a need for more transparency and traceability, plus a need for specific training. By adapting a cautious approach, the GECES proposes a flexible framework of indicators, rather than a single methodology. Regarding controls, here again, the GECES has identified a long list of pitfalls in achieving effective controls. There are at least three options (Validation, Review & Audit) but none of them are completely satisfactory.

Also, although central, the notion of social utility remains subject to technical uncertainty. And alternative systems stemming from the PACTE law could create real competition to the ESS sector.

4.2 Exogenous Competition from the Private Sector

The strongest attack on the ESS sector is represented by the interest of the public authorities in a reformed private sector, with a risk of reclaiming ESS values. The future of the ESS sector will depend on the capacity of ESS organisations to maintain their specificities and independence in a socio-economic environment marked by profound transformations that are redrawing the contours of the private, public and social economy spaces. These developments could ultimately raise the question of the permanence of the ESS model.

As D. Demoustier[27] rightly noted, many for-profit companies have long sought to expand their markets by trying to absorb social economy enterprises. Today, the existence of this sector is jeopardised by major reforms recently made to the private sector.

[27] Demoustier (1996).

The PACTE law (acronym for "Plan of Action for the Growth and Transformation of enterprises") is based on the triptych of efficiency, justice and clarification. It aims to rethink the place of business activities in society, create jobs and strengthen the competitiveness of French companies.[28] To this end, by modifying cardinal articles of common company law, it requires managers to take into account the social and environmental issues of the company activities (Article 1833 para. 2 of the Civil Code). It also offers companies the possibility of including their "raison d'être" in their articles of association (Article 1835 of the Civil Code). In including a new Article L.210–10 in the Commercial Code, it allows commercial companies to state their status as a "mission company".[29] It should be noted that the PACTE Act represents progress compared to the reform of 31 July 2014. At the origin of the parliamentary work prior to the PACTE Act, the Sénard-Notat report[30] highlighted the consequences of the congenital imperfection of the ESS law by proposing a legal framework dedicated to profit-making companies pursuing social and environmental objectives: "If the ESS has constituted a "third way" between the State and the market, or between Marxism and liberalism, the demand for this new status seems to draw another path between classical capitalism and the ESS sector, that of a responsible market economy. The creation of wealth remains at its core but, taking into account the social and environmental consequences, must avoid endangering the natural heritage and human rights, so that the search for productive efficiency never falls into the capture of resources". Thus, while respecting the imperative of value creation, the company with a mission—referred to in the report as an "entreprise à mission"—would pursue a collective interest without the constraints imposed by the ESS law. The constraints would be freely consented to by the shareholders, who would have accepted the inclusion in the articles of association of a "raison d'être" accompanied by a mission, with the company's managers then being subject to a dual internal and external control.

It remains to be seen whether private companies will follow suit. On the one hand, the law, when supplemented by the decree of 3 January 2020, makes no mention of what the impact of the status of a company with a mission will be on governance from the point of view of both shareholders and managers. By increasing the number of interests to be respected, the pursuit of a mission may exacerbate conflicts of interests and make it difficult to determine the hierarchy of interests. Moreover, the notion of mission remains ambiguous. A "mission" evokes a responsibility for the future, unlike accountability, which is focused on the past. To recognise that a company has a mission is to imply that this mission confers upon the company a responsibility towards all of civil society. Without defining the notion, the law specifies that the mission consists of pursuing "one or more social or environmental objectives in the context of its activity". These objectives are proclaimed in major

[28] V. Hatchuel (2012).

[29] V. Magnier and Paclot (2021).

[30] Report "L'entreprise, objet d'intérêt collectif, de Sénard J-D, Notat N. https://www.economie.gouv.fr/mission-entreprise-et-interet-general-rapport-jean-dominique-senard-nicole-notat.

international texts such as the United Nations Global Compact and the OECD Guidelines, which promote the fight against climate change, world peace, education, respect for labour standards and health. By making social and environmental objectives the goal of the company with a mission, the law assigns it the pursuit of a collective interest that goes beyond the social interest. But the Sénard-Notat report struggles to define the "object of collective interest"!

The company with a mission therefore constitutes a new form of hybridisation. Only the future will tell which side the organisations and those who fund them will choose!

5 Conclusion

Ultimately, what will be the future of ESS? Since it did not seem possible to the 2014 legislator, based exclusively on a legal criterion, to exclude *a priori* from the ESS sector all structures that do not use an associative status, the relativisation of the importance of the legal criterion runs the risk of marginalising organisations from the ESS sector. This risk could be countered by better highlighting the economic and social added value of solidarity actions. This valuation would imply an assessment that could be carried out in monetary terms, based on the increase in income-wages of the people helped, by means of indicators relating to the cost avoided for the community due to these very same actions. These developments should be able to rely on the international movement in favour of a third sector. The French sociologist, J.-L Laville, underlines more than ever the reality of the movement at the international level: "The Social and solidarity economy is not a marginal sector, nor a public sub-service, nor a cheap private enterprise, contrary to the common view that prevails in France. For several decades, on all continents, solidarity-based initiatives have been boosting the social economy, while a North-South dialogue has been established, revealing a potential for emancipation and economic, social and political transformation".[31] Participating in the collective debate is, in itself, evidence of this movement.[32]

[31] Laville (2019), pp. 52–60.

[32] European Commission (2011) Social Business Initiative: Creating a favourable climate for social enterprises, key stakeholders in the social economy and innovation, Communication to the European Parliament, the Council, the European Economic and Social Committee and the Committee of the Regions, COM (2011), 682 final; Fici A (2017) European Study for Social and Solidarity-Based Enterprise – Study for the Juri Committee, available at: http://www.europarl.europa.eu/RegData/etudes/STUD/2017/583123/IPOL_STU(2017)583123_EN.pdf.

References

Archambault E (1996) Le secteur sans but lucratif, associations et fondations en France [The non-profit sector, associations and foundations in France]. Economica

Boltanski L, Chiapello E (1999) Le nouvel esprit du capitalisme [The new spirit of capitalism]. Gallimard, Paris

Boltanski L, Thévenot L (1991) De la Justification. Les économies de la grandeur [On Justification. The economies of greatness]. Gallimard, Paris

Demoustier D (1996) Economie sociale et construction européenne. Rapports au marché et à la concurrence [Social economy and European construction. Relationship to the market and competition]. Revue internationale de l'économie sociale Recma 261:3e. trimester

European Commission (2011) Social Business Initiative: Creating a favourable climate for social enterprises, key stakeholders in the social economy and innovation, Communication to the European Parliament, the Council, the European Economic and Social Committee and the Committee of the Regions, COM (2011), 682 final

Fici A (2017) European Study for Social and Solidarity-Based Enterprise – Study for the Juri Committee. Available at http://www.europarl.europa.eu/RegData/etudes/STUD/2017/583123/IPOL_STU(2017)583123_EN.pdf

Garabé M, Bastide L, Fas K (2001) Identité de l'économie sociale et de l'économie solidaire, [Identity of the social economy and the solidarity economy]. Revue internationale de l'économie sociale, Recma, p 280

Hatchuel A (2012) Refonder l'entreprise [Re-founding the entreprise]. Seuil, la république des idées

Laville J-L (2016) L'Économie sociale et solidaire [Social and solidarity economy]. Pratiques, théories, débat, 2nd edn. Points

Laville J-L (2019) L'économie sociale et solidaire: pour une sociologie des émergences, in Informations sociales [The social and solidarity economy: for a sociology of emergences, in Informations sociales] 1(199):52–60

Lipietz A (2001) Pour le tiers secteur. L'économie sociale et solidaire: pourquoi et comment, [For the third sector. The social and solidarity economy: why and how]. La Découverte, La Documentation française

Magnier V, Paclot Y (2021) Le clair-obscur de la loi PACTE: Vers un nouveau paradigme de la gouvernance? [The chiaroscuro of the PACTE law: towards a new paradigm of governance?]. Mélanges Alain Couret, Dalloz

Nogués H (2014) Les associations à l'heure de l'ESS. Juris Associations 506:18

Rapport "L'entreprise, objet d'intérêt collectif". [The company as an object of collective interest], de Sénard J-D, Notat N https://www.e.conomie.gouv.fr/mission-entreprise-et-interet-general-rapport-jean-dominique-senard-nicole-notat

Chapter 4
Law in Transition: Reforming the Legal Framework of the Third Sector in Germany

Florian Möslein

Contents

Abstract The legal framework of the third sector in Germany is in a state of transition. While this transition has previously been driven by case law and specific legislative changes, much more substantial legal reforms are currently emerging, in particular with the plans to introduce a new legal form for social entrepreneurship. Within the concept of the third sector, the legislative proposal for a company in steward-ownership represents an extreme: The proposal aims at a legal form with a very strict non-profit orientation but without any legal commitment to specific public interest objectives defined by the legislator. It is based on the assumption that entrepreneurial goals will almost inevitably serve the common good if entrepreneurial activities are not aimed at making profits. The proposal builds on basic trust in individual purposes, but at the same time shows scepticism towards state definitions of public welfare goals. With this departure from specific public purposes, the legislative proposals ultimately challenge the very concept of the third sector

Florian Möslein is Professor, dr.jur at the Department of Law at the Philipps-Universität.

F. Möslein (✉)
Philipps-Universität, Department of Law, Marburg, Germany
e-mail: Florian.Moeslein@jura.uni-marburg.de

A. Fici (ed.), *The Law of Third Sector Organizations in Europe*,
https://doi.org/10.1007/978-3-031-41744-3_4

which traditionally oscillates in a vague spectrum between non-profit and public interest orientation.

1 Constituting the Third Sector

The legal framework of the third sector in Germany is undergoing a phase of fundamental change. It is difficult, however, to delineate even the contours of this area of law, mainly because the notion of a 'third sector' is not used as a legal term in German law. Nonetheless, that term has become increasingly common in political, economic and also legal debates, albeit often with basically, or at least partially, different meanings. It is therefore appropriate to first attempt a clarification of terms before subsequently addressing questions of economic relevance and historical roots.

1.1 Organisations Beyond Market and State

To begin with, a clarification is necessary. On the basis of the so-called three-sector model, macroeconomic statistics still used to divide the economy into different sectors in accordance with specific type of activities, namely extraction of raw materials (primary), manufacturing (secondary), and service industries (tertiary sector).[1] Nowadays, the term is much more commonly used, however, in the sense of non-profit organisations, social enterprises or the voluntary sector, and this is also the understanding underlying this book and chapter. In German legal discourse, it has become widespread at least since 1987 when various prominent foundation law conferences were organized under the headings "third sector" and "non-profit sector".[2] Shortly after, a ground-breaking contribution entitled "State, Market, Third Sector – and even more?" set the tone by assuming that the third sector is to be located somewhere between the State and the Market.[3] At its core, this notion of sectors goes back to earlier international research and namely to *Amita Etzioni*'s piece "The Third Sector and Domestic Missions", published in the early 1970s.[4] It aims at categorizing a complex and sometimes confusing multitude of very different types of organisations that do not fit neatly in either of the two boxes of the market and the state, inter alia para-governmental organisations, non-governmental

[1] The model goes back to Fisher (1939); for an earlier account see id. (1933). Nowadays in the same sense, for example, Latzel (2020), para. 17 et seq.

[2] Cf. Neuhoff (1988).

[3] Schuppert (1989); for an abbreviated English version see id (1991); cf. also id (1995).

[4] Etzioni (1973).

organisations, non-profit organisations, voluntary organisations and self-organisations. In addition, another approach has been considered as an alternative to such concept of sectors, namely to place these different types of organisations "on an imagined state-private continuum, with the end points labelled *purely private* and *core public bureaucracy*".[5] Both approaches have in common the fact that they stress the existence of organisations that defy categorization into either the public or the private sector because they operate neither according to the logics of markets nor to that of the state.

The German legal system, however, builds on a particularly pronounced distinction between public law and private law. Accordingly, the idea of organisations between (or beyond) market and state gave rise to an intense academic debate on whether such mixed forms can exist at all within the traditional dichotomy, with prominent authors arguing in favour of *tertium non datur*.[6] At a less fundamental, more detailed level, the breakup of that dichotomy triggered legal questions on which rules to apply to such hybrid forms, most importantly with regard to direct (or, alternatively, only indirect) effects of fundamental rights.[7] Both within constitutional law and statutory law, numerous rules are applied differently according to the public or private nature of the addressees, for example in tax or public procurement law, and it is therefore particularly challenging to deal with something that appears to be a "third element" between the market and the state. Despite these dogmatic difficulties, however, it can hardly be denied that such organizations do in fact exist.

1.2 Non-Profit Vs. Purpose Orientation

However, to stress that third-sector organisations belong neither to the sphere of the market nor to that of the State provides only a negative definition. To define which criteria positively distinguish these organizations raises more difficult questions. Building on community, market and the State as the three models of social order,[8] German social scientists stress the characteristic of spontaneous solidarity as opposed to dispersed competition and hierarchical control.[9] In other words, the appeal of third-sector organisations "is to voluntarism, whereas the other sectors depend on law and commercial pressure".[10] Among legal scholars, a somewhat different understanding has prevailed according to which the third sector is

[5] Schuppert (1991), p. 126 (emphasis in original).

[6] Di Fabio (1999), at pp. 586 et seq.; see also the monograph by Weiß (2000). Cf. on the other hand Sachs (1988): "tertium datur".

[7] See, for instance, Kahl (2002), at pp. 724 et seq.

[8] Streeck and Schmitter (1985).

[9] Görlitz and Voigt (1985), pp. 173, 183 et seq.

[10] Levitt (1973), p. 53.

composed, in particular, of privately-held organisations that contribute to the public (or common) good.[11]

Alternatively, however, the term 'non-profit sector' is frequently used in the legal sphere and in particular by corporate law scholars.[12] By taking the intent not to generate economic gains as a starting point,[13] that term uses a somewhat different perspective, closer to the social science concept of voluntarism. Nonetheless, both approaches draw the line in a fairly similar fashion: Whenever a private organisation's purpose does not consist in profit-making, it does not seem unlikely that it is aimed at some contribution to the common good. As long as it is realistic to assume that people are good,[14] it is hard to imagine any other motivation than either making profits or creating some sort of positive impact for the common good. As a consequence, the two terms of 'third sector' and 'non-profit sector' at least point into a similar direction of a social or common-good-oriented purpose.[15] Taking the separation of ownership and control into account, however, it is important to distinguish the level at which such non-profit intent is relevant: Does the respective organisation itself exclusively act for non-economic purposes or does it even operate outside of the commercial sphere? Or does the non-profit orientation rather characterize its members, for example if distributions of profits are limited or even excluded? It is such ban on profit distributions that is usually understood to be the key component of non-profit organisations.[16] Note that this ban does not prevent the organisation itself from operating in the economic sphere and even from pursuing profit-oriented goals.

Due to the fact that the third sector is commonly characterized by a lack of profit orientation, there is an increasing debate about an emerging fourth sector, (also) among German legal scholars.[17] Organisations of this additional sector are characterized by a dual purpose in that they operate on goods or service markets just like conventional companies, but combine profit making and contributions to the common good in their economic activities. Very often this fourth sector is understood to be synonymous with the (similarly vague) concept of social enterprises.[18] In addition to social purposes, however, economic and governance considerations are increasingly gaining in importance. As a consequence, the even broader notion of sustainable companies ("nachhaltige Kapitalgesellschaften") is used increasingly often in the German legal debate.[19] With their sustainable purpose—that does not, however,

[11] See, for instance, Anderheiden (2006), pp. 197–199; Droege (2010), p. 301; similar from the perspective of political economy Neumärker (2003).

[12] Hopt et al. (2005), s. also Hansmann (1980).

[13] Schuppert (1989), p. 52; more extensively Rose-Ackerman (1986).

[14] Bregman (2021), pp. 266-280.

[15] Walz (2002), p. 270 et seq.

[16] von Hippel (2005), pp. 38 f.

[17] Möslein (2017), p. 176; Rast (2018), p. 142; initially cf. Sabeti and Fourth Sector Network Concept Working Group (2009). For a different use of the term, however, see Walz (2002), p. 269.

[18] Möslein (2017), p. 175 et seq.; Möslein and Mittwoch (2016), p. 6.

[19] Burgi and Möslein (2021).

exclude profit-making—such companies are decidedly different from traditional non-profit organisations. Nonetheless, sustainability goals contribute to the common good.

Accordingly, the two criteria of non-profit-orientation on the one hand, and contributions to the common good on the other hand, coincide in many cases but can also differ in other important case groups. For the purposes of this chapter, the term third sector will be limited to organisations that are non-profit in the sense that distributions to its members or shareholders are prohibited.[20] In addition, it is assumed, but not required, that these organisations (usually) also have a social or sustainable purpose, however this may be defined.

1.3 Relevance and Roots

Due to these difficulties in definition and the resulting vagueness of boundaries, the economic relevance of the third sector is difficult to assess. Several attempts have been made to estimate the size and significance of this sector in Germany. Most of the information on its development and relevance is still based on data collected in the 1990s in the international comparative "John Hopkins Comparative Nonprofit Sector Project".[21] More recently, the project "Zivilgesellschaft in Zahlen (ZiviZ)" (Civil Society in Numbers) has been set up jointly by the Stifterverband für die Deutsche Wissenschaft, the Bertelsmann Foundation and the Fritz Thyssen Foundation.[22] It aims to establish an information system on civil society in order to permanently provide internationally comparable reporting on key data, structures and trends in German civil society. The project operates on the basis of the standards and guidelines provided by the UN Handbook of Nonprofit Institutions in the System of National Accounts,[23] and it builds on data of the "Statistisches Unternehmensregister" (business register at the Federal Statistical Office).[24] Since the main challenge was to assign the companies to the third sector, a machine algorithm filtered the data according to certain criteria, for example company name, ownership structure and legal form. On this basis and supplemented by individual case research, it was possible to assign all companies in the statistical business register.[25] According to this research, in 2007 about 105,000 enterprises

[20] For a similar definition cf. Salamon and Sokolovski (2018), pp. 36–42.

[21] Salamon and Anheier (1997); with specific focus on Germany: Zimmer and Priller (2007), pp. 29–116.

[22] More details available at https://www.ziviz.de/.

[23] United Nations (2003).

[24] https://www.destatis.de/DE/Themen/Branchen-Unternehmen/Unternehmen/Unternehmensregister/_inhalt.html.

[25] In detail Rosenski (2012), at pp. 211–213.

belonged to the third sector in Germany, with about 2.3 million employees subject to social insurance and about 300,000 marginally employed.[26] This corresponds to about 3% of the enterprises, 9% of the employees subject to social insurance and 7% of the marginally employed. In terms of gross value added, the third sector contributed about 89 billion EUR, which corresponds to a share of about 4.1%.[27] On the other hand, more recent and comprehensive studies show that associations are the most frequently used legal form of organised civil society in Germany, with more than 600,000 registered associations, whereas foundations are the legal form of organised civil society with the highest growth rates in the last 20 years, with a total of about 20,000 foundations.[28] In addition, about 11,000 charitable limited liability companies and more than 1000 cooperative organisations have been counted.[29] While the large discrepancies in numbers have to do with the fact that some of these organisations are not listed in the business register, the figures at least illustrate the high social relevance of the third sector. At the same time, they show the great diversity of the organisational landscape of the third sector in Germany. In addition to the variety of legal forms, the financial resources and also asset sizes differ markedly.[30] In fact, this heterogeneity has given rise to the question of whether the third sector can be captured in a theoretically meaningful way at all.[31]

Research on its historical roots reveals more distinctive features of Germany's third sector: One study concludes, for example, that it is "highly integrated into the country's administrative set-up. [...] Non-profit organizations are cooperating closely with state entities at every level of government, thereby forming a part of the German state rather than being an independent and critical part of civil society".[32] These roots go back to the Middle Ages when many church-affiliated foundations active in healthcare and social service delivery were founded.[33] The development intensified under the peace treaty of Westphalia: Contrary to the emergence of centralized, secular states seen in England and France, it established a highly fragmented political system in which regional and local monarchs considered traditional guilds and associations, but also new voluntary organisations, as useful political instruments, while also aiming at avoiding their escape from political control.[34] It was only under the German Empire in the late nineteenth century that the legal framework for third-sector organisations was established, in particular with the codification of the Bürgerliches Gesetzbuch (Civil Law Code, 1900), and the GmbH-Gesetz (Limited Liability Companies Act, 1892). Building on Hegel's

[26] Rosenski (2012), at p. 214.

[27] Rosenski (2012), at p. 217.

[28] Krimmer (2018), at pp. 5–54.

[29] Primmer et al. (2017), at pp. 50 et seq.

[30] For more details Hüttemann (2018), at p G 13.

[31] Bauer (2015).

[32] Zimmer et al. (2004), at p. 689.

[33] Strachwitz (2001), at p. 133.

[34] Anheier and Seibel (2001), at pp. 31–36.

concept of civil society as a public sphere independent from—but not on a par with—the state,[35] this legislation is influenced by the idea that "while society is entitled to form legal entities for public as well as private ends, the state is inherently superior and thus legitimized to exercise control including supervision by the police force".[36] Even today, founding third-sector organisations is relatively burdensome, and it is the state (rather than societal bodies) which is deemed to be in charge of determining what is legally considered to be socially beneficial.[37] At the same time, the so-called principle of subsidiarity emerged, establishing a system of large welfare associations with close ties to either the Church or to political parties.[38] They were granted privileged legal status and funding by the welfare legislation of the 1920s. These privileges were later incorporated into the Federal Republic's social and welfare laws after the Second World War, and they became a driving force for the development of so-called neo-corporatism.[39] Similar mechanisms of strong cooperative relationships between private third-sector organisations and the government for the purpose of implementing economic and social policies can also be observed beyond the areas of healthcare and social services, although to a less pronounced extent (for example, without guaranteed public funding in other policy fields such as sports and culture).[40] In addition, the German "Vereinskultur" is based on smaller, member-based associations with fewer, but still some ties, to either the government or the church.[41] Despite such exceptions, one can still conclude that Germany's third sector in general is highly integrated into the public sphere: "There is a specific form of German etatism that resulted in a very special governance structure or public-private partnership with nonprofit organisations [...], working on equal footing or even replacing government entities in service provision".[42]

In sum, the organisational landscape of the third sector in Germany is particularly heterogeneous. With a wide variety of legal forms being used, it is already difficult to assess whether or not an organisation belongs to the third sector. As a result of deep historical rules, the German third sector has, moreover, particularly strong ties with the public sphere.

[35] Hegel (1821), §§ 182–256.

[36] Zimmer et al. (2004), at p. 689.

[37] Cf. again Zimmer et al. (2004), at p. 689.

[38] Anheier (1992), at p. 33; see also Sachße (1994).

[39] Sachße (1995); Zimmer (1999).

[40] In more detail: Zimmer (1999), p. 41.

[41] Zimmer (1996).

[42] Zimmer et al. (2004), at p. 689.

2 Lex Lata of Third-Sector Organisations

In view of these close links between state institutions and the third sector in Germany, public support plays a particularly important role. Public funding and tax incentives in particular even shape the organisational forms that are being used in this sector. This determining impact makes it necessary to outline the tax law framework first before giving an overview of the different corporate forms that are currently being used in Germany's third sector. This current legal framework is undergoing a process of dynamic change, however. According to the coalition agreement of the new government, this process of change is likely to continue in the years to come. The outline of the lex lata in this section will therefore be relatively brief, in order to then be further supplemented with a look into what will likely be the lex ferenda in the next section.

2.1 Tax Law as the Organisational Law of the Third Sector

The status of a charitable organisation forms the core prerequisite for obtaining tax benefits. These benefits favour not only the tax-exempt organisation itself, but also their donors: Entitled organisations are exempted from income tax insofar as their income is generated by economic activities that relate to their charitable purpose. In addition, they enjoy further tax advantages according, for example, to the provisions of gift and inheritance tax law or real estate tax law.[43] Donors, on the other hand, are entitled to deduct donations made to tax-exempt organisations from their personal or corporate income tax subject, however, to certain limitations (for individuals up to 20% of the yearly income, for companies alternatively up to 4‰ of the sum of gross revenue and salaries per year). Against the historical background that has been described, it is telling that these tax benefits have usually been justified with the argument that charitable organisations deserve tax relief because they engage in areas where otherwise the state itself would have to become active.[44] In contrast, however, it has been argued that the third sector also complements and enriches the state's offerings.[45] Its organisations know individual preferences better than the state, so that civic engagement serves as a discovery process ("Bürgerengagement als Entdeckungsverfahren").[46]

The requirements of the status of a charitable organisation are also defined by tax law. In principle, the status is granted regardless of the corporate form.[47] It is

[43] More extensively Hüttemann (2021a), para. 1.26 et seqs.

[44] Seer (2003), p. 11 et seqs.; Droege (2010), pp. 315 et seqs.

[45] Isensee and Knobbe-Keuk (1988), p. 346 et seq.; see also Hüttemann (2018), p. G 88.

[46] Paqué (2007), pp. 12–16.

[47] Sec. 51 para. 1 of the German Abgabenordnung (AO, Fiscal Code) refers to "a corporation, an association or a pool of assets as defined in the Corporation Tax Act", and the respective legal forms

therefore available for all sorts of third sector organisations: In addition to associations and foundations, limited liability companies and even companies limited by shares can therefore operate as charitable organisations. Natural persons and partnerships, however, form an exception because they do not have legal personality and are not subject to corporate tax.[48]

Within this field of personal application, the core requirement is that the organisation in question has to promote a public-benefit purpose as defined in section 52 of the German Abgabenordnung (AO, Fiscal Code). According to para. 1 of this provision, the activity needs to be dedicated to the altruistic advancement of the general public in material, spiritual or moral respects. Such advancement is excluded in cases where the group of beneficiaries is limited, for instance, by membership of a family or the workforce of an enterprise, or where that group is necessarily small as a result of its definition, especially in terms of geographical or professional attributes. Art. 52 para. 2 AO then provides for a detailed catalogue of purposes that are regarded as public benefit purposes, namely the advancement of (1.) science and research, (2.) religion, (3.) public health and public hygiene, (4.) assistance to young and old people, (5.) art and culture, (6.) the protection and preservation of historical monuments, (7.) education, (8.) environmental protection, coastal and flood defence, (9.) public welfare, (10.) relief for people persecuted on political, racial or religious grounds and for refugees and war and disaster victims, (11.) lifesaving, (12.) fire and accident prevention, (13.) internationalism and tolerance, (14.) protection of animals, (15.) development cooperation, (16.) consumer counselling and consumer protection, (17.) rehabilitation of former prisoners, (18.) equal rights for women and men, (19.) protection of marriage and the family, (20.) crime prevention, (21.) sports, (22.) local heritage and traditions, (23.) animal husbandry, plant cultivation, allotment gardening, traditional customs including regional carnivals, amateur radio, aeromodelling and dog sports, (24.) the democratic political system, and (25.) active citizenship in support of public-benefit, charitable or religious purposes. This list is almost, albeit not entirely, exhaustive: If an organisation pursues a purpose that does not fall under the list, but similarly advances the general public altruistically in material, spiritual or moral aspects, this purpose can be declared as being for the public benefit in accordance with Art. 52 para. 2 AO. However, the tax authorities rarely grant such exemptions. Applying for them requires a lot of effort and means uncertainty, even though the Federal Fiscal Court has ruled that the margin of discretion of the tax administration is limited.[49] In any event, the requirements for the charitable status are relatively narrow. An illustration has been given recently when the activist organisation ATTAC (Association for the Taxation of financial

are enumerated in Sec. 1 para. 1 of the German Körperschaftssteuergesetz (KStG, Corporate Income Tax Act).

[48] In more detail Hüttemann (2018), p. G 24 et seq.

[49] With respect to an association with the purpose of advancing tournament bridge, the Court ruled that bridge is not a sport but needs to be treated in analogy to chess, for which Art. 52 para. 2 no. 21 AO provides that it shall be considered to be a sport: BFH, judgment of 9 February 2017 (V R 70/14), BStBl. II 2017, 1106.

Transactions and Citizen's Action) was denied the status of a charitable organisation: The Federal Fiscal Court (Bundesfinanzhof, BFH) has approved this decision, mainly on the grounds that the pursuit of political purposes by influencing the formation of political will and shaping public opinion is not one of the purposes mentioned in Art. 52 AO.[50] Against the background of this case law, there are legitimate concerns about "shrinking spaces for the third sector".[51] Given that charitable purposes are determined by the detailed and basically exhaustive list of Art. 52 AO, one can in any case conclude that the conditions for the status of a charitable organisation are relatively narrow in Germany.

In addition to the promotion of a public-benefit purpose, tax law requires further conditions to be met by non-profit organisations in order to qualify for tax exemption.[52] While these various conditions are defined by tax law, they shape the corporate governance of third sector organisations: Tax law operates as the organisational law of the third sector.[53] Firstly, the charitable status requires certain specifications in the articles of association: According to Art. 59 AO, the articles must specify the purpose of the corporation, that this purpose complies with the requirements of Arts. 52 to 55 AO and that it is pursued exclusively and directly; the actual management must comply with these provisions of the articles.[54] Secondly, tax law requires exclusivity which presupposes that the organisation only pursues its tax-privileged statutory purposes (Art. 56 AO). As a consequence, tax-exempt organisations must not distribute assets to their members, directors or other non-beneficiaries without adequate compensation. Thirdly, Art. 55 AO requires selflessness of charitable organisations, thereby prohibiting the promotion of the economic interests of its members and requiring both a non-distribution constraint and a promptly and timely use of funds for the tax-privileged purposes set out in the statutes. Finally, charitable organisations must pursue and realise their tax-privileged statutory purposes themselves (Art. 56 AO), even if there are exceptions to this principle of directness where the articles of association provide for planned cooperation with certain other entities. With these manifold requirements and, in particular, with the restrictions on profit distributions and participations in other corporations, German tax law largely predefines the corporate governance framework of charitable organisations. The qualification of tax law as the organisational law of the third sector is therefore very accurate.[55]

---

[50] BFH, judgment of 10 January 2019 (V R 60/17), NJW 2019, 877. A decision by the Federal Constitutional Court in this matter is still pending: BVerfG – 1 BvR 697/21.

[51] Leistner-Egensperger (2019).

[52] For an overview see von Hippel (2010), pp. 206–208.

[53] Hüttemann (2017); see also Hüttemann (2018), pp. G 17 et seqs., G 67 et seqs.; Weitemeyer (2018), p. 2776.

[54] More extensively Hüttemann (2017), pp. 628 et seqs.

[55] See n. 53 again.

2.2 Corporate Forms

Even if the governance framework of charitable organisations is therefore largely predefined by German tax law, that status is granted regardless of a specific corporate form. Apart from the organisational requirements of tax law that have just been described, third-sector entrepreneurs therefore enjoy freedom of choice with respect to the legal form in which their charitable organisations operate. As has been mentioned, limited liability companies and even companies limited by shares can also be chosen in order to establish such organisations, in addition to associations and foundations.[56] Moreover, within these different legal forms, contractual freedom prevails, albeit to varying degrees, most extensively within limited liability companies. This freedom of organisational choice and design contributes to the difficulties experienced when efforts are made to clarify the vague boundaries of the third sector and also to assess its economic relevance.[57] The resulting diversity of corporate forms also implies that only a very general overview can be given.

The private limited company (GmbH), to begin with, is designed for organising for-profit business activities and is subject to the provisions of commercial law. Yet German law on private limited companies is characterized by a particularly far-reaching freedom of organisational design: "Wide ranging party autonomy for shareholders has been a hallmark of the German GmbH Act since its entry into force in 1892".[58] As a consequence of this autonomy, shareholders can freely decide upon their company's purpose: According to Art. 1 of the German Limited Liability Companies Act (Gesetz betreffend die Gesellschaften mit beschränkter Haftung, GmbHG), GmbHs can be established for any lawful purpose. By choosing a non-profit purpose and by also complying with all other organisational requirements of tax law, shareholders can therefore also form charitable GmbHs.[59] It should be noted, however, that shareholders are also free to unanimously amend the purpose at some later stage, for instance after a change in ownership. Such amendments can transform the company into a for-profit organisation which will then lose its charitable tax status.[60] The non-profit character of charitable GmbHs is therefore not fixed in perpetuity. Upon formation, the company acquires legal capacity by entry in the commercial register. Registration requirements are minimal: The founding director must provide the commercial register through a public notary with the notarised deed of formation, the signed articles of association, as well as a list of all shareholders. In addition, they must declare and confirm that the minimum contributions to the share capital have been paid in and are at the free disposal of the GmbH, and that there are no obstacles to their appointment.[61] Above all, there is

[56] Above, at Sect. 2.1.

[57] See above, at Sect. 1.3.

[58] Fleischer (2018), at p. 688.

[59] For a practice-oriented introduction cf. Weidmann and Kohlhepp (2020).

[60] Gilberg (2020), at p. 207 et seq.

[61] In much more detail, for instance: Gerner-Beuerle and Schillig (2019), pp. 159–161.

no discretionary approval requirement, but the court has to register the company if all legal requirements are met.[62] Moreover, there is no state supervision of limited companies apart from financial monitoring for tax purposes.[63] In practice, limited liability companies are mainly used for the economic activities of non-profit organisations, for example as subsidiaries of either associations or foundations.[64]

Registered associations, on the other hand, are by far the most popular legal form in Germany's third sector. The prime rationality of these membership organisations is reciprocity and voluntary engagement.[65] While in principle associations may also be established for any lawful purpose, the law draws a fundamental and significant distinction between commercial and non-commercial associations: According to Arts. 21 et seq. of the German Civil Code (Bürgerliches Gesetzbuch, BGB), non-commercial associations acquire legal personality by their mere entry in the register of associations (similar to the GmbH), whereas commercial associations are granted legal personality only by state grant which is subject to the discretion of the competent authority. Unless expressly provided for by law, most authorities consider such granting legal only if, due to specific, individual circumstances, it is unreasonable for the association to organise itself in one of the other forms (such as a limited liability company or cooperative) in order to obtain legal capacity.[66] Economic associations therefore exist almost only in the agricultural and forestry sectors, where they are provided for by law.[67] Drawing the line between the two categories of associations has proven to be very difficult, however, in particular for third-sector organisations. In a landmark decision of 2017, the Federal Court of Justice (Bundesgerichtshof, BGH) had to decide on the status of an association that operated several day care centres for children.[68] According to this decision, the non-commercial character according to Art. 21 BGB is not equivalent to the status of a charitable organisation for tax purposes, but the Court stressed that this tax status has an indicative effect, in particular due to the tax law requirement of altruism, as well as the corresponding prohibition of profit distributions and the requirement of timely use of funds. As a consequence, non-commercial associations are permitted to engage in economic activities in order to raise funds: An association cannot be prevented from fulfilling its idcal, non-commercial purpose directly with its economic activities.[69] While this judgment has prevented the legislator from reforming

[62] von Hippel (2010), p. 204.

[63] Zimmer et al. (2004), at p. 692.

[64] von Hippel (2010), p. 204.

[65] Zimmer et al. (2004), at p. 692.

[66] Werner (2000), at para. 44.

[67] Only one federal state, namely Rheinland-Pfalz, has adopted a more generous practice and, for example, also grants village shops the possibility to obtain legal capacity as an economic association: Gumbach (2010).

[68] BGH, Order of 16 May 2017 (II ZB 7/16), Neue Juristische Wochenschrift (NJW) 2017, p. 1943.

[69] BGH, NJW 2017, p. 1943, at p. 1945.

the access to the legal form of the commercial association,[70] the case law of lower courts continues to make it difficult for third sector organisations to establish non-commercial associations. Only recently, a Higher Regional Court ruled in a very controversial decision that an association which, according to its statutes, pursues social purposes in rural areas by operating a village pub in a non-profit oriented manner, cannot be regarded as a non-commercial association if it does not have charitable tax status.[71] Even though tax law only has an indicative effect, it substantially restricts the choice of legal form for third-sector organisations.

A third option for these organisations is the establishment of a foundation. The German parliament has recently passed a far-reaching reform of German foundation law.[72] Although the new legal provisions do not reinvent the very fundamentals of foundation law, they aim at creating a more coherent legal framework by bundling its entire content, which was previously partly spread across numerous state laws, in Sections 80-87d of the German Civil Code.[73] In substance, the new rules still introduce the most fundamental change in foundation law since that Code was enacted over a century ago. They have entered into force in July 2023. Both the current and the future foundation law conceptualize foundations as legal entities based on an endowment and thereby offer the possibility to permanently determine the purpose for which income from the endowed assets is used. Due to the absence of members and shareholders, the governance of foundations is dominated by the board of directors, but otherwise their internal structures can be designed quite flexibly. The new law introduces, however, new provisions on the composition, tasks and management and representation powers of the foundation bodies.[74] Establishing a foundation requires not only a foundation deed, a draft of the foundation's statutes and an initial endowment which is sufficient for the fulfilment of the purpose, but also the approval of the competent state authority (Stiftungsaufsichtsbehörde).[75] While this approval is not discretionary, the authority will examine whether all legal requirements are met. In this respect, the foundation's purpose plays a leading role as it defines what should and may be done with the foundation's funds: the foundation exists only for the sake of fulfilling its purpose. According to Art. 80 para. 2 BGB, however, foundations can be established for any purpose that "does not endanger the common good". Current and also future German law therefore follows the guiding principle of the all-purpose foundation in conformity

[70] German Parliament Document (BT-Drs.) 18/12998, p 19. According to the committee on legal affairs, entrepreneurial initiatives in the third sector can be registered as non-commercial associations regardless of the charitable tax status as long as they pursue an idealistic purpose and are not profit-oriented or aimed at profit distribution.

[71] Oberlandesgericht (OLG) Celle, Decision of 6 October 2021 (9 W 99/21), Neue Zeitschrift für Gesellschaftsrecht (NZG) 2022, 223; in more detail and very critical Hüttemann (2021b).

[72] Federal Law Gazette (BGBl.) 2021 I No. 46, pp. 2947 et seqs.

[73] For first overviews, see for instance Pruns (2021); Schauhoff and Mehren (2021).

[74] Stricter governance requirements were discussed intensively, but have not been adopted, cf. Markworth (2021), at pp. 102 et seq.

[75] von Hippel (2010), p. 202.

with the common good (Leitbild der gemeinwohlkonformen Allzweckstiftung),[76] so that in principle all types of foundations are permissible, including family foundations and company-affiliated foundations. Nevertheless, so-called self-purpose foundations are deemed to be prohibited so that the mere operation of companies or the administration of shareholdings in companies do not count among the permissible purposes.[77] Moreover, in the case of charitable foundations, the formulation of the foundation's purpose in the statutes must ensure that the foundation fulfils all respective tax law requirements.[78] While foundation law therefore provides some substantive scope for third sector organisations, there are often insurmountable hurdles in practice because the administrative efforts that are necessary to establish a foundation are considerable.[79] Moreover, sufficient endowments are a necessary precondition for establishing a foundation.

Fourthly and finally, cooperatives are sometimes discussed as an organisational form of the third sector.[80] Whilst the German cooperative movement had, in fact, originally been promoted by social activists aiming at a solidarity-based economy,[81] today's cooperatives are said to "have lost their non-profit character".[82] From a legal point of view, Art. 1 para. 1 of the German Law on Cooperatives (Genossenschaftsgesetz, GenG) provides that the purpose of cooperatives is to "promote the acquisition or the economy of its members or their social or cultural interests through joint business operations". Organisations that primarily serve the interests of their members can, in fact, hardly be counted as being in the third sector if that sector's constitutive characteristics, vague as they may be, are taken seriously.

3 Lex Ferenda for Social Enterprises

As this brief overview of current law has shown, the legal framework of the third sector in Germany has been undergoing several changes in recent years. This transition is driven partly by case law, such as the judgment on day care centres, and partly by legislative changes, such as the reform of the law on foundations. Despite these changes, however, German law still does not provide legal forms that are a really good fit for entrepreneurial initiatives within the third sector, in particular for companies that want to combine profit and purpose. Unlike in many other countries, Germany has so far lacked more fundamental reforms and especially the

---

[76] Explicitly German Parliament Document (BT-Drs.) 14/8765, 9.

[77] See, for instance, Schlüter (2004), pp. 203 et seq.; Jakob (2006), pp. 51 et seqs.; von Homeyer and Reiff (2020), pp. 228 et seq.

[78] In more detail: Fischer and Ihle (2008), p. 1697 et seq.

[79] Cf. Hüttemann, Rawert (2020), at pp. 245–247.

[80] Zimmer and Priller (2019), discussing "Genossenschaften als Teil des Dritten Sektors".

[81] Steding (2002), at pp. 449 et seqs.

[82] Zimmer et al. (2004), p. 682 (n. 1).

introduction of new, specifically tailored legal forms.[83] However, at least with the last change of the federal government, the discussion about such reforms has gained new momentum, supported by corresponding announcements in the coalition agreement.

3.1 National Strategy for Social Entrepreneurship

"Social enterprise lawmaking is a growth industry".[84] With these words, an American author accurately summed up the boom in new corporate forms, with numerous states offering social enterprises suitably tailored legal forms under names such as (Public) Benefit Corporation, Social Purpose Corporation or even Low Profit Limited Liability Company, alongside a private certification scheme that has established itself under the name B Corp.[85] At the same time, social entrepreneurship law-making is also becoming a growth industry in Europe, where no less than 18 member states have introduced special company law regimes.[86] Moreover, the European Parliament launched an own-initiative procedure for a Statute for social and solidarity-based enterprises which would offer an opportunity to establish a broader EU-level legal basis for various types of social economy actors.[87] Such a statute would complement numerous other European measures to promote social entrepreneurship, namely the introduction of European Social Entrepreneurship Funds through the so-called EuSEF Regulation.[88]

Since Germany had been slow to enter this booming legislative field for a long time, the introduction of new legal forms in German law is currently being discussed all the more intensively. No less a person than Holger Fleischer, the managing director of the Max Planck Institute in Hamburg, even announced a "beauty contest" for a new corporate form related to sustainability in a recent article.[89] The starting signal for this contest has been given by the coalition agreement negotiated by the current government parties, i.e. the Social Democratic, the Green and the Liberal Party, which was published in November 2021 and defines the key policy goals for

[83] More extensively Möslein (2017).

[84] Galle (2013), p. 2025.

[85] In detail Möslein and Mittwoch (2016).

[86] Cf. Fici (2017), pp. 15 et seqs and Annex; see also Momberger (2015), pp. 233–300.

[87] For more details, see https://www.europarl.europa.eu/legislative-train/theme-deeper-and-fairer-internal-market-with-a-strengthened-industrial-base-services-including-transport/file-statute-for-social-and-solidarity-based-enterprises.

[88] Regulation (EU) No 346/2013 on European social entrepreneurship funds, OJ EU 2013 L 115, p 18; see also European Commission (2011).

[89] Fleischer (2022).

the period up to 2025.[90] According to this document, one key policy goal concerns support for start-ups and innovation.[91] For this purpose, the government intends to develop a national strategy for social enterprises in order to provide stronger support for public benefit oriented enterprises and social innovations.[92] Part of this strategy is to improve the legal framework for public welfare oriented businesses, such as cooperatives, social enterprises, and integrative organisations.[93] By expressly stressing that a modern corporate culture also includes new corporate forms, such as social enterprises or companies with steward-ownership, the coalition agreement sets the tone for the *lex ferenda* that can be expected to become the *lex lata* in the years to come.

3.2 Towards a New Legal Form for Steward-Ownership

While the coalition agreement leaves open the possibility of introducing other legal forms, for example along the lines of the French société a mission,[94] the text establishes the introduction of a specific legal form as a mandatory legislative task for this legislative period: For companies in steward-ownership, the signatory parties want to create a new appropriate legal basis that excludes tax savings structures ("Für Unternehmen mit gebundenem Vermögen wollen wir eine neue geeignete Rechtsgrundlage schaffen, die Steuersparkonstruktionen ausschließt").[95] With this declaration of commitment, the government coalition refers to an initiative of the Stiftung Verantwortungseigentum (Responsible Ownership Foundation) which has been propagating such a legal form since 2017,[96] and to the preliminary work of an independent group of professors who have already prepared a relevant (and now revised) legislative proposal.[97] Their proposals have triggered a very intense debate among German corporate law scholars and practitioners.[98] Currently, the Federal Ministry of Justice, in cooperation with the Federal Ministry of Finance and the Federal Ministry of Economics and Climate Protection, is working intensively on

[90] The coalition agreement under the title "Mehr Fortschritt wagen – Bündnis für Freiheit, Gerechtigkeit und Nachhaltigkeit" is available at https://www.bundesregierung.de/breg-de/service/gesetzesvorhaben/koalitionsvertrag-2021-1990800.

[91] Coalition agreement, pp. 29–31.

[92] Ibid., para. 917.

[93] Ibid., para. 919 et seq.

[94] Fleischer and Chatard (2021).

[95] Coalition agreement, para. 920–922.

[96] https://stiftung-verantwortungseigentum.de/.

[97] The group includes Anne Sanders, Barbara Dauner-Lieb, Rüdiger Veil, Simon Kempny and the author of this chapter. For their proposals with comments, see Sanders et al. (2020, 2021).

[98] See only, among many others: Arnold et al. (2020); Fischer and Fischer (2020); Habersack (2020); Henn (2021); von Homeyer and Reiff (2020); Hüttemann et al. (2020); Sanders (2020); Reiff (2020); Reiff (2021); Loritz and Weinmann (2021).

these legislative proposals. An official draft bill is about to be prepared. Against this background, numerous details of the new legal form are still the subject of an ongoing legal policy discussion, but at the same time it is both possible and important to outline the key characteristics of that new legal form for steward-ownership already. After all, the "Gesellschaft mit gebundenem Vermögen" is a legal innovation that is strikingly different from other, even foreign, legal forms.

Primarily, the proposed legal form is characterized by a mandatory and unalterable asset lock: Profits and assets must exclusively serve the long-term development of the company and therefore cannot be distributed to shareholders, not even as hidden distributions. On the other hand, profit-sharing by third parties is allowed for the purpose of equity-like corporate financing. If no distributions are made due to the asset lock, distributions do not have to be taxed. Also, with regard to other types of taxation, the new legal form can and should be treated in the same way as other companies. It is only entitled to the benefits of charitable status if it fulfils the relevant (additional) requirements that have been described above.[99] Secondly, there is no obligation to retain assets at the company level. Unlike foundations, the aim is not to preserve those assets, but to secure long-term entrepreneurial freedom across generations. Entrepreneurial assets should therefore be allowed to be used sensibly in competitive markets. Since it is not the goal to tie assets irrevocably to a company, it is permitted to sell assets while maintaining the asset lock. Disinvestments and entrepreneurial realignments are therefore also permissible. Thirdly, the formation of companies in steward-ownership should be simple and straightforward. Complex constructions such as foundations with subsidiaries are often too complicated and too expensive, especially for start-up companies. Unlike the foundation, the "Gesellschaft mit gebundenem Vermögen" is not about creating and monitoring perpetual assets anyway. Therefore, the establishment and, while maintaining the asset lock, also the dissolution, must be as simple as with other entrepreneurial company forms. Apart from the principle of the asset lock, the legal form also offers the greatest possible scope for freedom of contractual design and organizational change. Finally, the draft law does not provide for a commitment to any specific corporate purpose beyond economic activity. The new legal form can thus be used for all kinds of entrepreneurial goals. This absence of any legal commitment to a specific public interest objective defined by the legislator is based on the conviction that entrepreneurial initiative always contributes to the common good, all the more so when personal profit-seeking is not its primary driving force. Any public definition of non-profit purposes would contradict the entrepreneurial character and also the dynamic change in needs that we can currently observe in our society. Therefore, there should be the greatest possible freedom with regard to the entrepreneurial purposes that companies in steward-ownership are allowed to follow.

[99] See above, Sect. 2.1.

4 Conclusion

The legal framework of the third sector in Germany is in a state of transition. Up to now, this transition has been driven partly by case law and partly by specific legislative changes, but it has not yet led to a fundamental change of the legal framework. Currently, significantly more substantial legal reforms are on the horizon, in particular with the plans to introduce a new legal form. Within the spectrum between non-profit and public interest orientation in which the third sector oscillates,[100] the legislative proposal for a company in steward-ownership represents an extreme. The proposal aims at a legal form with a very strict non-profit orientation but without any legal commitment to specific public interest objectives defined by the legislator. One driving force of the upcoming reform is certainly the observation that existing legal forms, such as the foundation, were neither created for social enterprise, nor are they particularly well suited for entrepreneurial ventures. The core of the proposal, however, is the idea that people who do not engage in business for the sake of making profits will have set themselves other, idealistic goals. The legal form is based on the assumption that these goals will almost inevitably serve the common good, precisely because the entrepreneurial activity is not aimed at making a profit. The proposal builds on basic trust in individual purposes, but at the same time also shows scepticism towards state definitions of public welfare goals. Inter alia, the recent discussion about the addition of nuclear energy activities to the list of economic activities covered by the EU sustainability taxonomy[101] illustrates how differently social and sustainability purposes are understood and also how quickly they are subject to change. The new legal form for steward ownership is therefore not subject to any state-defined purpose. Steward-ownership ultimately means a radical departure from the Hegelian image of civil society as a public sphere, where third sector organisations primarily relieve the state of its tasks. In contrast, steward-ownership is thoroughly characterised by private autonomy. With the introduction of the respective legal form, the third sector will form part of a civil society that has finally been transformed into a genuine private law society.

References

Anderheiden M (2006) Gemeinwohl in Republik und Union. Mohr Siebeck, Tübingen

Anheier HK (1992) An elaborate network: profiling the third sector in Germany. In: Gidron B, Kramer RM, Salamon L (eds) Government and Third Sector. San Francisco. pp 31–56

[100] See above, Sect. 1.2.

[101] Cf. Draft of the Commission Delegated Regulation amending Delegated Regulation (EU) 2021/2139 as regards economic activities in certain energy sectors and Delegated Regulation (EU) 2021/2178 as regards specific public disclosures for those economic activities, available at https://ec.europa.eu/info/publications/220202-sustainable-finance-taxonomy-complementary-climate-delegated-act_en.

Anheier HK, Seibel W (2001) The nonprofit sector in Germany. Between state, economy and society. Manchester University Press, Manchester/New York

Arnold A, Burgard U, Roth G, Weitemeyer B (2020) Die GmbH im Verantwortungseigentum – eine Kritik, Neue Zeitschrift für Gesellschaftsrecht (NZG). 1321–1328

Bauer (2015) Ist der "Dritte Sektor" theoriefähig? Anmerkungen über Heterogenität und Intermediarität. In: Birkhölzer K, Klein A, Priller E, Zimmer A (eds) Dritter Sektor/Drittes System – Theorie, Funktionswandel und zivilgesellschaftliche Perspektiven. Verlag für Sozialwissenschaften, Wiesbaden, pp 105–112

Bregman R (2021) Humankind: a hopeful history. Bloomsbury, London

Burgi M, Möslein F (eds) (2021) Zertifizierung nachhaltiger Kapitalgesellschaften: "Good Companies" im Schnittfeld von Markt und Staat. Mohr Siebeck, Tübingen

Di Fabio U (1999) Privatisierung und Staatsvorbehalt. Juristenzeitung (JZ) 1999:585–592

Droege M (2010) Gemeinnützigkeit im offenen Steuerstaat. Mohr Siebeck, Tübingen

Etzioni A (1973) The third sector and domestic missions. Public Adm Rev 33:314–323

European Commission (2011) Social Business Initiative: Creating a favourable climate for social enterprises, key stakeholders in the social economy and innovation, Communication to the European Parliament, the Council, the European Economic and Social Committee and the Committee of the Regions, COM (2011), 682 final

Fici A (2017) European Study for Social and Solidarity-Based Enterprise – Study for the Juri Committee, available at: http://www.europarl.europa.eu/RegData/etudes/STUD/2017/583123/IPOL_STU(2017)583123_EN.pdf

Fischer DJ, Ihle J (2008) Satzungsgestaltung bei gemeinnützigen Stiftungen, DStR, pp 1692–1698

Fischer H-J, Fischer K (2020) Die GmbH in Verantwortungseigentum (VE-GmbH) im Rahmen der Umsetzung globaler Nachhaltigkeitsziele – eine mögliche neue Rechtsform für den Mittelstand

Fisher AGB (1933) Capital and the growth of knowledge. Econ J 43:379–389

Fisher AGB (1939) Production, primary, secondary and tertiary. Econ Rec 15:24–38

Fleischer H (2018) Comparative corporate governance in closely held corporations. In: Gordon J, Ringe WG (eds) The Oxford handbook of corporate law and governance. Oxford University Press, Oxford, pp 679–718

Fleischer H (2022) Ein Schönheitswettbewerb für eine neue Gesellschaftsform mit Nachhaltigkeitsbezug: zur rechtspolitischen Diskussion um eine GmbH mit gebundenem Vermögen. Zeitschrift für Wirtschaftsrecht (ZIP):345–355

Fleischer H, Chatard Y (2021) Gesetzliche Zertifizierung nachhaltiger Unternehmen: Die französische "société à mission" als Vorbild für Deutschland?, Neue Zeitschrift für Gesellschaftsrecht (NZG). 1525–1532

Galle B (2013) Social enterprise: who needs it? Boston Coll Law Rev 54:2025–2045

Gerner-Beuerle C, Schillig M (2019) Comparative company law. Oxford University Press, Oxford

Gilberg A (2020) Die gemeinnützige GmbH in der notariellen Praxis, Rheinische Notar-Zeitschrift (RNotZ). pp 193–210

Görlitz A, Voigt R (1985) Rechtspolitologie. Eine Einführung, Opladen: Westdeutscher Verlag

Gumbach D (2010) Dorfläden als wirtschaftliche Vereine. In: Zentralverbandes deutscher Konsumgenossenschaften e.V. (ed) Wirtschaftliche Vereine, Books on Demand: Norderstedt

Habersack M (2020) "Gesellschaft mit beschränkter Haftung in Veranwortungseigentum" – ein Fremdkörper im Recht der Körperschaften. GmbH-Rundschau (GmbHR):992–997

Hansmann H (1980) The role of nonprofit enterprise. Yale Law J 89:835–901

Hegel GWF (1821) Grundlinien der Philosophie des Rechts. Nicolaische Buchhandlung, Berlin

Henn L (2021) Gesellschaft mit beschränkter Haftung mit gebundenem Vermögen (GmbH-gebV) – Ein Überblick, Zeitschrift für die notarielle Beratungs- und Beurkundungspraxis (NotBZ), pp 241–246

Hopt KJ, von Hippel T, Walz WR (2005) Nonprofit-Organisationen in Recht, Wirtschaft und Gesellschaft: Theorien, Analysen, Corporate Governance. Mohr Siebeck, Tübingen

Hüttemann R (2017) Gemeinnützigkeitsrecht als Organisationsrecht des Dritten Sektors. In: Festschrift für Theodor Baums. Mohr Siebeck, Tübingen, pp 623–640

Hüttemann R (2018) Empfiehlt es sich, die rechtlichen Rahmenbedingungen für die Gründung und Tätigkeit von Non-Profit-Organisationen übergreifend zu regeln?, Gutachten G zum 72. Deutschen Juristentag. CH Beck, München
Hüttemann R (2021a) Gemeinnützigkeits- und Spendenrecht, 5th edn. Otto Schmidt, Köln
Hüttemann R (2021b) Die kleine Kneipe und das Vereinsrecht, Zeitschrift für Wirtschaftsrecht (ZIP). pp 2524–2526
Hüttemann R, Rawert P (2020) Gründungsaufwand bei Stiftungen und Vereinen, Zeitschrift für Wirtschaftsrecht (ZIP). pp 245–251
Hüttemann R, Rawert P, Weitemeyer B (2020) Zauberwort "Verantwortungseigentum". Zeitschrift für das Recht der Nonprofit Organisationen (npoR):296–298
Isensee J, Knobbe-Keuk B (1988) Gutachten der Unabhängigen Sachverständigenkommission zur Prüfung des Gemeinnützigkeits- und Spendenrechts. Schriftenreihe des Bundesministeriums der Finanzen, Bonn
Jakob D (2006) Schutz der Stiftung: Die Stiftung und ihre Rechtsverhältnisse im Widerstreit der Interessen. Mohr Siebeck, Tübingen
Kahl W (2002) Die rechtliche Bedeutung der Unterscheidung von Staat und Gesellschaft. Juristische Ausbildung (JURA):721–729
Krimmer H (2018) Datenreport Zivilgesellschaft, Pringer VS, Wiesbaden
Latzel C (2020) Vorbemerkung zu § 611. In: von Staudinger J (ed) Kommentar zum BGB, 16th edn. Sellier, de Gruyter, Berlin
Leistner-Egensperger A (2019) Shrinking spaces für den Dritten Sektor: Reformbedarf zur Abgabenordnung, Zeitschrift für Stiftungs– und Vereinswesen (ZStV). 205–210
Levitt T (1973) The third sector: new tactics for a responsive society. Amacom, New York
Loritz KG, Weinmann PS (2021) Die GmbH mit gebundenem Vermögen – Kreative Idee oder Legitimation zum Betreiben eines Unternehmens ohne typische Unternehmerpflichten? Deutsches Steuerrecht (DStR):2205–2211
Markworth D (2021) Das Stiftungsrecht am Scheidweg: Der Entwurf eines Gesetzes zur Vereinheitlichung des Stiftungsrechts aus unternehmensrechtlicher Perspektive. Neue Zeitschrift für Gesellschaftsrecht (NZG):101–110
Momberger B (2015) Social Entrepreneurship – im Spannungsfeld zwischen Gesellschafts- und Gemeinnützigkeitsrecht. Bucerius Law School Press, Hamburg
Möslein F (2017) Reformperspektiven im Recht sozialen Unternehmertums, Zeitschrift für Rechtspolitik (ZRP). pp 117–119
Möslein F, Mittwoch AC (2016) Soziales Unternehmertum im US-amerikanischen Gesellschaftsrecht: Benefit Corporations und Certified B Corporations. Rabels Zeitschrift für ausländisches und internationales Privatrecht (RabelsZ) 80:399–434
Neuhoff K (1988) Stiftung und Unternehmen – Zur Diskussion über das Stiftungsrecht, Zeitschrift für öffentliche und gemeinwirtschaftliche Unternehmen (ZögU). Journal for Public and Nonprofit Services:329–335
Neumärker KJB (2003) Die politische Ökonomie der privaten Bereitstellung öffentlicher Güter. In: Frankfurt M et al (eds) Lang
Paqué KH (2007) Gemeinnützigkeit und Steuerbegünstigung: Neue ökonomische Gedanken zu einem alten rechtlichen Problem, Non Profit Law Yearbook, pp 1–19
Primmer J, Krimmer H, Lavigne A (2017) ZiviZ-Survey 2017: Vielfalt verstehen, Zusammenhalt stärken, available at https://www.ziviz.de/ziviz-survey
Pruns M (2021) EIn Überblick über das neue Stiftungsrecht, Zeitschrift für die Steuer. und Erbrechtspraxis (ZErb), pp 301–308
Rast F. (2018) Perspektiven der Förderung sozialen und nachhaltigen Unternehmertums im Rahmen des EU-Beihilfenrechts – Zugleich ein Beitrag zum Kriterium der Selektivität, Europäisches Wirtschafts– und Steuerrecht (EWS). pp 142–148
Reiff M (2020) Entwurf eines Gesetzes für die GmbH im Verantwortungseigentum (VE-GmbH) vorgelegt. Zeitschrift für Wirtschaftsrecht (ZIP):1750–1754

Reiff M (2021) Verantwortungseigentum "mit gebundenem Vermögen": Überarbeiteter Gesetzentwurf zur Erweiterung des GmbHG vorgelegt, Neue Juristische Online-Zeitschrift (NJOZ), pp 609–611
Rose-Ackerman S (1986) Introduction. In: id. (ed) The economics of nonprofit institutions. Studies in structure and policy. Oxford, Oxford University Press, pp 3–17
Rosenski N (2012) Die wirtschaftliche Bedeutung des Dritten Sektors, in: Statistisches Bundesamt (ed.), Wirtschaft und Statistik. pp 209-217., available at https://www.destatis.de/DE/Methoden/WISTA-Wirtschaft-und-Statistik/2012/03/wirtschaftliche-bedeutung-3-sektor-032012.html
Sabeti H, Fourth Sector Network Concept Working Group (2009) The Emerging Fourth Sector – A New Sector of Organizations at the Intersection of the Public, Private and Social Sectors. https://assets.aspeninstitute.org/content/uploads/files/content/docs/pubs
Sachs W (1988) Mannigfaltigkeit der Situationen. Über Wilhelm von Humboldts Versuch, die Grenzen der Wirksamkeit des Staates zu bestimmen. In: Schmidt T (ed) Entstaatlichung. Wagenbach, Berlin, pp 26–37
Sachße C (1994) Subsidiarität: Zur Karriere eines sozialpolitischen Ordnungsbegriffs. Zeitschrift für Sozialreform 40(11):717–738
Sachße C (1995) Verein, Verband und Wohlfahrtsstaat. Entstehung und Entwicklung der dualen Wohlfahrtspflege. In: Rauschenbach T, Sachße C, Olk T (eds) Von der Wertgemeinschaft zum Dienstleistungsunternehmen. Frankfurt, Suhrkamp, pp 123–149
Salamon LM, Anheier HK (1997) Defining the nonprofit sector: a cross-national analysis. Manchester University Press, Manchester
Salamon LM, Sokolovski W (2018) Beyond nonprofits: in search of the third sector. In: Enjolras B, Salamon LM, Sivesind KH, Zimmer A (eds) The third sector as a renewable resource for Europe: concepts, impacts, challenges and opportunities. Palgrave Macmillan, pp 7–48
Sanders A (2020) Eine Gesellschaft in Verantwortungseigentum im GmbHG, Zeitschrift für Rechtspolitik (ZRP). GmbH-Rundschau (GmbHR):140–143
Sanders A et al (2020) Eckpunktepapier zum Gesetzesentwurf zur Einführung einer Gesellschaft in Verantwortungseigentum mbH (VE-GmbH) in das GmbHG. GmbH-Rundschau (GmbHR), pp R228–R230
Sanders A et al (2021) Gesetzentwurf GmbH mit gebundenem Vermögen – Verantwortungseigentum 2.0, 285–290
Schauhoff S, Mehren J (2021) Die Reform des Stiftungsrechts, Neue Juristische Wochenschrift (NJW). pp 2993–2999
Schlüter A (2004) Stiftungsrecht zwischen Privatautonomie und Gemeinwohlbindung. C.H. Beck, München
Schuppert GF (1989) Markt, Staat, Dritter Sektor – oder noch mehr? Sektorspezifische Steuerungsprobleme ausdifferenzierter Staatlichkeit, Jahrbuch zur Staats- und Verwaltungswissenschaft. pp 47–87
Schuppert GF (1991) State, market, third sector: problems of organizational choice in the delivery of public services. Nonprof Volunt Sect Q 20:123–136
Schuppert GF (1995) Zur Anatomie und Analyse des Dritten Sektors. Die Verwaltung 2:137–200
Seer R (2003) Gemeinwohlzwecke und steuerliche Entlastung. DStJG 26:11–48
Steding R (2002) Die Genossenschaft und ihr ambivalentes Verhältnis zum Aktienrecht: Überlegungen zur juristischen Annäherung der eG an die AG, Neue Zeitschrift für Gesellschaftsrecht (NZG), pp 449–455
Strachwitz RG (2001) Germany. In: Schlüter A, Then V, Walkenhorst P (eds) Foundations in Europe. Bertelsmann, Gütersloh, pp 133–144
Streeck W, Schmitter P (1985) Community, market, state – and associations? The prospective contribution of interest governance to social order. Eur Sociol Rev 1(2):119–138
United Nations, Department of Economic and Social Affairs, Statistics Division (2003) Handbook on non-profit institutions in the system of Nationa accounts. New York, Studies in Methods Series F. No. 91

von Hippel T (2005) Begriffsbildung und Problemkreise der Nonprofitorganisationen aus juristische Sicht. In: Hopt KJ, von Hippel V, Walz WR (eds) Nonprofit-Organisationen in Recht, Wirtschaft und Gesellschaft: Theorien, Analysen, Corporate Governance. Mohr Siebeck, Tübingen, pp 268–275

von Hippel T (2010) Nonprofit organizations in Germany. In: Hopt KJ, von Hippel V, Walz WR (eds) Comparative corporate governance of non-profit organizations. Cambridge University Press, Cambridge, pp 197–227

von Homeyer O, Reiff M (2020) Verantwortungseigentum ante portas? – Erste Betrachtungen einer weitreichenden Idee, Zeitschrift für das Recht der Nonprofit Organisationen (npoR). pp 224–232

Walz WR (2002) Die Selbstlosigkeit gemeinnütziger Non-Profit-Organisationen im Dritten Sektor zwischen Staat und Markt. Juristenzeitung 20:268–275

Weidmann C, Kohlhepp R (2020) Die gemeinnützige GmbH: Errichtung, Geschäftstätigkeit und Besteuerung einer gGmbH. Springer, Wiesbaden

Weiß W (2000) Privatisierung und Staatsaufgaben. Mohr Siebeck, Tübingen

Weitemeyer B (2018) Reformbedarf für den Dritten Sektor? Neue Juristische Wochenschrift (NJW):2775–2780

Werner A (2000) Verein. In: Winheller S, Geibel S, Jachmann-Michel M (eds) Gesamtes Gemeinnützigkeitsrecht, 2nd edn. Nomos, Baden-Baden

Zimmer A (1996) Vereine – Basiselement der Demokratie. Leske & Budrich, Opladen

Zimmer A (1999) Corporatism revisited – the legacy of history and the German nonprofit sector. Voluntas 10(1):37–49

Zimmer A, Priller E (2007) Gemeinnützige Organisation im gesellschaftlichen Wandel, 2nd edn. Verlag für Sozialwissenschaften, Wiesbaden

Zimmer A, Priller E (2019) Genossenschaften als Teil des Dritten Sektors, Zeitschrift für öffentliche und gemeinwirtschaftliche Unternehmen (ZögU). pp 280–299

Zimmer A et al (2004) The legacy of subsidiarity: the nonprofit sector in Germany. In: Zimmer A, Priller E (eds) Future of civil society. Verlag für Sozialwissenschaften, Wiesbaden

Chapter 5
Third Sector Organisations in Ireland: Assembling the Regulatory Jigsaw Pieces of an Evolving, If Fragmented, Sector

Oonagh B. Breen

Contents

Abstract Ireland is home to a rich and vibrant tapestry of third sector organisations. The legal regulation of these organisations, however, does not form a seamless web of enabling legislation. Most recent legislative attention has focused on charitable organisations in light of the tax exemptions and benefits that often flow from attaining this legal status. While efforts have been made to modernise the charity regulatory framework with the introduction of the Charities Act 2009, much work remains to be done before the transparency and accountability promised by that Act

---

Oonagh B. Breen is Professor of Law at the Sutherland School of Law at University College Dublin.

O. B. Breen (✉)
Sutherland School of Law, University College Dublin, Dublin, Ireland
e-mail: Oonagh.breen@ucd.ie

A. Fici (ed.), *The Law of Third Sector Organizations in Europe*,
https://doi.org/10.1007/978-3-031-41744-3_5

is attained. Outside of the world of charities, which form a smaller subset of the non-profit world, the legal and regulatory treatment of non-profits is both fragmented and functional, depending on the legal structure underpinning the third sector organisation with little allowance made for environmental differences experienced by non-profits compared to their for-profit counterparts. Legislation aimed at non-profits is often arcane and badly in need of reform—note particularly the nineteenth century legislation governing trusts (The Trustee Act 1893) and industrial and friendly societies (The Industrial and Provident Societies Act 1893). National policy discussions on the promotion of social enterprises and the modernisation of the law relating to cooperatives are steps in the right direction but action is now required to move from policy ideal to practical implementation.

1 Introduction

Ireland is a common law country in the midst of its civil law neighbours in the European Union. It is more common to speak of the "community and voluntary sector" or to speak of "charities" than it is to speak of third sector organisations in this jurisdiction. Nevertheless, there is a strong non-profit sector present in Ireland, which at the last count (by Benefacts in 2021) numbered in excess of 34,331 organisations, of which approximately one-third are registered as charities. According to Benefacts' fifth annual non-profit sectoral report in June 2021,[1] the non-profit sector in Ireland had a turnover of €13.9 billion and received €6.2 billion in state funding—accounting for 8.1% of all government funding in 2019 (the financial year on which the 2021 report was based). The sector employed more than 164,922 employees. Since 2017, when the first Benefacts Nonprofit Sector analysis was published, the number of third sector organisations mapped by Benefacts grew from a starting number of 19,505 (forty percent of which were charities) and an annual turnover of €10.9 billion.

Despite the significance of its contribution, the non-profit sector in Ireland is not well served in terms of legally enabling frameworks. Organisations active in this non-government, non-market space typically adopt one of an array of legal forms ranging from the corporate form of a company limited by guarantee, trusts, or unincorporated associations with a smaller number taking the form of cooperatives or friendly societies. Presently, there is no bespoke legal form to facilitate non-profits that wish to engage in social enterprise and unlike the United Kingdom, there is no bespoke charitable incorporated form such as the charitable incorporated organisation.

[1] Benefacts (2021) Nonprofit Sector Analysis 2021. June. https://benefactslegacy.ie/wp-content/uploads/2022/03/benefacts-nonprofit-sector-analysis-2021.pdf.

2 Historical Background

In the late 19th century, religious charities provided many essential services in the fields of health care, education and social welfare in Ireland. In the 20th century, many of these voluntary organizations partnered with the state to provide these services on its behalf while receiving its funded support. In terms of the non-profit sector classification of Salamon and Anheier,[2] the relationship between the state and the non-profit sector in Ireland can be classified by the corporatist model. In line with this model, Irish non-profits work closely with the State in the provision of public services and are largely funded by the State, resulting in a sizeable non-profit sector (based on numbers employed) and extensive government social welfare spending. Today, the greatest number of non-profits continue to be found in the local development, recreation/sports, and education/research sectors.[3]

2.1 The Difference Between Being a Non-Profit and Being a Charity

Before we delve into the legal regulation of third sector organisations in Ireland, it is necessary to say a few words about dividing lines between charities, which form a small but important subset of the larger non-profit sector in Ireland, and non-profits more generally. We normally distinguish the "non-profit sector" from both the "for-profit" or market sector and from the state. It is known by many names in many different regions, including "the community and voluntary" sector, "the not-for-profit" or "non-governmental organisation (NGO)" sector, the "third sector" or "the social economy." One of the most widely accepted definitions of a non-profit organisation was developed by the Johns Hopkins Comparative Non-profit Sector Project in 1991.[4] This project sought to develop a common base of data about a similar set of "non-profit" or "voluntary" institutions in a disparate set of more than 45 countries and covering all five continents. To this end, it identified five key structural and operational characteristics that seemed to define the range of entities most associated with the non-profit or voluntary sector in countries throughout the world.

Non-profits often provide much good in their local communities and enrich civil society, but they are not all necessarily charities as they will not meet the charity test (discussed below). This may be because they won't have exclusively charitable purposes or perhaps, they will not meet the standards of the public benefit test.

[2] Salamon and Anheier (1998), pp. 213–248.

[3] Benefacts (2021) Nonprofit Sector Analysis 2021. June. https://benefactslegacy.ie/wp-content/uploads/2022/03/benefacts-nonprofit-sector-analysis-2021.pdf.

[4] Johns Hopkins Comparative Nonprofit Sector Project (CNP), Methodology and Data Sources, available at https://ccss.jhu.edu/publications-findings?did=105.

Non-profits are not required to register with or be regulated by the Charities Regulatory Authority (CRA) and they are not entitled to charitable tax-exempt status. These organisations may take many forms, again discussed below, ranging from mutual societies, cooperatives, social enterprises, community sports associations, trade unions and organisations otherwise set up not to distribute any profits made to their founders and controllers.

The defining characteristics of a non-profit entity, as explained by the Johns Hopkins methodology,[5] are that the entity must be:

(1) Organised, i.e., institutionalised to some extent.
(2) Private, i.e., institutionally separate from government.
(3) Non-profit-distributing, i.e., not returning profits generated to their owners or directors.
(4) Self-governing, i.e., equipped to control their own activities.
(5) Voluntary, i.e., involving some meaningful degree of voluntary participation.

For many non-profit organisations mission matters more than profit, but they do not necessarily meet the stricter tests set down in the Charities Act to be registered as charities. In other words, a non-profit organisation is a catch-all term for organisations that are, unsurprisingly, "not for profit", meaning that their activities are not for the financial benefit of any individual or board of directors. Non-profits must choose a legal form upon establishment and as we shall see, they may choose to be incorporated or unincorporated.

The main benefit of being a not-for-profit organisation is that these organisations are much freer to carry out their activities as they do not have to comply with charity law. They can, therefore, engage in political activities and other non-charitable purposes to a much greater extent than charities can; they enjoy greater freedom in their commercial activities than charities, and because they do not have to satisfy the public benefit test, they can choose to limit those who benefit from their activities on a mutual benefit basis.

2.2 *What Is a Charity?*

The smaller subset of the charity sector sits within this broader sphere of non-profits. The key factor that differentiates the charity sector from non-profit organisations more generally is whether the organisation is eligible to register as a charity with the CRA. While not every non-profit will be a charity, every charity will be a non-profit.

Section 2 of the Charities Act 2009 provides that:

'charitable organisation' means

[5] Ibid.

(a) the trustees of a charitable trust, or
(b) a body corporate or an unincorporated body of persons –

(i) that promotes a charitable purpose only,
(ii) that, under its constitution, is required to apply all of its property (both real and personal) in furtherance of that purpose, except for moneys expended –

(I) in the operation and maintenance of the body, including moneys paid in remuneration and superannuation of members of the staff of the body, and
(II) in the case of a religious organisation or community, on accommodation and care of members of the organisation or community,

and

(iii) none of the property of which is payable to the members of the body.

The Act goes on in section 3 to define a charitable purpose as being one of the listed purposes in that section of the Act and that each of those purposes must be for the public benefit. Charitable purposes must also be "exclusively charitable."[6]

The main benefits of being a charity include the public trust and recognition that comes with this status, the associated tax exemptions and benefits (e.g., exemption from income and corporation tax, etc), and the preference of some public funders to work with and fund charities because of the regulatory regime with which they comply. Charities can also legally last in perpetuity and when they come to an end, any remaining charitable assets or funds are not lost to the charitable sector but are applied to another charitable purpose as near as possible to that of the defunct charity (under the doctrine of cy près).

All charities that meet the charity test in the 2009 Act are required by law to register with the CRA regardless of size, legal form, purpose, or activities. Section 39(3) of the 2009 Act clearly states, "a charitable organisation that intends to operate or carry on activities in the State shall . . . apply to the Authority to be registered in the register, and it shall be the duty of the charity trustees of the charitable organisation concerned to make the application on behalf of the charitable organisation." Registered charities must then comply with the annual reporting and governance requirements of the CRA.

3 Legal Framework and Legal Forms

Regulation of non-profits more generally in Ireland has been piecemeal and sporadic in the past. While the Charities Act 1961–1973 provided a regulatory framework for charitable organisations, the Acts did not provide for a public register of charities or for annual reporting by charities. The Commissioners for Charitable Donations and Bequests, established in 1844, had statutory responsibility for the oversight of Irish charities and the Commissioners carried out their role until they were dissolved by

[6]For further details on the requirements for charitable status see Breen and Smith (2019).

the Charities Act 2009 with their powers being transferred to the new regulator, the Charities Regulatory Authority ('CRA'). While the Commissioners had certain investigation powers on the face of the Charities Acts 1971–1973, in truth, they had no real enforcement powers to regulate charities and their role was more of an enabling one.[7] The Commissioners assisted charity trustees who lacked the necessary powers in their trust deeds to effectively carry out their charitable purposes. The Commissioners could grant a power of sale over trust property and could authorise actions by the charity trustees in instances where the charity trust deed was otherwise silent. Acting on the sanction of the Commissioners provided charity trustees with indemnity in relation to their actions that would not have otherwise existed. The Commissioners also played an important role in framing cy près schemes for charities that could no longer continue to function for whatever reason. This important cy près jurisdiction has now passed to the Charities Regulatory Authority.[8] The High Court also enjoys jurisdiction to frame cy près schemes.

Past regulation of non-profit activities was very much the preserve of a fragmented functionary regulatory system.[9] If a non-profit took a corporate form, its regulation was the preserve of the Companies Registration Office (CRO) and the Office of the Director of Corporate Enforcement. If a non-profit enjoyed charitable tax exemption, then the Revenue Commissioners played an important role in regulatory oversight in the absence of a bespoke charity regulator. Where a non-profit was engaged in public fundraising endeavours, An Garda Síochána played an important role in licensing such public collections or local lotteries and ensuring that the fundraised sums were applied to the purpose for which they were raised. Many non-profit organisations, particularly if they are unincorporated and not claiming tax relief, fall under the regulatory radar entirely and have no statutory requirements imposed upon them but equally do not enjoy enabling provisions to accommodate their non-profit missions.

3.1 Trusts

The trust is typically used in the context of asset holding entities engaged in charitable endeavours and in the past has been the favoured legal form for many religious congregations and grant-making foundations that are not otherwise heavily involved in employing staff or entering contractual relations so as to expose themselves to liability. The register of charities currently lists over 600 registered charities that self-identify as trusts. A common law trust differs from a civil law foundation in that a trust does not enjoy separate legal personality from the trustees charged with administering it. The primary legislation governing trusts in Ireland is the Trustee

[7] O'Halloran and Breen (2000), pp. 6–14.

[8] Breen and Smith (2019), pp. 499–505.

[9] See Breen (2020), pp. 155–177.

Act 1893, an Act developed at a time of gentlemen trustees in a far gone era. The Irish Law Reform Commission has recommended a complete statutory revision of trust law in Ireland and produced a draft Trustee Bill to assist the government but to date no government has taken action in this area.[10] With the introduction of the Charities Act 2009, charitable trusts were required to send copies of their trust deeds to the CRA. These founding documents, however, have not been published on the Register of Charities by the regulator to date. Thus, unless a trust voluntarily shares its governing instrument with the public, it is difficult to review the provisions under which it operates.

3.2 Companies

Just over 10,000 of Ireland's non-profits are incorporated while approximately 44.3% of charities take this legal structure with the most common form being the company limited by guarantee ('CLG'). A CLG does not have a share capital. Instead, its members' liability is limited to the amount they have undertaken to contribute to the assets of the company, in the event it is wound up, not exceeding the amount specified in the memorandum. This 'guarantee' is often for a nominal sum of €1. A CLG shares many of the same terms and processes as a company limited by shares. Like such companies, it enjoys limited liability and separate legal personality, it has directors and members and holds AGMs, because all companies are governed by company law contained in the Companies Act 2014. However, there are also differences—for example, the 'optional'provisions for a CLG's constitution include rotation of one third of the directors each year unless the constitution expressly provides otherwise.[11]

A CLG is governed by the Companies Act 2014 and its governing instrument or 'constitution'. Since the Companies Act 2014, the constitution is officially a single document—however, it comes in two parts: the memorandum and the articles of association. These two parts of the constitution are essentially the same as the pre-Companies Act 2014 'Memorandum and Articles'. Many of the terms used in a company's memorandum and articles of association have special meanings set out in that Act. Some of those terms also have meanings which are governed by case law relating to cases before the courts on past ambiguities involving companies.

A second form of company which is sometimes used in the not-for-profit sector is the 'designated activity company' ('DAC'). This form of company tends to be used in the relatively rare circumstances where a non-profit company was a simple private company limited by shares with charitable objects prior to the introduction of the

[10] Irish Law Reform Commission (2008) Trust Law: General Proposals. (LRC 92).

[11] Companies Act 2014, s.1196 – there is no equivalent provision for an LTD company in Part 4 of the Act.

Companies Act 2014.[12] After the end of the transitional phase for the introduction of the Companies Act, the objects clauses of ordinary private companies were deleted by operation of law. As a charity needs its objects clause to remain charitable (to ensure that its objects remain wholly and exclusively charitable), any charities that simply wished to retain their objects clause converted to a designated activity company, which is the new corporate form most nearly equivalent to a private limited company retaining its objects clause.

3.3 Unincorporated Associations

The vast majority of Ireland's non-profit organisations take the form of unincorporated associations with Benefacts categorising two-thirds of its mapped non-profits as unincorporated entities in its 2021 Report. As with trusts, legal responsibility and legal liability for the actions of unincorporated associations rest with the individuals who set up and run the organisation, as the organisation has no separate legal personality of its own. To contract with or sue the organisation it is necessary to contract with or sue the individuals who control the organisation. Many non-profits start life as unincorporated associations—as it is the simplest association to establish—but later convert to corporate forms for the greater protection offered by company law.

Not being a company has three important consequences: firstly, by virtue of the fact of not being incorporated, unincorporated organisations, like trusts, enjoy neither separate legal personality nor limited liability. So, if liability befalls the organisation, the personal assets of those controlling the association are at risk—in legal terms, they are 'personally liable' and in the absence of express contractual wording in the constitution there is no limit on this liability. Secondly, the relationship between the people involved in the organisation is overned by contract law according to the rules (or constitution) they have drawn up between them. Thirdly, the property of the organisation has to be held by the individuals who are controlling the organisation (because the organisation has no legal personality and cannot own property in its own name).

3.4 Cooperatives and Friendly Societies

Cooperatives, friendly societies and industrial and provident societies developed as part of the mutual self-help movement in nineteenth century Ireland. Today, they take many forms ranging from co-operatives, building societies, savings banks,

[12] DACs are governed by Parts 1 to 14 of the Companies Act 2014 as varied by Part 16 of the Act.

credit unions and trade unions. The primary legislation governing these entities are the Industrial and Provident Societies Acts 1893–2018; the Friendly Societies Acts 1896–2018; and the Trade Union Acts, 1871–1990. The Companies Registration Office acts as the statutory regulator and maintains the Register of Friendly Societies. According to the most recent Annual Report of the Registrar of Friendly Societies, at the end of 2020 there were 960 industrial and provident societies, 46 friendly societies and 53 trade unions on the register, making a combined total of 1059 registered entities. As such, 2020 saw an increase of 4 in the number of societies/trade unions on the register compared to the end of 2019.[13] The industrial and provident societies comprise mainly various agricultural co-operatives, group water schemes and housing co-operatives but also include societies involved in a wide range of other activities.

There is no specific legislation dealing with co-operatives in Ireland. The Industrial and Provident Societies Acts 1893–2021 provide the statutory basis for the formation and general operation of industrial and provident societies and is the primary legislation within which co-operatives operate. The legislative framework is a largely Victorian era statutory code incorporating a number of antiquated provisions. Various piecemeal amendments have been introduced over more than 120 years but the fundamental requirements are as set out in the original Industrial and Provident Societies Act, 1893.

Currently, co-operatives can register and operate under the aforementioned IPS legislation or alternatively under the Companies Act 2014. Co-operatives usually define themselves as such by reflecting the distinguishing features of the co-operative model in their rules, if registered as an industrial and provident society, or in their constitution, if registered as a company.

The Industrial and Provident Societies Acts 1893–2018 are widely regarded as being significantly outdated with many of their provisions predating the establishment of the State. The Department of Enterprise, Trade and Employment is engaged in a long awaited extensive overhaul of the legislation governing co-operatives in Ireland with work nearing completion on proposed legislation to repeal the Industrial and Provident Societies legislation and to provide in its stead a modern and effective legislative framework suitable for the diverse range of organisations using the co-operative model in Ireland. To this end, in January 2022, the Department launched a targeted public consultation on the reform and modernisation of the legislation governing co-operative societies.[14]

[13] Registrar of Friendly Societies Annual Report 2020 (June 2021), at p. 5.

[14] See Dept of Enterprise, Trade and Employment (2022), https://enterprise.gov.ie/en/Consultations/Consultations-files/Public-Consultation-Reform-Legislation-Co-operative-Societies.pdf.

4 Legal Reform: Charities Act 2009

In 2009, the Charities Act was signed into law by the President of Ireland but the Act was not commenced until October 2014 when the Charities Regulatory Authority (CRA) was established and the Register of Charities was created. All organisations that enjoyed charitable tax exemption on the date of the Register's creation were automatically placed on the register and deemed registered. Any new charity established after the commencement date of the Act must apply to the CRA for registration prior to operation, as must any existing charity that now meets the charity test in the 2009 Act but which was not previously availing of charitable tax exemption so as to be automatically registered as a deemed charity in 2014. It is an offence to carry out activities or to hold property in Ireland as a charity and not be registered with the CRA.

The long title of the Act sets out the legislative intent to provide for the better regulation and protection of charitable organisations and charitable trusts in Ireland. The Act requires that all charities—regardless of legal form—submit an annual report to the CRA.[15] Unincorporated charities are also required to file their annual financial returns directly with the CRA, while charitable companies continue to file their annual returns with the CRO under company law and the CRO, in turn, shares these returns with the CRA.

To date, the promised transparency and accountability that the Charities Act 2009 was to provide has not materialised in practice. While unincorporated charities shared both their governing instruments with (whether in the form of a written constitution or a trust deed) and submit their annual returns to the charities regulator, this information is not made public on the Register of Charities. There is power for the relevant Minister to make regulations setting out the format of accounting returns for unincorporated charities under the Act but the Minister has never exercised this power.[16] Thus, the level of visibility in relation to the 56% of charities that identify as unincorporated is extremely poor when it comes to governing instruments and financial accounts.

The reason proffered by the charities regulator for the failure to proceed with the promulgation of accounting regulations has been the regulator's preference to first seek amendment of the 2009 Act so as to enable the regulator also to set similar accounting rules for incorporated charities (which currently fall under the remit of company law for reporting purposes). This desire to have a level playing field has had a paradoxical outcome in that it has always been possible to view a charitable company's governing instrument and annual returns via the CRO and this has continued to be the case since the introduction of the 2009 Act. However, the Act has not made the promised inroads in creating greater transparency and accountability for unincorporated charities.

---

[15] Charities Act 2009, s.52.

[16] Charities Act 2009, s.48.

The Charities Amendment Bill is listed on the current Programme of Government as being at "heads of Bill in preparation" stage and while the regulator states in its Statement of Strategy for 2022–2024[17] that it will "continue to advocate for the introduction of the Charities (Amendment) Bill to strengthen the regulatory framework for charities in Ireland", the lack of political will and interest to advance this legislative reform is unlikely to see a timely passage of new law in the coming year.

4.1 *Tax Treatment*

The taxation reliefs available to non-profit organisations in Ireland are associated with having charitable status. Charities are exempt from income and corporation tax, from capital gains tax and capital acquisitions tax. Charities do not pay deposit interest retention tax ('DIRT') on investment savings; nor do they pay stamp duty on land transactions. While charities must pay VAT, they may in certain instances be eligible to apply for the Government's VAT compensation refund scheme which sets an annual sum of €5 million aside to refund charities who meet conditions laid down by the Revenue Commissioners on qualifying VAT expenses incurred in the previous financial year. The Irish scheme is modelled on an earlier Danish scheme to a similar effect.

Charities that have been registered with the Revenue Commissioners for tax exempt purposes for a period of two years or more can apply to the Revenue Commissioners for recognition to benefit under the Charitable Donations Scheme. Under this scheme, recognised charities can reclaim the tax paid by their donors on gifts to that charity provided that that gift equals €250 or more in a financial year. Thus, instead of incentivising individuals to give to charities by making it tax efficient for the individual, the Irish approach is to gross up the donation made to the charity at a blended rate of tax (31%) sitting midway between the standard and marginal rate of tax. The return of the tax to the charity happens when a PAYE worker or a self-assessed worker makes an eligible gift to a recognised charity. When a company makes a donation to a charity, it writes this gift off as a trading expense, thereby continuing to provide an incentive for corporate giving. In 2022, there were approximately 2680 charities availing of the Charitable Donations Scheme.[18] In 2009, the cost to the Exchequer of the gift deduction was approximately €50 million per annum, according to the Commission on Taxation.[19]

---

[17] Charities Regulatory Authority, Third Statement of Strategy 2022-24 (October 2021), p. 13.

[18] See https://www.revenue.ie/en/corporate/information-about-revenue/statistics/other-datasets/charities/resident-charities.aspx.

[19] See Breen and Carroll (2015), pp. 190–210.

4.2 Charitable Accountability

As mentioned in 4 above, the level of charitable accountability promised by the Charities Act 2009 has not materialised in practice. While draft charity and accounting regulations were prepared in 2016 by an expert group in consultation with the CRA, these regulations have never been promulgated. Section 47 of the Charities Act 2009 provides that all unincorporated charities have a duty to keep proper books of accounts. Section 47(11) specifically excludes charitable companies from the remit of s.47, leaving these entities fully subject to company law. While s.48 of the Charities Act requires that charity trustees of a unincorporated charities (with an annual gross income or expenditure greater than €50,000) prepare a statement of accounts in respect of each financial year in such form and containing information relating to such matters as may be prescribed by regulations made by the Minister, these regulations have never been promulgated. Even if introduced, these regulations would not apply to incorporated charities or to education bodies, both of which are expressly excluded from the scope of the section by s.48(6).

Between 2017 and March 2022, a non-profit organisation called Benefacts provided a very useful resource for understanding the broader landscape of non-profits beyond strictly charities. Benefacts mapped and classified Irish non-profits using the International Classification of Non-profit Organisations (ICNPO) developed by the Comparative Nonprofit Sector Project at Johns Hopkins University, Baltimore under the leadership of Professor Lester Salamon.[20] It then used open source data to build an empirical and often forensic account of the funding sources, governance structures and annual expenditures of many of the 34,000 organisations on its database. It made all of this information publicly available as well as providing research services for government departments, statutory agencies and philanthropic foundations who wanted a better understanding of the non-profit organisations that they were funding or partnering with.

The data produced by Benefacts provided the first true picture of Ireland's third sector landscape since the initial and decidedly less empirical efforts that formed part of Ireland's contribution to the John's Hopkins non-profit mapping project.[21] Benefacts was funded by a combination of state and philanthropic funding. When the lead department (the Dept for Public Expenditure and Reform) decided in 2021 that it no longer wished to champion the cause of Benefacts and a substitute 'parent' department could not be identified, other government departments who were ready to fund Benefacts found that they could not. Benefacts was forced to voluntarily wind up in March 2022 as a result.

The loss of the accountability that Benefacts brought to the non-profit sector will be severely missed and the insights provided previously by Benefacts will still be required by funders, most notably government departments who will have to attempt, at much higher cost, to replicate what Benefacts was doing. A legacy

[20] Benefacts (2016) Classification of Irish Civil Society Organisations: Disclosure Draft. January.

[21] Donoghue et al. (1999).

website houses the reports of Benefacts and its published reports shine a spotlight on many areas of non-profit life where previously there was none.[22] In addition to its five annual non-profit sectoral analysis reports 2017–2021, Benefacts also published an online directory showing the sources, levels and beneficiaries of grants to non-profits in Ireland and overseas from nine State bodies (known as the 'Who Funds What'project) in 2020, two reports on Charitable Giving and Philanthropy in Ireland in 2020 and 2021, and a report on charity regulatory filings in 2021 based on the published regulatory filings of 5,364 corporate charities. Its last publication in November 2021 was an online National Lottery Directory, detailing for the first time the sources, levels and beneficiaries of State grants to non-profits in Ireland and overseas using net proceeds of the Irish National Lottery. Benefacts has made all of these previous publications available through its legacy website.[23]

5 Social Enterprises in Ireland

In 2019, the Irish government published its first ever National Social Enterprise Policy for Ireland.[24] The National Social Enterprise Policy is complemented by two other government strategies, the Sustainable, Inclusive and Empowered Communities: A five year Strategy to Support Community and Voluntary Sector in Ireland 2019–2024 and the National Volunteering Strategy (2021–2025). It seeks to create an enabling environment for social enterprise to grow, both in terms of scale and impact.

5.1 National Policy on Social Enterprises

The National Social Enterprise Policy defines a social enterprise in the following way:

> A Social Enterprise is an enterprise whose objective is to achieve a social, societal or environmental impact, rather than maximising profit for its owners or shareholders. It pursues its objectives by trading on an ongoing basis through the provision of goods and/or services, and by reinvesting surpluses into achieving social objectives. It is governed in a fully accountable and transparent manner and is independent of the public sector. If dissolved, it should transfer its assets to another organisation with a similar mission.

---

[22] See https://benefactslegacy.ie/.

[23] Ibid.

[24] National Social Enterprise Policy for Ireland 2019-2022 available at https://s3-eu-west-1.amazonaws.com/govieassets/19332/2fae274a44904593abba864427718a46.pdf.

This definition is consistent with definitions of social enterprises at EU level[25] and distinguishes social enterprises from enterprises that operate for private profit and from other social economy entities. The national policy is built around three key objectives, namely to, (1) build awareness of social enterprise; (2) grow and strengthen social enterprises; and (3) achieve better policy alignment.

In its Annual Report 2020 on the implementation of the national policy,[26] the Minister for Community and Rural Development highlighted the steps taken in its first year of operation to implement that national policy through activities to raise awareness of social enterprises. These included the convening of a second National Social Enterprise Conference in November 2020 and the development of a new Awareness Strategy to highlight the critical role social enterprises play in responding to challenges such as COVID-19 and climate adaptation and to emphasise their potential to shape a more sustainable and inclusive future.

The Annual Report also highlights increased investment with the allocation of €800k for a Training and Mentoring Pilot and €2m for a Small Capital Grants Scheme, funded by the Dormant Accounts Fund. Approximately 220 social enterprises benefited from the small capital grants pilot, which provided grants of between €2000 and €15,000 for equipment, repairs or refurbishments which enabled social enterprises to improve their service delivery. This support was in addition to the Social Enterprise Development Fund (SED Fund), which is delivered by Rethink Ireland and also funded through the Dormant Accounts Fund. Significant support was also provided through the Community Services Programme (CSP), the Social Inclusion and Community Activation Programme (SICAP) and LEADER programmes.

5.2 Legal Structures

There is currently no bespoke legal structure for social enterprises in Ireland. A social entrepreneur can use one of the existing incorporated or unincorporated structures discussed earlier in this chapter in establishing his or her new social enterprise. The absence of a bespoke legal form that equates with the English 'community interest company (CIC) has been noted. In 2020, the Department for Rural and Community Development commissioned the Thompson Reuters Foundation and Mason Hayes Curran Solicitors to produce a legal structures guide for social enterprises in Ireland. This guide sets out the existing legal structures available to social enterprises, detailing the advantages and disadvantages of each type along

[25] See European Commission, A Map of Social Enterprises and their Ecosystems in Europe: Synthesis Report (2015), available at https://ec.europa.eu/social/BlobServlet?docId=12987&langId=en.

[26] Government of Ireland (2020), National Social Enterprise Policy for Ireland 2019-2022: Annual Report.

with a brief discussion of the governance, regulation, tax treatment, establishment costs and treatment of liability, financing and fundraising for each model.[27]

In 2021, the Department, along with Rethink Ireland, published jointly-commissioned research on the need for dedicated legal form for social enterprises.[28] The report, by Tanya Lalor and Gerard Doyle, sought to explore the barriers relating to legal form experienced by social enterprises in Ireland; to inquire whether a dedicated legal form would benefit the sector and, if so, what form it should take.

The authors undertook desk research, a survey of social enterprises in Ireland (resulting in 179 responses), semi-structured interviews with 32 individuals from 27 organisations[29] and two focus groups (comprising 10 participants). The majority of the survey respondents (71.8%) were incorporated as a company limited by guarantee without share capital (CLG) and the second most prevalent form (5.7%) was that of co-operative. Almost three-quarters (73.4%) were standalone local organisations, and 19.7% were part of or associated with 'parent'organisations. Most respondents had applied for charitable status (60.3%) to access grants and social investment funding, to safeguard the social enterprises' social mission, to gain charitable tax exemption, and to safeguard their reputation. The majority of respondents believed that the legal form of their social enterprise met their current or future requirements (59%). However, close to one-quarter believed that it did not. Two-thirds of respondents (66.9%) believed that a distinct legal form was required for the social enterprise sector.

The findings of the report make for interesting reading. The key barriers relating to legal form experienced by social enterprises related to a lack of recognition of social enterprises as a legitimate form by funding agencies, coupled with a perception that charitable status was necessary for them to operate. Difficulties in securing equity finance arising from the CLG legal form (as this form does not enable private shareholding) was also noted. A certain tension arose between those respondents who saw a definite need for a dedicated legal form and those who feared that the introduction of such a model would place a straitjacket on the evolution of social enterprises in Ireland. Those who sought a bespoke legal vehicle were predominantly in favour of the introduction of a corporate form equivalent to the English community interest company ('CIC'), welcoming its characteristic features of an asset lock and a limit on the distribution of profits. Amongst those who did not welcome a new legal form, the fear was expressed that a dedicated legal form would become the de-facto legal form for social enterprises, even if its characteristics were at odds with the predominant structure and governance of social enterprises currently constituted.

---

[27] Social Enterprises in Ireland: Legal Structures Guide (October, 2020), available at https://assets.gov.ie/120048/46975c06-152f-44e5-9036-d6d58c3d72d0.pdf.

[28] Lalor and Doyle (2021).

[29] The participants were drawn from policymakers, social enterprises, network and advocacy organisations, academics, local development organisations, social finance/social impact investors, regulators, and funders.

Drawing on survey responses, the report authors noted respondents' general concerns related to funders' attitudes and understanding of social enterprise, access to finance, the need for recognition and greater awareness of the sector, clarity around identity issues, administrative burdens, and the limitations of charitable status on enterprise development. From the perspective of the majority of those surveyed, a dedicated legal form would resolve many of these issues and would benefit the sector. However, among those surveyed, and across the wider consultation process, there was no consensus about what features a dedicated legal form could provide. There was also a view that existing legal forms might be able to address these barriers. For others, it was not yet possible to demonstrate the necessity of a dedicated legal form at this point in the sector's development.[30]

5.3 *Certification*

Social enterprises that wish to highlight their social economy credentials have had to find other voluntary accreditation methods to distinguish themselves and their organisations from other for-profit or non-profit entities. To date, non-profits have chosen to either become certified 'B Corps'or have applied for a social enterprise accreditation mark.

B Corp certification is a private certification regime for for-profit social enterprises. It is run by a non-profit organisation named 'B-Lab', founded in Pennsylvania in 2006.[31] B Corps are certified by B-Lab to meet standards of social and environmental performance, accountability and transparency. There are currently nine B Corps headquartered in Ireland (the most prominent of which include Danone Dairy Ireland and Cully & Sully) and a further 130 B Corps operating in Ireland (the most prominent of which includes the food company, Innocent).

In November 2020, Social Impact Ireland announced that it had partnered with Social Enterprise Mark CIC (an organisation which accredits social enterprises in the UK). The mark is an independent, externally assessed guarantee that a business is operating as a social enterprise. The mark launched with 5 social enterprises undertaking the certification process.[32]

5.4 *Tax Treatment*

There are a range of fiscal and taxation arrangements, including tax relief, that apply to all enterprises, including those legal forms that can be adopted by social enterprise such as Company Limited by Guarantee (CLG) and including social enterprises

[30] Lalor and Doyle (2021).

[31] See https://www.bcorporation.net/en-us/.

[32] See https://socialimpactireland.ie/social-enterprise-mark/.

holding charitable status approved by the Revenue Commissioners. It has been noted that charitable tax status can "act as a deterrent to investment" as the Revenue Commissioners require that a body with charitable tax status applies its income and property towards the promotion of its main charitable object as set out in the charity's governing instrument. The directors or trustees of a social enterprise with charitable tax status are generally not permitted to receive any remuneration from the social enterprise other than reimbursement of out-of-pocket expenses.

Entrepreneurs who start-up and work full-time in their own company, can claim back income tax paid in the previous six years to invest equity into the company (subscribed as shares) under Start-Up Relief for Entrepreneurs (SURE), previously known as the Seed Capital scheme. The amount of relief is restricted to the amount of the investment.[33] The general conditions for eligibility are that you must:

(1) establish a new company carrying on a new qualifying trading activity
(2) have mainly Pay As You Earn (PAYE) income in the previous four years
(3) take up full-time employment in the new company as a director or an employee
(4) invest cash in the new company by purchasing new shares
(5) keep the purchased shares for at least 4 years.

The Employment and Investment Incentive (EII) (which replaced the Business Expansion Scheme) is a tax relief incentive scheme aimed at unquoted micro, small and medium-sized trading companies. It provides for tax relief of up to 40% in respect of investments made in certain corporate trades.[34] The scheme allows an individual investor to obtain income tax relief on investments for shares in certain companies up to a maximum of 150,000 EUR per annum in each tax year up to 2019. Initially relief is allowed on thirty fortieths [30/40] of the EII investment in the year the investment is made. Potentially, this can result in a tax saving for the investor of up to 30% of the investment. Relief in respect of the further ten fortieths [10/40] of the EII investment will be available in the fourth year after the EII scheme investment was made provided that certain conditions are met. The scheme has the potential to result in a further tax saving for the investor of up to 10% of the investment.[35] The tax relief is provided to enable companies to raise finance for the purpose of expansion, create and/or retain jobs. Several conditions must be satisfied in order to be eligible for this tax relief. These relate to the investor, the company and its trade, how the company uses the money invested and the shares purchased. In its 2013 report, Forfás noted that the EII's predecessor, Business

[33] See https://www.revenue.ie/en/personal-tax-credits-reliefs-and-exemptions/investment/relief-for-investment-in-corporate-trades-for-in/start-up-relief-for-entrepreneurs.aspx. See also Forfás (2013) Social Enterprise In Ireland Sectoral Opportunities and Policy Issues.

[34] See https://www.revenue.ie/en/personal-tax-credits-reliefs-and-exemptions/investment/relief-for-investment-in-corporate-trades-for-in/employment-investment-incentive.aspx.

[35] O'Shaughnessy (2020).

Expansion Scheme, was considered an expensive source of finance, particularly for small projects and, therefore, believed to be of limited use for social enterprises.[36]

6 Conclusion

In conclusion, from a legal perspective the regulation and facilitation of non-profit activity has predominantly been viewed through the lens of charitable activity. The general public and funders alike recognise and for the most part view charities as trusted legitimate organisations, deserving of support, financial and otherwise. The public perception of what constitutes a charity is often much broader than the legal definition of 'charity' actually accommodates, a perception which consequently brings its own difficulties. While progress has been made on the modernisation of the regulatory framework for charities, significant and identifiable gaps remain that hinder the full and effective functioning of this subsector.

When it comes to the broader landscape of third sector organisations in Ireland, there is a rich and vibrant tapestry of organisations active across a broad spectrum of areas with a wide geographic distribution across the country.[37] These non-profit organisations take many legal forms but are not well supported through modern regulatory and enabling frameworks. While these problems have been identified as far back as 2008 (in the case of trusts) and there is ongoing policy discussion about the need to introduce new legislation (particularly for cooperatives and charities) and to consider the possibility of dedicated legal forms (in the case of social enterprise), political will and political attention seems, so far, to be absent when it comes to moving from the policy paper basis to the implementation of reforming legislation.

References

Benefacts (2016) Classification of Irish Civil Society Organisations: Disclosure Draft. January

Benefacts (2021) Nonprofit Sector Analysis 2021. June. https://benefactslegacy.ie/wp-content/uploads/2022/03/benefacts-nonprofit-sector-analysis-2021.pdf

Breen OB (2020) Redefining the regulatory space? The first forays of the irish charities regulatory authority. In: Picton J, Sigafoos J (eds) Debates in charity law. Hart Publishing, London, pp 155–177

Breen OB, Carroll J (2015) Giving in Ireland: a nation of givers in a largely unregulated arena. In Wiepking P, Handy F (eds) The Palgrave handbook of global philanthropy. Palgrave McMillan, Hampshire, pp 190–210

Breen OB, Smith PA (2019) Law of charities in Ireland. Bloomsbury, Dublin

Charities Regulatory Authority (2021) Third Statement of Strategy 2022-24. October

[36] Forfás (2013), p. 82.

[37] Benefacts (2021).

Department of Enterprise, Trade and Employment (2022) Public Consultation on Reform and Modernisation of Legislation regarding Co-operative Societies, https://enterprise.gov.ie/en/Consultations/Consultations-files/Public-Consultation-Reform-Legislation-Co-operative-Societies.pdf.

Donoghue F, Anheier HK, Salamon LM (1999) Uncovering the nonprofit sector in Ireland: its economic value and significance. Baltimore

European Commission (2015) A Map of Social Enterprises and their Ecosystems in Europe: Synthesis Report, https://ec.europa.eu/social/BlobServlet?docId=12987&langId=en

Forfás (2013) Social Enterprise In Ireland Sectoral Opportunities and Policy Issues

Government of Ireland (2020) National Social Enterprise Policy for Ireland 2019-2022: Annual Report

Government of Ireland, National Social Enterprise Policy for Ireland 2019-2022, https://s3-eu-west-1.amazonaws.com/govieassets/19332/2fae274a44904593abba864427718a46.pdf

Irish Law Reform Commission (2008) Trust Law: General Proposals. (LRC 92)

Johns Hopkins Comparative Nonprofit Sector Project (CNP), Methodology and Data Sources, https://ccss.jhu.edu/publications-findings?did=105

Lalor T, Doyle G (2021) Research into the need for a dedicated legal form for social enterprises. October

O'Halloran K, Breen OB (2000) Charity law in Ireland and Northern Ireland—registration and regulation. Irish Law Times 18:6–14

O'Shaughnessy M (2020) Social Enterprises and their Ecosystems in Europe: Report on Ireland

Registrar of Friendly Societies Annual Report 2020 (June 2021)

Salamon LM, Anheier HK (1998) Social origins of civil society: explaining the non-profit sector cross-nationally. Voluntas 9:213–248

Thompson Reuters Foundation and Mason Hayes Curran (2020) Social Enterprises in Ireland: Legal Structures Guide. https://assets.gov.ie/120048/46975c06-152f-44e5-9036-d6d58c3d72d0.pdf

Chapter 6
The New Italian Code of the Third Sector. Essence and Principles of a Historic Legislative Reform

Antonio Fici

Contents

Abstract In 2017, a new law on third sector organizations, including social enterprises, was introduced in Italy. Known as "the Reform of the third sector", this legislation is based on a Code of the third sector which introduces a new legal qualification or status, namely that of a "third sector entity", which is available to organizations that meet the expected legal requirements. The status of third sector entity confers upon the organization that holds it not only fiscal benefits, but also other benefits. After having highlighted the constitutional relevance of third sector

---

Antonio Fici is an Associate Professor of Private Law at the University of Rome Tor Vergata and the Scientific Director of the Terzjus Foundation – Observatory on the Law of Third Sector, Philanthropy and Social Enterprise.

A. Fici (✉)
University of Rome Tor Vergata, Department of History, Cultural Heritage, Education and Society, Rome, Italy
e-mail: antonio.fici@uniroma2.it

A. Fici (ed.), *The Law of Third Sector Organizations in Europe*,
https://doi.org/10.1007/978-3-031-41744-3_6

organizations, this chapter presents and discusses the notion of a third sector organization and the particular typologies thereof, including that of social enterprise. The chapter then describes the promotional treatment awarded to third sector organizations and the aims and forms of public control to which third sector organizations are subject. Conclusions follow.

1 Introduction

In Italian law, the category of "third sector organizations" (hereinafter also "TSOs") is recognized and regulated by Legislative decree no. 117/2017 on the Code of the Third Sector (hereinafter also "Code" or "CTS"), and other related laws such as, notably, Legislative decree no. 112/2017 on "social enterprises", which are, as we shall see, a particular type of TSOs.

In short, the legal category of TSOs comprises associations and foundations (and in certain instances also companies and cooperatives) that carry out one or more activities of general interest for civic, solidaristic and social utility purposes rather than for profit.

It is a kind of private organizations that has attracted the attention of the Italian legislator for a long time, even though not always in a systematic way. This has led to a large-scale production of special laws on specific subjects, which began immediately after the unification of Italy.

Law no. 753 of 3 August 1862 meticulously regulated "*opere pie*", namely, charitable institutions and other legal entities whose purpose was to help disadvantaged persons, assist them, provide them with an education or initiate them into professions, arts or crafts.[1]

Law no. 3818 of 15 April 1886, established "mutual aid societies", whose main objective was (and still is)[2] to offer their members a subsidy in the event of illness or inability to work or old age, as well as to help the families of deceased members.

Along similar lines, in the 1990s there was a new wave of special laws on particular TSOs, such as "voluntary organizations" (Law no. 266/1991), "social cooperatives" (Law no. 381/1991) and "associations of social promotion" (Law no. 383/2000).[3] Of particular importance in this period was Legislative Decree no. 460/1997, which introduced specific tax measures in favour of "non-profit organizations of social utility", known as "ONLUS" from the Italian acronym. Legislative decree no. 155/2006 on "social enterprises" further enriched the already broad and complex pre-existing Italian legal framework on TSOs.

[1] Cf. Zamagni (2000).

[2] Indeed, mutual aid societies and their respective laws have survived and, as we shall see, have been included into the new third sector legal framework.

[3] Cf. Vaccario and Barbetta (2017), p. 445 ff.

Some of these special laws, like those on social cooperatives of 1991 and on social enterprises of 2006, became models for foreign legislators since many countries followed Italy in introducing similar laws on these subjects.[4]

The myriad of special laws was seen as an obstacle to the further development of what was already known at that time as the "third sector". This was the main reason behind the legislative reform that, initiated with Delegation law no. 106/2016, finally led to the "Code of the third sector" of 2017.[5] The Code repealed a number of pre-existing laws and reorganized the entire category of organizations on new grounds without, however, breaking the connections with the past.

2 On the Great Impact of a Historic Legislative Reform

There are several reasons why the new legislation on the Third Sector, centred on the homonymous Code of 2017, is of great importance not only for TSOs but for the Italian community at large. Among the main reasons, the following deserve special mention.

Firstly, although the Italian Constitution of 1948 does not refer to TSOs, which are a subsequent conceptual and legislative creature, there is no doubt that the specific legal nature of TSOs place them in a leading position in the Italian constitutional order. TSOs implement fundamental constitutional principles and contribute to the pursuit of specific constitutional objectives, which makes the Code of the Third Sector a law of direct application of the Italian Constitution, mainly with regard to its articles 2, 3, para. 2, and 118, para. 4. This law comes with a significant delay and fills an unjustifiable gap, especially if one considers the wide and sophisticated legal frameworks that, for many years, have been provided for categories of entities, such as for-profit companies, whose constitutional salience is far lower than that of TSOs.

Indeed, TSOs are *ad hoc* legal vehicles for citizens wishing to undertake activities of general interest for the common good, which the Italian Republic has the duty to favour in accordance with the constitutional principle of (horizontal) subsidiarity (art. 118, para. 4). These communitarian initiatives represent a possible way for citizens to fulfil their mandatory duties of solidarity towards other citizens (art. 2 Cost.), thus helping to remove the economic and social obstacles that, by limiting *de facto* the freedom and equality of citizens, prevent the full development of human beings and the effective participation of all workers in the political, economic and social organization of the country (art. 3, para. 2, Cost.).

The stability and resilience of TSOs, especially in times of crisis (if compared to other types of entities), which is the effect of their institutional concern for the

[4] See, for references Fici (2017, 2020b) as well as Fici (2021).

[5] Available at https://www.normattiva.it/uri-res/N2Ls?urn:nir:stato:decreto.legislativo:2017-07-03;117.

community rather than for profits and their distribution, demonstrate the TSOs'positive contribution also to the economy of a country and not only to human promotion and social cohesion (ever if it is possible to distinguish the two aspects).

Secondly, to the extent that this new legislation contemplates organizational structures specifically conceived of for people not aiming at the maximization of their own (financial) interest, but at the pursuit of the common good, this legislation favours the development of a legal environment inspired by a "positive anthropology" rather than by a "negative anthropology" (the Holmesian "bad-man" or the Hobbesian "homo hominis lupus"). This suggests that a new approach to legislation and legal theory is possible, namely an approach aimed at the well-being of peoples and communities, which is equally or even more important than the more traditional approach.

From this point of view, the Code of the Third Sector may be seen as "a good law that tries to make good people".[6] It represents a novelty in Italian organizational law, whose focus had been kept, thus far, on the typical structures of action of the "homo oeconomicus" rather than on the structures of the "homo donator" or the "homo reciprocans", in other words on for-profit companies rather on non-profit and public benefit organizations.

Indeed, the Italian Civil Code of 1942 devoted, and still devotes in its first "Book", a handful of provisions to associations and foundations which are non-profit legal entities, whereas companies, which are for-profit legal entities, have always enjoyed an extensive regulation in the Fifth "Book" of the Civil Code (last updated in 2003).

Italian private law on organizations had not so far experienced the renewal that had already affected other sectors of private law. It had remained tied to the idea of the "modern private law ... as a juridical form of capitalism" and as a regulation exclusively at the service of economic and patrimonial interests of an individualistic nature.[7] The invention of the shareholder company, which was "one of the most important elements of the construction, by the State, of a legal system adequate to the development of capitalism", was not followed by parallel inventions aimed instead at the advancement of the organizational needs of civil society.[8] These organizational needs remained dependent on the extremely limited regulation found in the first Chapter of the Civil Code. It is clear and evident that the Code of the third sector has profoundly changed this situation, opening private organizational law up to the protection and enhancement of non-financial interests of persons and communities, as well as to the constitutional principle of horizontal subsidiarity.

Finally, by creating a new general legal category of organizations whose borders are clearly delineated, the Code of the Third Sector has attributed a very well-defined

[6] Cf. Stout (2011) and Feldman (2018).

[7] Cf. Salvi (2015).

[8] Ibidem.

common image to all the organizations belonging to the sector. This specific legal identity carries potential benefits of various kinds.

Notably, TSOs may now be easily distinguished from other organizations, including (simple) non-profit entities, and thus become recipients of specific public policies which, in turn, are easier to justify than before.

In the private sphere, under Italian organizational law, four general categories of organizations may now be identified:[9]

(i) for-profit organizations (of which joint-stock and limited liability companies are the prominent legal forms);
(ii) mutual purpose organizations (most notably, cooperatives);
(iii) non-profit organizations (mainly associations and foundations incorporated pursuant to the Civil Code);
(iv) third sector organizations established in accordance with the Code of 2017.

Therefore, TSOs are different not only from organizations with a profit purpose (i.e., to divide profits among their owners-members) and with a mutual purpose (i.e., to act with and in the interests of their owners-members as users, providers or workers), but also from simple non-profit organizations. Indeed, as we shall see, for an organization to qualify as a TSO, not only profit non-distribution but further requirements—most notably the performance of activities of general interest for civic, solidaristic and social utility purposes—are necessary, which contribute to their distinction from organizations whose sole legal feature is the prohibition regarding the distribution of profits.

Focusing on this precise legal identity, the Italian Constitutional Court has recently ruled that the particular form of interaction (defined as "shared administration") between TSOs and public administrations, which is found in article 55 of the Code of the Third Sector, is legitimate both under Italian law and EU law. The fact that this public-private relationship is removed from the ordinary regime of public procurements is justified by the legal nature of TSOs, which makes their interests "common" to those of the State and other public entities, thus legitimating cooperative relationships whose regime may diverge from that applicable to ordinary exchange relationships.[10]

---

[9] The need to simplify the discourse explains why, in this list, hybrid organizations, such as "benefit companies" of Law no. 208/2015, have been omitted. Benefit companies are dual-purpose companies that, in carrying out their economic activities, pursue, in addition to the aim of distributing profits, one or more aims of common benefit, and operate in a responsible, sustainable and transparent manner vis-à-vis individuals, communities, territories and the environment, cultural and social heritage, entities and associations, as well as other stakeholders. "Common benefit" means the pursuit of one or more positive effects, or the reduction of negative effects, for the company's benefited stakeholders.

[10] Cf. Italian Constitutional Court no. 131/2020. "Shared administration" between public administrations and TSOs is now explicitly mentioned in the new regulation of public contracts: see art. 6, Legislative Decree 31 March 2023, no. 36.

In conclusion, TSOs are "third" not certainly because they are less important than other organizations,[11] nor because they are a valid alternative to the solution of social problems only when the "first" and the "second" sectors fail,[12] but only because they are distinct from the public sector and from the traditional private sector, including the non-profit sector.

The legal identity of TSOs is useful not only for legal purposes but also for other purposes, including the elaboration of more precise statistics on the sector. According to the Italian National Institute of Statistics ("ISTAT"), there were more than 363, 499 active non-profit organizations in Italy on 31 December 2020. Their number has been constantly increasing over recent decades (the ISTAT reported only 235,000 active NPOs at the end of 2001). Among these non-profit organizations, the ISTAT also includes TSOs. But TSOs, as previously stated, do not coincide with non-profit organizations. Therefore, the reform of 2017 will make it possible to obtain specific figures on the third sector, also thanks to the existence of an ad hoc register for TSOs (named "RUNTS"). Indeed, there are more than 115,000 TSOs currently registered in the RUNTS, which means almost one third of all NPOs (which raises to more than one third, excluding those NPOs that, according to the existing legislation, being "excluded entities", could never acquire the status of TSO).

3 Sources and General Features of the New Legal Framework on TSOs. "TSO" as a Legal Qualification or Status

The Italian regulation of TSOs, as a particular legal category of organizations, is found in Legislative Decree no. 117/2017 on the "Code of the Third Sector".

Although formally separate from the Code, other laws shape the overall legal framework regarding TSOs. The main ones are:

- Legislative Decree no. 112/2017 on social enterprises, which are a particular type of TSOs;
- Law no 381/1991 on social cooperatives, which are social enterprises *ope legis* (and consequently TSOs *ope legis*); and
- Law no. 3818/1886 on mutual aid societies, which are another particular type of TSOs.

Several ministerial decrees have already been issued for the implementation of various parts of the Code. Among them, the ministerial decree on the functioning

[11] If the importance of a class of organization is evaluated according to the degree of constitutional relevance, TSOs, as explained in the main text, are inferior to none.

[12] For this economic justification of non-profit organizations, cf. Hansmann (1980) and Weisbrod (1986).

of the RUNTS assumes particular importance. Not less relevant are, in addition, the ministerial decree establishing (pursuant to art. 6 CTS) the limits within which TSOs can carry out activities other than those of general interest; the decree that (pursuant to art. 13 CTS) approved the formats of the balance sheets to be used by TSOs; and the decree that provides (pursuant to art. 14, para. 1, CTS) the guidelines for drafting the "social report" (which is compulsory only for some TSOs and for all social enterprises).

The prestigious name of "Code" assigned to the 2017 law on the third sector shows the legislative intention to provide a well-ordered, complete and self-sufficient regulation of TSOs, based on its own principles and values (expressed in its first two articles of the Code), and not limited to the organizational profiles of TSOs, but also including their tax treatment, relationships with public administrations, and other aspects. Indeed, the reform of 2017 aspired to remedy a very confused, scattered and uncertain legal framework, devoid of unity, and whose legislative sources did not communicate with each other. The pre-existing legal framework divided, rather than united, TSOs and did not regulate them in an in-depth and technically advanced way, thereby leaving several questions open and unresolved.

The Code is composed of 104 articles and divided into 12 parts ("titles"). As already mentioned, it provides an articulated regulation of the subject matter, which is not limited to its organizational law (mainly found in titles II-V), but also includes provisions of labour law, administrative law (titles VI and XI), public procurement law (title VII), and tax law (title X). Several measures in support of TSOs are contained in titles VIII and IX, while in title XI of the Code one may find some transitory provisions and provisions repealing previous laws.

From a substantial perspective, the principal characteristic of the Code is that it is not a law instituting a specific legal form of an entity's incorporation (i.e., a new legal type of entity) but rather a legal qualification or status, that of "third sector organization", available to several types or legal forms or types of organizations meeting the requirements for qualification laid down by the same Code.

The possession of the status is a condition for the organization to access a promotional legal regime, which contemplates, at the same time, burdens of a different nature for the organization to obtain and maintain its qualification/status as a TSO.

In brief and to summarize:

(i) the Code has introduced a legal status or qualification, that of "third sector organization", available to different legal types of entities[13] that meet the requirements provided for by the Code and are registered in the RUNTS (only organizations registered in the RUNTS are TSOs; and it is with this registration that the status is formally assumed);

[13] Individuals may not assume the qualification. Only organizations may do so.

(ii) the status of TSO is optional, which means that no organization is obligated to acquire the status; indeed, the acquisition of the status is the result of a free choice by a given organization wishing to obtain it and thus gain access to the specific (and promotional) legal framework for TSOs;
(iii) as it may be freely acquired, the status may be lost either voluntarily (the organization asks to be cancelled from the RUNTS) or by sanction from the authority in charge of the control of TSOs (TSOs not acting in accordance with the law are cancelled); the loss of the status has only patrimonial consequences for the organization (it must devolve disinterestedly, to other TSOs, the assets accumulated after its registration in the RUNTS or even all residual assets in the case of social enterprises, but only following deduction of the paid-up capital in the case of social enterprises), but it does not necessarily imply termination or dissolution of the legal entity (which may continue operating without the status);
(iv) the status of TSO provides several opportunities, ranging from tax-breaks to specific forms of relationships with the public administrations that may be established without applying the Code of public contracts (which lays down the ordinary regime of public procurements); an easier way of acquiring the juridical personality (and thus the full limited liability of members, directors and legal representatives) is among these promotional measures.
(v) at the same time, to maintain the legal status and benefit from the supportive legislation, a TSO has to respect all governance rules provided for in the Code, and is subject to public control (to check compliance with those rules); more precisely, these rules are not properly rules of conduct, because respecting them is necessary (only) for maintaining the status and gaining access to a specific legal regime; therefore, they are requirements (for qualification) rather than duties (of conduct) in the strict legal sense;
(vi) the Code provides for a general status/qualification of TSO and some more particular statuses/qualifications, which are those of voluntary organizations; associations of social promotion; philanthropic entities; social enterprises (including social cooperatives and their consortia); associative networks; and mutual aid societies; each legal status of the third sector is distinct from the others and based on some special requirements. The RUNTS, as we shall see, reflects this plurality of organizational models.

As regards the sources of regulation of TSOs, it must be finally underlined that—for what is not provided for by the Code of the third sector, and therefore for what is not necessary for the acquisition and maintenance of the TSO status (or TSO statuses)—the organizations holding the status are subject to ordinary organizational law, i.e. to the provisions laid down by the Civil code for each individual legal form of incorporation, or, as is most commonly stated in Italian legal theory, for each "legal type of entity" (e.g. association, foundation, cooperative, and company).

To provide only an example, an association with the status of TSO is first subject to the rules of the Code of the third sector, whose respect is necessary to obtain and maintain the status of TSO, and secondly to the rules of the Civil code regarding associations, which is to say, to the rules that concern its legal form of incorporation.

4 The Requirements for the Qualification of an Organization as a TSO

As previously stated, TSO is a legal status or qualification which may be obtained and maintained only by entities meeting certain requirements (art. 4 CTS). These legal requirements relate to a variety of aspects of a different nature.

For an organization to possess the status of TSO, it must simultaneously:

(i) have the legal form of an association, with or without juridical personality, or a foundation (while social enterprises may also have the legal form of a company or a cooperative);
(ii) be independent from “excluded entities”, i.e., not be directed or controlled by those entities that may never acquire the status of TSOs, namely, public administrations, political parties, trade unions, professional associations, associations representing economic categories, and representative organizations of employers (special rules apply to social enterprises in this particular regard);
(iii) carry out, exclusively or at least prevalently, one or more activities of general interest;
(iv) distribute no profits (although special rules apply to social enterprises set up as companies or cooperatives) and exclusively pursue civic, solidaristic and social utility purposes;
(v) be registered in a register denominated “RUNTS” (special rules apply to social enterprises also in this regard).

Some of these requirements need a more in-depth analysis.

4.1 Activities of General Interest

First of all, as regards the activities of general interest, the Code specifies them very clearly. It does not adopt a general clause but provides a long list of activities that, for the purposes of this law, are deemed to own this nature (art. 5 CTS). The list can be updated over time, as recently happened with the inclusion of the use of "green" energy for self-consumption among the activities in lit. e). This list includes the following activities:

(a) social services;
(b) health services;
(c) socio-health services;
(d) education, instruction, and professional training;

(e) services aimed at safeguarding and improving the conditions of the environment and the prudent and rational use of natural resources, the protection of animals and prevention of stray animals, as well as production, accumulation and sharing of energy from renewable sources for self-consumption sources;
(f) services for the protection and enhancement of the cultural heritage and the landscape;
(g) university and post-university training;
(h) scientific research of particular social interest;
(i) organization and management of cultural, artistic or recreational activities of social interest, including activities, among them editorial activities, for the promotion and dissemination of culture and the practice of voluntary work and of activities of general interest;
(j) radio broadcasting of a community nature;
(k) organization and management of tourist activities of social, cultural or religious interest;
(l) extra-curricular training aimed at the prevention of early school leaving and promotion of academic and educational success, at preventing bullying and at combating educational poverty;
(m) instrumental services to third sector entities provided by entities composed of no less than 70% of third sector entities;
(n) development cooperation;
(o) fair trade;
(p) services aimed at the insertion or reintegration into the labour market of disadvantaged workers and persons;
(q) social housing, as well as any other temporary residential activity aimed at satisfying social, health, cultural, training or working needs;
(r) humanitarian reception and social integration of migrants;
(s) social agriculture;
(t) organization and management of amateur sports activities;
(u) charity, remote support, free sale of food or products, or provision of money, goods or services in support of disadvantaged people or of activities of general interest;
(v) promotion of the culture of legality, peace between peoples, non-violence and unarmed defence;
(w) promotion and protection of human, civil, social and political rights, as well as the rights of consumers and users of activities of general interest, promotion of equal opportunities and mutual aid initiatives, including time banks, and joint purchasing groups;
(x) management of international adoption procedures;
(y) civil protection;
(z) requalification of unused public assets or assets confiscated from organized crime.

TSOs are not obligated to perform only general interest activities, but they must do so at least prevalently. Therefore, they may conduct activities "other" than those of general interest, but only on the condition that their statutes allow them to do so, and these activities are secondary and instrumental relative to the activities of general interest (art. 6 CTS and Regulation no. 107/2021).

4.2 *Profit Non-Distribution Constraint, Asset Lock and Prioritization of the Social Mission*

In the Italian legal system, the "profit purpose" of an organization is a precise concept. An organization driven by this purpose aims at the distribution, among its members, of the profits generated by the economic (or, more precisely, entrepreneurial) activity that it carries out. This is the ordinary purpose of companies pursuant to the general provision in art. 2247 of the Civil code. Companies are therefore "organizations with a profit purpose".

In contrast, "organizations without a profit purpose", such as associations and foundations, are not allowed by law to distribute profits to their founders, members, workers, directors, etc., which does not mean, however, that they are not allowed to conduct activities that generate a profit (i.e., "profit-making activities"), but only that they cannot distribute the potential profits from their activities (a full profit non-distribution constraint applies to them). On the other hand, since their purpose is not positively defined by law, and provided that no distribution of profits take place, associations and foundations may, in principle, pursue either the public or the private benefit.

The legislator's approach to TSOs is more detailed and sophisticated.

Indeed, not only have TSOs to act "without a profit purpose", but they must also "exclusively pursue civic, solidaristic and social utility purposes" by undertaking one or more activities of general interest.

Therefore, from a theoretical point of view, in TSOs'regulation, the "social" mission requirement prevails over that of the non-distribution constraint, which is only instrumental in ensuring the prioritization of the "social" mission of TSOs.

Moreover, the non-distribution constraint is, more precisely, an "asset lock", which applies not only during, but also at the end of the existence of a TSO (*rectius*, of the qualification of an organization as a TSO).

Therefore, to safeguard their institutional purpose, the Code prescribes that the assets of a TSO, including any profits, income, proceeds, revenues however denominated, must be used to carry out the statutory activity for the exclusive pursuit of civic, solidarity and social utility purposes (art. 8, para. 1, CTS).

For this reason, a TSO is barred from distributing, directly or indirectly, profits and operating surpluses, funds and reserves, however denominated, to founders, associates, workers and collaborators, directors and other members of the corporate bodies, etc., also in the case of withdrawal or any other hypothesis of individual dissolution of the associative/organizational relationship (art. 8, para. 2, CTS).

The law goes on to identify some situations that are qualified, under any circumstances, as an "indirect distribution" of profits and assets by a TSO (art. 8, para. 3, CTS). These hypotheses are:

(a) the payment to directors, auditors and all those who hold an organizational role, of an individual remuneration which is not proportionate to the activity carried out, to the responsibilities borne and to their specific competence, or which is, in any case, higher than that provided by entities operating in the same or similar sectors and conditions;
(b) the payment to dependent or self-employed workers of wages or payments 40% higher than those established, for the same qualifications, by the collective agreements referred to in Article 51 of Legislative Decree 15 June 2015, no. 81, except for proven necessities relating to the need to acquire specific skills for the purpose of carrying out activities of general interest;
(c) the purchase of goods or services for considerations that, without valid economic reasons, are higher than their normal value;
(d) the sale of goods and the provision of services under more favourable conditions than those of the market, to shareholders, associates or participants, to founders, to the members of the administrative and control bodies, to those who, in any capacity, work for the organization or are part of it, to persons who provide gifts to the organization, to their relatives within the third degree and to their relatives in law within the second degree, as well as to the companies directly or indirectly controlled or connected by them, exclusively by reason of their quality, unless such sales or provisions constitute the object of the activity of general interest performed by the TSO;
(e) the payment to persons, other than banks and authorized financial intermediaries, of interest rates, due on loans of all kinds, four points higher than the annual reference rate.

The asset lock also operates upon a TSO's dissolution, in which case its residual assets must be devolved to other TSOs, subject to the positive opinion of the public office that runs the RUNTS. The acts of devolution of the residual assets concluded in the absence, or in contrast, with the office's opinion are null and void (art. 9 CTS).

The same happens when an entity is cancelled from the RUNTS and thus loses its qualification as a TSO, although in this event the assets to be devolved are only those accumulated in the period of registration in the RUNTS (art. 50, para. 2, CTS).

4.3 Registration

The formal registration with a public register, named "RUNTS", is one of the requirements of the TSO status. Obviously, only the organizations holding the other requirements may be registered in the RUNTS. The qualification as TSO is acquired from the day of the registration.

Applications are examined by the (national and regional) public offices of the RUNTS. The status is maintained only if registration is maintained. De-registration may depend either on an organization's free choice or on the authority's decision after having ascertained that the organization has lost the necessary requirements for qualification or has violated the rules regarding the organization and management of a TSO, which are contained in the same Code.

By registering in the RUNTS, TSOs may also acquire the "juridical personality" and thus enjoy the "full patrimonial autonomy" that excludes the liability of their directors and legal representatives for the organization's debts.[14] To that end, they must be incorporated by a notarial deed (the public notary shall also present the request for registration of the organization in question) and demonstrate minimum net assets at the time of registration of 15,000 EUR, in the case of associations, or 30,000 EUR, in the case of foundations. In the event that assets decrease by more than 1/3, the minimum shall be reconstituted.

5 Sections of the RUNTS and Particular Types of TSOs

The possession of the requirements described above allows an organization to enrol in the RUNTS and thus obtain the qualification as a TSO, as well as the benefits associated with this qualification. When applying, each organization must indicate the section of the RUNTS in which it wishes to register. An organization may be registered only in one section of the RUNTS, but it may subsequently change the section of registration through a procedure called "migration" and may do so on

[14]While foundations must have juridical personality to exist as such, associations may ("recognized associations") or may not ("non-recognized associations") have juridical personality. The majority of Italian associations are associations without juridical personality. This is due to the fact that non-recognized associations have the same legal capacity as recognized ones and, moreover, enjoy more organizational freedom than recognized associations, being directly subject only to a few provisions of the Civil code (articles 36-38), one of which stipulates that they are regulated by their members' agreements. The legal personality, therefore, does not affect the organization's legal capacity.

On the other hand, the persons who act in the name and on behalf of a non-recognized association are also personally and jointly liable for the association's obligations (art. 38 Civil code). The juridical personality of associations and foundations is therefore necessary only for excluding the liability of their directors and legal representatives for the organization's debts. However, the ordinary procedure for obtaining the juridical personality (as regulated by Presidential Decree no. 361/2000) is lengthy and the requirements for its concession are stringent (associations must have minimum assets of around 40,000 EUR, while foundations'minimum assets vary from 60,000 to 120,000 EUR approximately), so that most Italian associations prefer to act without legal personality (foundations do not have any alternative, since the legal personality is necessary for their very existence).

As pointed out in the main text, the situation is different for TSOs, which may acquire the legal personality by registering in the RUNTS and with lower minimum assets.

more than one occasion. Only associative networks can be registered in a further section of the RUNTS in addition to their own (sect. "e").

The RUNTS is divided into seven sections (art. 46, para. 1, CTS), which are:

(a) voluntary organizations;
(b) associations of social promotion;
(c) philanthropic entities;
(d) social enterprises, including social cooperatives;
(e) associative networks;
(f) mutual aid societies;
(g) other entities of the third sector.

The plurality of sections in the RUNTS is due to the plurality of third sector statuses (or qualifications), which in turn shows the legislative desire to make various organizational models available to those who wish to enter the third sector, thus seeking to satisfy different needs and expectations.[15]

More precisely, the Code recognizes:

- third sector organizations in general, which are those that meet the general requirements of the status of TSO examined earlier in this chapter and that register in the last section of the RUNTS (sect. "g"); and
- six particular types of third sector organizations, which are those that satisfy the special requirements of each sub-status of TSO and that register in one of the sections from "a" to "f" of the RUNTS.

Therefore, each particular type of TSO has its own characteristics, which mainly relate to the type of activity conducted or the manner in which the activity is conducted, but may also include governance aspects.[16] The Code subjects each particular type of third sector organization to a specific regulation, which may also concern the promotional aspect. Hence, the choice of the section of the RUNTS in which to register is a very important choice for the organizations that make it. The choice must be made in an informed manner, knowing, first of all, the special requirements that typify each particular type of TSO (and that are necessary for the entity's registration in the corresponding section of the RUNTS).

Voluntary organizations (sect. "a" of the RUNTS)—also known as "ODVs" from their Italian acronym—are associations (with or without juridical personality) that must be composed of a minimum number of members (at least seven natural persons or at least three other voluntary organizations), and that must run their activity by availing themselves prevalently of the voluntary activity of their members or people associated with member organizations (art. 32, para. 1, CTS). Consequently, they may make use of paid workers only in the presence of certain conditions and within

[15] Admittedly, the plurality of models is also due to the legislators' will to respect the past, notably to avoid the cancellation of the pre-existing types of organizations through the application of the reform of 2017.

[16] Cf. Fici (2018), p. 91 ff.; Fici (2020a), p. 31 ff.

specific limits established by the law (art. 33, para. 1, CTS). ODVs must provide their services mainly to third parties (art. 32, para. 1, CTS), and in exchange for their services they may not, in principle, receive more than the reimbursement of the expenses actually incurred and documented for the provision of the services. As regards governance, all the members of the board of directors must be members of the organization and cannot be paid for the execution of their function.

Associations of social promotion (sect. "b" of the RUNTS)—also known as "APSs" from their Italian acronym—are associations (with or without juridical personality) that, like ODVs, must be composed of a minimum number of members (at least seven natural persons or at least three other associations of social promotion). Unlike ODVs, APSs may provide their services either to their members (and their relatives) or to third parties (art. 35, para. 1, CTS), and may receive in return for the services provided considerations exceeding their expenses. However, like ODVs, APSs must predominantly avail themselves of the voluntary activity of their members or people associated with member organizations and may employ paid workers only within certain limits and conditions.

Philanthropic entities (sect. "c" of the RUNTS) are associations or foundations with legal personality whose typical activity is "to provide money, goods or services, including investment services, in support of disadvantaged categories of people or of activities of general interest".

Mutual aid societies (sect. "f" of the RUNTS) are TSOs whose specific regulation is found in Law no. 3818 of 15 April 1886 (as modified in 2012). Their main characteristic lies in the activity performed, which is to provide assistance in the event of accident, illness and disability at work, to provide subsidies for the coverage of the expenses related to the prevention or treatment of illnesses and accidents, or to provide assistance or financial contributions in case of need. These activities may also be carried out through the establishment of "supplementary health funds" as provided for by a law of 1992. In addition, mutual aid societies must provide their services only to their members and their relatives (they cannot provide their services to non-members).

Associative networks (sect. "e" of the RUNTS) are associations (with or without juridical personality) that group together at least 100 TSOs (or at least 20 TSOs with the legal form of foundation) with registered or operative offices in at least five Italian regions or autonomous provinces, and that carry out activities of "coordination, protection, representation, promotion or support of the third sector organizations associated with them and their activities of general interest, also for the purpose of promoting and increasing their representativeness before institutional subjects" (art. 41, para. 1, CTS).

Associative networks may conduct several activities in favour of their members, such as, for example, submit their applications for registration in the RUNTS and draw up standard statutes which, if approved by the Ministry of Labour, facilitate the registration of TSOs that adopt them.

Representatives of the associative networks sit on the National Council of the Third Sector, which is a consultative organism established with the Ministry of Labour.

Among the associative networks, "national" associative networks receive specific treatment. National associative networks are those networks that group together at least 500 TSOs (or at least 100 TSOs with the legal form of foundation) with registered or operative offices in at least 10 Italian regions or autonomous provinces (art. 41, para. 2, CTS). Among other things, national associative networks may be authorised by the Ministry of Labour to control their associate TSOs on behalf of the Ministry.

As previously mentioned, associative networks may be registered in another section of the RUNTS in addition to their own, and thus obtain the related pertinent status and consequent legal treatment. Associative networks APSs (i.e., organizations contemporarily registered in sections "e" and "b" of the RUNTS) are the most common.

6 Social Enterprises and Social Cooperatives

Among the various types of TSOs, social enterprises (and among them, social cooperatives) deserve particular attention for many reasons, and not only because they are, in Italian law, the most *sui generis* category of TSOs.[17] In fact, they represent an organizational model that is widespread across Europe, as different jurisdictions explicitly recognize and regulate social enterprises (although the legal denomination may vary from country to country). Social enterprises are also known at the EU level. Explicitly referred to in some EU Regulations,[18] they were at the centre of the European Commission's "social business initiative" of 2011, which triggered a new wave of European national legislation on the subject.[19] They are covered by the recent action plan of the European Commission on the social economy.[20] Social enterprise legislation is constantly developing worldwide.[21]

Within the category of social enterprises, social cooperatives occupy a special place, as they were the first type of social enterprise recognized by Italian law and remain the most widespread (there are more than 15,000 social cooperatives).[22] Italian Law no. 381/1991 on social cooperatives has inspired many foreign

---

[17] Cf. Fici (2020a), p. 43 ff.

[18] Cf. Reg. no. 346/2013 (art. 3(1)(d)) on European social entrepreneurship funds ("EuSEF") and Reg. no. 1296/2013 (art. 2(1)) on a European Union Programme for Employment and Social Innovation ("EaSI") later replaced by Reg. no. 1057/2021 establishing the European Social Fund Plus (ESF+), where the definition of a social enterprise is found in art. 2(1) n. 13.

[19] Cf. Fici (2020b).

[20] Cf. COM(2021) 778 final of 9 December 2021 on "Building an economy that works for people: an action plan for the social economy", according to which "social enterprises are now generally understood as part of the social economy" (p. 3).

[21] Cf. Defourny et al. (2021).

[22] More precisely, 15,489 active social cooperatives as of 31 December 2019, according to the National Institute of Statistics (ISTAT).

legislators.[23] Therefore, Italian social cooperatives and their law are known almost everywhere in the world and continue to be a term of reference for the regulation of social enterprises in general.

Italian social enterprises find their particular regulation not in the Code of the Third Sector, but in a formally separate act, which is Legislative decree no. 112/2017.[24] Although Legislative decree no. 112/2017 is a formally distinct act, it must be considered as a substantial part of the Code of the third sector, just as social enterprises belong to the third sector.

Compared to the other types of TSOs, social enterprises have the following distinguishing features:

- social enterprises may be established in any available legal form; therefore, not only associations and foundations, but also companies of any kind (including cooperatives[25]) may qualify as social enterprises; the status is also available to companies composed of a single shareholder, provided that the sole shareholder is not an individual, a public entity or a for-profit organization, which are the "excluded entities" in the specific area of social enterprises (in the sense that they may not acquire the status nor exercise the control of a social enterprise);
- social enterprises carry out the activities of general interest in an entrepreneurial way, i.e., they sell their services rather than provide them for free; moreover, social enterprises can be characterized, rather than by the performance of a general interest activity, by the work integration in any entrepreneurial activity of disadvantaged persons and workers, who shall be at least 30% of a social enterprise's total workforce;
- like other TSOs, social enterprises also have a non-profit aim and act for civic, solidaristic and social utility purposes, but companies (with the status of) social enterprises may remunerate shareholders within certain limits (precisely, no more than 50% of the annual profits may be used for the remuneration of shares and no shareholder may receive more, on the paid-up shares, than the maximum interest of postal bonds increased by 2.5 points);
- to acquire the status, social enterprises must register in a specific section of the Register of enterprises rather than in the RUNTS, to which, however, data on social enterprises flow from the Register of enterprises; in the event of de-registration, social enterprises must devolve all their assets disinterestedly to other social enterprises, after the deduction, in the case of social enterprises in the company form, of the shareholders' paid-up shares;
- social enterprises are subject to specific governance requirements and a specific form of public control.

Social cooperatives referred to in Law no. 381/1991 (and their consortia) are recognized as social enterprises by law (art. 1, para. 4, Legislative decree

[23] Cf., also for references, Fici (2017, 2020b).

[24] Legislative decree no. 112/2017 replaced Legislative decree no. 155/2006.

[25] Indeed, under Italian law, cooperatives are formally a particular type of company.

no. 112/2017). Like social enterprises, social cooperatives must either carry out an activity of general interest ("type A social cooperatives") or provide the work integration of disadvantaged persons ("type B social cooperatives").

Social enterprises in the company form, and social cooperatives as *ex lege* social enterprises, belong to the third sector, and as such they must be kept distinct from "benefit companies" (which are not part of the third sector), which is another optional status or qualification made available by Italian law to companies (including cooperatives) that want to commit themselves to the pursuit, in addition to the purpose of profit distribution (which remains their main purpose), of one or more purposes of "common benefit".[26]

7 Principles of Governance and Transparency

The new Italian legislation on the third sector also deals with the governance of TSOs. The governance of TSOs is not extensively regulated and essentially refers to those aspects that are deemed by law necessary to ensure the consistency of the governance of the organization with its particular purposes and to reduce the risks of abuse of the legal status. The remaining aspects are regulated by the law applicable to the TSO on the basis of its legal form of incorporation (association or foundation, or also company or cooperative, in the case of social enterprises). It must be underlined here again that even the prescriptions regarding governance, as well as those related to transparency, are not rules of conduct in the strict sense, but requirements to be respected in order to maintain the status of TSO. Indeed, if these rules are violated, the sole and final consequence is the cancellation of the TSO from the RUNTS and the consequent loss of the status.

Although freedom of organization was one of the guiding principles of the reform of 2017, governance requirements are unavoidable legal burdens for organizations, such as TSOs, that benefit from public funding and public trust, moreover in contexts of strong "information asymmetry" such as those in which TSOs usually operate (social services, socio-health services, health services, etc.). However, to avoid imposing an excessive burden on small organizations, organizational requirements are graded according to the size of the organization. Violation of governance rules affects the organization's recognition as a TSO and can therefore lead to its cancellation from the RUNTS (or the Register of enterprises in the case of social enterprises) and the consequent loss of qualification.

TSOs must have a governance structure in which the appointment of certain organs is compulsory. The applicable law takes into account the structural difference between associations and foundations.

---

[26] Cf. https://www.societabenefit.net/wp-content/uploads/2017/03/Italian-benefit-corporation-legislation-courtesy-translation-final.pdf.

Associations recognized as TSOs shall have a members'general meeting, a board of directors (a sole director is not admitted) and, in certain cases, also a supervisory board. The powers of the members'general meeting are such that this organ effectively becomes the "supreme" body of the organization. It has the power to appoint (and remove) the directors, to approve the accounts of the association and to make the fundamental decisions, such as those regarding amendments to the statutes and dissolution of the association. All members have the right to vote in the general meeting according to the principle "one member, one vote". The supervisory board, composed of one or more professionals, must be appointed when the association exceeds, for two consecutive financial years, certain thresholds set by law with regard to the number of employees (five on average), annual profits (220,000 EUR) and net assets (110,000 EUR) (art. 30 CTS). Among other general aspects, the supervisory board must also control compliance with the purposes of the association. If other, higher thresholds are exceeded (art. 31 CTS), the association must also appoint an auditor of the accounts, unless the supervisory board is charged with this task (in which case it must be entirely composed of auditors of accounts).

Foundations recognized as TSOs must necessarily appoint a board of directors (or a sole director) and a supervisory board (also monocratic). If the thresholds of art. 31 CTS are exceeded, the foundation must also appoint an auditor of the accounts, unless the supervisory board is charged with this task.

The governance of social enterprises mainly depends on their legal form of incorporation, although associations and foundations that are social enterprises are subject to the previously examined rules that apply to all associations and foundations of the third sector. There are, however, a few common rules applicable to all social enterprises regardless of their legal form of incorporation, including the obligation to appoint a supervisory board (also monocratic) and the obligation to involve workers, users and other stakeholders in the management, in accordance with guidelines provided by the Ministry of Labour and Social Affairs. In this regard, it is significant that in larger social enterprises, stakeholders must be entitled to appoint at least one member of the board of directors and at least one member of the supervisory board (art. 11 Legislative decree no. 112/2017).

Transparency is equally considered by Italian law as fundamental to guarantee ex ante, and verify ex post, substantial compliance of a TSO with its specific regulation and institutional purpose. Also in this case, the Italian legislator has tried to provide sustainable burdens for the organization, so that not all TSOs are subject to them or that TSOs are subject to different burdens.

TSOs with revenues exceeding one million EUR (and all social enterprises, including social cooperatives) must draw up a "social balance sheet" in accordance with ministerial guidelines and file it with the RUNTS (art. 14, para. 1, CTS) or the Register of enterprises (in the case of social enterprises, including social cooperatives).

TSOs are also obligated to draw up and file with the RUNTS (or the Register of enterprises in the case of social enterprises) a financial statement in accordance with forms defined by ministerial decree. The statement has the form of a cash report for TSOs with revenues not exceeding 220,000 EUR, while the financial statement of the other TSOs has a more articulated structure (statement of assets, management report with indication of income and expenses, and mission report). On the other hand, TSOs that mainly or exclusively carry out entrepreneurial activities, and all social enterprises, must draw up their financial statements in accordance with the regulation on companies, found in the Civil Code.

In addition, TSOs are required to keep certain books and a register of volunteers. TSOs with revenues exceeding 100,000 EUR must also publish data on their website regarding emoluments and fees paid to members of the organs, managers and members.

More in general, TSOs must publish other information in the RUNTS regarding their organizational structure, number of members and volunteers, number of paid workers, etc.

8 Taxation and Promotional Measures

The Code of the third sector and Legislative decree no. 112/2017 may be classified as "promotional laws" inasmuch as their principal objective (unlike organizational laws, whose main purpose is to facilitate the organization and functioning of an entity) is to favour the growth and development of the concerned category of organizations, namely TSOs and social enterprises among them. To achieve this objective, these laws act in the way already highlighted above in this chapter: They establish certain requirements that are necessary for an organization to acquire the status of TSO or more specifically of social enterprise, and then grant specific and favourable treatment to the organizations that decide to obtain the status. This favourable treatment represents a sort of reward and compensation for organizations that, having opted for the third sector qualification, accept to carry out activities of general interest without a profit aim and to assume the various organizational and management burdens that the law imposes on TSOs.

Promotional measures in support of TSOs are disseminated throughout the Code (and Legislative decree no. 112/2017) and differ in nature.

The possibility of making exclusive use of the label of "third sector organization", which is a denomination reserved for entities registered in the RUNTS (art. 12, para. 3, CTS), must already be taken as a promotional measure, if one considers its ability to attract volunteers, ethical consumers and investors, public administrations, etc.

The possibility of obtaining the juridical personality (and the consequent limited liability of members and directors) by registering in the RUNTS (art. 22 CTS) is another opportunity for associations and foundations with the status of TSOs, if compared to all other associations and foundations which are subject, in this regard, to the ordinary (and more severe) regime provided by Presidential Decree no. 361/2000.

The possibility of undertaking, in the perspective of the "shared administration", special relationships with the public administrations that are not subject to the ordinary rules of public contracts (articles 55-57 CTS) is another great opportunity for TSOs.

There can be no doubt that taxation plays a fundamental role in the promotion of TSOs and also in favouring their access to resources.

The first requirement is that TSOs be subject to an ad hoc tax regime which takes their particular legal nature into specific consideration.

In this regard, Italian law adopts a peculiar distinction between "commercial entities" and "non-commercial entities". TSOs (other than social enterprises) may be "commercial" or "non-commercial" depending on the ratio of the volume of their non-commercial activities to that of commercial activities (art. 79 CTS). Revenues from non-commercial activities are not subject to taxation and non-commercial TSOs may also opt for a specific (and particularly advantageous) tax treatment regarding the profits generated by their commercial activities (art. 80 CTS). This fiscal regime, however, is not yet in force, since it is subject to the authorization of the European Commission which has yet to be granted.[27]

Social enterprises are "commercial entities" by definition, even when they have the legal form of associations or foundations. However, their particular law provides that profits re-invested in the activity do not constitute taxable income (art. 18 Legislative decree no. 112/2017). This measure is also still not in force since it is subject to the authorization of the European Commission. However, the same rule already applies to social cooperatives of Law no. 381/1991.

VAT does not apply to non-commercial activities of non-commercial entities (art. 4, para. 3, Presidential decree no. 633/1972).

In addition, there are some services (such as socio-health services or home assistance of disabled persons and other disadvantaged people) that, if provided by non-commercial TSOs, are VAT exempt (art. 10, para. 1, n. 27 *ter*, Presidential decree no. 633/1972). However, at the moment, this provision applies to entities with the fiscal status of ONLUS, but in the future, once the new fiscal regime of TSOs is approved by the European Commission, will only apply to non-commercial TSOs.[28]

A reduced VAT rate (5% rather than the ordinary 22%) applies to social cooperatives that provide specific health, socio-health, assistance and educational services (Table A), Part II *bis*, no. 1, Presidential decree no. 633/1972).

Furthermore, there are some services usually provided by TSOs, such as, for example, those pertaining to childcare facilities or retirement homes for the elderly, whose provision is exempt from VAT (art. 10, para. 1, n. 21, Presidential decree no. 633/1972).

Among the tax measures aimed at favouring private support to TSOs, reference must first of all be made to the tax-privileged regime of donations to TSOs. 30% of the amount of cash donations or of the value of in-kind donations to non-commercial

---

[27] Still to be requested by the Italian Government.

[28] Pursuant to art. 89, para. 7, lit. b), CTS, which will enter into force beginning from the fiscal year following that in which the authorization of the European Commission for the new tax regime of TSOs is granted.

TSOs (as well as to social cooperatives) may be deducted from the gross income tax of individuals, for a total amount, in each fiscal year, not exceeding 30,000 EUR (art. 83, para. 1, CTS). Cash or in-kind donations to non-commercial TSOs (as well as to social cooperatives) may be deducted from the total net income of individuals, legal entities and companies within the limit of 10% of the total declared income (art. 83, para. 2, CTS).

Another relevant measure (in this case not only in favour of TSOs but also of other entities) is called "5 per thousand". It is a sort of tax allocation mechanism. When declaring their income for the purposes of tax payment, any individual may decide to allocate to TSOs (or even to a specific TSO identified by its fiscal code) 5 per thousand of the income tax due for the preceding year. This 5 per thousand is not retained by the State, which receives the payment of taxes, but is forwarded directly to the TSO indicated by the taxpayer on the tax declaration. There are TSOs that receive huge amounts of money (even millions of Euros) each year thanks to this mechanism, and for this reason invest in the promotion of the instrument (also through campaigns in the media), especially in the period just before the deadline for the submission of income tax declarations.

With particular regard to social enterprises, art. 18, paragraphs 3-4, Legislative decree no. 112/2017 encourages investments in social enterprises by providing tax benefits for physical and legal entities that buy shares of "new" social enterprises (namely, of entities that have acquired the qualification of social enterprise no more than five years earlier) and hold these shares for at least five years. The benefit consists in the deduction from the gross income tax of individuals, or from the taxable income of legal entities, of an amount equal to 30% of the sum paid up for the shares (up to 1 million EUR per tax period in the case of individuals or up to 1.8 million EUR per tax period in the case of legal entities). This way, the Reform of 2017 tries to boost social enterprises, knowing that in the absence of these tax breaks, only social cooperatives are attractive, and it is therefore unfortunate that even these measures are not yet in force (they are also subject to the European Commission's approval).

9 State Supervision

TSOs are subject to external control by public administrations. This is aimed at verifying that they act in conformity with the applicable law (principally the Code of the third sector in the case of TSOs and Legislative decree no. 112/2017 in the case of social enterprises), which in the context of promotional laws such as those on the Italian third sector, is necessary to ensure that state-supported organizations do not abuse the qualification by pursuing purposes other than those that justify state support. Safeguarding the trust of the various stakeholders of TSOs (donors, volunteers, ethical investors, etc.) is another reason for instituting an effective system of legal enforcement.

Public control is exerted by the same public offices that are in charge of the management of the RUNTS and the registration of TSOs (the offices of the RUNTS). Social enterprises are controlled by the Ministry of Labour and Social Affairs, while social cooperatives are controlled by the Ministry of Economic Development (currently denominated Ministry of Enterprises and Made in Italy).

If irregularities are found and are not duly remedied, the organization is cancelled from the RUNTS (or from the Register of enterprises in the case of social enterprises) and loses its status as a TSO (or as a social enterprise). Upon cancellation, assets accumulated after registration must be disinterestedly devolved to other TSOs subject to the positive opinion of the competent office of the RUNTS, but the cancelled organization may continue to operate as an ordinary organization (of course, without the status of TSO).

In order to promote self-control by their representative organizations, the law provides that the power of control can be delegated to associative networks of TSOs and other large secondary associations among TSOs (the "service centres for volunteering"), which may exercise it with regard to their member TSOs (art. 93 CTS). A similar provision also exists for social enterprises (art. 15 Legislative decree no. 112/2017). These provisions, however, are not yet in force due to the lack of a ministerial decree providing for specific regulation.

10 Conclusions

The Italian legal framework on TSOs is an excellent example of how this particular group of organizations can be taken seriously by the legislator. Italian law had previously concentrated on for-profit organizations, widely and meticulously regulated in the fifth "Book" of the Civil code, while very few rules (articles 14-42-*bis*) were (and still are) devoted, in the first "Book" of the Civil code, to associations and foundations as non-profit entities. But there is no apparent reason why the state should provide a specific legal framework for collective actions based on a profit motive and not also do so for collective actions aimed at the common good. Both structures of action, those for the "homo oeconomicus" and those for the "homo donator" or "reciprocans", should be recognized and carefully regulated by law. Indeed, organizations with a higher degree of constitutional salience such as TSOs, which perform such an important social and economic function, helping the State in the provision of general interest services and the community to self-organize for the fulfilment of needs unmet by the state (the first sector) and traditional for-profit producers (the second sector), should deserve even more attention than other categories of organizations.

The Italian legislator has therefore changed its approach since 2017, taking care of the legislation on the third sector and enriching it compared to the past. The main effect is that, in Italian law, TSOs are now "third" not because they are less important than other organizations, but because they are distinct from them, thanks to a legislation capable of highlighting their specific characteristics and safeguarding them.

Italian law has followed a particular regulatory approach, which consists in taking "third sector organization" as a legal qualification or status, rather than as a particular type of legal entity. The status is available to associations and foundations that meet specific legal requirements related to the purpose pursued, the activity carried out, the use of profits, governance and transparency. Just as it may be acquired, the status may also be lost either by a decision of the organization that holds it or by sanction of the controlling public authority. The status confers on the organization that holds it benefits of various kinds, not only of a fiscal nature. Privileged relationships with public administrations in keeping with the notion of the "shared administration" are the new and most significant frontier in this regard.

"Social enterprise" is also a legal qualification or status. More precisely, given that social enterprises are a particular typology of TSOs, that of "social enterprise" is a third sector sub-status (or sub-qualification). It is a particular status for several reasons, including the fact that it may be acquired not only by associations and foundations, but also by (commercial) companies and cooperatives, and that it is partly compatible with the distribution of profits to shareholders (or rather, with a limited remuneration of the share capital). Social cooperatives of Law no. 381/1991 are the first and most diffuse form of social enterprise in Italy.

Social enterprises are not simply "sustainable and socially responsible businesses", but enterprises acting for the common good, to which they give priority over any other purpose. Like similar entities (though with a different legal denomination) in other countries, social enterprises are the group of business enterprises on which one can, and should, increasingly count for a safe and sustainable economic development in Europe. The history of Italian social cooperatives can be particularly illuminating in this specific regard.

References

Defourny J et al (2021) Testing social enterprise models across the world: evidence from the "International Comparative Social Enterprise Models (ICSEM) Project". Nonprofit and Voluntary Sector Quarterly 50(2):420 ff

Feldman Y (2018) The law of good people. Cambridge University Press, Cambridge

Fici A (2017) A European statute for social and solidarity-based enterprise. European Union, Brussels. https://www.europarl.europa.eu/RegData/etudes/STUD/2017/583123/IPOL_STU%282017%29583123_EN.pdf

Fici A (ed) (2018) La riforma del terzo settore e dell'impresa sociale. Una introduzione. Editoriale scientifica, Napoli

Fici A (2020a) Un diritto per sil terzo settore. Studi sulla riforma. Editoriale scientifica, Napoli

Fici A (2020b) Social Enterprise Laws in Europe after the 2011 "Social Business Initiative". A Comparative Analysis from the Perspective of Worker and Social Cooperatives. CECOP, Brussels, https://cecop.coop/uploads/file/bzuQI79nF5yrrwoDvUNUg47Ro7iaHA6wAxsvK9yo.pdf

Fici A (2021) A statute for European cross-border associations and non-profit organizations. Potential benefits in the current situation. European Union, Brussels

Hansmann HB (1980) The role of nonprofit enterprise. Yale Law J 89/5:835 ff

Salvi C (2015) Capitalismo e diritto civile. Itinerari giuridici dal *Code Civil* ai Trattati europei. Il Mulino, Bologna

Stout L (2011) Cultivating conscience. How good laws make good people. Princeton University Press, Princeton

Vaccario C, Barbetta GP (2017) Legal aspects of civil society organizations and their relation with government: Italy. In: Van der Ploeg TJ et al (eds) Civil society in Europe. Minimum norms and optimum conditions of its regulation. CUP, Cambridge, p 445 ff

Weisbrod BA (1986) Toward a theory of the voluntary nonprofit sector in a three-sector economy. In: Rose-Ackerman S (ed) The economics of nonprofit institutions. Oxford University Press, New York, p 21 ff

Zamagni V (ed) (2000) Povertà e innovazioni istituzionali in Italia. Dal Medioevo a oggi. Il Mulino, Bologna

Chapter 7
The Legal Infrastructure of the Third Sector and the Social Economy in the Netherlands

Ger J. H. van der Sangen

Contents

Abstract In the taxonomy of organizational forms in the Netherlands, the concepts of the third sector and social economy are not well-known and not often used. Organizational forms with a social objective, however, can be found in three distinctive areas: (1) semi-public organizations in health care, education and social housing, commonly incorporated as foundations and regulated under sectoral laws, (2) civil society organizations, commonly incorporated as associations and foundations, which under strict conditions qualify for the fiscal status of *Public benefit organization*, and (3) social enterprises, in practice incorporated in a variety of organizational forms. To date, social enterprises are not regulated in the Netherlands. A legal infrastructure is missing. There are no tax incentives or other financial inducement for social enterprises. Recent legislative proposals only address social enterprises incorporated as private companies. So far, the legislator has shown little

---

Ger J.H. van der Sangen is Associate Professor of Company Law with the Department of Private, Business & Labor Law at Tilburg University.

G. J. H. van der Sangen (✉)
Tilburg University, Department of Private, Business and Labor Law, Tilburg, Netherlands
e-mail: g.j.h.vdrsangen@tilburguniversity.edu

A. Fici (ed.), *The Law of Third Sector Organizations in Europe*,
https://doi.org/10.1007/978-3-031-41744-3_7

attention to the potential of cooperatives and their principles of mutuality and solidarity, as applied in the growing number of cases of socio-labor insertion.

1 Introduction

The term 'social economy' or 'social and solidarity-based economy' (SSBE) is not as well-known and as often used in the Netherland as it is in many other European countries. This might have to do with the fact that the Netherlands does not have a distinctive legal framework that applies to social enterprises.[1] According to the former Dutch Government in their Coalition Agreement of 2017, appropriate legislation aims to stimulate social enterprises, while safeguarding an equal and level playing field for all enterprises.[2] Hence, the Dutch government has so far chosen to support social entrepreneurship as an approach (in a similar way to other ambitious types of entrepreneurship), rather than social enterprises as a specific type of business organization. Therefore, government support is available through channels for all enterprises and there are no particular fiscal treatments, exemptions or advantages that apply for social enterprises as such.[3]

Nevertheless, the last decade has witnessed an upsurge of social enterprises in the Netherlands. Social enterprises have grown in number and have attracted much more visibility then some 10 years ago.[4] This rise in popularity of social enterprises—though still small in number—can be situated against a shift in a number of public tasks from the national government to the local level, which has made Dutch local governments increasingly aware of the value of collaborating with social enterprises as a way to achieve their public tasks.[5] As reported by Bosma, in 2018 about 40% of

[1]Tailor made legislation regarding social enterprises has been introduced in the majority of EU countries (19 out of 28, including Italy, Greece, Belgium, Portugal, the UK, and France). See European Commission (2015) A Map of Social Enterprises and their Eco-systems in Europe (Synthesis Report) Luxembourg, Publications Office of the European Union; Lambooy and Argyrou (2014), pp. 71–76.

[2]https://www.kabinetsformatie2017.nl/documenten/publicaties/2017/10/10/regeerakkoordvertrouwen-in-de-toekomst.

[3]Bosma (2019). Commissioned by the European Commission. Luxembourg: Publications Office of the European Union, p 69. However, the most important lobbying organization for social enterprises in the Netherlands, Social Enterprise NL, aims, with a common code of conduct/governance, to support social enterprises to position themselves and more easily express their impact.

[4]McKinsey, Company (2016). OECD/EU (2019).

[5]The Dutch Public Procurement Act 2012 (*Aanbestedingswet 2012*) offers opportunities for stimulating social enterprises, both in terms of including specific criteria in the tenders and in the possibility to award contracts to social enterprises (with specific characteristics, following the EU directives set out in 2014). This is often referred to as Social Return on Investment (SROI). See Oden (2015), pp. 579–593, and Bosma (2019), pp. 47–51.

Dutch municipalities[6] had developed some kind of support policy targeted at social enterprises.[7] Among the main legal forms used by social enterprises in the Netherlands are the Foundation (*Stichting*), Association (*Vereniging*), Cooperative (*Coöperatie*), and the Private company with limited liability (*Besloten Vennootschap; BV*).[8] Currently, almost half of Dutch social enterprises focus their activities on socio-labor insertion, while the other half are involved in the circular economy and activities designed to address problems in global value chains.[9]

This chapter describes the legal infrastructure of the third sector and the social economy in the Netherlands primarily from a business organizational point of view. After defining the third sector and the social economy in the context of Netherlands society in paragraph 2, paragraph 3 gives an overview of the menu of business forms available for third sector and social economy activities, addressing the question of which business form is most adequate and efficient to incorporate a third sector enterprise or social enterprise. In paragraph 4, the underdeveloped legal infrastructure of the social economy is described and analyzed, while in paragraph 5 a recent legislative instrument—though rudimental in its current form—is analyzed, questioning whether the introduced business form of the so-called *Besloten vennootschap met een maatschappelijk doel* (hereinafter: *BVm*) will be an adequate vehicle to incorporate a social enterprise, addressing its mandatory scope, the overlap with semi-public enterprises and public benefit organizations in tax law (*ANBIs*). Paragraph 6 discusses the role that cooperatives can play in organizing third sector and social enterprises. The potential of the cooperative model in this respect seems to be overlooked by the Netherlands legislator. Paragraph 7 concludes.

2 Defining the Third Sector and Social Economy in the Context of Netherlands Society

To date, the concept of social economy and social enterprises is a relatively new phenomenon in Netherlands society. Although in the past, before 2015, enterprises existed that also had a social or societal objective, the absence of the concept of social economy and a legal definition and a registration facility of social enterprises

---

[6]Most policy and network activities aimed at stimulating social enterprises appear to take place in the four biggest cities (Amsterdam, Rotterdam, Utrecht, Den Haag). However, medium-size municipalities (collaborating in the so-called G40) also stimulate social entrepreneurship and smaller municipalities increasingly follow this example.

[7]Bosma (2019), pp. 13, 36–37, 73–75.

[8]According to Bosma (2019), p. 37, drawn from Argyrou (2018).

[9]According to Bosma (2019), p. 31, the 2018 Social Enterprise Monitor grouped their activities into four main fields: most social enterprises could be classified as work integration social enterprises (WISES: 44%). Other categories included climate (circular economy, food, environmental waste: 24%), well-being (neighbourhood/cohesion, health, other: 26%) and international development (value chain interventions, other: 6%).

in the Netherlands made social enterprises invisible from a 'regulatory and legal'point of view and difficult to identify as such. At this moment, however, a specific legal infrastructure of the social economy is still absent,[10] although the social economy sector is growing, and future business organizational regulation has been announced by the government. Hence, at the moment enterprises involved in social economy activities have access to all business organizational forms available in Netherlands law. The menu of legal business forms consists of sole proprietorship, general and limited partnership, private company limited by shares, public company, and cooperative. Mutuals are not available for social enterprises since their activities are mandatorily restricted to insurance.[11] Furthermore, associations and foundations—although by nature and legal mandate not for profit—may operate as an enterprise and make a profit provided the profit is not distributed to investors or members of its organs, while any distribution must fall within the objective of the association or the foundation.[12]

It is worth noting that in the Netherlands social-economic context the third sector is mainly dominated by what are called *maatschappelijke ondernemingen* or societal organizations that operate—under state supervision and regulated by mandatory sectoral laws[13]—in the fields of social housing, education, and health care. They are also called *semi-publiekrechtelijke* organizations. The common definition of semi-public law organizations stems from the legal characteristic that—although being private organizations—they are mandated by sectoral laws to perform a public state task in the field of social housing, education, or health care. Commonly, these third sector organizations are legally established as foundations or—in fewer cases—as public companies, but rarely as cooperatives.[14] It is also important to consider that the legal business form of the cooperative in the Netherlands has no obligation to include social or societal interests as a legal objective in the articles of association, since its mandatory legal objective is defined solely in economic terms.[15]

To make the non-profit sector in the Netherlands even more diffuse, civil society organizations, with or without an ideological or religious background, abound in Netherlands society, encompassing all kinds of activities like sports, welfare, culture, trade unions, political organizations, special interests'groups etc. However, while normally organized as associations or as foundations, the law allows these organizations to have an enterprise in order to fulfill their non-profit objective, but

[10] European Economic and Social Committee, Chaves Ávila and Monzón Campos (2012), p. 40, and Karré (2021), pp. 149–165.

[11] Article 2:53.2 NCC.

[12] Article 2:26.1 and 3 and 2:285.1 and 3 NCC.

[13] An overview is provided in: Laseur-Eelman and Mars (2018), pp. 469–498.

[14] See on this distinction with social enterprises in the social economy Karré (2021).

[15] Cooperatives Europe, van der Sangen (2021) Legal Framework Analysis, National Report: The Netherlands, available at https://coops4dev.coop/sites/default/files/2021-08/Netherlands%20Legal%20Framework%20Analysis%20Report.pdf. See also van der Sangen (2022), pp. 159–171.

they are not allowed to distribute the profit. From a tax point of view, some of the non-profit organizations may—under strict conditions—qualify as public benefit organizations (*algemeen nut beogende instellingen*, hereinafter: ANBIs)—a general interest organization established either as a foundation or as an association—as a result of which gifts and donations to these organizations are exempted from taxation for the donor.[16]

3 The Menu of Business Forms Available for Third Sector and Social Economy

As said above, the Netherlands at this moment has no specific regime for business forms in the social economy. Nor are there tax incentives or other financial inducements for social enterprises. Hence, for social enterprises active in the social economy sector there is no specific legal business form. One reason for this lies in the fact that Netherlands law on legal persons as a general principle does not prescribe the use of a specific legal entity for a specific activity. Netherlands law on legal persons adheres to the principle of freedom of incorporation and association, provided that the minimum formal requirements for the establishment of the legal entity are met.[17] However, there are some, although few, exemptions to this principle. Semi-public organizations in the health care, education and social housing sectors must be established as foundations or as public companies, while mutuals are restricted to insurance activities. Apart from these examples, Netherlands law on legal persons is based on formal requirements upon establishment, rather than on material norms. In the event that a legal person is in conflict with its mandatory definition and legal form or the prohibitions of that form,[18] the legal person is not null and void, but rather the Public Prosecutor or any stakeholder with a direct interest may petition the court to declare the legal person dissolved.[19] However, in practice the court will grant a 'grace period'in order to allow the legal person to alter its behavior or to convert into a more suitable legal form. Given these principles, the menu of business forms available for third sector and social economy enterprises vis-à-vis other business forms can be summarized in the chart below.

The problem here is that the legislation on legal business forms in the Netherlands does not lead directly to a specific legal form for social enterprises based on their activities, contrary to semi-public organizations in the field of health care, education, and social housing. However, looking at the scope and definition of the legal persons

[16] See Overes (2017), as well as Idsinga and Wessels (2018), pp. 545–569.

[17] Dijk and Van der Ploeg (2017), pp. 17–19.

[18] Like the prohibition to distribute profit for associations and foundations in article 2:26.3 and 2: 285.3 NCC respectively or in the event that a cooperative does not comply with its mandatory legal objective in article 2:53.1 NCC.

[19] Article 2:21 NCC.

available in Netherlands law, private company limited by shares, cooperative, foundation, and association seem to be the most suitable for social economy activities. This is reflected in the Chart of business forms below (see Table 7.1).

Some empirical studies show that social enterprises are commonly incorporated as private companies limited by shares, as foundations, as sole proprietorships, as associations, and, surprisingly, only a small number as cooperatives. According to Bosma,[20] the results from a Social Enterprise Monitor show that social enterprises—those responding to the survey—do not usually use the cooperative statute for their organization (4% in the most recent survey in 2018). The private company limited by shares presents the most popular legal form (46%), whereas another 10% applies a combination of limited liability and association or foundation. Foundations account for 21%, sole proprietorships 10% and—as already mentioned—cooperatives 4%.

The dominant position of the private company limited by shares as the legal business form for social enterprises corresponds with the definition of social enterprises used by policymakers in the Netherlands, building on the definition of the European Commission's Social Business Initiative.[21] Here, a social enterprise is defined as an operator in the social economy whose main objective is to have a social impact, rather than to make a profit for its owners or shareholders. It operates by providing goods and services for the market in an entrepreneurial and innovative fashion and uses its profits primarily to achieve social objectives. It is managed in an open and responsible manner and, in particular, involves employees, consumers and stakeholders affected by its commercial activities. This definition has subsequently been used by policymakers and the legislative bodies in the Netherlands since 2015, the year in which the *Sociaal-Economische Raad* (Social Economic Council, hereinafter: SER) produced an in-depth study on social enterprises and the social economy in the Netherlands.[22] As such, social enterprises can be viewed as part of the third sector enterprises between government and the market.

4 The Ill-Designed Legal Infrastructure of the Social Economy in the Netherlands

The 2015 SER Report identified five aspects to be targeted by future policy measures and legislation.[23] These include (1) problems with measuring societal impact of social enterprises, (2) the low level of legal recognition of the specific nature of social enterprises and its visibility, (3) problems in financing, (4) restrictions due to

---

[20] Bosma (2019), p. 34.

[21] See https://ec.europa.eu/growth/sectors/proximity-and-social-economy/social-economy-eu/social-enterprises_en.

[22] Sociaal-Economische Raad (2015) Sociale Ondernemingen: een verkennend advies. Advies nr. 15/03, May. The Hague (hereinafter: SER-Report (2015).

[23] SER-Report (2015), p 14.

Table 7.1 Chart of business forms

Public Government	Semi-public organization	Investor-owned enterprise	Member-owned enterprise	Social enterprise	Civil society organization	ANBI organization
State-owned Not for profit	Public task Not for Profit	For profit	For profit	Social objective For profit with cap	Social objective Not for profit	Social objec-tive Not for profit
NV	NV Foundation	Sole proprietor Partnership BV/NV	Cooperative Mutual*	BV Foundation Association Cooperative	Association Foundation Cooperative	Association Foundation
	Health care Education Social housing		* Mutual restricted to insurance	*Voluntary restriction on profit distribution		
	Third sector			*Third sector*	*Third sector*	

rules and regulations hampering (social) entrepreneurship, and (5) problems with regard to public procurement procedures to create a level playing field vis-à-vis investor-owned enterprises. Similar conclusions and recommendations are to be found in a 2019 OECD Report[24] and the 2019 Bosma Report commissioned by the European Commission.[25]

The growing number of social enterprises, as well as the growing awareness of the Netherlands legislators since the 2015 SER Report, that there is—what is defined as—a social economy sector in the Netherlands, has led to a preliminary proposal to design a specific legal business form for social enterprises, but solely based on the existing foundations of the private company limited by shares. In the preproposal, other business forms are *ab initio* excluded from the possibility to be labelled as a social enterprise (sic?). The Ministry of Economic Affairs published the *'Aanzet voor een wettelijke regeling voor een besloten vennootschap met maatschappelijk doel'*[26] on 9 March 2021, introducing a *BVm*, a private company limited by shares with a societal objective. The deadline for consultation on this preproposal was set as 7 May 2021.

Although the preproposal itself does not give a legal definition of a social enterprise, the preproposal refers to a 2020 KMPG Report[27] commissioned by the Ministry of Economic Affairs on which the preproposal is based. The preproposal uses the following definition of a social enterprise: an enterprise that delivers a service or a product with a market-driven business model, primarily to achieve a societal goal, of which the distribution of profits is limited, which operates independently without government support, and with an inclusive governance, actively involving all stakeholders, and that is transparent about its societal impact.[28]

I cannot stress this enough: the preproposal only addresses social enterprises incorporated as private companies limited by shares and draws heavily on the 2020 KPMG Report. This report estimated that there are 5000 social enterprises in the Netherlands. The report conducted an inquiry into the problems social enterprises encountered in practice and sent questionnaires to 240 enterprises. 220 respondents called themselves a social enterprise. The respondents were incorporated as follows: private company (48%), public company (2%), sole proprietor (5%), foundation (29%), association (4%), cooperative (2%), general partnership (3%), other (7%).[29] The 220 respondents answered that they lacked recognition and awareness in day-to-day business of the fact that they are a social enterprise vis-à-vis contracting partners, investors, and banks. They also lacked legal recognition of their specific nature. Although the inquiry was not restricted to social enterprises incorporated as private

[24] OECD/EU (2019).

[25] Bosma (2019).

[26] https://internetconsultatie.nl/bvm.

[27] KMPG/Nyenrode Business University (2020).

[28] Reference 2 of the Preproposal, referring to the KPMG Report 2020, defining the social enterprise on p. 24.

[29] KPMG Report 2020, p. 20.

companies, the Minister of Economic Affair only intends to regulate these social enterprises.

5 Future Business Form of the BVm for Social Enterprises: An Assessment

Existing social enterprises incorporated in a private company limited by shares (48%) claimed a lack of awareness and recognition as a business form with a social objective and a limited for-profit objective, distinct from the common private company limited by shares with a purely for-profit objective.[30] This in itself is a valid point. Although any private company may adjust the objective of the company in the articles of association to operate (partially) on a not-for-profit basis in combination with a restriction on the distribution of profits (dividends and net proceeds upon liquidation),[31] according to current Netherlands law, there is no means to make this visible in the name of the company and to indicate this in the commercial register. To overcome this lack of awareness and legal recognition, the Netherlands government has put forward the preproposal for a draft act on a private company limited by shares with a societal objective, the so-called *Besloten vennootschap met een maatschappelijk doel (BVm).*[32] As said above, the preproposal has been submitted for consultation until 7 May 2021. Further legislative actions are pending.

To be sure, the announced future regulation of the *BVm* will not be supported with any additional financial, tax or subsidy inducements upon compliance with the regime for the *BVm.* To become a *BVm*, the articles of association must nominate the private company as such, must contain a cap on the distribution of profits up to 50% by means of a guiding principle (not even as a default rule), the objective must indicate that the profit is primarily used for the benefit of the social objective of the enterprise. Furthermore, the *BVm* is mandated to produce and file—in addition to financial accounts—a social annual account to inform all stakeholders involved. Also, the Netherlands inquiry procedure will be made available for social stakeholders.[33] Similar to other social enterprise regulations in EU member states, there is a mandatory rule on a disinterested distribution of profits in the event of dissolution.

[30] SER Report 2015 and https://internetconsultatie.nl/bvm, as well as, only focusing on existing social enterprises incorporated as private company limited by shares, KPMG Report 2020.

[31] Art. 2:216.1 NCC and art. 2:23b.1 NCC.

[32] Ministry of Economic Affairs, 'Aanzet voor een wettelijke regeling voor een besloten vennootschap met maatschappelijk doel', 9 March 2021, introducing a *BVm*, a private company limited by shares with a societal objective. See https://internetconsultatie.nl/bvm.

[33] Art. 2:346 NCC. This would be a major adjustment since only shareholders, trade unions and the Public Prosecutor, the management board, the supervisory board and the insolvency receiver have the right to request an inquiry into the affairs of the legal person and its enterprise. So far, with the exception of the Public Prosecutor, this involves only direct internal stakeholders based on the mandatory bodies for that legal person.

The consultation of the preproposal resulted in 60 reactions in total. Although most reactions are positive in regard to the legislator's ambition to regulate social enterprises, overall, the reactions to the consultation are critical, questioning, in particular, why its label as social enterprise (the label *maatschappelijk*) is only available for private companies since social enterprises also use other legal forms.[34] The reasoning and the motivation given by the legislator falls short of expectations. Cooperatives are excluded—according to the Minister—because of the mandatory patronage with its members and the fact that members must benefit economically from it, which according to the Minister is contrary to the principle of the *BVm* to distribute profit to be used for the benefit of the social objective of the enterprise.[35] The Minister has a misconstrued view on the legal definition, scope, and objective of the cooperative according to Netherlands law.[36] He made no further assessment in this respect or any legal analysis. Similarly, the foundation and the association are ruled out, because—according to the Minister—[37] they both have a not-for-profit objective, ignoring the fact that foundations and associations may operate as an enterprise and Netherlands company law even regulates this possibility.[38] According to the Minister, they would have to convert themselves into a *BVm* on the basis of article 2:18 NCC to obtain the label. A second critique is the lack of further financial and/or tax inducements and support measures.[39] A third critique is the fear that the label will lead to green washing.[40] Apart from these critiques, the restriction that the 'social enterprise' label (*maatschappelijk*) can only be obtained by social enterprises that are incorporated as private companies limited by shares, appears to be an unjustified discrimination.

Given the pivotal premise that social enterprises operate to a certain degree on the basis of principles of solidarity, mutuality and not-for-profit, the association,[41] the

---

[34] See KPMG Report 2020, p. 20. See also Flamman (2022), pp. 9–11 questioning why the cooperative has not been taken into consideration by the legislator.

[35] Preproposal, p. 3.

[36] This will be elaborated further in paragraph 6.

[37] Preproposal, p. 4.

[38] It triggers the application of accounting rules and the publication of annual accounts, the application of the law on works councils and the law on the inquiry procedure. As said, the associations and foundations may generate a profit but are bound by the asset lock and the prohibition to distribute profits. An association or foundation may even operate as a holding. See Court of Appeal Amsterdam, Enterprise Chamber 6 June 2014, ECLI:NL:GHAMS:2015:4454 (*Meavita*).

[39] There is some basis for this in EU law based on the joint cases ECJ 8 September 2011, Joint Cases C-78/08 to C-80/08.

[40] See for legal comments on the BVm-proposal Stokkermans (2021), pp. 97–108, van Uchelen-Schipper (2020), pp. 713–726, Zillikens-Loos et al. (2021), pp. 109–119, Heesakkers (2021), pp. 679–687, as well as Helder (2021), pp. 140–144.

[41] Art. 2:26 NCC.

foundation[42] and the cooperative[43] seem also to be well equipped to incorporate social economic activities. In this respect, it is important to mention once more that associations and foundations are allowed to operate as an enterprise and to make a profit provided the profit is not distributed to investors or members of its organs, while any distribution must fall within the objective of the association or foundation.[44] This mandatory cap on the distribution of profits of associations and foundations, however, can be circumvented in practice by either incorporating the enterprise to be operated in a fully owned subsidiary of the association or foundation—which is not forbidden—,[45] or to use the technique of a subordinated loan instead of equity titles. In addition, with regard to associations, the mandatory member base may constitute a legal problem—who are the members?[46]—but also an economic problem of collective action given the heterogeneity of the member base and an agency problem due to potential information asymmetries between the management and stakeholders, for example given the nature of the individual problems employees in a socio-labor insertion enterprise encounter.[47]

Turning back to the preproposal of the *BVm*, to pinpoint the societal impact (*maatschappelijk belang*), the objective and the activity of the *BVm* in the articles of association are restricted to activities listed in article 5b, section 3, Algemene wet inzake rijksbelastingen, regulating the *algemeen nut beogende instelling* (hereinafter: *ANBI*). The statutory objective in the articles of association of the *BVm* must lay in the following fields: well-being (*welzijn*), culture, education, science and research, protection of nature and environment, including the enhancement of sustainability, health care, youth care and geriatric care, development cooperation, animal care, religion, the enhancement of democracy, social housing. There are two additional categories: human rights and labor market participation for the most vulnerable in society (socio-labor insertion). Charity, though, is not mentioned. It is clear from the mandatory scope of the *BVm*, that there is an overlap with semi-public organizations in health care and education, but not with social housing since the latter is not mentioned. As already mentioned, the scope is derived from the mandatory activities

[42] Art. 2:285 NCC.

[43] Art. 2:53.1 NCC.

[44] Art. 2:26.3 and 285.3 NCC.

[45] The mandatory prohibition of profit distribution does not apply to a private company controlled by the foundation or association. See Dijk and Van der Ploeg (2017), pp. 23–25 en Asser/Rensen 2-III (2017), nr. 323 en 324.

[46] If members benefit primarily through economic transactions with the association, the association falls within the legal definition of a cooperative pursuant to art. 2:53.1 NCC and will have to either change its legal form into a cooperative or is to be dissolved by court order. See art. 2:21 NCC.

[47] That is also the reason semi-public organizations in the field of education, social housing and health care are not organized as associations but as foundations or as companies with share capital. See van der Sangen (2013a), pp. 223–254.

for *ANBIs*. However, private companies are exempted from the ANBI-status, which includes the *BVm*.[48]

The *BVm*-label is protected by the following measures: only the *BVm* is allowed to use the label in the name of the company and register the company as such in the commercial register. Any stakeholder may request a court order that obliges the abuser of the label to abstain from using the label. Abuse can be prosecuted by the Public Prosecutor and fined as a criminal offence. Also, any stakeholder can request the dissolution of the *BVm*.[49]

Given the preliminary status of the preproposal, I will only summarize the main characteristics of the *BVm* to be met upon incorporation. The *BVm* is established by a notarial deed, either ex novo or by adjusting the name of the private company and the articles of association to that end. The articles of association contain a description of the scope of the societal objective. The preproposal obligates the *BVm* to reserve a certain part of the annual profits for the achievement of the societal objective and to draw up a distribution policy. However, the preproposal does not mandate a strict norm in this respect or any prefixed ratio, but gives as a guideline to be taken into consideration the option to choose 50%, 20–25% or an adjustable ratio. Also, it states in accordance with standing case law that shareholders of the *BVm* may not be barred generically from a part of the profits. They are entitled to a reasonable dividend.[50] Normal restrictions on the distribution of profits applicable to all private companies to protect creditors apply.[51] The *BVm* should be transparent on, and be held accountable for, the results of the societal impact and therefore has the obligation to draw up an annual societal report while stakeholder organizations have the right to start an inquiry procedure in the event that the company does not act in conformity with its societal objective. In the case of liquidation, the net assets shall be distributed in accordance with the principle of disinterested distribution to another *BVm* or any other organization with a similar social objective. This feature would be a novelty in Netherlands company law because company law does not mandate

[48]Preproposal, p. 6 and further. Public benefit organizations (ANBIs) incorporated as associations or foundations must meet the following cumulative requirements: The organization's efforts must be almost entirely focused on the public benefit. This is the 90% requirement. The organization and the persons directly involved in the organization must meet with the integrity requirements. A natural or legal person may not manage the organization's assets as it is its equity. Directors and policymakers cannot have majority control over the assets of the organization. An ANBI may not have more assets then necessary for the organization's work. For this reason, the organization's assets must remain limited. The directors'remuneration must be restricted to an expense allowance or a minimum attendance fee. An ANBI must possess an up-to-date policy plan. The ANBI's costs must be in reasonable proportion to its expenditure. Funds remaining after the dissolution of the organization must be allocated to a general good objective identical to the organization's objective. An ANBI is governed by specific administrative obligations. An ANBI must publish information about the organization on its own website or on a communal website of, for example, a trade organization. See Idsinga and Wessels (2018), pp. 545–569.

[49]Preproposal, p. 9.

[50]High Court 5 July 1990, *NJ* 1991/51 (*Sluis BV*).

[51]Like a balance sheet test and liquidity test according to article 2:216.1 and 2 NCC.

disinterested distribution, not even for associations, foundations, the cooperative or the 'Netherlands'SCE.

6 The Potential of the Cooperative to Incorporate Social Enterprises and Their Activities: The Case of Socio-Labor Insertion

As mentioned above, social enterprises in the Netherlands are not only incorporated as private companies. However, the data show a small number of cooperatives that are used as the legal business form in the social economy so far. This is also the case for initiatives in the field of socio-labor insertion designed to include the most vulnerable people in employment. These initiatives are clearly considered part and parcel of the third sector and social economy—also by the legislator given the addition of this activity to the mandatory scope of the *BVm*. However, the cooperative may provide an adequate model.

For example, according to Oden and others,[52] entrepreneurs prefer to set up labor pools in the legal form of a foundation. An advantage of a foundation is that it has no members,[53] so the board can act instantly. Also, a foundation is easily accessible for companies to join through contracts or through positions on the board. However, as said above, a foundation has no profit that can be distributed among those who are affiliated with the foundation. Another disadvantage of the foundation is that the affiliated entrepreneurs cannot take part in the formal decision-making process since the foundation's mandatory decision-making body is the board. Granting decision-making rights to entrepreneurs to appoint and dismiss board members, to change the objective or the articles of association, the right to merge, split or convert, to approve the annual account and major board decisions in a foundation will lead to trespassing on the legal boundaries of the foundation and a violation of the prohibition to have members.[54] By doing so, the foundation enters the area of the common association. Because of these restrictions of the foundation, there is less involvement of affiliated partners and they can withdraw if they wish to. If too many companies withdraw, the continuity within the labor pool can be at risk, because the affiliated companies have to provide the work (experience) places. If the labor pool cannot provide workplaces, the potential employees again end up in a social benefit situation, which is contrary to the aim of a labor pool.

The cooperative has several benefits compared to the foundation. A cooperative can make a profit[55] and is mandated to let members benefit economically from it, although there is no indication of how this should happen. Labor pools may use the

[52] Oden et al. (2018).

[53] Article 2:285.1 and 2 NCC.

[54] Article 2:285.1 and 2 NCC.

[55] Art. 2:53a NCC exempting the prohibition to distribute profits as laid down in art. 2:26.3 NCC.

profit for insurance purposes, training and pensions for the employees (in an employers'cooperative) and for the members (in a workers'cooperative). The profits may also be used to address downturns in periods with fewer projects where workers can be allocated to work. However, the members in a cooperative are free to join the cooperative but also to terminate their membership.[56] This may also affect the capital of the cooperative, although Netherlands cooperative law does not mandate that members are entitled to be paid a yearly dividend or have a right of refund upon withdrawal, unless the articles of association stipulate otherwise. Because the members are bound by the rules within the cooperative, it is possible to regulate under what conditions members are allowed to terminate their membership.[57] In this way, the continuation of work (experience) places is better guaranteed. Members of a cooperative have control over the functioning and operations of the cooperative through the general meeting and the right to appoint and dismiss board members. All members have an equal say in the cooperative as a default rule.[58] In an employer's cooperative, the companies have a say; in a workers' cooperative, the employees have a say. Conceptually, cooperatives are highly democratic and there is a strong involvement of the members. However, we must keep in mind that in larger cooperatives the involvement of the members and the internal democracy may decrease.[59] Another, yet theoretical, disadvantage of a cooperative is that the members are liable for the deficit upon liquidation. However, this default rule on member liability can be changed in the articles of association into a limited liability upon liquidation or into a complete exemption of liability.[60] In any event, members of a cooperative are not directly liable towards creditors.

The example of the case of the labor pool already showed that the cooperative might be an adequate vehicle for socio-labor insertion enterprises and their activities. Although Netherlands cooperative law has no specific provisions in this respect, nor specific laws on social economy and worker cooperatives, from a business organizational point of view the cooperative law statute is one of the most flexible business forms in the Netherlands,[61] including the possibility to introduce different multi-stakeholder memberships or an investor membership.[62] However, specific mandates

---

[56] Art. 2:36 NCC jo. 2:53a NCC.

[57] Art. 2:60 NCC. However, any restriction in this respect must meet the rule of reason-criterion of economic necessity and may not lead to an absolute restriction to withdraw from the membership of the cooperative. Also, national and EU competition law rules may apply. See van der Sangen (1999), p. 499 and Asser-Rensen 2-III (2017), nr. 243.

[58] Art. 2:38.1 jo. 53a NCC.

[59] It is the distinction between formal and effective control Henry Hansmann referred to in: Hansmann (1996), p. 11.

[60] Art. 2:55 and 56 NCC.

[61] van der Sangen (2013b), pp. 541–561, van der Sangen (2019), pp. 39–56 and van der Sangen (2022).

[62] The voting rights of an investor membership are, however, limited to half of the votes actually cast in the general assembly. Art. 2:38.3 NCC.

and inducements—particularly in tax law[63] or social security law—are missing. Although the Dutch government has launched a consultation on the feasibility of a specific legal business form for social economy initiatives, the cooperative was not included in that preproposal.

As mentioned above, the legal business form of the cooperative in the Netherlands has no mandatory obligation to include social or societal interests as a legal objective in the articles of association or adherence to the ICA Principles. But it does not mean that a cooperative cannot be organized with a social objective. This decision is left to the incorporators or the subsequent members who may choose to amend the articles of association.[64] The mandatory legal objective of the cooperative is to enhance and further the economic position of its members by engaging in economic transactions with them. The remainder of this section is dedicated to the question of how the cooperative as a legal business form could contribute to socio-labor insertion and inclusiveness, in particular with regard to the new phenomenon of the so-called *participation cooperative*.

The participation cooperative is a new phenomenon that only recently came into practice in the Netherlands[65] and triggered the question whether the cooperative is an adequate model for the socio-labor insertion of the most vulnerable people in the Netherlands. The main stakeholders of the participation cooperative are the unemployed who rely on social assistance benefits and have an obligation under the Participation Act 2015[66] to (re)integrate in the work process without wages but are not able to do so on their own account and need assistance from the government as the social security public agent. The ultimate goal is to achieve full employment with the help of the local government (municipalities) and a social enterprise established to achieve that aim, either through a labor contract or through self-employment.

In practice, several so-called *participation cooperatives* have been identified that fulfill this function in some 25 trajectories of re-integration of the most vulnerable people into the work process. They organize themselves as follows (see Fig. 7.1):

The clients or members of the cooperative are (re)integrating employees and employers. In some cases, the municipality is also a formal member.

The participation cooperative is not a special type of cooperative. This type of cooperative needs to be established under the statute for cooperatives in the Second Book of the Netherlands Civil Code, as defined in article 53, paragraph 1 (hereinafter: art. 2:53.1 NCC). The participation cooperative, therefore, has to comply with the mandatory objective of the cooperative prescribed in article 2:53.1 NCC and the characteristics that follow from that law. Article 2:53.1 NCC stipulates in this

[63] Although cooperatives are exempted from Dividend Withholding Tax and under strict conditions can also deduct profits from the Corporate Income Tax, provided the profits are only generated in economic transactions with its members being natural persons and the profits are distributed after closing of the financial year to the members in proportion to the economic transactions. See van der Sangen (1999), pp. 309–313 and van der Sangen (2013b), pp. 541–561.

[64] van der Sangen (2022) as well as van der Sangen (2019), pp. 39–56.

[65] Flamman (2020), pp. 12–14.

[66] See on the Participation Act 2015: Eleveld (2014), pp. 204–224 and Eleveld (2019), pp. 110–113.

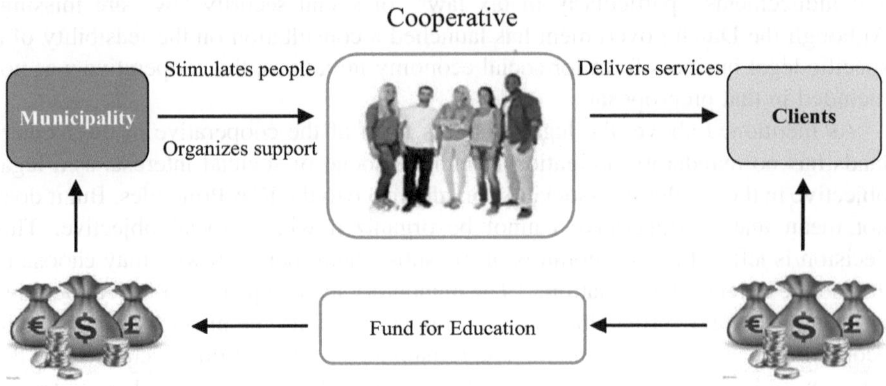

Fig. 7.1 Transactions within the participation cooperative

respect: *'under its articles of association, the statutory objective of the cooperative must be to provide for certain material needs of its members under agreements, other than insurance agreements, concluded with them in the business it conducts or causes to be conducted to that end for the benefit of its members.'* From the parliamentary proceedings, it follows that worker cooperatives specifically are meant to be covered by this legal definition, although Netherlands'cooperative law has no specific provisions or a law on worker cooperatives.[67]

To comply with the legal definition of the cooperative and its mandatory objective, the participation cooperative must meet four distinctive characteristics:

1. Unemployed persons need to be members (membership) to be able to use the services of the cooperative.
2. The members need to enter into contracts with the cooperative and maintain a patronage relationship with the cooperative. What type of contract covers the patronage relationship between the member and the cooperative is left to be defined in the articles of association. In the case of the participation cooperative, it is most likely to be a contract sui generis combining labor contract elements, educational, financial, and administrative support, and other services to facilitate the proficiency of the member towards full employment.
3. The participation cooperative needs to have an enterprise to fulfill the mandatory legal objective and to establish the patronage relationship with its members in that enterprise. It is permitted for the enterprise to be operated on behalf of the cooperative in a fully controlled subsidiary. The enterprise could run the workplace itself or be a platform or intermediary for other enterprises that supply workspaces.
4. The economic results of the cooperative need to be economically beneficial for the members. This requirement means that the profits of the cooperative should be

[67] See on the historic evolution of the definition of the cooperative van der Sangen (1999), chapter 3.

> redistributed to its members to achieve the objective of the cooperative and its patronage relationship with its members. Redistribution in this context means that the members benefit economically from the cooperative in the broadest sense. However, the law does not mandate that members are entitled to a yearly dividend unless the articles of association stipulate otherwise. Within the existing legal framework of Netherlands cooperative law, it is already possible to design the articles of association in such a way that the profits of the cooperative are not distributed but are fully reserved to the benefit of the continuity of the cooperative, provided members have a patronage relationship with the cooperative and benefit economically from this. As previously mentioned, the objective of the cooperative may also include a social objective.[68]

In the participation cooperative, the people to insert are the members of the cooperative. As already indicated above, this is a quintessential element of the legal definition of the cooperative. The question may arise whether it is permitted for the municipality to participate in the cooperative. From a cooperative law point of view, it is worth noting that article 2:38.1 NCC provides the possibility of different types of memberships provided that all members have equal voting rights in the general assembly. Also, the municipality could take the role of investing member on the basis of article 2:38.3 NCC. Whether and how the municipality participates in the cooperative, however, depends on the policy of the municipality.[69] The designated municipality is the municipality that has a public duty under the Participation Act 2015 and the Decree on Social Assistance of Self-Employed Persons, to develop re-integration policies and programs. However, these laws do not mandate the use of cooperatives as a social economy business form. So, in practice, only a few municipalities have developed a policy in which the use of the cooperative is promoted. In these few cases, the municipality is co-establisher and co-member of the cooperative. This is the case in the cities of Breda, Eindhoven and Zaanstad. In the majority of the still small number of cases, a group of self-employed persons in receipt of social assistance benefit has established the participation cooperative voluntarily and the cooperative has entered into agreements with the municipality without obtaining formal membership of the cooperative. A couple of commercial intermediaries act as consultants and advisors to set up this type of cooperative in this niche market.

However, other formats are available as well, like the franchise model of Brownies & Downies (51 franchisees, one of which is in South-Africa).[70] The franchisees take different business forms: sole proprietor, partnership or private company limited by shares, all of which employ people with Down's syndrome.

[68] van der Sangen (2019), pp. 39–56.

[69] In its country report on The Netherlands, Bosma (2019), pp. 43–44, points to the recognition of the concept of social enterprises by municipalities, which has led to a certain level of support at local levels. A study by PwC (2018) shows about four in every ten municipalities are developing policies to stimulate social enterprises. PwC (2018).

[70] https://www.browniesanddownies.nl/franchisenemer-worden.

At this moment there is no conclusive evidence whether, or to what extent, these franchise branches get assistance from the municipality.

As indicated above, the participation cooperative may also allow equity partners. According to article 2:38.3 NCC, it is possible for a cooperative to introduce non-user members, members who do not make use of the services provided and grant restricted voting rights to these members in the general assembly. The voting rights of these members are restricted to half of the total amount of votes actually cast at the general meeting by the ordinary members. From this provision and from the provision of the Implementation Act of the SCE Statute and the parliamentary proceedings thereof,[71] it follows that these members, who exist notably in the form of equity providers, are allowed under cooperative law in the Netherlands.

Like any enterprise, a participation cooperative needs financing to fulfil their objective. According to cooperative law in the Netherlands, cooperatives are financed by a technique of a postponed obligation of the members to contribute to pay off any deficit upon dissolution of the cooperative to the receiver in the liquidation procedure. However, this rule of joint and several liability upon liquidation is not mandatory and, in most cases, excluded in the articles of association, limiting the members'liability in this respect to nil.[72] Other ways of financing the cooperative are not provided for by law, but need to be outlined in the articles of association. This would also be an important part of future research to list the techniques of financing participation cooperatives because to date the small number of examples of participation cooperatives are tailor-made for a specific purpose.

Social enterprises operate in competition with for-profit organizations. As indicated in the introduction, the policy of the Netherlands government in this respect is to maintain a level playing field between all market actors. In the absence of an articulated legal infrastructure for social enterprises, there are no public promotion measures provided for by law for social enterprises in general. Instruments in the Participation Act 2015 are financial support in the form of a salary supplement up to the minimum wage (*loonkostensubsidie*) and financial assistance for enterprises that create so-called *beschutte werkplekken*: designated workplaces for the most vulnerable people that meet certain requirements that enable them to work. Every municipality—while executing the Participation Act 2015—is developing its own policy, and further research is required to indicate how many municipalities stimulate the use of cooperatives in this respect, or any other form of business organization that enables socio-labor insertion of the most vulnerable people.[73] The main challenges for these entities are to create and maintain a durable business concept and

[71] See van der Sangen (2013b), p. 550 and reference 35.

[72] Articles 2:55 and 2:56 NCC.

[73] Bosma (2019) in his country study on The Netherlands, p. 44, points to a specific support scheme for social enterprises in Amsterdam (*Ondersteuning voor sociale firma's*). Social enterprises in this support scheme concern WISEs: enterprises that support the employment of people with a work limitation and provide daytime activities for vulnerable groups, which provides one of the biggest challenges for the municipality of Amsterdam. In return for the social support, the municipality has initiated a support program, consisting of the following activities: investment fund, promoting

model, to attract financing, management support, to manage taxation, to get support with business administration and the development of work related educational programs to facilitate full employment/entrepreneurship. It is odd that they will not be able to obtain the label *social enterprise*, even though organized as a cooperative, if and when the preproposal on the *BVm* becomes legislation.

7 Conclusion

There is a lot of legislative work to be done in the Netherlands to create the legal environment in which social enterprises may come to fruition and reach maturity. In practice, some municipalities have developed a policy with regard to the promotion of social enterprises, but not as a result of a national policy agenda so far. In general, Netherlands law lacks incentives for municipalities to actively promote the establishment of social economy enterprises, with the exception of mandatory procurement rules in executing the so-called Participation Act 2015. Netherlands law lacks incentives to establish voluntarily social enterprises as well. This lacuna will not be solved with—if that is the case—the entering into force of the Act introducing the *BVm*. As said, the Netherlands law lacks a specific tax treatment for businesses that have a social economy objective. Looking at the preproposal of the *BVm*, it seems that the Netherlands legislator has little awareness of the role a cooperative can play to incorporate social enterprises and their social economy activities. The chapter has outlined several applications of the cooperative model with regard to socio-labor insertion and also showed that—from a business organizational point of view—cooperative law in the Netherlands provides an adequate and flexible model to organize social enterprises. Overall, there seems to be little awareness of the legislator of the potential of the cooperative model, especially when cooperatives'principles of mutuality and solidarity are applied in a similar fashion to the ICA Principles and the current Netherlands *Coöperatie Code 2019*.[74]

References

Argyrou A (2018) Social enterprises in the EU: law promoting stakeholder participation in social enterprises. Utrecht University, Doctoral dissertation

social firms, promoting social return using social firms towards suppliers, as well as providing guidance and advice. Next to that, the city of Utrecht runs a program called 'Working together for work' (*Samen werken aan werk*). With this program, Utrecht aims to collaborate with social entrepreneurs, provide funding (Local Economic Fund) and income tax benefits, in particular for social entrepreneurship relating to job creation for people excluded from the labor market.

[74] Available at: https://www.cooperatie.nl/wp-content/uploads/2019/10/Folder-Co%C3%B6peratie-Code-2019-sept-2019-Platform.pdf.

Asser/Rensen 2-III (2017) Wolters Kluwer Deventer

Bosma N (2019) Social enterprises and their ecosystems in Europe. Updated country report: The Netherlands. Commissioned by the European Commission. Publications Office of the European Union, Luxembourg

Cooperatives Europe, Sangen G van der (2021) Legal framework analysis. National Report, The Netherlands

Dijk/Van der Ploeg (2017) Van vereniging en stichting, coöperatie en onderlinge waarborgmaatschappij, 3rd edn. Wolters Kluwer Deventer

Eleveld A (2014) The duty to work without wage: legal comparison between social assistance legislation in Germany, The Netherlands, and the United Kingdom. Eur J Soc Secur 16(3): 204–224

Eleveld A (2019) Werken met behoud van uitkering in de Participatiewet en in de werknemersverzekeringen. Ars Aequi 2:110–113

European Commission (2015) A map of social enterprises and their eco-systems in Europe (synthesis report). Publications Office of the European Union, Luxembourg

European Economic and Social Committee, Chaves Ávila R, Monzón Campos J (2012) The social economy in the European Union. European Economic and Social Committee. Brussels

Flamman M (2020) Sociale coöperaties gericht op arbeidsparticipatie. Coöperatie 642:12–14

Flamman M (2022) De BVm: een overbodig wetsvoorstel. Coöperatie June 2020, 651:9–11

Hansmann H (1996) The ownership of enterprise. Belknap Press of Harvard University Press, London England/Cambridge

Heesakkers R (2021) De BVm-aanzet en hervorming van het ondernemingsrecht: pionier of dwaalspoor? Ondernemingsrecht 108:679–687

Helder R (2021) Een rechtsvorm voor sociaal ondernemerschap. TvOB, 140–144

Idsinga N, Wessels J (2018) Bijzondere verschijningsvormen van de stichting en de vereniging. In: Hamers J et al (eds) Handboek Stichting en Vereniging. Uitgeverij Paris Zutphen, pp 545–569

Karré P (2021) Social enterprise in The Netherlands. Between hope and hype. In: Defourny J et al (eds) Social enterprise in Western Europe. Routledge, New York, pp 149–165

KMPG/Nyenrode Business University (2020) Stimuleren van (h)erkenning van sociale ondernemingen. The Hague

Lambooy T, Argyrou A (2014) Improving the legal environment for social entrepreneurship in Europe. Eur Comp Law 11(2):71–76

Laseur-Eelman S, Mars A (2018) Maatschappelijke ondernemingen. In: Hamers J et al (eds) Handboek Stichting en Vereniging. Uitgeverij Paris Zutphen, pp 469–498

McKinsey&Company (2016) Scaling the impact of the social enterprise sector

Ministry of Economic Affairs (2021) Aanzet voor een wettelijke regeling voor een besloten vennootschap met maatschappelijk doel. 9 March. Available at https://internetconsultatie.nl/bvm

Oden P (2015) SMEs cooperate to meet social procurement conditions. Understanding small enterprises (USE). 2015 conference proceedings, pp 579–593

Oden P et al (eds) (2018) Partnerschap door regelruimte. De samenwerking van ondernemers met gemeenten bij de Participatiewet. Groningen Hanzehogeschool/SIA

OECD/EU (2019) Boosting Social Entrepreneurship and Social Enterprise Development in the Netherlands. In-depth Policy Review. OECD LEED Working Papers 2019, OECD Publishing, Paris

Overes H (2017) The Netherlands. In: Van der Ploeg P et al (eds) Civil society in Europe. Minimum norms and optimum conditions of its regulation. Cambridge University Press, Cambridge. chapter 13

Price Waterhouse Coopers (2018) Prille kansen: de samenwerking tussen sociale ondernemingen en gemeenten in Nederland. Price Waterhouse Coopers. March

Sociaal-Economische Raad (2015) Sociale Ondernemingen: een verkennend advies. Advies nr. 15/03. May. The Hague

Stokkermans C (2021) Naar een wettelijke verankering van de maatschappelijke onderneming. Maandblad voor Ondernemingsrecht. 3–4:97–108
van der Sangen G (1999) Rechtskarakter en financiering van de coöperatie. Tjeenk Willink Zwolle
van der Sangen G(2013a) Privaatrechtelijke waarborgen bij financieringsmodellen in de zorg. In: Berden B et al (eds) Financiering van zorginstellingen. Vakmedianet Deventer, pp 223–254
van der Sangen G (2013b) The Netherlands. In: Cracogna D et al (eds) International handbook of cooperative law. Springer, Berlin, pp 541–561
van der Sangen G (2019) The principles of European cooperative law and their impact on future law-making on cooperatives. The case of The Netherlands. Int J Cooperat Law II:39–56
van der Sangen G (2022) The hybridization of cooperatives and cooperative law. Insights from The Netherlands. In: Tadjudje W, Douvitsa I (eds) Perspectives on cooperative law. Singapore, Springer Nature, pp 159–171
van Uchelen-Schipper M (2020) Sociale ondernemingen in Nederland: is het BV-recht nog flexibel genoeg? WPNR 7298:713–726
Zillikens-Loos J et al (2021) De nieuwe juridische jas voor de maatschappelijke onderneming komt eraan: de BVm. Maandblad voor Ondernemingsrecht 3–4:109–119

Chapter 8
Third Sector in the Third Republic: An Overview of the Law and Practice in Poland

Arkadiusz Radwan, Marcin Mazgaj, and Przemysław Żak

Contents

Arkadiusz Radwan is professor at Vytautas Magnus University in Kaunas and president of the Allerhand Institute of Advanced Legal Studies in Kraków.
Marcin Mazgaj is assistant professor of commercial law at the University of the National Education Commision in Kraków, attorney-at-law and partner in JWMS Jakubowski Wiese Mazgaj Staszek law firm in Kraków.
Przemysław Żak is a lawyer and partner in Pajaczkowska i Wspolnicy law firm in Kraków and a legal expert on NGO law in working group on NGO law at National Federation of Polish NGOs.

A. Radwan (✉)
Vytautas Magnus University, Kaunas, Lithuania
e-mail: arkadiusz.radwan@vdu.lt

M. Mazgaj
University of the National Education Commission, Kraków, Poland
e-mail: marcin.mazgaj@up.krakow.pl

P. Żak
Pajaczkowska i Wspolnicy Law Firm, Kraków, Poland
e-mail: przemyslaw@obywatelzak.pl

A. Fici (ed.), *The Law of Third Sector Organizations in Europe*,
https://doi.org/10.1007/978-3-031-41744-3_8

Abstract In this chapter we discuss and evaluate the regulatory framework for the Third Sector in Poland, including its philosophical and constitutional underpinning. We do not however stop at the dogmatic or theoretical level but instead go on to offer insights from practical application and interpretation of the laws by public authorities and the courts. We point out to difficulties TSOs encounter and to problems and shortcomings of the existing law and practice. We attempt to offer a cross-sectional presentation of key aspects related to the functioning of the Third Sector in Poland. The chapter is divided into four sections. In the first one we provide an overview of the functioning of NGOs in Poland. In the second, we discuss their impact on the economy and society, using, among other things, available statistical data. In the third section we focus on the legal aspects of organization of TSOs, while in the fourth one we analyse various aspects related to TSOs' finance and funding.

1 Introduction

At the time this text was written, Russian aggression against Ukraine continued. In February and March of 2022, i.e. during the first weeks of the war, hundreds of thousands of war refugees crossed Ukrainian-Polish border seeking shelter in Poland. As of September 1, 2022, Border Guard officers in Poland have cleared over 5.9 million people fleeing war-stricken Ukraine at border crossings with Poland's eastern neighbour.[1] This unprecedented migration caused a major humanitarian challenge. That we can speak of a *challenge* rather than of a crisis is owed to a number of actions and initiatives, both bottom-up and top-down, many of which have been inspired, implemented and coordinated by Polish NGOs, supported through massive donations from the general public as well as by their foreign and international peers. At one point Poland was even proclaimed to have turned itself into world's largest NGO.[2] This phrase conveys a very positive notion of civic and charitable organisations. It remains to be seen if this extreme experience will have a lasting reinvigorating impact on the Third Sector in Poland. Admittedly, in this chapter we discuss the legal framework for the Third Sector Organisations in Poland, yet we do not entirely disregard a broader societal and economic background and context in which Third Sector Organisations in Poland operate.

[1] https://www.statista.com/statistics/1293228/poland-ukrainian-refugees-crossing-the-polish-border.

[2] Tweet by former US ambassador to Poland – Daniel Fried, https://twitter.com/AmbDanFried/status/1506259481839157249.

2 Mapping the Third Sector in Poland: Typologies, Definitional Problems, History

2.1 Introduction

In this section, prelusive and general remarks are made in order to introduce the regulatory framework for NGOs in Poland. First, an attempt is made to present three main groups of regulations of the sector, with particular attention paid to legal forms which qualify as non-governmental organisations. Next, selected aspects of the Act on Public Benefit Activity and Volunteerism,[3] crucial for the Third Sector in Poland, are described, focusing on the notion of non-governmental organisation and cooperation with public authorities. In the last piece of this section, we attempt to bring some conceptual clarity when it comes to the relationship between non-governmental organisations and social economy entities.

2.2 Polish NGO Law as a Multilayer System

At the outset, it is necessary to refer to the constitutional provisions of Article 12 and Article 58 of the Constitution of the Republic of Poland,[4] which will be discussed in more detail in Sect. 4.2 of this chapter. The respective provisions read as follows:

"The Republic of Poland ensures the freedom to establish and operate trade unions, socio-professional organisations of farmers, associations, civic movements, other voluntary associations and foundations." (Article 12 of the Constitution).

"Everyone shall be guaranteed freedom of association" (Article 58 sec. 1 of the Constitution).

At this point it must be emphasised that while Article 58 sec. 1 in a classical way is a source of affirmation and guarantee of the state's protection of the freedom of association, Article 12 puts emphasis on the guarantee of establishment and operation of the types of organisations enumerated therein, including associations and foundations.

While looking at the system of Polish NGO law, it is necessary to refer to the conceptual grid and definitions developed by M. Kisilowski in his 2009 monographic study "Law of the non-governmental sector. A functional analysis",[5] which is a milestone contribution to the theory of Polish NGO law.

In the context of the aforementioned constitutional provisions, M. Kisilowski points out that already at the constitutional level the concept on which the legislator is to base the regulation of the Third Sector is not prejudiced, and the *prima facie*

---

[3] Act of 24 April 2003 on Public Benefit Activity and Volunteerism (hereinafter: "Public Benefit Act").

[4] Constitution of the Republic of Poland of April 2nd, 1997 (hereinafter: "Constitution").

[5] Kisilowski (2009).

impression of reliance on freedom of association as a founding principle is misleading.[6] In elaborating further on to the concepts behind the adopted models for statutory solutions, we will make references to the study by M. Kisilowski.

Polish legislation on the Third Sector may, for cognitive purposes, be divided into three categories or groups. The first group are organic or institutional provisions setting out governance and structural design for any given legal forms. The second group is made up of regulations that focus mainly on the relationship between the organisations and public authorities, including conditions for obtaining and maintaining special statuses conferring upon the status-holding organisations a number of additional benefits and rights of preferential nature. The third group are general regulations to which NGOs are often subjected on an equal footing with business associations. Save for their relationships and interactions with public authorities, non-governmental organisations in Poland, are subject to the vast majority laws and regulations that apply to business associations. NGOs are not, however, covered by some protective regulations, e.g. provisions limiting the maximum length of inspections by various public authorities, neither are they entitled to request binding upfront interpretations of laws and regulations, which offer safe harbours to business associations under the Entrepreneurs'Law,[7] unless they themselves carry out business activities and hence qualify as entrepreneurs within the meaning of the said law.[8]

In the first group, the Law on Associations[9] and the Law on Foundations[10] are the organic acts laying down the bedrock for the functioning of 4 basic legal forms of NGOs in Poland: registered associations (*stowarzyszenie rejestrowe*) with legal personality, ordinary associations (*stowarzyszenie zwykłe*) as of 2016 enjoying restricted legal personality, unions of associations (*związek stowarzyszeń*) and foundations (*fundacja*). All but one, i.e. except for ordinary association, are subject to mandatory entry and disclosure in the National Court Register—this for the sake of transparency and legal certainty. In addition to these, there is a number of other legal acts that, while introducing some specific forms, refer to the aforementioned Law on Associations. These acts are foundational for a number of specific organisations, such as rural housewives'associations, voluntary fire brigades, student sports clubs, sports clubs in the form of associations, local action groups, local tourist organisations.

[6] Kisilowski (2009), Part II, Ch. 8.

[7] Act of March 6th, 2018 – Entrepreneurs'Law.

[8] As an aside, it should be mentioned that in the Polish system organisations face two regimes of economic activity. A general one on the basis of the Entrepreneurs'Law, from which most of their, i.e. NGOs'activities are excluded under Article 6 of the Public Benefit Act, and a specific one on the basis of the VAT regulations, which uses a legally autonomous definition of economic activity, in the light of which part of the organisation's activity is qualified for VAT purposes as economic activity. This is a situation with a high potential of legal risks for running organisations in Poland.

[9] Act of April 7th, 1989 – Law on Associations.

[10] Act of April 6th, 1984 – Law on Foundations.

It is worth mentioning that unions of associations, contrary to what their name suggests, may be formed by organisations other than associations, e.g. a federation of foundations may avail itself of such legal form, which may be a bit misleading. Putting it differently: the legal vehicle of union of associations may be utilised in order to bring about federalisation of heterogenous legal forms. However, there is a legal requirement for a minimum number of members who actually wear a legal robe of registered associations for the union to be established—the said number is three. Even though this requirement appears random and arbitrary, the reality is that, without at least three registered associations, no other legal forms can avail themselves of the federalization by means of union of association as the legal vehicle thereto.

In contrast to the Code of Commercial Companies,[11] which is the fundamental legal act in Poland under which business organizations operate, the above regulations designed for NGOs are, in principle, characterised by a very high degree of generality. To varying degrees, they leave up to the founders a great deal of freedom with respect to the shaping of organisation's internal affairs and governance structure. Putting it differently, the organic NGO laws are either dominated by default provisions or simply limit themselves to a wireframe, while leaving the rest up to the charters and bylaws the organisations are bestowed with or adopt for themselves.

The common denominator for all legal forms of NGOs lies in their being inapt for profit-making: there is a legal ban on profit-orientation and on distributing of any surpluses to the founders, stakeholders and any other individuals behind the organisation. However, this does not imply a prohibition of business activities, subject to a few exceptions.

For more detailed analysis of the two above-mentioned organic acts for the legal forms of organisations in Poland we refer to Sect. 4 *infra*.

It is worth emphasising that the Polish system is thus marked by a specific corporatism, characteristic of models based on the theory of subsidiarity. However, the two basic legal acts mentioned above are partly based on different regulatory philosophies. The Act on Foundations, by leaving full freedom to shape the internal structure of foundations, combined with no minimum assets'requirement, meets the demands of a model based on freedom of association.[12] Consequently, the regulatory model of foundations follows the liberal economic theory rather than a democratic theory of civil society. At the same time, however, it incorporates an anachronism from the previous system under which it was enacted, that is, the requirement that the objectives comply with the fundamental interests of the state, and the requirement that they be socially or economically useful. In practice, the former requirement is generally not examined by the courts of registration, although there is some anecdotal evidence to the contrary. The Law on Associations, on the

[11] Act of September 15th, 2000 – Code of Commercial Companies.

[12] It is worth quoting a succinct account of the essence of such a model "it is not the sector that needs to justify the purpose of its existence, but it is society that needs to justify any limitation of the sector's reach" – Kisilowski (2009), Part I, Chapter 6.

other hand, does not provide any rationing of the objectives the associations are allowed to pursue. However, it limits the possibilities of shaping internal relations, clearly focusing on enforcing a democratic, associative form of the association's constitution, with a number of mandatory provisions (*ius cogens*) pertaining to the governance, e.g. by vesting the supreme authority over the organization with the members'general assembly. This in turn moves this regulation towards a model based on the theory of civil society.

The second group (category) of NGO laws are statutes addressing the junction of the civic and the public, i.e. the cooperation of organisations with public authorities. This embraces also requirements and benefits of obtaining special statuses and enjoying special rights of a preferential nature resulting thereof. The key legal act here is the Public Benefit Act. The rules set out therein are more prescriptive and characterised by greater attention to details. Moreover, contrary to the repeated declarations, the said act maintains a considerable inequality in the organisation-authority relationship. This mainly concerns the financial dimension. We will further discuss two fundamental terms of this Act, i.e. "non-governmental organisations" (NGOs) and "public benefit activity".

Separately in this group, tax law is worth mentioning, mainly the Legal Persons' Income Tax Act[13] (the CIT Act). The CIT Act does not take sufficiently into account the specificity of entities, which, after all, by law, cannot operate for profit. As a result, if the organisations want to avoid paying CIT on the private funds they raise or earn with a view on spending on their activities, they need to resort to exemptions that the law provides. These exemptions have a rather anachronistic design, focusing on objectives that were important from the state's point of view 25–35 years ago. One exception to this is the exemption for organisations that have been granted a public benefit organization status (see Sect. 2.4 below).

2.3 Terminology

The term "third sector organization" is not a legal term in Poland. On the other hand, under Polish law there are two similar terms close to each other, i.e. "social organisation" and "non-governmental organisation", with a noticeable tendency for the former to be replaced by the latter. Social organisation is a general term, with its origins in legal acts enacted in the period of the communist People's Republic of Poland, referred to in laws such as the Code of Civil Procedure[14] or the Code of Administrative Procedure,[15] whenever they provide for a possibility for civic actors to take part in the proceedings. Over the last 20 years, i.e. since the enactment of the

[13] Act of February 15th, 1992 – Legal Persons'Income Tax Act.

[14] Act of November 17th, 1964 – Code of Civil Procedure.

[15] Act of June 14th, 1960 – Code of Administrative Procedure.

Public Benefit Act, it has been gradually replaced in legislation and interpretation by the concept of a non-governmental organisation.

In 2003, the concept of NGO was defined at the statutory level. It became a legal notion, it ceased to be merely a colloquial, sociological term, naming a phenomenon, without attempting to define it in the legal sense. The "upgrade" of the notion from colloquial to a legal definition has influenced the understanding of the Third Sector, the NGO sector. This is due to the statutory context in which it was established. While the definition itself is broad, the context in which it appears is the junction of the civic and the public, i.e. of the relationship between the NGO sector and public administration, predominantly the executive branch of the government, both central and local.

At the outset, however, it is important to emphasise the wide range of subjects covered by the legal definition itself, setting aside the context in which it is placed. According to Article 3 sec. 2 of the Public Benefit Act, NGOs are legal persons or organisational units without legal personality which are granted legal capacity by a separate act, including foundations and associations, provided they are not operating for profit neither are they units of the public finance sector within the meaning of the Act on Public Finance,[16] nor enterprises, nor research institutes, nor banks nor state-owned or local government owned commercial companies. This general definition as well as subsequent provisions make it possible to conclude that not only organisations traditionally numbered among the non-governmental actors, such as registered associations, ordinary associations, unions of associations, and foundations[17] should be seen as embraced by the said definition, but also entities established under other legal regimes, such as political parties, European political parties, political foundations, European political foundations, trade unions, employers'organisations, and professional associations.

The Act also singles out entities labelled as "entities referred to in Article 3(3)" as the ones that also may conduct public benefit activity.[18] This not very clear inclusion means a number of entities which are either close to the definition of a non-governmental organisation or could even fall under it and their separate listing was intended to exclude them from the definition. These are legal persons and organisational units operating on the basis of the laws on the relation of the State to the Catholic Church in the Republic of Poland, the relation of the State to other churches and religious associations and the guarantees of freedom of conscience and religion, if their statutory objectives include conducting public benefit activity. These will also include associations of local government units, social cooperatives, joint-stock companies and limited liability companies, as well as sports clubs that are companies operating under the provisions of the Sports Act—which do not operate for profit and allocate their entire income to the pursuit of their statutory objectives

[16] Act of August 27th, 2009 on Public Finance.

[17] As well as those mentioned when discussing the first group of regulations discussed in Sect. 2.2 *supra*.

[18] As regards the term „public benefit activity" – see Sect. 2.4 of this chapter below.

and do not allocate their profit for distribution among their members, stakeholders, managers or employees.

Although the definition itself does not explicitly refer to a requirement of carrying out a certain type of activity or to cooperate with public authorities, it is located in an act dedicated to this. It therefore becomes crucial to examine now the notion that is fundamental for the Public Benefit Act, namely: the concept and the definition of public benefit activities.

2.4 Public Benefit Activity and Cooperation with Public Administration

The status of a public benefit organisation ("PBO") is a key notion of the Polish NGO law. This is due to the fact that an organization that qualifies as PBO enjoys certain special preferences, at the same time being, however, obliged to fulfil some additional requirements. According to the Public Benefit Act, each NGO may apply to obtain this status after 2 years of conducting public benefit activity (we will clarify this term below). The PBO status is granted on the basis of a decision issued by a registry court. Having the PBO status entails a number of reporting obligations,[19] but involves also potentially significant benefits—inter alia: full exemption from CIT of income allocated to the statutory activities of such an organisation, eligibility to raise funds from tax deductions allocated by individuals in their personal income tax returns (1% of PIT, recently increased to 1.5%[20]), free access (within a limited scope) to public media etc.

It has to be highlighted that this kind of organisation has to change some of its governance aspects. The Public Benefit Act requires PBOs to introduce internal, collective control body (independent from management board). There is also a significant number of legal requirements pertaining to management of organisation's assets.[21]

The legal notion of public benefit activity, which is central to the aforementioned cooperation of organisations with public administration, although not a defining

[19] Those organisations are obliged to send their financial and activity yearly reports to special base of public benefit organisation's report base (available via the following website: https://sprawozdaniaopp.niw.gov.pl/).

[20] See Sect. 5.3 *infra* – the so-called 1,5% financing.

[21] I.e. the Public Benefit Act prohibits "granting loans or pledging the organisation's property to secure any financial liabilities of such organisation's members, members of management bodies, employees, or their spouses, domestic partners, next of kin or relations in lineal or collateral affinity thereto, or persons related to them on the basis of adoption, custody or guardianship, all of whom jointly referred to as "relatives", as well as transfer of the organisation's property to its members, members of its management bodies, employees or their relatives under terms and conditions other than those applying to unrelated third parties, in particular should such transfer be free of charge or on preferential terms, and others".

element of the NGO term, has become a functional component of it. In our opinion this is due to the location of the definition in the law dedicated to the cooperation of NGOs with public administration and to the conduct of public benefit activities by organisations. Moreover, it is due to the explicit exclusion from the possibility of participation in the statutorily regulated cooperation of NGOs with public administration, as governed by the pertinent act, of a number of entities that otherwise fall under the definition of an NGO recapitulated above. This explicit exclusion embraces political parties, European political parties, trade unions, employers'organisations, professional associations, political foundations and European political foundations.[22] Here we again emphasise a broad understanding of the concept of public benefit activities—in practical terms it seems difficult to carry out social activities that do not fall into any of the public benefit spheres that define the concept of public benefit activities.

It is worth mentioning at this point that under the Public Benefit Act, public administration bodies are even ordered to implement tasks from the sphere mentioned in the Act in cooperation with NGOs.[23]

The definition of public benefit activity, as provided by the Public Benefit Act, is tripartite: "Public benefit activities are socially useful activities carried out by non-governmental organisations in the sphere of public tasks specified in the Act".[24]

The sphere of public tasks is defined in Article 4 sec. 1 of the Public Benefit Act. Among others it embraces tasks in the field of: social welfare benefits, including assistance to families and individuals in difficult life situations and creating equal opportunities for such families and individuals; support for the family and the foster care system; creation of conditions for satisfying the housing needs of the local communities; providing free legal aid and increasing the legal awareness of the society; charitable activity; maintenance and dissemination of national tradition, cultivation of Polishness and development of national, civic and cultural awareness; activity for the benefit of national and ethnic minorities and regional languages; activity for the benefit of integration of foreigners; activity for the benefit of equal rights of men and women; activity supporting economic development, including the development of entrepreneurship; activity supporting the development of local communities; culture, art, protection of cultural goods and national heritage; ecology and protection of animals as well as protection of natural heritage. In total, the Act now enlists, taking into account all the Act's amendments over the last 20 years, 40 different spheres of public tasks—an increase from the initial catalogue of 33.

Cooperation between the public and the civic, although possible in various forms, usually boils down to allocating public funds along with the assignment of certain

---

[22] Article 3 sec. 4 of Public Benefit Act.

[23] "Public administration bodies shall carry out activities in the sphere of public tasks referred to in Article 4 in cooperation with non-governmental organisations and entities mentioned in Article 3, paragraph 3, conducting, according to the territorial scope of activities of public administration bodies, public benefit activities within the scope corresponding to the tasks of these bodies" Article 5 sec. 1 of Public Benefit Act.

[24] Article 3 sec. 1 of Public Benefit Act.

public tasks by the authority to the NGOs. The mechanics of such a cooperation is based on the concept of public financing of public tasks combined with "outsourcing" of the implementation of these tasks to NGOs as service providers. This practice is referred to as "entrusting of public tasks or services" and the underlying agreement is a contract signed by the governmental unit and the NGO. The said contract is the basis of funds allocation to the implementing NGO. The contract is governed by the Civil Code,[25] yet the overlap of prescriptive mandatory provisions of the Public Benefit Act as well as executive ordinances enacted on the basis of the Act is quite significant and limits parties'contractual freedom. Additional layer of mandatory legal provisions are the public finance regulations. Also the very selection of organizations to be entrusted with a public task is subject to binding legal provisions: the law prescribes open call (tender or competition) as a mandatory procedure for selection of service providers. Grants allocated to the entities selected in the said procedure usually do not cover 100% of the estimated costs of a task (project). Hence requirement for an own contribution is a widespread practice. Organisation's own contributions may be financial or non-financial, including in-kind or personal resources (e.g., work of volunteers).

It is crucial to emphasise that the Public Benefit Act contains a normative demand to base cooperation on the principles of subsidiarity, sovereignty of the parties, partnership, efficiency, fair competition and openness. This is ostensibly fostered by the system of selection of offers, the civil law nature of the contract, or the principles of consultation or the institution of annual and multi-annual cooperation programmes.

Nonetheless, organisations entering into cooperation with public administration have to reckon with a very strict legal regime governing funds returns in cases of contract violations or other irregularities on the part of the organization implementing the public task. Ex-post monitoring on how the fund recipients (organisations) used (spent) the funds granted to them, and possible questioning the findings made in the course of this monitoring—all this is not covered by guarantees and rules on the statutory level, but is governed by the contract concluded between the authority and the organisation. It is until (and if) the funds return order is issued by the task entrusting authority that the organization would have a chance to challenge the underlaying findings in the course of administrative and then court proceedings. However, this is a difficult path for organisations with limited resources, as embarking on the court trial does not by itself entail the suspension of the effectiveness of the funds return order and hence does not preclude the authority from enforcing it. Consequently, the organization runs a risk of not surviving up to the point when it gets the charges of alleged contract violation or other irregularities dismissed by the court. This is where the problem arises, due to the fact that such organisations in Poland, unless they are engaged in economic activity, do not have insolvency capacity, i.e. there is no legal path for a court administrated liquidation in the course of insolvency proceedings. The lack of

---

[25] Act of April 23rd, 1964 – Civil Code, hereinafter: "Civil Code".

insolvency capacity essentially means that managers run the risk of personal liability towards the fiscus for "public debts", i.e. obligations arising from e.g. grants subject to return, tax debts or unpaid social security contributions. On the other hand, managers of organisations not conducting business activity, are structurally free of any risk of wrongful trading liability vis-à-vis organisations'creditors (e.g., contractual or tort creditors), as this liability regime does not apply to entities not carrying out economic (business) activities.

We wrap up this section by concluding that the regulatory philosophy underlying the legal framework for NGOs in Poland focuses on organisations as entities entitled to and carrying out cooperation with public administration in the sphere of public tasks of the latter, or at least carrying out not-for-profit activities in the sphere of the so-called "state interest".

2.5 NGOs and Social Economy Actors

The purpose of this section is to offer a mere sketch of the two concepts and their mutual relationship: non-governmental organization and social economy entity, without discussing in detail the subject of social economy entities and social economy in Polish law and practice. There is certainly no obvious equal sign between NGOs, the Third Sector, public benefit activities and social economy entities or social economy.

The Public Benefit Act does not refer in any way to the concept of social economy or social economy entities. However, Poland, like some other EU Member State, has on its agenda the development of the social economy. Nevertheless, for many years, legal regulations in this area had been fragmented and punctual. One of these few regulations is the Act on social cooperatives.[26] Social cooperatives have so far been considered as a representative example of social economy entities. This has changed in 2022, when a government draft of Act on Social Economy, after being prepared by the Polish Parliament for a significant period of time, has eventually been adopted on August 5th, 2022.

Nonetheless, in order to understand the context of issues fundamental to the social economy in Poland, it is necessary to first refer to the key document to date—KPRES,[27] i.e. "The National Programme for the Development of the Social Economy up until 2023". Its importance is due to the fact that both the ending perspective and the next perspective of the EU funds in Poland have been—to the extent that

[26] Act of April 27th, 2006 on social cooperatives.

[27] KPRES (Polish: *Krajowy Program Rozwoju Ekonomii Społecznej*) – National Programme for the Development of the Social Economy up until 2023. Social Solidarity Economy, https://www.ekonomiaspoleczna.gov.pl/download/files/EKONOMIA_SPOLECZNA/KPRES.pdf.

they relate to the development of the social economy—not coupled with the aforementioned Act on Social Economy.[28]

According to KPRES (which is a governmental strategy document), the social economy entities in Poland are considered to be entities whose common denominator is a number of principles related to their operations. The said principles are enlisted as follows: "the primacy of social goals over economic goals; the primacy of service provision to members, employees or the community over absolute profit categories; autonomous management and participatory decision-making; the carrying out of activities on a regular basis by means of economic instruments coupled with the bearing of economic risks in connection with these activities"[29] .

From the above it follows, that the distinction between non-governmental organisations and social economy entities is by no means dichotomous—we should rather speak of different categories defined on the basis of separate sets of criteria. The relationship may thus be overlapping at least for a subset of organisations—some of the NGOs may be qualified as social economy entities, provided that they carry out activities based on the principles outlined above, whereas some others may not. Admittedly, the document cited above (KPRES) overly simplistic assumes (which at the same time, for the purposes of illustrating the potential of the social economy sector, seems to include as social economy entities) all NGOs to be counted as a part of social economy sector,[30] maybe just in order to highlight, if not magnify, sector's potential.

The novelty of the Polish approach to social economy may be seen in singling out the concept of "solidarity economy" (*ekonomia solidarna*) as a subset of social economy. Below we find the definitions, as found in KPRES, of the social economy and its subcategory—the solidarity economy.

"Social economy – is a sphere of civic and social activity which, through economic and public benefit activities, serves: professional and social integration of individuals at risk of social marginalisation, job creation, provision of social services of public interest (for the general interest) and local development".

"Solidarity economy – is a part of social economy, the primary objective of which is professional activation and social integration, including professional and social reintegration of individuals at risk of social exclusion, and social and professional rehabilitation of persons with disabilities".[31]

In the cited excerpts from the KPRES, one can discern attempts to combine the concepts of NGOs and public benefit activities with the social economy and social economy entities. However, this is not self-evident in relation to the operating principles cited above. Not all non-governmental organisations avail themselves of economic instruments, not all have any paid staff whatsoever or rely on participatory

[28] The provisions implementing the new perspective and the provisions of this Act do not relate to each other.

[29] KPRES, p. 12.

[30] KPRES, p. 14.

[31] KPRES, p. 12.

decision-making (e.g., foundations usually have little or no participatory element in their governance system).

In addition, within the framework of the solidarity economy, which also *de facto* defines the main area where the state support for the development of the social economy is allocated, the key entities are no longer non-governmental organisations. Here, KPRES itself indicates very specific entities such as social enterprises, social cooperatives, cooperatives of the disabled, sheltered work entities (*zakład pracy chronionej*), and a whole group of statutorily regulated reintegration units. Characteristically, legal forms of legal persons (such as social cooperatives) are mixed at this level with organisational units that can also be established and run by non-governmental organisations (such as a social enterprise or the aforementioned reintegration units).

Finally, the understanding of a social enterprise should be cited. These are entities of the social economy which, by carrying out economic or paid-for public benefit activities, professionally activate hard-to-employ persons, do not privatise profit or balance sheet surplus and are managed in a participatory way, can be awarded the status of social enterprise.[32] The need to undergo verification in order to obtain the said status is clearly emphasised in this case. Organisations (NGOs) can therefore be recognised as social enterprises under these conditions, but more often a model is used where they are the operator of the social enterprise, which is not as onerous on the organisation as a whole.[33]

As we indicated above, the government draft Act on Social Economy[34] has, after having pended before the Polish Parliament for quite some time, been eventually adopted on August 5th, 2022.[35] Although, on the one hand, the need for it was raised, including the introduction of legal definitions of the above-mentioned triad of concepts (social economy, social economy entities, social enterprises), at the same time a number of remarks and objections was formulated against the bill, which, however, has not met with the understanding of the authorities, amendments, and final version of this Act.

It is worth quoting the definition of social economy that the Polish legislator has introduced. In accordance with the Act on Social Economy (art. 2 pt 1) it "should be understood as the activity of social economy entities for the benefit of the local community in the scope of social and professional reintegration, creating jobs for people at risk of social exclusion and providing social services, realised in the form of economic activity, public benefit activity and other paid activity".

As regards social economy entities, the Act has explicitly opted for a subjective definition through a closed catalogue of types of entities, without legalising requirements of a subjective nature. For instance, according to the Act, social economy entities are to be, without meeting additional requirements, non-governmental

[32] KPRES, p. 13.

[33] It does not require the entire organisation to be subject to the aforementioned requirements.

[34] https://www.sejm.gov.pl/Sejm9.nsf/PrzebiegProc.xsp?nr=2321.

[35] Act of August 5th, 2022 on Social Economy.

organisations within the meaning of the previously discussed definition from the Public Benefit Act. At the same time, it excludes the aforementioned entities that were also excluded from cooperation with public administration in the regulation on benefit activity. Still, social economy entities do include non-profit companies referred to in the Public Benefit Act.

The Act also introduces the concept of the status of a social enterprise, as a qualified form of social economy entity. The granting of such status is a result of proceedings and a decision of the competent governmental authority (voivode). This introduces a great deal of confusion, as the Act does not provide for any transitional provisions or reconciliation of the entry into force of its norms with the existing environment of social enterprises created in the framework of the implementation of EU funds for the development of social economy.

It has to be highlighted that, as of today, the Act on Social Economy, on the one hand, and the regulations implementing the new EU perspective, on the other hand, do not foresee how the new Act should be applied to the development of social economy financed by EU funds in the near future. The strategic and programming documents of the new perspective use their own definitions of key terms and do not provide for a new law (such as KPRES). In turn, the Act ignores not only the operational programmes of the new perspective, but above all the whole environment of social enterprises developed so far in the strict sense, as well as support organisations.

It is not clear which direction the Polish legislator will choose with respect to both public benefit and social economy as well as social enterprises. Nevertheless, the palpable relationship of competition and, at the same time, strong interpenetration in the introduced regulations as well as in the practice of operation of the concepts of public benefit activity, social economy, NGOs and social economy entities will have a strong impact on the understanding and formation of the NGO sector, as well as the concept of a non-governmental organisation in Poland.

3 Economic and Societal Impact of Third Sector Organisations

By the end of 2021 there were 138 thousand non-governmental organizations registered in Poland. This figure breaks down into 107 thousand (77.5%) associations and 31 thousand (22.5%) foundations.[36] These figures embrace all legally established organisations, regardless whether they are operational or merely zombies, i.e. idled organisations with no activities at all—solely existing on paper.

[36] Klon/Jawor, Kondycja organizacji pozarządowych 2021, at p. 15, https://kondycja.ngo.pl/.

A 2020 count involving solely active organisations reveals 66.8 thousand (80.7%) registered associations and 16 thousand (19.3%) foundations.[37] This data demonstrates that roughly 60% of legally existing entities are operational and conduct any activities.

9.3 thousand organisations enjoyed the legal status of public benefit organization (PBO)—a status making the "PBO badge"-holder eligible to compete for the 1% PIT[38] and access other benefits restricted to the officially accredited public benefit organizations.

Even though the associations clearly prevail over foundations in terms of sheer numbers, many of the biggest and richest entities are formed as foundations. For example, among the largest beneficiaries of the 1% PIT, we solely find foundations—no single association makes it to the top 15. What is even more telling, the slice these 15 foundations take in the 1% PIT pizza accounts for as much as 46.3%—a remarkable share, given the fact that a total number of organisations benefiting from the 1% PIT money pot amounted to 8694 in 2021 (PIT collected from 2020 and allocated in 2021).[39] This is explained by the fact, that many of these foundations are not big social ventures, they are rather mere managers of individual subaccounts collecting taxpayers 1% that is later transmitted directly to the needy ones. One more reason for opting out for the foundation rather than association is the fact that foundations have stronger anti-takeover design. Whenever the need is strong for maintaining control over resources (wealthy organisations) or ideas (think-tanks), founders are often inclined to choose a foundation as the legal vehicle.

Non-profit organizations are characterized by carrying out various and multi-disciplinary activities. In 2020, as part of their statutory activities, most organizations dealt with sports, tourism, leisure and pastime (26.9%), and then—rescue/lifesaving services (15.3%). A large group consisted of organizations indicating culture and art as their main field of activity (12.4%), education and research (10.5%) or welfare—social and humanitarian aid (8.3%). Entities qualified as public benefit organization (PBO) operate mainly in the field of social and humanitarian aid (24.7% of the PBO-organisations compared to 8.3% in the entire cohort) and health protection (12.9% among the PBO-entities versus 3.9% in the entire cohort).[40]

As is evidenced by the data reproduced in Fig. 8.1, Third Sector Organisations not only provide socially beneficial services such as charity to vulnerable groups (chronically ill, homeless, orphans, minorities) but also contribute to strengthening

---

[37] Statistics Poland (GUS), Działalność stowarzyszeń i podobnych organizacji społecznych, fundacji, społecznych podmiotów wyznaniowych oraz samorządu gospodarczego i zawodowego w 2020 r. – wyniki wstępne, https://stat.gov.pl/obszary-tematyczne/gospodarka-spoleczna-wolontariat/gospodarka-spoleczna-trzeci-sektor/dzialalnosc-stowarzyszen-i-podobnych-organizacji-spolecznych-fundacji-spolecznych-podmiotow-wyznaniowych-oraz-samorzadu-gospodarczego-i-zawodowego-w-2020-r-wyniki-wstepne,3,9.html, hereinafter "Statistics Poland".

[38] See Sect. 5.3. of this chapter."

[39] Own calculations based on official data from the Ministry of Finance https://www.gov.pl/web/finanse/1-procent-podatku-dla-opp.

[40] Statistics Poland (GUS), *supra*.

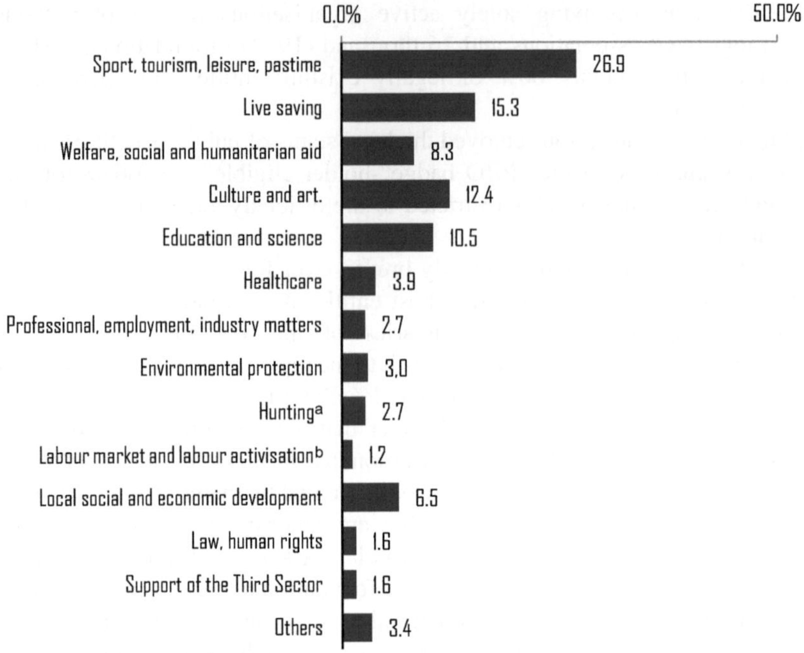

Fig. 8.1 Activity of Polish TSOs broken down into areas. *Source of Data*: Statistics Poland (*Główny Urząd Statystyczny*—Central Statistical Office)

of societal bonds by activating local communities around undertakings of common interest.

In the political sphere, advocacy organisations, watchdogs and think tanks are becoming increasingly visible. Unlike Germany, Poland does not have a tradition of political foundations, i.e. resourceful and influential entities affiliated with political parties. The existing ones cannot compare with their German equivalents. Even though Polish advocacy, watchdog and think-tank organisations are relatively underfinanced, they are very efficient when it comes to their outreach by means of electronic platforms.

On the other side, the comparatively bigger charitable organisations not always engage in collective undertakings such as infrastructure building or provision of services. As it was mentioned above, many of them serve as vehicles transmitting financial resources directly to their beneficiaries. This is due to the nature of the aforementioned 1% PIT financing. The business model of these charities is to set up subaccounts to which family and friends of the needy ones allocate 1% of their PIT and they also turn into a legion of campaigners for their cause.

The vast majority (81.4%) of organizations provided solely unpaid services to the public. The remaining 18.6% of entities declared to carry out paid activities or business activity whereby goods and/or services are offered to their recipients against compensation.[41]

As of the 2020 data, nearly two-thirds (61.6%) of the non-profits operated solely on the basis of voluntary (unpaid) work of their members or other persons involved. Organisations which at least partially hired paid staff account for over one-third (38.3%). They were more inclined to rely on service contracts under the Civil Code (24.1%) rather than offering employment contracts under the Labour Code[42] (14.2%).[43]

The problem of work stability (service contracts provide lesser degree of protection) and salaries (often low) long have been among the factors negatively affecting the non-profit sector.

More than half of the revenues generated by non-profit organizations came from non-market sources (6.0%). In this subcategory, public funds accounted for the largest share (45.2%), including subsidies from local government administration (19.6%). The fraction of revenues from market sources was estimated 28.5%, which in turn breaks down into paid statutory activity (14.8%) and business activity (11.6%). Membership fees and other financial resources accounted for mere 8.6% all revenues generated by the non-profits.[44]

Organisations'average revenues fell for the first time in almost a decade—in 2020 they amounted to 26 thousand złoty (approx. 6 thousand Euro by the average 2020 PLN/EUR exchange rate). At the same time there was an increase of the fraction of organisations with lowest revenues (up to 1 thousand złoty per year which in 2020 equalled approx. 230 EUR).

4 Legal Design of Foundations and Associations Under the Polish Law: Structure, Governance, Assets

4.1 Introductory Remarks

As it has already been outlined in Sect. 2 of this chapter, on the grounds of Polish law there is considerable diversity in the legal design of law provisions on TSOs. It is possible to distinguish among them both those in respect of which the legislator regulates the structure and governance in a rather meticulous manner (registered associations) and those in respect of which the legal requirements in these aspects are limited to the minimum (foundations and ordinary associations), and their founders are left with a far-reaching freedom to shape the governance structure of the organisation.

---

[41] Statistics Poland (GUS), *supra*.

[42] Act of June 26th, 1974 – Labour Code.

[43] Statistics Poland (GUS), *supra*.

[44] Statistics Poland (GUS), *supra*.

As already indicated in Sect. 2 of this chapter, in Poland there is a wide range of legal forms that could be classified as the third sector organisations. Undoubtedly, however, the key among these forms are associations and foundations. Due to the volume limitations of this publication, not all types of TSOs will be the subject of analysis in this section, but only the two legal forms mentioned above. In fact, however, it can be assumed that not two but three different legal forms will be analysed here. This is due to the fact that while foundations are essentially a homogeneous legal form, the same cannot be said of associations. Indeed, Polish law distinguishes two forms of associations: the "registered associations" (*stowarzyszenie rejestrowe*)[45] and "ordinary associations" (*stowarzyszenie zwykłe*).[46] There is a number of differences between them (some of which will be described below[47]), nevertheless the key one boils down to the liability and risk exposure. Members of an ordinary association may be held liable for its obligations without limitation, with their own assets, jointly and severally with the other members and with the association (whereby this liability arises as soon as the execution from the assets of the ordinary association proves ineffective). Contrary to this, no similar liability rule exists for members of registered associations, whose private assets are hence shielded from liability vis-à-vis organisation's creditors. Consequently, registered association is not such a risky venture for its members as the ordinary association is. Beyond the liability issue, the legal design of these two forms of association is so different that it makes them separate, distinct legal forms, albeit bearing the same name ("association"). The adoption of such a method by the Polish legislator does not seem to be an apt solution, although—on the other hand—it should be admitted that the indicated differentiation of associations does not generate significant problems in practice (mainly due to the ease of qualifying a given association under the one or the other category).

4.2 Constitutional Law Basis and Regulatory Philosophy

The liberty to engage in collective undertakings is enshrined in Poland's 1997 Constitution. According to Article 12 "*The Republic of Poland shall ensure freedom for the creation and functioning of trade unions, socio-occupational organizations of farmers, societies, citizens'movements, other voluntary associations and*

[45] The name stems from the fact that these associations are registered in the National Court Register (PL: *Krajowy Rejestr Sądowy*) – i.e. the same register in which all companies and foundations, among others, are registered.

[46] This name is used by the legislator itself—see articles 40–43 of the Law on Associations. Ordinary associations, unlike registered associations, are not registered in the National Court Register. However, this is only one of many differences, which are described in detail later in this chapter.

[47] See also the broader analysis by Suski (2018), sec. 5, chapter III, part I (accessed digitally via LEX legal information system on July 4th, 2023).

foundations". Article 58 guarantees everyone the freedom of association and provides for certain limitations as well as formalities that must be complied with in order to enjoy the said liberty in institutionalized forms. In accordance with Article 58 Sec. 2 "*Associations whose purposes or activities are contrary to the Constitution or statutes shall be prohibited. The courts shall adjudicate whether to permit an association to register or to prohibit an association from such activities*". According to Article 58 Sec. 3 "*Statutes shall specify types of associations requiring court registration, a procedure for such registration and the forms of supervision of such associations*". From these constitutional provisions it follows that associations are understood as the primary legal form of voluntary civic engagement and that the libertarian (*pro libertate*) spirit should dominate the legislative action. The laws (statutes) should be meant as necessary framework needed to facilitate the liberty that—although guaranteed to everyone individually—is by its very nature designed to be exercised collectively. In terms of legislative techniques this basic assumption let us expect the prevalence of default provisions (*ius dispositivum*) over the mandatory ones (*ius cogens*).[48] Contrary to this legitimate expectation, much of the legislation on associations is mandatory law. Where much more freedom is left up to the founders is the Act on Foundations. This Act provides little details and is confined to providing some core elements of what makes foundation a distinct organizational form and a legal person. Anything beyond these core mandatory elements is up to the founders to be regulated in the foundation charter, although the registration courts sometimes tend to demonstrate judicial precaution in identifying what is and what is not "in the spirit" of a foundation as a legal form and reject the draft charters that do not meet their understanding of foundations.

4.3 Formation Requirements

Formation requirements that apply to TSOs may be split into two categories: asset requirements and organisational requirements. Asset requirements will be described in Sect. 5.1 *infra*, while in this section we focus on the organisational requirements. What, however, could be said here is that while in the case of associations the founders are free to decide on what organisation's initial and further assets should be, in the case of foundations the law imposes certain requirements. The situation is, however, quite the opposite if we turn to the organisational requirements to be met for a given entity to be established. In the case of foundations there are no limitations as to the identity of the founders—the provisions explicitly state that foundations may be established by natural persons irrespective of their citizenship and place of

[48] Maciej Kisilowski sees this as a manifestation of priority setting by the legislator: democratisation of the associations goes over the freedom of creating structures that would best suit the needs of the founders – c.f. Kisilowski (2009), at p. 196.

residence or legal entities having their seat in Poland or abroad[49] (however the foundation itself must have its seat in the territory of Poland). Likewise, no restrictions are found when it comes to the number of founders—a foundation may therefore be established by one or more founders.

In case of associations, the situation is different. Three types of restrictions may be distinguished here:

- restrictions as to the identity of the founders;
- restrictions as to the nationality of the founders;
- restrictions concerning the (minimum) number of founders.

The restrictions as to the identity of the founders boil down to the fact that only natural persons may be founders of an association. It is therefore not permissible for an association to be formed, for example, by a company, by a foundation or by another association. However, the possibility for legal persons to participate in associations is not completely excluded, although the legal regulations in this respect are extremely enigmatic and vague. Indeed, the legislator indicates—in Article 10(3) of the Law on Associations—that "*A legal person may only be a supporting member of an association.*" Thus, the statutory provisions differentiate the nature of membership in associations—as one can simply be a "member" or a "supporting member", with only the latter possibility being offered to legal persons. The problem is that the legislator fails to define the term "supporting member", neither it explains the differences (if any) between "ordinary" and "supporting" membership. Consequently, this issue is left up to the charter (articles of association) and bylaws. If a given organization wants to accept legal persons as their members, the only way of doing so is by providing for the category of "supporting members" in the association's constitution, where their rights and obligations in relation to "ordinary" members are defined. From a practical point of view, this differentiation generally consists in limiting (or excluding) certain membership rights, e.g. the right to vote at general meetings of the association's members. In this regard, the literature points out that legal persons cannot be founders of an association, but can only join it once it has been established.[50]

The second category of restrictions, i.e. the restriction on the nationality of the members of the association, is particularly relevant at the stage of formation of associations. This is due to the fact that they may be established only by:

- natural persons who are Polish citizens;
- persons who do not have Polish citizenship, but have their place of residence in Poland.

In turn, persons who have neither Polish citizenship nor residence in Poland may only join associations whose charters provide for such a possibility. Thus, such persons may become members of an association not at the stage of its formation, but

[49] Art. 2 sec. 1 of the Act on Foundations.

[50] Hadrowicz (2020), art. 10, sec. 18.

only after its establishment. If they do not have a place of residence in Poland, then they may only join associations whose charters provide for such a possibility. Leaving aside the question of the compliance of such differentiation with the law of the European Union, it should be pointed out that this differentiation is criticised in the literature as weakening the competitiveness of the Polish law.[51]

The third category of limitations, i.e. limitations as to the number of founders, varies for registered associations and ordinary associations. A registered association has to be established by at least seven founders,[52] whereas in case of an ordinary association there have to be at least three founders.[53]

4.4 *Internal Structure and Governance*

The above-described differences concerning the manner of shaping the organisational requirements to be met when establishing foundations and associations are further reflected in the regulations relating to their organisational structure. While in the case of foundations these regulations are limited to an absolute minimum (thus giving the founders a significant scope of discretion in the design of this structure), with respect to associations the legislator imposes a rather precise set of rules.

The document laying down the structure of a given organisation is, for both foundations and associations, the charter. However, this information should be supplemented with two reservations:

- in the case of foundations, in addition to the charter (or, in fact, before the charter is drawn up), the founders sign a deed of establishment of the foundation[54] in which the objectives of the foundation are set out; the objectives set out later in the charter (or at least in its first wording) must be consistent with those indicated in the deed of establishment of the foundation;
- in the case of ordinary associations, instead of the charter, the association's rules of operation are drawn up (which in practice is a simplified version of the charter).

In the case of a foundation, the only real requirement for its organisational structure comes down to the obligation to establish a management board. This board may consist of one or more persons.[55] There is no obligation to establish any other bodies.

[51] Radwan (2005), pp. 55–62.

[52] Art. 9 of the Law on Associations.

[53] Art. 40 sec. 2 of the Law on Associations.

[54] Which has to be drawn up as a notarial deed.

[55] Although there are some opinions in the literature (see Kępa and Podgórska-Rykała (2020), art. 10, sec. 7) that the management board should be collegial (and therefore there could not exist a one-person management board), this view is not endorsed by the authors of this chapter, and the functioning of one-person management boards of foundations is a very common practice in Poland, which is accepted by registry courts.

At the same time, the legislation does not even specify the rules for the appointment of the management board. As a result, in practice there exists a variety of approaches on how to handle this issue in the charter. A frequently applied solution is the appointment of an additional body (referred to e.g. as a council, foundation council, supervisory board, founders' council or in a similar manner) that performs supervisory role and is authorised to appoint and dismiss members of the management board. However, this is only an exemplary solution, not mandated by law, but applied in the framework of contractual freedom. Nonetheless, other solutions are also possible, such as the appointment of new board members by the existing management board, granting the right to appoint the board to the founder etc.

In the case of registered associations, on the other hand, the organisational structure is much more precisely regulated and the scope of contractual freedom in this area is limited. Indeed, such associations must have an established board of directors and an "internal control body" (which may be variously named under the charter—e.g. as "supervisory board", "association council" or otherwise). Furthermore, according to the law, registered associations must have—as its supreme organ—a general assembly of members, composed of all members of the association[56] and to which the presumption of competence applies (i.e., it has the power to decide on matters not allocated otherwise by the charter). Even though the general rule is that the general assembly brings together all members of the association, for bigger associations with crowds of members, the charter may provide that, instead of a general assembly of members, a meeting of delegates will be held. For this modification to be triggered a pre-defined number of members must be exceeded. The charter also hast to specify the manner by which the delegates should be elected or appointed. This solution is practical to simplify the governance of large associations with massive membership.

In ordinary associations, on the other hand, the organisational structure can be shaped much more flexibly. Indeed, the requirements merely amount to the following:

- "an ordinary association that intends to have a management board shall specify in its rules of operation the procedure for its election and completion of its composition, its competences, the conditions for the validity of its resolutions and the manner in which the ordinary association is represented, in particular the contracting of property obligations" (Article 40 sec. 3 of the Law on Associations);
- "an ordinary association that intends to have an internal control body shall determine in the rules of operation the procedure for its election, supplementation of its composition and its competences" (Article 40 sec. 4 of the Law on Associations).

Since the cited provisions refer only to an ordinary association "which intends to have" a management board or an internal control body, it should be inferred from

[56] Art. 11 sec. 1 of the Law on Associations.

this wording that the establishment of a management board or an internal control body is not mandatory for an ordinary association. Who then represents an ordinary association in which no management board has been established? This person is the representative, who must be defined in the association's rules of operation.[57]

5 Assets, Finance and Funding

5.1 Asset Requirements

As it has been mentioned in Sect. 4 of this chapter, the initial requirements that must be met for the establishment of a foundation or an association under Polish law can be split into two categories, i.e. asset requirements and organisational requirements.

Asset requirements are formulated by the legislator only with regard to foundations, albeit in a not entirely clear manner. Indeed, according to Article 5 sec. 5 *in fine* of the Act on Foundations: "If the foundation is to carry out business activities, the value of the foundation's assets earmarked for business activities may not be less than one thousand zlotys." This provision, however, only applies to foundations that carry out business activities (while not all foundations do so) and refers only to the funds allocated to business activities, not to the entire foundation's assets. At the same time, there is no provision specifying a minimum value of the foundation's assets. This distinction is important insofar as the economic activity of the foundation should not constitute its "core" activity, but should only be complementary to its statutory activity. Summarising the whole, one can conclude at this point that the purpose of a foundation's activity is non-profit activity; whereas the business activity, as undertaken for profit, is only supposed to play an auxiliary role to the non-profit activity, e.g. allowing the foundation to raise funds which will then be allocated to the non-profit activity. However, what is crucial, a foundation is not obliged to carry out business activity and a large number of foundations in Poland do not carry out such activity.

All these circumstances lead to the following conclusions:

- Firstly, Polish law does not specify in a general way (for all foundations) the minimum amount of contributions that the founders have to make to their foundation in order for it to be established. Article 3 sec. 2 of the Act on Foundations only indicates that in the deed of establishment of the foundation "the founder should indicate the purpose of the foundation and the assets intended for its realisation"—thus, some contribution must be made, but its minimum amount is not specified. Theoretically, therefore, it is possible to establish a foundation with an initial fund of, for example, 1 PLN (= ca. 0.21 EUR). In practice, due to the risk of the deed of establishment of the foundation providing

[57] Art. 40 sec. 2 of the Law on Associations.

for such a low initial fund being deemed to be an act aimed at circumventing the law (by circumventing the regulation providing for the obligation to allocate assets to the accomplishment of the foundation's objective), foundations with such a low initial fund are not likely to be established, and the assets contributed by the founders upon the establishment of the foundation are usually worth at least several hundred PLN, which is still way below a serious threshold, yet considered acceptable

– Secondly, if the foundation intends to carry out business activities, the value of the assets allocated for this purpose should be at least 1.000 PLN (=ca. 215,08 EUR).[58] For this reason, in the case of such foundations, in the deed of establishment of the foundation the founder should not only indicate the amount of assets allocated for the establishment of the foundation, but also earmark within these assets a part allocated for business activity (which is required, among others, so that the registration court, in the course of the foundation establishment procedure, could verify whether the asset requirement in this respect is met). Again, the said amount seems to be arbitrary as it hardly corresponds to any credible commitment to embarking upon any meaningful business activity.

The above assertions must be supplemented by one important caveat. In view of the fact that, in case of foundations, business activities should be complementary to the statutory activities (and thus consisting in the pursuit of objectives for which the foundation was established),[59] there is a known practice whereby the registry courts require that, if a foundation is to carry out business activities, the part of its assets allocated to statutory activities must, at the stage of its establishment, be larger than the part allocated to business activities. It is a mere court practice and thus case-law rather than a statutory requirement, yet the founders would be ill-advised if not told to pay attention to the established jurisprudence.

With respect to associations, as it has already been indicated above, the Polish legislator does not formulate any asset requirements. There is not even a requirement for the founders of an association to make any contributions – the law only requires that the charters specify "the manner of obtaining financial means and establishing membership fees".[60] Therefore, it is formally permissible even to establish an association which—at the time of its establishment—will not have any assets whatsoever.

[58] In accordance with the official PLN-EUR exchange rate published by the National Bank of Poland on 14 April 2023.

[59] See, for a broader analysis in this respect (in Polish), Rzetecka-Gil (2018), art. 5, sec. 16–19.

[60] Art. 10 sec. 1 (7) of the Law on Associations.

5.2 Financing Existing Organisations

There are no major restrictions as to the sources of raising funds by foundations and associations in the course of their operation. Although both the regulations relating to foundations and those relating to associations require the inclusion in the charter of a given entity of a provisions specifying "assets" (Art. 5 sec. 1 of the Act on Foundations) or "the manner of obtaining funds and establishing membership fees" (Art. 10 sec. 1 (7) of the Law on Associations), in practice these provisions do not play a major role, as they are usually reflected in the charters only in short, very general sentence simply indicating that the assets of a given TSO come from donations and profit-making activities.

Foundations and associations in Poland may raise income in particular by carrying out business activities. These activities do not have to be related to the subject of the statutory activity (so, for instance, a foundation whose statutory objective is to support a specific branch of medicine may generate income by, for example, running a restaurant or an online shop). However, there are certain limitations in this respect, namely:

- A foundation may carry out business activities "to the extent that they serve the foundation's objectives".[61] This restriction is so vague that in practice it does not play any significant role (the authors of this chapter are not aware of any cases in which a foundation would face any negative consequences if, for instance, the size of its business activity exceeded the size limited by the quoted provision).
- In the case of associations, there is a norm according to which "The income from the economic activity of the association serves the realization of the statutory objectives and may not be intended for distribution among its members."[62] This restriction has a more important practical dimension than the one existing in foundations, since a possible action (e.g. a resolution of the general assembly of the association's members) providing for the distribution of profits from the association's business activities to the association's members would be unlawful and the payment made on the basis of it would be subject to return to the association's assets by virtue of law.

5.3 "1,5%" Financing

A characteristic element of Polish NGO law is the possibility for NGOs to obtain funding through the allocation of 1,5% of personal income tax by individuals. In

[61] Art. 5 sec. 5 of the Act on Foundations.

[62] Second sentence of art. 34 of the Law on Associations.

practice, when filling in the annual tax return,[63] each individual may (but is not obliged to) indicate an NGO to which the amount corresponding to 1,5% of the tax paid by the individual should be transferred. In this field it is possible (but not mandatory) to indicate the specific purpose (e.g., a common practice is that in the case of organisations carrying out charitable activities for chronically ill or disabled persons, the field with the specific purpose is a place where the name of a particular person, to whom the organisation should allocate the funds coming from a given tax deduction, is indicated). In practice, therefore, the mechanism described above serves not so much as a funding mechanism for TSOs, but mostly as a platform for the provision of charitable assistance targeted at specific individuals as ultimate beneficiaries and fund recipients.

The above observations should, however, be supplemented by some additional information:

- Firstly, not all NGOs are entitled to raise funding in the above-described manner, but only those of them that earned a PBO status[64] (such status may be held by, among others, foundations and associations).
- Secondly, due to the significant increase of the PIT-exempted annual income implemented in 2022, which resulted in a reduction in tax deductions transferrable to NGOs, in June 2022 the Polish parliament, in order to remedy this potential drop, enacted an amendment, whereby from 2023 on (i.e. starting with the tax returns for 2022) every taxpayer has a right to transfer to the NGO of her choice 1.5% instead of the previously applicable rate of 1% of personal income tax.[65]

As for statistical data related to the described funding mechanism, on the example of 2021 data (i.e. concerning the 2020 tax returns) they are as follows[66]:

- Approximately 15.3 million taxpayers (out of the total number between 25 and 26 million[67]) decided to allocate 1% (which was the then-applicable rate) of their tax to the eligible NGOs.

[63] For some individuals (i.e., as a general rule, those who have only one source of income and that is an employment contract), such a return is automatically produced by the Ministry of Finance, but requires electronic approval by the individual concerned.

[64] As regards public benefit organisation statuts—see Sect. 2.4. of this chapter.

[65] Act of 9 June 2022 on amending the Act on personal income tax and certain other acts (Journal of Laws of 2022, pos. 1265).

[66] All the statistical data below (with the exception of data on the total number of taxpayers in Poland) is presented on the basis of the official data published by the Ministry of Finance and available (in Polish) at: https://www.gov.pl/web/finanse/1-procent-podatku-dla-opp. The calculations of the indicated amounts from PLN to EUR was made on the basis of PLN-EUR official exchange rate, published by the National Bank of Poland on 14 April 2023.

[67] According to the official data published by the Ministry of Finance and available (in Polish) at: https://www.podatki.gov.pl/pit/abc-pit/statystyki/. More precise information on the total number of taxpayers is not available due to the fact that the Ministry of Finance publishes the data on the number of taxpayers with a breakdown by mode of taxation. The problem is, however, that many individuals derive income from a number of different sources and thus apply several taxation

- The total amount raised by NGOs through the described mechanism was PLN 972.7 million (= ca. EUR 209.2 million), of which the organisation that received the most funds received PLN 194.1 million (= ca. EUR 41.75 million).
- The average amount donated by one taxpayer was PLN 63 (= ca. EUR 13.55).

6 Conclusions

The Polish experience with creating efficient legal framework for TSOs is marked by some successes but is still an unfinished business. Nowadays it seems to be the result of mixed visions on how civil society should be organized and serve private and public interests. Conceptions based on the freedom of association, civil society and effectiveness meet regulatory philosophies aiming at subordinating the TSOs to public goals and interests, as extension of public administration in its general interest (social) services sphere of activity.

It must be reminded that Third Sector in Poland, as vibrant as it is today, is still relatively young—despite its reach and long traditions, dramatically broken by the World War II and ensuing period of Soviet-installed communism. The five decades between 1939 and 1989 proved devastating for the Polish civil society. The last 34 years, counting since the 1989 beginning of Poland's transformation were full of social, economic and technological changes. Today, more than three decades down the road, Third Sector in Poland has grown significantly and benefited from innovative arrangements, such as e.g. the 1% (currently 1,5%) PIT funding. Yet there is still scope for improvement, specifically when it comes to further strengthening the position of TSOs vis-à-vis public administration. This may be done by some technical, yet practically important, punctual reforms, such as easing the onerousness of public monitoring in form of inspections and by addressing the problems arising around financial cooperation between the TSOs and the government, specifically in conflict situations. Also tax regulations should be updated to make them safer and more foreseeable for TSOs. Mutual benefit organizations have to be recognized by law, which is related to the need of social economy and "social enterprise" regulations as well.

Any reform endeavours should be accompanied by a public debate and inclusive, participatory process, involving stakeholders, predominantly representatives of the TSOs community. It is worth mentioning here the TSOs initiatives like #prosteNGO[68] or good law for foundations,[69] which are aiming at animating public debate and working-out law changes postulates.

---

methods at the same time (as a result of which simply adding up the figures provided by the Ministry would lead to an overestimation of the number of taxpayers relative to the actual number).

[68] https://proste.ngo.

[69] https://www.forumdarczyncow.pl.

For the meantime, the Act on Social Economy has been passed. Regretfully, the feedback received from the TSO community along the legislative process has largely been ignored and did not translate into the final wording of the Act.[70]

References

Hadrowicz E (2020) Prawo o stowarzyszeniach. Komentarz, Legalis
Kępa M, Podgórska-Rykała J (2020) Ustawa o fundacjach. Komentarz, Legalis
Kisilowski M (2009) Prawo sektora pozarządowego. Analiza funkcjonalna
Radwan A (2005) Wolność zrzeszania się cudzoziemców według prawa polskiego, wspólnotowego oraz postulatów polityki prawa. Państwo i Prawo 5:55–62
Rzetecka-Gil A (2018) Ustawa o fundacjach. Komentarz, LEX
Suski P (2018) Stowarzyszenia i fundacje. Wolters Kluwer Polska, 2018

[70] https://publicystyka.ngo.pl/uchwalono-ustawe-o-ekonomii-spolecznej.

Chapter 9
The Legal Regime of the Social Economy Sector in Portugal

Deolinda Meira

Contents

Abstract In Portugal, the organisational reality of the third sector is called the "Social Economy." This term refers to a set of entities that are legally determined both in the Constitution of the Portuguese Republic and in the Framework Law on Social Economy. These entities have a specific social objective, expressed in an

Deolinda Meira is Coordinator Professor of Commercial and Cooperative Law at the Polytechnic of Porto/ISCAP/CEOS.PP.

D. Meira (✉)
CEOS.PP, ISCAP, Polytechnic of Porto, Porto, Portugal
e-mail: meira@iscap.ipp.pt

A. Fici (ed.), *The Law of Third Sector Organizations in Europe*,
https://doi.org/10.1007/978-3-031-41744-3_9

economic and social activity pursuing a general interest. Their organisation and operation are based on a set of guiding principles. The Social Economic sector comprises a market sector and a non-market sector. The first shall include the entities providing goods and services on the market, in competition with the other entities of the for-profit private sector. The non-market sector shall include social economy entities fulfilling an exclusively social function based on the principle of solidarity. In this sector, the beneficiaries receive free of charge benefits or compensation not proportional to the costs incurred. The pursuit of a general interest objective, directly or indirectly, justifies the positive discrimination that these entities enjoy, with a more favourable tax regime and public financial support. They are subject to specific rules of supervision and public procurement.

1 Introduction

In Portugal, the organisational reality of the third sector is called the "Social Economy." This term refers to a set of organisations that, in the case of Portugal, are legally determined both in the Constitution of the Portuguese Republic (CRP) and in the Framework Law on Social Economy (LBES) as approved by Law 30/2013 of 8 March.

According to the data from the latest Satellite Account for the Social Economy (CSES), this sector in Portugal consists of 71,886 entities from various groups, namely: cooperatives (3.3%), mutual associations (0.1%), charities (Misericórdias) (0.5%), foundations (0.9%), community and self-managed sub-sectors (2.3%) and associations with altruistic purposes (92.9%). Their main activities focus on culture, communication, and recreation (46.9%), followed by religious activities (11.9%), and social services (9.7%). The Social Economy represents 6.1% of Salaried Employment in the National Economy, and its contribution to Gross Value Added (GVA) is 3.0%.[1]

2 Constitutional Framework of the Social Economy

In Portugal, the legal substrate of the Social Economy is to be found in the Constitution, as this sector is subject to an autonomous legal treatment by the Constitution of the Portuguese Republic (CRP), even though the constitutional text does not use this exact term, referring to it as the "cooperative and social sector."

[1] The National Statistics Institute (INE) and the António Sérgio Cooperative for the Social Economy (CASES) have published in 2019 the results of the third edition of the Social Economy Satellite Account (CASES) for the year 2016. The data is available at https://www.cases.pt/contasatelitedaes/.

The CRP protects this sector through a set of principles, such as the principle of co-existence of three sectors (public, private and cooperative and social), the principle of freedom of cooperative initiative, the principle of protection of the cooperative and social sector, the principle of the obligation of the State to stimulate and support the creation of cooperatives, the principle of compliance with the cooperative principles of the International Cooperative Alliance (ICA).

Among these, the principle of co-existence of three sectors and the principle of protection of the cooperative and social sector are of major relevance to the Social Economy sector.

The principle of co-existence of three sectors enshrined in Article 82 guarantees the co-existence of three economic sectors—the public sector, the private sector, and the cooperative and social sector—at the same level and with the same constitutional dignity, as structures required for an economic model enshrined in the Constitution, which can be characterised as a social market economy. Under the terms of Article 82(4) of the CRP, the cooperative and social sector is divided into four sub-sectors corresponding to two approaches: the cooperative (which includes the cooperative sub-sector) and the social (which contains the self-managed, community and solidarity-based sub-sectors).

The principle of protection of the cooperative and social sector is the basis for the positive discrimination of this sector and the provision of material measures to enable its development. Following this principle, Article 85(1) states that "the State shall stimulate and support the creation and activity of cooperatives", and Article 85(2) guarantees that "the law shall define the tax and financial benefits of cooperatives, as well as more favourable conditions for obtaining credit and technical assistance". The "stimulus" involves mainly legislative measures to increase interest in the cooperative activity, while the "support" is mostly based on administrative measures aimed at facilitating the performance of that activity.[2]

3 Definition, Legal Forms and Guiding Principles of Social Economy

In Portugal, the Framework Law of the Social Economy limits the concept of Social Economy, using a combined technique where the definition of Social Economy in Article 2 is supplemented by an open list of Social Economy entities (art. 4) and the statement of its guiding principles (art. 5).

Thus, under the terms of art. 2 of the LBES, "social economy is understood to be the set of economic and social activities, freely undertaken by the entities referred to in art. 4 [. . .]," activities that "aim to pursue the general interest of society, either directly or by pursuing the interests of its members, users and beneficiaries, when socially relevant."

[2] Cf. Namorado (2017), *passim*.

This definition highlights two criteria delimiting the concept of Social Economy: the activity performed and the purpose pursued. The legislator associates the notion of Social Economy to a specific social object, translated into the exercise of an economic and social activity pursuing a general interest objective.

According to Rui Namorado, the term economic activity means an activity of "production of goods and services, under the aegis of a rationale that implies the maximisation of results, cost containment and replicability of productive potentialities."[3] In other words, social economy entities are guided by efficiency in allocating resources needed to produce goods or provide services. Having an economic activity is a requirement for an entity to be part of the Social Economic sector. However, this activity must be both economic and social in nature. It is believed that by combining the words "economic" and "social" with a hyphen, the legislator wanted to point out that the activity developed by Social Economy entities is not done for profit, but rather to satisfy the needs of the members, through their participation in the said activity (mutuality) and/or to satisfy the community needs.[4]

As regards the criterion of the purpose pursued, namely the general interest, this is considered to be related not only to the fact that these entities pursue social purposes, emerging as partners of the Social State, cooperating with it on ensuring a minimum vital level of economic, social and cultural rights of the citizens, but also to their peculiar mode of organisation and operation, which is distinct from the public sector and the for-profit private sector and is reflected in their guiding principles, in particular that of "conciliation between the interest of the members, users or beneficiaries and the general interest,"[5] as further detailed. With regards to the pursuit of this general interest, the legislator admits that it may be achieved directly or indirectly through the interests of members, users and beneficiaries.

The definition of Social Economy is supplemented by an open list of the entities listed in Article 4, according to which: "(. . .) the following entities, provided they are established on the national territory, are part of the Social Economy (a) cooperatives; (b) mutual associations; (c) mercies (Misericórdias); (d) foundations; (e) private social solidarity institutions not covered in the previous subparagraphs; (f) associations with altruistic purposes operating in the cultural, recreational, sports and local development fields; g) entities covered by the community and self-management sub-sectors, integrated under the terms of the CRP in the cooperative and social sector[6]; h) other entities endowed with legal personality that respect the guiding principles of the Social Economy foreseen under Article 5 of the Framework Law on Social Economy and included in the Social Economy database.

[3] Cf. Namorado (2007), pp. 10–11.

[4] Cf. Meira (2013), p. 28 ff.

[5] Cf. Meira (2013), p. 30.

[6] The community sub-sector covers "community means of production, owned and managed by local communities" (art. 82(4)(b) of the CRP). The self-managed sub-sector comprises "the means of production subject to collective exploitation by workers" (Article 82(4)(c) of the CRP).

Thus, the LBES does not adopt the legal form of the entities as the exclusive criterion for subjective delimitation. In addition to the legal forms corresponding to the traditional delimitation of Social Economy families (cooperatives, mutual associations, associations and foundations), the legislator also refers to a legal status (the Status of Private Social Solidarity Institutions – IPSS).

In addition to these entities, which we may call *ex lege* Social Economy entities, the legislator foresees, in point h) of Article 4, the possibility of integrating other entities in the Social Economy sector provided that they comply with three requirements, namely: have legal personality, respect the guiding principles of the Social Economy and be included in the Social Economy database (a *sine qua non* requirement).

First and foremost, it should be noted that we believe the legislator acted well in assuming that the Social Economy should not be defined only by its traditional families (cooperatives, mutual associations, associations and foundations), given that the sector can integrate other organisations if they meet the aforementioned requirements. These entities will then be Social Economy entities "by concession" and may take the legal form of commercial companies, as long as they respect the guiding principles set out in the LBES, which will be addressed below.

The guiding principles supplementing the concept of Social Economy are listed in Article 5 of the LBES, according to which: "(...) Social Economy entities are autonomous and act within the scope of their activities in accordance with the following guiding principles: (a) the primacy of the person and the social objectives; (b) free and voluntary membership and participation; (c) democratic control of the respective bodies by their members; (d) conciliation between the interest of members, users or beneficiaries and the general interest; (e) the respect for the values of solidarity, equality and non-discrimination, social cohesion, justice and equity, transparency, shared individual and social responsibility and subsidiarity; (f) autonomous and independent management of public authorities and any other entities outside the Social Economy; (g) the allocation of surpluses to the pursuit of the objectives of Social Economy entities in accordance with the general interest, without prejudice to the respect for the specificity of the distribution of surpluses, proper to the nature and substratum of each Social Economy entity, as enshrined in the Constitution.

The guiding principle of the primacy of the person and the corporate purpose over the capital refers to the general interest purpose that these entities pursue directly or indirectly, linking to the principle of the conciliation between the interest of the members, users or beneficiaries and the general interest.

According to the principle of free and voluntary membership, anyone who is interested and meets the statutory admission requirements should be able to become a member of the entity and benefit from the services it provides. In other words, to become a member, it is not necessary to acquire the share participation of another member or wait for the entity to increase its capital.

The principle of democratic control of the respective bodies by their members, designed for association-based entities, imposes a governance model and a decision-making process that ensure the balanced participation of members, employees, customers and other stakeholders.

The principle of autonomous and independent management of these entities compared to the public authorities and other external entities has a double meaning. On the one hand, it means the guarantee that the relations of Social Economy entities with the State do not lead to their instrumentalization. The State will determine the legislative framework that will regulate the functioning of these entities. The law, specifically, should define the tax and financial benefits and establish the privileged conditions regarding, among other things, access to credit and technical assistance. To this end, Article 9 of the LBES sets out that the State, in its relationship with these entities, shall: "stimulate and support the creation and activity" of these entities (art. 9(a) of the LBES); "ensure the principle of cooperation, considering, namely in the planning and development of the public social systems, the installed material, the human and economic capacity of Social Economy entities, as well as their levels of technical expertise, and insertion in the economic and social structure of the country" (art. 9(b) of the LBES); and "ensure the necessary stability of the relationships established with Social Economy entities" (art. 9(d) of the LBES). In short, the State should stimulate the Social Economy sector, but may not exercise tutelage. On the other hand, this autonomy will aim to ensure that the entry of capital from external sources does not jeopardise the independence or the democratic control of these entities by their members, which is highly relevant given that many Social Economy entities need external funds, public or private, to develop their activities.[7]

The principle of respect for the values of solidarity, equality and non-discrimination, social cohesion, justice and equity, transparency, shared individual and social responsibility and subsidiarity refers primarily to the internal and external solidarity that characterises these entities, as well as the fact that their governance should be aligned with the fundamental principles of Corporate Social Responsibility (CSR). We believe that, as far as social economy entities are concerned, CSR is not voluntary, and their governance should be based on the best practices concerning organisation, equal opportunities, social inclusion and sustainable development.[8]

The principle of "allocating surpluses to the pursuit of the purposes of social economy entities following the general interest, without prejudice to respect for the specific nature of the distribution of surpluses, proper to the nature and substratum of each social economy entity, as enshrined in the Constitution" results in a mode of distributing surpluses that prioritises people and labour over capital. The Portuguese legislator expressly safeguards the specificities of the distribution of surpluses inherent to cooperatives by including in the wording of the principle "without prejudice to the respect for the specificity of the distribution of surpluses, inherent to the nature and substratum of each social economy entity, constitutionally consecrated." In cooperatives, the surplus results from operations of the cooperative

[7] Cf. Meira (2017), pp. 195–229.

[8] Cf. Meira (2012), pp. 293–305.

with its members and is generated at their expense, thus being defined as an amount provisionally overpaid by the members to the cooperative or underpaid by the cooperative to the members in return for their participation in the activity of the cooperative.[9] However, there may be a return of surplus by virtue of the provisions of Article 100(1) of the Portuguese Cooperative Code.[10]/[11] This does not apply to social solidarity cooperatives where all surpluses must revert to reserves (Article 7 of Decree-Law 7/98 of 15 January) and housing cooperatives (Article 15 of Decree-Law 509/99 of 19 November).

The term "surpluses" in this context means a positive economic result, including profits. By determining in this subparagraph g) that such surpluses must be allocated to the pursuit of the goals of Social Economy entities following the general interest, the legislator enforces the collective allocation of surpluses, if there are any, to continue the goals of the entity, which is satisfying the needs of its members and/or of the community.

Finally, in line with what is stated by Montesinos Oltra about the Spanish Framework Law,[12] it is also understood that the entities mentioned in subparagraphs a) to g) of Article 4 of the LBES must be considered *ex lege* Social Economy entities, the underlying nature and legal regime of these entities being the observance of the guiding principles. In addition to these Social Economy entities *ex lege*, the Social Economy entities "by concession" (which provides the possibility for other entities endowed with legal personality and included in the Social Economy database to become part of this sector) are also found in the Framework Law on Social Economy, as pointed out above. Regarding the latter, the legislator expressly states in Article 4(h) the need for them to comply with the guiding principles of the Social Economy.[13]

In this context, even though the Social Economy Law does not mention the social enterprise or the commercial company by name, a certain doctrine considers that commercial companies are not definitely excluded from the Social Economy sector under the aforementioned Article 4(h).[14]

---

[9]Cf. Fajardo and Meira (2017), pp. 89–92.

[10]The legal regime for cooperatives is contained in a Code, called the Cooperative Code, approved by Law No. 119/2015 of 31 August, with the amendments contained in Law No. 66/2017 of 9 August.

[11]Cf. Meira (2018), p. 539 ff.

[12]Cf. Montesinos (2012), pp. 13–19.

[13]Cf. Meira (2013), p. 32 ff.

[14]Cf. Meira and Ramos (2019), p. 1 ff; Farinho (2015), p. 265 ff.

4 Social Enterprises in Portugal

The first legal regime nominally designated as social enterprise in Portugal corresponds to the regime of the social insertion enterprises, which are part of a European tradition of social enterprises aimed at ensuring the integration of the long-term unemployed and other types of unemployed with specific characteristics.

Under the terms of the Resolution of the Council of Ministers No. 49/2008 of 6 March, the social insertion enterprises, regulated by the Ministerial Order No. 348-A/1998 of 18 June (now revoked by subparagraph m) of art. 25 of Decree-Law No. 13/2015), are considered social enterprises. In paragraph 1 of Article 3, the Ministerial Order defines social insertion enterprises as non-profit legal persons whose purpose is the socio-professional reinsertion of the long-term unemployed or people in a situation of disadvantage in relation to the labour market. They may take the following forms: cooperative, association, foundation and private institution of social solidarity. They must also operate according to "business management models" (Article 5(1) of the Ministerial Order). It follows that the legislator restricts social insertion enterprises to non-profit making entities.

There is also an explicit reference to social enterprises in the Draft Framework Law on the Social Economy No. 68/xii of 16 September 2011. Article 13(2)(c) of the aforementioned project states that the legislative reform of the Social Economy sector will also involve "the creation of the legal regime of social enterprises as entities engaged in a commercial activity with primarily social purposes and whose surpluses are essentially mobilised to fulfil those purposes or reinvested in the Community". However, after overall discussion, this rule was removed from the final text of the draft.

Finally, we find a definition of social enterprise in Article 250-D(7) of the Public Procurement Code.[15] This Article refers to "contracts reserved for certain services" (health, social, educational and cultural services), which may include social enterprises. These are defined in paragraph 7 of the Article, in the following terms: "(...) for the purposes of this Article, social enterprises are considered those engaged in the production of goods and services with a strong component of social entrepreneurship or social innovation, and promoting integration into the labour market, through research, innovation and social development programmes, in the areas of the services set out in paragraph 1."

This is, to date, the only legal definition of a social enterprise in Portugal, although it is only sectoral in nature. It should be noted that it does not prevent the pursuit of profit, thus revealing an understanding of the social enterprise that covers both for-profit and non-profit entities, as in the case of commercial companies.[16]

---

[15] Decree-Law No. 18/2008, of 29 January, amended and republished by Decree-Law No. 111-B/2017 of 31 August (rectified by rectification statements No. 36-A/2017 of 30 October and No. 42/2017 of 30 November).

[16] Cf. Meira and Ramos (2019), pp. 1–33.

5 The Non-Market Sector of the Social Economy. Special Reference to the Private Institutions of Social Solidarity (IPSS)

Although not explicitly stated in the LBES, we can make a distinction between a market sector and a non-market sector within the Social Economic sector. The first shall include the entities providing goods and services on the market, in competition with the other entities of the for-profit private sector. This sector comprises cooperatives (except social solidarity cooperatives), mutual associations and social enterprises. The non-market sector shall include social economy entities fulfilling an exclusively social function, based on the principle of solidarity, on a non-profit basis. The beneficiaries receive free of charge benefits or a compensation not proportional to the costs incurred.[17]

In Portugal, the Private Institutions of Social Solidarity (IPSS) stand out in the non-market sector. They are referred to in Article 63(3) of the CRP as follows: "The organisation of the social security system shall not prejudice the existence of non-profit private institutions of social solidarity, which shall be permitted, regulated by law and subject to the supervision of the State".

The legal regime of IPSS is outlined in a special status featuring the activity of various legal forms of entities—the Status of Private Institutions of Social Solidarity (EIPSS), approved by Decree-Law No. 119/83, of 25 February, as amended by Decree-Law No. 172-A/2014 of 14 November.

According to data from the Satellite Account, IPSS entities take up most space and importance in the universe of the Social Economy, with 5622 entities with IPSS or equivalent status identified, operating mainly in the area of social services (56.3%), followed by health (26.3%) and education (6.5%).

5.1 Definition, Object and Activities of the IPSS

Article 1 of the IPSS Status defines IPSS as: "private social solidarity institutions (...) with a non-profit purpose, established exclusively at the initiative of private individuals, to give organised expression to the moral duty of justice and solidarity, contributing to the enforcement of the social rights of citizens, provided that they are not administered by the State or by another public body."

[17] This distinction between social market economy and non-market economy is made in the Social Economy Charter of 2002, revised in 2015, defining the identity, core values, and characteristics of all social economy actors. This Charter was adopted on 10 April 2002 by the main European social economy actors, represented by the CEP-CMAF (European Standing Conference of Co-operatives, Mutuals, Associations and Foundations), the predecessor of Social Economy Europe. Cf. Chaves and Monzón (2018), p. 13 ff.

As to their object, it is clear that the IPSS pursue purposes of general interest, which are achieved through the development of a set of activities, which the legislator divides into primary activities, secondary activities and instrumental activities.[18]

With regards to the primary activities, Article 1-A of the EIPSS states that the objectives of the IPSS are achieved by granting goods, providing services and other initiatives to promote the well-being and quality of life of individuals, families and communities, particularly in the following areas: support to children and youth, including children and youngsters at risk; support to the family; support to the elderly; support to disabled or impaired people; support to social and community integration; social protection of citizens in case of illness, old age, disability and death, as well as in all situations of deprivation or decrease of means of subsistence or capacity to work; health prevention, promotion and protection, namely through preventive, curative and rehabilitative healthcare services and pharmaceutical assistance; education and vocational training of citizens; solving the housing problems of the population; other social responses not included in the previous subparagraphs, provided that they contribute to the enforcement of the social rights of citizens.

These activities fulfil the general interest purpose of the IPSS, justifying the positive discrimination accorded to them by the State. We are thus in the presence of private institutions whose mission is to provide support in situations of economic and social weakness aimed at a specific public.[19]

Besides their primary activities, the IPSS may secondarily pursue other non-profit purposes provided they are compatible with the primary purposes (Article 1-B). To delimit the scope of these secondary purposes, it is understood that, although not limited to those set out in Article 1, they should be related and follow the same fields of activity.

The IPSS may also conduct activities of an instrumental nature as set out in No. 2 of Article 1-B. As the name suggests, these activities are instrumental for non-profit purposes and may be carried out by other entities created by the IPSS. The economic results generated by these activities are mandatorily reinvested in the IPSS, thus contributing to its funding.

The IPSS Status shall not apply to all that exclusively concerns the secondary purposes and the instrumental activities conducted, provided that this does not affect the competence of the services with supervisory or inspection roles to verify the secondary or instrumental nature of the activities and to apply the corresponding regime of administrative sanctions.[20]

[18] Cf. Saraiva (2018), pp. 69–97.

[19] Lopes (2009), p. 81 ff.

[20] Aguiar (2018), pp. 229–235.

5.2 Form and Legal Nature of the Entities That Can Obtain the IPSS Status

As for the legal forms of the entities that can obtain the IPSS status, Article 2(1) of the EIPSS admits the following forms or groups: social solidarity associations; social solidarity cooperatives accredited under the terms of Article 9 of Decree-Law No. 7/98 of 15 January; mutualist or mutual aid associations; social solidarity foundations; and brotherhoods of mercy (*Irmandades da Misericórdia*).

Moreover, under the terms of the Concordat established between the Holy See and the Portuguese Republic on 18 May 2004, the IPSS can take the form of Catholic Church institutions, namely parish social centres and diocesan and parish Caritas organisations (Article 2(2)).

Under the terms of Article 2(4), the IPSS can also group themselves into unions and federations.

The law distinguishes between IPSS entities that automatically acquire the IPSS status and entities that acquire the status by equivalence. The equivalent entities are granted the same rights, duties and benefits, namely tax benefits.

In the following sections we shall analyse the legal forms, grouping them into two sets: the IPSS with an associative basis and those of a foundational nature.

5.3 Association-Based IPSS

The IPSS which adopt the legal form of associations may do so as social solidarity associations and mutual or mutual aid associations.

5.3.1 Social Solidarity Associations

Social solidarity associations are legal persons of an associative nature governed by private law, established for the purpose of giving organised expression to the moral duty of justice and solidarity, contributing towards the enforcement of citizens'social rights (Article 52(1) of the EIPSS).

Their legal regime is set out in Articles 52 to 67 of the EIPSS.

Social solidarity associations acquire legal personality in the act of incorporation, which must be set out in a public deed or equivalent act. An association whose number of members is less than twice the number of members established for the respective bodies cannot be considered a social solidarity association.

5.3.2 Mutual Associations

Mutual associations are "private institutions of social solidarity with an unlimited number of members, undetermined capital and indefinite duration which, essentially through the contribution of their members, fulfil, in their interest and that of their families, mutual aid purposes" (Article 1 of the Mutual Associations Code (CAM), approved by Decree-Law No. 47/2018 of 2 August).

Mutual associations have mutual aid as their general purpose (Art. 1(1) of the CAM). The mutual aid purpose is pursued in the interest of their members and their families in the framework of complementarity of public social security and health systems.

Under the terms of Article 2 of the CAM, the main purpose of mutual associations is to grant social security and health benefits intended to remedy the consequences of contingent events relating to the life and health of members and their families and to prevent, as far as possible, the occurrence of such events (main purposes). Cumulatively, mutual associations may pursue other purposes of social protection and promotion of quality of life through the organisation and management of social support equipment and services, as well as other social works and activities aimed especially at the moral, intellectual, cultural and physical development of the members and their families (cumulative/secondary purposes).

According to the provisions of Article 76 of the EIPSS, mutual associations are governed "by the provisions of special legislation and, subsidiarily, by the Statute's provisions." In the same vein, Article 145(a)(b)(c) of the Mutual Associations Code notes that "in all that is not regulated by the present diploma, the Status of the Private Institutions of Social Solidarity and complementary legislation shall apply, mutatis mutandis."

Besides the EIPSS, the Mutual Associations Code must be combined, under the terms of Article 7, with social security supplementary occupational schemes (Decree-Law No. 225/89 of 6 July). In the aforementioned diploma, the specific discipline dedicated to mutual associations is foreseen in Articles 18 to 20.

Mutual associations acquire legal personality in the act of incorporation (Article 23 of the CAM). Acts of incorporation, statutes, benefit regulations and other acts relating to mutual associations specified by law, are subject to registration (Article 25 of the CAM; Article 6 of Ministerial Order 135/2007 of 26 January). The registration of the statutes and benefit regulations is a *sine qua non* condition for collecting dues and granting benefits.

Mutual associations must have a number of members and a financing system to ensure the technical and financial balance required to grant the benefits pursued by the entity (Article 22 of CAM).

Mutual associations are subject to State supervision of legality and financial supervision by the entity legally competent for this purpose (Articles 126 to 139 of CAM).

5.3.3 Brotherhoods of Mercy (Misericórdia)

The brotherhoods of mercy or Santas Casas da Misericórdia are IPSS of an associative nature "recognised in the canonical legal order to satisfy social needs and practise acts of Catholic worship in harmony with their traditional spirit as informed by the principles of Christian doctrine and morality" (Article 68 of the EIPSS). Articles 68 to 70 of the EIPSS apply to the brotherhoods of mercy in addition to the articles concerning social solidarity associations (Articles 52 to 67 by virtue of Article 69(2) of the EIPSS).

Under the terms of Article 68 of the EIPSS, the brotherhoods of mercy serve a dual purpose—a religious purpose and a social purpose. In addition to the IPSS Status applicable to the social purpose, the brotherhoods of mercy are governed by the terms of the Commitment (*Compromisso*) established between the Union of Portuguese Mercies and the Episcopal Conference, or the bilateral document replacing it (Article 69(2)).[21]

5.4 *The IPSS with a Foundational Basis*

IPSS that adopt the legal form of a foundation may only do so as social solidarity foundations. Their legal regime is set out in the Framework Law on Foundations (Law No. 24/2012 of 9 July, in the version of Law No. 36/2021 of 14 June) and subsidiarily the EIPSS.

From the combination of the EIPSS with Article 39 of the Framework Law, we can define social solidarity foundations as collective private persons of foundational nature, created exclusively at the initiative of private individuals and established to give organized expression to the moral duty of justice and solidarity, thus contributing to the enforcement of the social rights of citizens.

Regarding the acquisition of legal personality, Article 6 of the Framework Law states that "foundations acquire legal personality through recognition," referring to the special scheme of Article 39 and following of the diploma. Article 40-(1) empowers the Prime Minister to recognise social solidarity foundations, with an option of delegation. The competent entity for the recognition must request the competent services of the Ministry of Solidarity, Employment and Social Security to issue a binding opinion on the recognition request. In the case of foundations of social solidarity with main or exclusive purposes of promotion and protection of health and foundations of social solidarity within the scope of the Ministry of Education, the competent services of the Ministry of Health or the Ministry of Education and Science, as the case may be, are also requested to issue a binding opinion. The absence of such opinions shall constitute grounds for refusal of recognition.

[21] Roque (2018), p. 842 ff.

5.5 *The IPSS by Equivalence*

5.5.1 Social Solidarity Cooperatives

The legal regime of social solidarity cooperatives is set out in a specific diploma, Decree-Law No. 7/98 of 15 January.

Pursuant to Article 2 of this decree law: "1 – Social solidarity cooperatives are those that, through the cooperation and mutual assistance of their members, in compliance with the cooperative principles, aim to satisfy their social needs, promotion and integration, without profit, namely in the following areas: a) Support to vulnerable groups, in particular children and youngsters, people with disabilities and the elderly; b) Support to socially disadvantaged families and communities with a view to improving their quality of life and socio-economic insertion; c) Support to Portuguese citizens living abroad, during their stay outside the national territory and upon their return, in a situation of economic deprivation; d) Development of support programmes directed towards target groups, namely in case of illness, old age, disability and serious economic need; e) Promotion of access to education, training and professional integration of socially underprivileged groups. 2 – In addition to those listed in the previous number, social solidarity cooperatives may conduct other actions identical in purpose to those foreseen in the previous number and, within the limits of the Cooperative Code, provide services to third parties."

In areas not covered by the regulations set out in Decree-Law 7/98 of 15 January, the more general rules of the Cooperative Code shall directly apply, mentioning the social solidarity cooperative branch in Article 4(1). Article 4(4) also states that "Social solidarity cooperatives that pursue the objectives set out in Article 1 of the Status of Private Social Solidarity Institutions, approved by Decree-Law 119/83 of 25 February, as amended by Decree-Law 172-A/2014 of 14 November, and which are recognised as such by the Directorate-General of Social Action, are comparable to private social solidarity institutions and subject to the same rights, duties and benefits, including tax benefits.

In this context, it is envisaged that social solidarity cooperatives will be treated in the same way as IPSS, with the same rights, duties and benefits provided for in the EIPSS. The recognition by equivalence granted to IPSS of social solidarity cooperatives that pursue the objectives set out in the IPSS Status shall follow the rules set out in Order No. 3859/2016 of the Ministry of Labour, Solidarity and Social Security. Under the terms of the aforementioned diploma (Article 1), such recognition may be requested by the cooperative itself to the Directorate-General of Social Security (DGSS), duly instructed (Article 2), followed by the issuance of a reasoned opinion regarding the request by the District Centre of Social Security of the area of the cooperative's head office (Article 3). Subsequently, the process will be forwarded to the DGSS which, after evaluation, shall decide whether to grant or reject the request for recognition (Article 4).

To be recognised as an IPSS-equivalent entity, the cooperative must submit: a copy of the incorporation act and the bylaws of the cooperative and an accreditation issued by the *António Sérgio Cooperative for the Social Economy* (CASES). This accreditation, foreseen in Article 117 of the Cooperative Code, besides confirming the cooperative nature of the entity and its legal functioning, will also confirm its social solidarity purposes. Technical and financial support from public entities, namely in integration and social security, will depend on that accreditation.[22]

5.5.2 The Casas Do Povo (People's Houses)

The Casas do Povo (People's Houses) that pursue the purposes assigned to IPSS can also be treated as IPSS. Their legal regime is established in the Decree-law No. 4/82 of 11 January, altered by Decree-laws No. 81/85 of 28 March and No. 246/90 of 27 July, which defines them as associations established for an indefinite period of time, promoting social support to the population and welfare, particularly in rural areas. They perform activities of a social and cultural nature, with the involvement of the interested parties, and collaborate with the State and the Local Authorities to help solve local problems. The area covered by each people's centre shall be the most appropriate for its purposes and the characteristics of the population, but less than that of the parish. The minimum number of members of a People's House shall be 50 (fifty).

The recognition granted by equivalence to IPSS is regulated by Decree-Law No. 171/98 of 25 June. Such recognition depends on the submission of a copy of the act (or charter) of incorporation and the bylaws of the Casa do Povo and a copy of the legal person's identification card.

5.6 The Status of Public Interest

It is also essential to analyse the legal framework of IPSS as legal persons of public interest. This status, set out in Law No. 36/2021 of 1 July (Framework Law on the Public Interest Status), may be attributed to legal persons pursuing purposes of general, regional or local interest and cooperating, within this scope, with the central, regional or local administration (Article 4(1) of Law No. 36/2021).

The status of public interest is granted by law, without the need for an administrative procedure, to private social solidarity institutions, equivalent social solidarity cooperatives and mutual associations (Article 28 of Law No. 36/2021).

This status of public interest exempts these entities from demonstrating the relevance of the general interest of the activity they carry out, resulting in the State's concession of benefits (tax exemptions, financial support, among others).

The attribution of this public interest status represents the recognition of the connection of interests between the IPSS and the State. Although they are entities

[22] Cf. Meira (2020), pp. 221–247.

governed by private law, the IPSS pursue social goals that materially coincide with the public interests pursued by the State. In other words, although they are private entities, they pursue public interests to the exact extent that they substitute the State in the provision of a set of services, namely social services, to fulfil the general interest.[23]

6 Tax Framework of the Social Economy

The promotion of the social economy is achieved by assigning these entities “a more favourable tax status, defined by law based on their substratum and nature” (Article 11 of the LBES). Two points emerge from this provision: firstly, the legislator makes a commitment of a tax nature by establishing that social economy entities will benefit from a more favourable differentiated tax regime (positive discrimination) than other private entities operating in the market; secondly, given the heterogeneity of the entities that make up the social economy sector, the tax regime will be differentiated among them, taking into account the degree to which they pursue general interest objectives.

Notwithstanding this legal provision, there is still no single tax status applicable to these entities. In fact, the tax and social security scheme applicable to social economy entities is spread across several legal diplomas in Portugal.

In terms of Corporate Income Tax (IRC), there is a division between the tax regime for Cooperatives and the tax regime for other Social Economy Entities (such as IPSS, Foundations, Associations, etc.).

For tax purposes, cooperatives are considered for-profit entities, which is why the IRC determination and quantification follow the general rules and principles applicable to business entities (subparagraph a) of No. 1 of article 2 of the IRC Code, as well as subparagraph a) of No. 1 of article 3 of the same Code).[24] The other Social Economy entities are qualified as entities not primarily engaged in a commercial, industrial or agricultural activity (i.e. they are not for-profit oriented), which is why the determination and quantification of IRC is based, alternatively, on the algebraic sum of the net income of the various categories determined under the terms of Personal Income Tax (IRS), as provided for in Articles 53 and 54 of the IRC Code.

However, there is one common aspect in the universe of social economy entities in Portugal, namely the fact that tax benefit provision (such as total or partial tax exemption) is closely linked to the effective pursuit of the social object defined in the bylaws of these entities and the effective performance of activities targeted to fulfil such object. This circumstance does not only apply to IRC, but also to other relevant taxes, such as Value Added Tax (VAT), Municipal Property Tax (IMI) and Municipal Property Transfer Tax (IMT). For example, as a rule, only properties or parts of

[23] Lopes (2009), p. 418.

[24] Cf. Aguiar (2022), p. 88 ff.

properties directly used to achieve the statutory purposes of Social Economy Entities are entitled to exemption from IMI and IMT, which leaves outside the scope of the exemption the properties or parts of properties rented or used as bar or restaurant facilities of the IPSS.[25]

There is also a tax regime in Portugal to encourage corporate patronage, which includes tax advantages for benefactors of social economy entities (articles 61 to 66 of the Statute of Tax Benefits).[26]

7 Supervision of the Social Economy

In Portugal, social economy entities are granted positive discrimination, enshrined in the Constitution of the Republic, in the aforementioned Article 85, and in the Framework Law on Social Economy (LBES).

The LBES states that public authorities should "foster the creation of mechanisms that allow for the reinforcement of economic and financial self-sustainability of Social Economy entities in accordance with Article 85 of the Constitution of the Portuguese Republic" (Article 10(2)(b)). The promotion of the social economy by the public authorities includes: "facilitating the creation of new social economy entities and supporting the diversity of initiatives specific to this sector, empowering itself as an instrument of innovative responses to the challenges faced by local, regional, national or other communities, removing obstacles that prevent the establishment and development of the economic activities of social economy entities" (Article 10(2)(c)); "encouraging research and innovation in the social economy, vocational training within social economy entities, as well as supporting their access to processes of technological innovation and organisational management" (Article 10(2)(d)); and the establishment, for these entities, of a more favourable tax status (Article 11).

The counterpoint to this positive discrimination is the need for an effective and appropriate supervision of social economy entities. Being aware of this need, the legislator, in Article 8 of the LBES, highlighted the importance of transparency and the consequent need for mechanisms to supervise the activity of social economy entities.

These supervision mechanisms cannot undermine the autonomy of social organisations vis-à-vis the public authorities and other external entities, as mentioned above.

Regarding the supervision of the cooperative sector, it is worth noting the role of the António Sérgio Cooperative for the Social Economy (CASES), created by

[25] See, in this regard, Article 6 of the IMT Code and Articles 44 and 66-A of the Tax Benefits Statute, as well as Article 9 of the VAT Code.

[26] Cf. Ribeiro and Santos (2013), passim.

Decree-Law 282/2009 of 7 October.[27] Pursuant to Articles 115 to 118 of the Cooperative Code, CASES is responsible for supervising, in accordance with the law, the use of the cooperative form, respecting the cooperative principles and the rules regarding their establishment and operation. For this purpose, cooperatives shall submit to CASES copies of the acts of incorporation and amendments to the bylaws, annual management reports, annual financial statements and balance sheets.[28]

Regarding the IPSS, special reference must be made to the supervisory regime foreseen in Article 34 and following of the EIPSS.

Article 34(1) of the EIPSS provides that "The State, through its competent organs and services, under the terms of the general law, exercises powers of inspection, audit and supervision over the institutions covered by the present Statute, and may therefore order enquiries, probes and inspections". Paragraph 2 of this rule adds that "The supervisory powers are exercised by the competent services of the ministry responsible for social security, in the exact terms defined in the respective statutes, to ensure the effective fulfilment of their objectives in compliance with the law."

Note that this supervision only applies if the IPSS receives public financial support resulting from cooperation or management agreements with the State. In these cases, the IPSS acts as a co-contractor of the State, justifying a supervisory action by the State.[29] However, this supervision is "only a supervision of legality"[30] translated into a set of a posteriori supervisory powers, thus not conflicting with the principle of autonomy and independence that characterises the management of these entities. The State supports the IPSS through the cooperation and management agreements. Still, this support from the State "cannot constitute a limitation to the right of free action of the institutions" (Article 4(2) and (4) of the EIPSS).[31]

These supervisory powers aim to correct and repair illegalities arising from free management decisions taken by the competent bodies of the IPSS. Such illegalities, translated into a "repeated practice of acts or systematic omission of compliance with legal or statutory duties by the management body that are prejudicial to the interests of the institution or its beneficiaries," may lead to a request for judicial dismissal of the holders of such body (Article 35 of the EIPSS). Out of respect for the principle of autonomy, judicial intervention is always required in a conflict between the State and the IPSS.[32]

---

[27] The legal regime for public interest cooperatives is set out in Decree-Law No. 31/84 of 21 January. Article 1(1) of this law defines public interest cooperatives as legal persons in which the State or other legal persons governed by public law and cooperatives, or users of the goods and services produced, or non-profit legal persons governed by private law associate to pursue their objectives.

[28] Cf. Meira (2016), pp. 281–327.

[29] Cf. Almeida (2011), p. 125 ff.

[30] Canotilho and Moreira (2007), p. 821.

[31] Cf. Saraiva (2017), p. 80 ff.; Farinho (2021), p. 142 ff.

[32] Cf. Farinho (2021), p. 140 ff.

8 Public Procurement and Social Economy

The question has been raised in the social economy sector as to whether the entities composing it are subject to public procurement rules or benefit from some particular regime in this area.

The question is particularly relevant for IPSS.

Article 2(2) of the Public Procurement Code extends the subjective scope of application of public procurement to legal persons that, although private, "have been created specifically to meet general interest needs, not having an industrial or commercial character" and "are financed for the most part by public entities, are subject to their management control or have an administrative, managerial or supervisory body composed mainly of members directly or indirectly appointed by those (public) entities."

The doctrine regards IPSS as non-contracting entities on the basis of the criteria provided for in Article 2(2), since they are entities governed by private law and with private initiative, as referred to in Article 1(1) and Article 3 of the EIPSS.[33] Although satisfying general interests, they are materially and formally private entities, are not entrusted with public functions, were not created by any public entity and do not act by delegation or instrumentally, but by their own right, recognised by the Constitution. In other words, they are not "bodies governed by public law," either by the criterion of management control or financing.

In fact, IPSS are not subject to any material management control. Article 1(1) of the EIPSS clearly states that only institutions that "are not administered by the State or any other public body" can be recognised as IPSS, and their statutes are freely drafted by them (Article 10(1) of the EIPSS). In addition to statutory autonomy, they have freedom of management, freedom to choose the holders of the bodies and freedom of passive electoral capacity regarding the holders of those bodies.[34] The State has no competence to interfere in the management orientation of the IPSS, their management and supervisory bodies are autonomous and are not appointed or dismissed by an act of Public Administration. Furthermore, the IPSS does not have representation of the State or minor public entities in its bodies, which are composed by the members of the IPSS.[35]

The supervision regime foreseen in Article 34 and following of the EIPSS does not represent a management control but only supervision of legality, as we have seen.

Regarding the criterion of majority funding (through subsidies or grants) by the public authorities, the doctrine considers that this does not apply to IPSS. The State support to the IPPS finds its basis in the fact that they pursue "private social goals that coincide materially with interests formally qualified as public by the legislator

[33] Cf. Farinho (2021), pp. 131–152;.

[34] Lopes (2019), pp. 67–92.

[35] Cf. Farinho (2021), pp. 131–152

and, as such, their pursuit is (also) the responsibility of the State"[36] (Article 63(2) of the CRP). The EIPPS recognises this connection of interests in Article 4(1), which states that the State "accepts, supports and values the contribution of the institutions in the enforcement of the social rights of the individual citizens". This support based on cooperation agreements is merely a "compensation for services rendered or contributions made in the State's direct interest."[37] The revenues from cooperation agreements have a contractual nature, as such agreements are bilateral contracts, freely and autonomously entered into. However, the funding referred to in Article 2(2)(a)(ii) refers to budgetary transfers and not payments for services provided to the State under cooperation agreements.[38]

Although the IPSS are not contracting entities according to the Public Procurement Code criteria, they are still contracting entities in respect of the public contracts identified in Article 23 of their Statute. Paragraph 1 of this article states: "The contracting of construction or major repair works belonging to the institutions must comply with the provisions of the Public Contracts Code, except works carried out by direct administration up to a maximum amount of 25,000 EUR". In turn, paragraph 3 states that "Sales or leases may be made by direct negotiation when it is foreseeable that there are advantages for the institution or for reasons of urgency, substantiated in minutes", and that "In any case, the prices and rents accepted cannot be lower than those in force on the normal market for real estate and leases, in line with the values established in an official appraisal" (paragraph 4).

In such cases, the IPSS perform acts equivalent to administrative acts, described in Article 23 of the EIPSS as awarding procedures for the establishment of contracts of an economic nature covering services that may be subject to market competition. In this way, the principles of transparency, free competition and publicity are ensured, which are also the raison d'être of the specific public procurement regime.[39]

Reference should also be made to the special regime for public contracts for health services, social services, education services and cultural services provided for in Article 250-D of the Public Contracts Code. Concerning these services, below the threshold of 750,000 EUR, contracting entities may initiate reserved contract establishment procedures, giving preference to entities that cumulatively meet the following requirements:

(a) Having as their object the pursuit of a public service mission linked to the provision of the services referred to in the previous number;
(b) Reinvesting their profits to achieve the objective of the organisation or, in case of distribution or redistribution, observe participatory considerations;

[36] Farinho (2021), p. 140.

[37] Gonçalves (2021), p. 190.

[38] The guiding principles of cooperation agreements are set out in Decree-Law No. 120/2015 of 7 June and their legal regime is enshrined in Ordinance No. 196-A/2015 of 1 July.

[39] Cf. Amorim (2021), pp. 350–353.

(c) Counting on the participation of employees in the capital stock of the organisation performing the contract or base their management structure on participative principles that require the active involvement of employees, users or interested parties;
(d) Not having concluded a contract under this Article with the same contracting party for the last 3 years.

The entities of the economic sector, considering the legal regime applicable, are covered by this provision. The legislator expressly adds social enterprises (Article 250-D(6)).

9 Conclusions

From a legal point of view, the term "Social Economy" has prevailed over the "Third Sector" in Portugal.

The Social Economy sector covers all the cooperative and social sectors enshrined in the Constitution, configured as an independent sector, parallel to the public and private for-profit sector.

The concept of social economy is legally determined in the Framework Law on Social Economy.

Social economy entities have a specific social object, consisting of an economic and social activity pursuing a general interest objective. Their organisation and operation are based on a set of guiding principles.

The pursuit of general interest purposes, directly or indirectly, justifies the positive discrimination that these entities enjoy, which translates into a more favourable tax regime and public financial support.

In the Framework Law, Social Economy is not only defined by its traditional families (cooperatives, mutual societies, associations and foundations) and by their legal status. The legislator acknowledges that the sector can incorporate other entities endowed with legal personality provided that they observe the guiding principles and are included in the social economy database. The fulfilment of these requirements allows social enterprises, under corporate form, to be considered social economy entities.

The Social Economic sector comprises a market sector and a non-market sector. The first shall include the entities providing goods and services on the market, in competition with the other entities of the for-profit private sector. This sector comprises cooperatives (except social solidarity cooperatives), mutual associations and social enterprises. The non-market sector shall include social economy entities fulfilling an exclusively social function based on the principle of solidarity. In this sector, the beneficiaries receive free of charge benefits or compensation not proportional to the costs incurred.

In the non-market sector, the IPSS entities stand out in number and importance. This is a legal status that encompasses a set of various legal form entities whose objective focuses on a clear mission to assist in situations of social and economic vulnerability, contributing to the enforcement of social rights. These private social purposes are materially coincident with the purposes pursued by the State, which, accordingly, supports the IPSS through cooperation agreements and a more favourable differentiated tax regime. This positive discrimination justifies the supervision of legality to which these entities are subject. However, despite serving general interests, they are materially and formally private entities.

References

Aguiar N (2018) Differentiation Between Primary and Secondary Activities by Non-Profit Entities and Its Relevance in Terms of Capital Taxes. Commentary on the Sentence of the Supreme Administrative Court, Second Section, of February 22, 2017, Procedure N.° 1658/15. Cooperativismo e Economía Social 40:229–235

Aguiar N (2022) The taxation of co-operatives'income: analysis of its rationale. Int J Cooperat Law 4:88–104

Almeida V (2011) As Instituições Particulares de Solidariedade Social. Almedina/CES, Coimbra

Canotilho JG, Moreira V (2007) Constituição da República Portuguesa anotada, Volume I, 4.ª edição. Coimbra Editora, Coimbra

Chaves R, Monzón JL (2018) The social economy facing emerging economic concepts: social innovation, social responsibility, collaborative economy, social enterprises and solidarity economy. CIRIEC España, Revista de Economía Pública, Social y Cooperativa 93:5–50

Fajardo G, Meira D (2017) Cooperative financial structure. In: Fajardo G, Fici A, Henrÿ H, Hiez D, Meira D, Münkner H-H, Snaith I (eds) Principles of European cooperative law. Principles, commentaries and national reports. Intersentia, Cambridge. pp 73–96. https://doi.org/10.1017/9781780686073.005

Farinho DS (2015) A sociedade comercial como empresa social – breve ensaio prospetivo a partir do direito societário português. Revista de Direito das Sociedades 7(2):247–270

Farinho DS (2021) Todas as IPSS são entidades adjudicantes? Contributo para uma interpretação constitucionalmente conforme do critério do controlo de gestão face ao Estatuto das IPSS: comentário ao Acórdão do TCA do Sul, de 10 de outubro de 2019, P.° n.° 836/19.9BELSB. Revista dos Contratos Públicos 25:131–152

Gonçalves P (2021) Direito dos Contratos Públicos, 5.ª edição. Almedina, Coimbra

Lopes L (2009) As Instituições Particulares de Solidariedade Social. Almedina, Coimbra

Lopes L (2019) Financial supervision of mutualist associations and freedom of association. Cooperativismo e Economía Social. 41:67–92

Meira D (2018) Artigo 100.°. In: Meira D, Ramos ME (eds) Código Cooperativo Anotado. Coimbra, Almedina, pp 539–547

Meira DA (2012) A responsabilidade social da empresa cooperativa. Uma análise jurídica e intercultural. In: Sarmento C (coord.) Diálogos interculturais: os novos rumos da viagem. Vida Económica, Porto, pp 293–305

Meira DA (2013) A Lei de Bases da Economia Social Portuguesa: do projeto ao texto final. CIRIEC España, revista jurídica de economía social y cooperativa 24:21–52

Meira DA (2016) A fiscalização das cooperativas à luz do novo Código Cooperativo Português. CIRIEC-España, Revista Jurídica de Economia Social y Cooperativa 28:281–327

Meira DA (2017) A governação da Economia Social. Uma reflexão a partir da Lei de Bases da Economia Social portuguesa (The Governance of the Social Economy. A reflection from the Law of Bases of the Portuguese Social Economy). In: Loureiro J, Silva S (Estudos, coord.) A economia social e civil. Vol. 1. Instituto Jurídico da Faculdade de Direito da Universidade de Coimbra. pp 195–229. https://doi.org/10.14195/978-989-26-1423-6

Meira DA (2020) O fim mutualístico desinteressado ou altruísta das cooperativas de solidariedade social. CIRIEC-España, Revista Jurídica de Economia Social y Cooperativa 36:221–247

Meira DA, Ramos ME (2019) Empresas sociais e sociedades comerciais: realidades convergentes ou divergentes? (Social enterprises and commercial companies: converging or diverging realities?). Cooperativismo & Desarrollo 27(1):1–33

Montesinos O (2012) Ley de Economía Social, interés general y regímenes tributários especiales. CIRIEC-España, Revista Jurídica de Economía Social y Cooperativa 23:9–35

Namorado R (2007) Renovar os quadros jurídicos da Economia Social? Oficina do Centro de Estudos Sociais, Coimbra

Namorado R (2017) A Economia Social e a Constituição, Economia Social em Textos, n.° 3,. CECES – Centro de Estudos Cooperativos e da Economia Social, Coimbra

Ribeiro F, Santos S (2013) A fiscalidade e as organizações da economia social. Vida Económica, Porto

Roque MP (2018) Misericórdias e conflito de jurisdições: a impugnação de deliberações das associações de religiosos. Revista da Ordem dos Advogados 78(3/4):835–878

Saraiva R (2017) A regulação pública das entidades da Economia Social. Cooperativismo e Economia Social 39:55–88

Saraiva VR (2018) As instituições particulares de solidariedade social. In Gomes CA et al (coord.) Organização Administrativa: novos actores, novos modelos, Vol. II. AAFDL Editora, Lisboa, pp 69–97

Chapter 10
Social Economy and Third Sector in Spanish Law. Convergences and Divergences

Gemma Fajardo-García

Contents

Gemma Fajardo-García is Professor of Commercial Law and member of the Institute for Research in Social Economy, Cooperativism and Entrepreneurship (IUDESCOOP).
My thanks to Professor Rafael Chaves for reviewing this text and his valuable contributions.

G. Fajardo-García (✉)
University of Valencia, Department of Commercial Law, Valencia, Spain
e-mail: fajardo@uv.es

A. Fici (ed.), *The Law of Third Sector Organizations in Europe*,
https://doi.org/10.1007/978-3-031-41744-3_10

Abstract In Spain, both the social economy sector and the so-called third sector have been legally recognised and promoted, or more accurately, the third social sector since it only integrates social initiative entities. There is a third cultural, sports, and environmental sector, but it has not been legally recognised. The social economy as regulated by Law 5/2011 includes both entities that pursue purposes of common interestof its members (cooperatives, associations, mutual societies, labour societies) and purposes of general interest (associations, foundations, special entities) and other entities that, whatever their legal form, have the purpose of integrating disabled people or people with difficult employability (social enterprises) into the labour market. The third social sector is identified in Law 43/2015 as a set of private organisations created by social initiative with purposes of general interest and non-profit. This law considers foundations and associations of general interest as part of the third sector, a scope extended by the laws of the Autonomous Communities to special entities, social initiative cooperatives and social enterprises. The third sector can be considered the non-market subsector of the social economy. They share the same goals and principles but have different representative structures (CEPES/Third Sector Platform) and their promotion depends on different government departments (Employment and Social Affairs).

1 Introduction

Social Economy and Third Sector are terms that, whilst at some point could have been used as equivalents, following their legal regulation their profiles have been defined and their similarities and differences have become evident. This is the issue we have set out to analyse: the evolution of both concepts, from their origins to the present day, in order to show what aspects they share and what differentiates them.

Our analysis is based primarily on legislation. This is a complex task, since both the Spanish State and the Autonomous Communities (CCAA) have exclusive or shared powers to regulate not only most of the legal entities under study, but also the categories of social economy and third sector.

We will begin by looking at the first legal references to the social economy and the third sector in Spain. We then analyse the most relevant aspects of the legislation on the social economy and the third sector, both at the State and Autonomous Community levels. We pay special attention to the concept, the principles that inspire them, the entities that are integrated, their representative organisations and their promotion.

Finally, we conclude by highlighting the similarities and differences between the two concepts, and the reasons that justify them.

2 First Legal References to the Social Economy and the Third Sector

The terms Third Sector and Social Economy have been used in Spain for years. At first, they were used as equivalent expressions to identify a sector of the economy different to the public sector and the capitalist private sector; it was also stated that the third sector was the meeting point between the "non-profit sector" and the "social economy" (Monzón et al. 2010, p. 32).

The term social economy was initially adopted by the public administration responsible for employment, mainly as an expression of collective self-employment. Thus, the social economy became the target of public employment aid and of other policies dependent on that public administration, such as the promotion of cooperativism. In 1990, the National Institute for the Promotion of the Social Economy, known as INFES,[1] was created as a successor to the General Directorate of Cooperatives and Labour Companies of the Ministry of Labour. Royal Decree 1836/1991 defined social economy companies as "those whose purpose is to provide goods and services to their members, with the latter participating directly and democratically in decision-making, and those in which the workers hold the majority of the capital stock. Likewise, those individuals or legal entities that conduct a socio-economic activity by means of any self-employment formula are also included". At this early stage, cooperatives, worker-owned companies and, on occasion, mutual benefit societies, were considered to be social economy companies, all of which are subject to promotion, control and supervision by the public administration responsible for labour matters.

Later, in 1999, when the current law on cooperatives was passed, the Higher Council of Cooperativism, present until then in cooperative legislation, was replaced by the Council for the Promotion of the Social Economy as an advisory and consulting body of the State administration for activities related to the social economy.[2]

From these first institutions, public policies in support of the social economy have been present in all the Autonomous Regions. Some of them, since 2006, have even

[1]Law 31/1990 of 27 December 1990 (art. 98). Later, by Royal Decree 140/1997, of 11 January 1997, the INFES was transformed into the General Directorate for the Promotion of the Social Economy and the European Social Fund.

[2]Law 27/1999 of 16 July 1999 (Additional Provision 2ª).

included in their Statutes of Autonomy the promotion of the social economy as a characteristic of their economic model.[3]

A further, and the most important step so far, was the recognition and regulation of the social economy in Law 5/2011. It is a law applicable throughout the Spanish State, which does not prevent the Autonomous Regions from passing their own social economy laws, allowing them to highlight local particularities, as in the case of Law 6/2016, of 4 May of the Social Economy of Galicia, or other laws currently being drafted in Aragon, the Canary Islands or Catalonia.

The term third sector, for its part, began to gain legal recognition in the early years of this century, as a new expression of identification of non-profit entities that pursue purposes of general interest, and more particularly of social initiative organisations collaborating with public administrations in the social services sector.[4]

The expression "non-profit entity" has been present in Spanish legislation since the second half of the nineteenth century as a characteristic of entities such as cooperatives, mutual societies, associations or foundations. The first two, because they do not seek profit in their economic activity (carried out with their members), are said to have an objective non-profit purpose[5]; and the others, because whether or not they seek profit in their economic activity, the profits they obtain cannot be distributed among their associates or patrons, are said in this case to have a subjective non-profit purpose (Ascarelli 1964, pp. 178–179).

Tax legislation has traditionally recognised a special regime for all of them, among other things because of this lack of profit motive. This can be seen in the law on the tax regime for cooperatives,[6] mutual societies[7] or in the laws regulating the taxation of foundations and associations.[8]

However, the lack of profit motive is not enough to obtain the main benefits, fiscal or otherwise, conferred by Spanish law; the entities are also required to pursue purposes of general interest. These purposes are specific to entities such as foundations and associations.

Article 34 of the Spanish Constitution recognises "the right of foundation for purposes of general interest". Based on this declaration, the current law on foundations[9] defines foundations as "non-profit organisations that, by the will of their creators, have their assets permanently assigned to the achievement of purposes of general interest" (art. 2); it requires that foundations pursue purposes of general

[3]This has been the case in Andalusia, Aragon, Castile and Leon, Catalonia and the Valencian Community.

[4]References in the literature begin at the end of the previous century, with contributions by De Lorenzo and Cabra de Luna (1993), Fuentes Rey (1996); Álvarez de Mon (1998), Herrera (1998) or Cabra de Luna (1999).

[5]Commercial Code of 1885 (art. 124) and Explanatory Memorandum.

[6]Law 20/1990, of 19 December 1990, on the tax regime for cooperatives.

[7]Cf. Fuster Asencio (2009).

[8]Law 30/1994, of 24 November 1994, on Foundations and tax incentives for private participation in activities of general interest.

[9]Law 50/2002, of 26 December 2002, on Foundations (art. 2).

interest (art. 3) and declares non-compliance with this obligation to be a cause for their extinction (art.31).

The current law on associations,[10] for its part, develops the right of association recognised in the Spanish Constitution (art. 22 EC) and establishes the legal regime of associations. It states that associations shall be non-profit organisations (art. 1) and that they pursue purposes of general or particular interest (art. 5). However, the law only orders the public administrations to promote and facilitate the development of associations "that pursue purposes of general interest". They may receive aid and subsidies and enter into collaboration agreements with the administration in programmes of social interest (art. 31). The law then goes on to regulate public utility associations, which it defines as those whose statutory purposes tend to promote the general interest; their activity is not restricted exclusively to benefiting their members; the members of their representative bodies who receive remuneration are not paid from public funds or subsidies; they have adequate personal and material means and the appropriate organisation to fulfil their purposes, and they are constituted, registered in the Registry and have been in operation uninterruptedly for at least 2 years immediately prior to the filing of their application for declaration as a public utility (art. 32). Authors and jurisprudence usually identify the concept of general interest with that of public interest, public utility, social interest or general economic interest, which are used in legal areas of public, private, social or community law (Acosta Gallo 2019, p. 174).

As to what is understood by purposes of general interest, the constitutional legislator refers to them, but does not define them. The Pan-Hispanic Dictionary of Legal Spanish (2020) defines general interest as those "functions that are constitutionally entrusted to the public authorities and that concern values and objectives that transcend the specific interests of citizens or groups". These values and objectives are usually reflected in the Constitutions of the States, but also in the general feeling of the people, and may vary over time. To facilitate their understanding, both the law on foundations and the law on associations give some examples. Thus, according to the former, the purposes of general interest are: "those of defense of human rights, victims of terrorism and violent acts, social assistance and social inclusion, civic, educational, cultural, scientific, sports, health, labour, institutional strengthening, cooperation for development, promotion of volunteering, promotion of social action, defense of the environment, promotion and care for people at risk of exclusion for physical, economic or cultural reasons, promotion of constitutional values and defense of democratic principles, promotion of tolerance, promotion of the social economy, development of the information society, scientific research, development or technological innovation and its transfer to the productive fabric as a driving force of productivity and business competitiveness" (art. 3).

[10] Organic Law 1/2002, of 22 March 2002, regulating the Right of Association.

In tax matters, there is a special regime for foundations and associations pursuing general interest purposes.[11] This regime is currently contained in Law 49/2002, of 23 December 2002, on the tax regime for non-profit entities and tax incentives for patronage. This law, in its preamble, highlights the degree of importance achieved in recent years by the so-called "third sector" and the need to recognise and reward private participation in activities of general interest, in its various legal forms. For the purposes of this law, these entities are foundations, associations declared to be of public utility, and their respective federations (art. 2), provided that they meet the following requirements: (1) That they pursue purposes of general interest; (2) That they allocate at least 70% of the income and profits obtained from economic activities, transactions of goods, etc., to the achievement of these purposes, excluding donations received as endowments; and (3) That the economic activity carried out is not unrelated to their statutory object or purpose (art. 3).

As can be seen, the third sector is associated with entities that pursue purposes of general interest and are not for profit.

But the first time the expression "third sector" was recognised in the text of a law was in 2006. On the one hand, reference was made to it in the Statute of Autonomy of Catalonia, and on the other, a definition of the third sector was offered in Law 39/2006, of 14 December, on the Promotion of Personal Autonomy and Care for Dependent Persons (known as the Dependency Law).

With Law 6/2006 of 19 July 2006, the Statute of Autonomy of Catalonia was reformed, and an article 45 was introduced that incorporates two new features of interest for our purposes. On the one hand, section 5 establishes that the Government of Catalonia must promote the actions of cooperatives and worker-owned companies and must stimulate social economy initiatives. On the other hand, section 7 adds that third sector associative entities must be consulted in the definition of public policies that affect them.

The Law on Care for Dependent Persons of 2006 recognised that third sector social action entities have been participating for years in the care of dependent persons and that they constitute a social network that prevents the risk of exclusion of the persons concerned. The Law provides a brief definition of the third sector (art. 2.8) and orders its promotion.[12] Specifically, it defines "third sector" as "organisations of a private nature arising from citizen or social initiative, under different modalities that respond to criteria of solidarity, with general interest purposes and are

[11] Associations pursuing purposes of particular interest also have certain tax advantages due to their non-profit nature in the Corporate Income Tax Law 27/2014 (Transitional Provision 34).

[12] It establishes as one of the principles of the law "the participation of the third sector in the services and benefits for the promotion of personal autonomy and attention to the situation of dependency" (art. 3 n); it orders the Autonomous Communities to establish the legal regime and the conditions of action of the subsidized private centres and that in their incorporation into the network, special consideration be given to the centres corresponding to the third sector (art. 16.2); that the public authorities should promote the collaboration of citizens in solidarity with dependent persons, through their participation in volunteer organisations and third sector entities (art. 16.4); and that the different public administrations should collaborate with the third sector (art. 36.3).

non-profit, which promote the recognition and exercise of social rights." The above definition, despite the title, does not define the entire third sector but only a part of it: the third sector of social action or third social sector, as it is also known.

We could therefore say that the third sector is made up of entities or organisations that pursue purposes of general interest and are non-profit; and what identifies the third sector of social action is that these entities are created by social initiative and their purpose is to promote the recognition and exercise of social rights.

From here, it should be noted that only the third social action sector has had legal recognition and regulation as such, either as social initiative entities or as entities of the third social sector. In 2015, the Third Social Action Sector Law was passed at the state level and, shortly thereafter, various Autonomous Communities passed their respective third social sector laws (Basque Country, Balearic Islands, Extremadura, Castilla-La Mancha, or Castile and León).

This does not mean that there are no other socially recognised areas of the third sector, such as the cultural, sports, environmental areas, etc., but that they have not been legally recognised or regulated.[13]

It should also be noted that, despite its name, the so-called Third Sector Platform, which we will discuss later because it represents third sector entities, only includes organisations in the social sphere.[14]

Finally, it should be added that the regulation of social economy entities and third sector entities is largely the responsibility of the Autonomous Regions, but they depend on different departments: in the first case, it is the responsibility of the department in charge of labour, and in the second, of the department in charge of social services. This distinction has an impact not only on different regulations, but also on different promotion policies, as we shall see below.

3 The Social Economy in Spain

As we saw earlier, the concept of social economy that began to be reflected in Spanish legislation was practically limited to cooperatives and worker-owned companies, whose regulation, control, and promotion corresponded to the labour department of the public administration. But this concept did not correspond to that used by academia, which conceived the social economy in a broader sense, similar to that used in the French Charter of the Social Economy in 1980, and later, the Charter of Principles of the Social Economy of 2002 (CEP-CMAF, now Social Economy Europe), and which encompassed cooperatives, associations, mutual societies and

[13] According to Chaves (2017, p. 25) in Spain there are 27,345 associations and 1644 foundations in the third social sector, while there are 124,380 associations and 2548 foundations, in the rest of the third sector.

[14] http://www.plataformatercersector.es/es/quienes-somos.

foundations.[15] The classification of the actors in the Spanish social economy drawn up by Professors Barea and Monzón in the early 1990s includes as social economy entities: cooperatives, labour and similar companies; savings banks, mutual and mutual benefit societies, associations, foundations, fishermen's guilds, mutual aid societies, the Red Cross, etc..[16]

3.1 Immediate Background of the Social Economy Law

In 2007, a Subcommittee on the Social Economy was set up in the Congress of Deputies to study the situation of the social economy in Spain. One of the conclusions of its work was to recommend, in 2009, the drafting of a social economy law. Other events of interest took place in the same year: the Parliament Resolution on the Social Economy (2008/2250/(INI)) was approved; the Spanish Confederation of Social Economy Enterprises (CEPES) submitted a report and a proposal for a framework law on the social economy to the Directorate General for the Social Economy; and the latter commissioned a committee of independent experts to prepare a report and a proposal for the text of a law to promote the social economy. It should be recalled that the 2009 European Parliament Resolution states that social economy enterprises are characterised by a form of entrepreneurship that differs from that of capital-based enterprises ("a different approach to business"); they are private enterprises, independent of public authorities, which provide responses to the needs and demands of their members and the general interest. Social economy enterprises—it continues—are defined by the characteristics and values they share, which are those included in the Social Economy Charter signed in 2002 by their representative organisations. The resolution identifies social economy enterprises with cooperatives, mutual societies, associations and foundations, as well as other enterprises and organisations that share the fundamental characteristics of the social economy. This resolution and the previous work conducted by the subgroup of deputies by CEPES and by the commission of experts, had an important influence on the drafting of the 2011 Social Economy Law, which was unanimously approved.

3.2 Law 5/2011, of 29 March 2011 on the Social Economy

The purpose of the Law is, as stated in its first article, "to establish a common legal framework for all the entities that make up the social economy, with full respect for the specific regulations applicable to each of them, as well as to determine the measures to promote them in consideration of their own purposes and principles".

[15] Cf. Monzón (1992, p. 15).

[16] Cf. Barea and Monzón (1994, p. 15), Barea and Monzón (1995, 2000).

It can be said that its main objective is to recognise and promote the social economy, but not to regulate the entities that make up the social economy. It is a law whose scope of application, without prejudice to the competences that may correspond to the Autonomous Regions, extends to all social economy entities operating within the Spanish State (art. 3).

The Law is structured in 13 articles that regulate the concept of social economy (art. 2); its guiding principles (art. 4); the entities that comprise it (art. 5 and 6); its organisation and representation (art. 7); its promotion and dissemination (art. 8) and the Council for the Promotion of the Social Economy (art. 13).

3.3 The Concept of Social Economy and Its Guiding Principles

The Law calls the social economy the set of economic and business activities conducted in the private sphere by those entities that, in accordance with the principles set out in Article 4, pursue either the collective interest of their members or the general economic or social interest, or both.

As we can see, for the law, the social economy is the economic and business activity conducted in the private sphere by certain entities. These are private law entities that conduct business activities and that, in addition, pursue the collective (or common) interest of their members or a general interest, or both, and are governed in their operation by the following principles:

(a) Primacy of the people and the social purpose over capital, which takes the form of autonomous and transparent, democratic, and participatory management, which leads to prioritising decision-making more in terms of the people and their contributions of work and services rendered to the entity or in terms of the social purpose, than in relation to their contributions to the capital stock.
(b) Application of the results obtained from the economic activity is mainly according to the work contributed and service or activity performed by the members or by its members and, if applicable, to the social purpose of the entity.
(c) Promotion of internal solidarity and solidarity with society that favours the commitment to local development, equal opportunities between men and women, social cohesion, the integration of people at risk of social exclusion, the generation of stable and quality employment, the reconciliation of personal, family and work life and sustainability.
(d) Independence from public authorities.

3.4 Social Economy Entities

Two criteria are used to determine which entities make up the social economy:

(a) On the one hand, a series of entities are listed which, due to their legal form or administrative qualification, form part of the social economy.
(b) On the other hand, it is stated that those entities that conduct economic and business activities, whose operating rules comply with the guiding principles listed in the law, and which are included in the catalogue of entities established in Article 6 of the Law, may also form part of the social economy.

The catalogue referred to in the Law has not yet been created, so that at present only those mentioned in Article 5 of the Law are considered social economy entities, i.e.: cooperatives, mutual societies, foundations and associations carrying out economic activities, labour companies, insertion companies, special employment centres, fishermen's guilds, agricultural processing companies and the special entities created by specific rules that are governed by the principles set forth in the preceding article. In any case, as the law goes on to say, the social economy entities will be regulated by their specific substantive rules.

The aforementioned social economy entities, for ease of analysis, could be grouped into the following categories:

(a) Entities pursuing general interests: Associations, Foundations and Special Entities.
(b) Entities pursuing the common interest of their members: Associations, Mutual Societies, Cooperatives, and related entities.
(c) Social Enterprises: Insertion Enterprises and Special Employment Centres.

3.4.1 Entities Pursuing General Interest Purposes

The law considers both associations and foundations to be social economy entities, but not all of them, rather only those that conduct economic activities. Let us recall that, by definition, social economy entities conduct economic and entrepreneurial activities (art. 2).

Both associations and foundations may conduct economic activities, either for their support or for the fulfilment of their social purposes, but they must comply with the limitations and conditions established by law, as we shall see below.

3.4.1.1 Associations

The right of association is recognised in Article 22 of the Constitution. This article also states that associations must be registered for the sole purpose of publicity, and that they may only be dissolved or suspended from their activities by virtue of a reasoned judicial decision. As the right of association is a constitutional right, the competence to regulate it lies with the State (art. 149.1.1 CE).

Organic Law 1/2002 of 22 March 2002 develops the right of association and establishes the legal regime applicable to state-level associations. This Law establishes, in its first final provision, which rules are of state competence and therefore must be respected throughout the State, which does not prevent the Autonomous Regions from having a certain margin to regulate associations and, of course, to regulate their registration, control and promotion.[17]

There are associations, such as sports associations or consumer and user associations, which are not governed by this law but by Law 10/1990 of 15 October 1990, on Sports and Royal Legislative Decree 1/2007 of 16 November 2007, on the Consolidated Text of the General Law for the Defense of Consumers and Users, respectively.

As for the registration of associations, it is merely declaratory, the legal personality is acquired from the very moment of its constitution, regardless of its subsequent registration (art. 10.1).

The law on associations regulates how they should be constituted, their operation, the rights and duties of their members, the registers of associations, the measures of promotion, jurisdictional guarantees, and the sectorial councils of associations, among other things.

As we have seen above, associations may pursue purposes of general interest or of particular interest, but they may not pursue purposes of profit, or of distribution among their associates (and persons related to them) of the "profits obtained" in the exercise of their economic activities, including the provision of services; these must be used exclusively for the fulfilment of the purposes of the association (art. 13), which will be expressly determined in its bylaws (art. 7).

We have also seen that only associations with general interest purposes can enjoy certain tax advantages and public aid, especially if they obtain the qualification as a public utility association. The tax regime for non-profit entities, to which we referred earlier, is only applicable to foundations and public utility associations.

The Ministry of the Interior's 2020 Statistical Yearbook compiles a list of the state-level associations and public utility associations registered both in the National Register and in the regional registers of associations (except for Catalonia, the Basque Country and Galicia).

Most of them correspond to Group I: Ideological, cultural, educational, and communication (22,923), followed by Groups VIII: Economic, technological, professional, and interests (10,883); VII: Solidarity (6410); IV: Environment and health (5897) and IX: Sports and recreational (5809). The Autonomous Communities where the registered offices of these associations are located are mainly the Community of Madrid (25,507); Andalusia (8191); Community of Valencia (6452); Catalonia (5052); Castile and León (3248) and Castilla-La Mancha (2099).

As for associations declared to be of public utility, there are 2455, of which 715 are in the National Register, 1692 in the regional registers (with the exceptions mentioned above) and 48 in other special registers (sports, consumer, religious, etc.). Of these, most are listed in Group VII: Solidarity (224), followed by Group V:

[17] The communities of Andalusia (Law 4/2006, of June 23), the Canary Islands (Law 4/2003, of 28 February), Catalonia (Law 7/1997, of 18 June), Valencia (Law 14/2008, of 18 November) and the Basque Country (Law 7/2007, of 22 June) have passed laws on associations.

Disability and Dependencies (155), I: Ideological, cultural, educational, and communication (121), IV: Environment and health (61) and III: Childhood, youth, elderly, family, and welfare (52). By Autonomous Communities, in the Community of Madrid there are 548, followed by Andalusia (408), Valencia (279); Catalonia (271) and Castile and León (205).

3.4.1.2 Foundations

Foundations in Spain, as we saw earlier, are only conceived as an instrument for the realisation of general interest purposes.

Foundations are governed by Law 50/2002, of 26 December 2002, on Foundations. The purpose of this law is twofold: on the one hand, to develop the rights of foundations, recognised in art. 34 of the Constitution, and on the other, to regulate foundations under state jurisdiction (art. 1). While respecting the basic rules, the Autonomous Regions may draw up their own laws on foundations.[18]

The law defines foundations as non-profit organisations which, by the will of their creators, have their assets permanently assigned to the realisation of general interest purposes (art. 2). Foundations must pursue purposes of general interest, purposes that benefit generic collectivities of persons, including the collectives of workers of one or more companies and their families (art. 3).

Unlike associations, foundations acquire their legal personality upon registration of their articles of incorporation in the corresponding Register of Foundations (art. 4).

The acts relating to foundations whose activity goes beyond the scope of an Autonomous Community will be registered in the Register of Foundations under the jurisdiction of the State, and those foundations whose activities are mainly conducted within the scope of an Autonomous Community will be registered in the registers of the Autonomous Communities (art. 36).

Regarding the implementation of foundations in Spain, in 2020 the Spanish Association of Foundations published the report "The foundational sector in Spain: fundamental attributes (2008-2019)". According to this report, in 2019 there were 14,729 active registered foundations, of which 8866 have economic activity and 5499 generate employment. Of the total number of foundations, 26.60% are state-wide, 38.67% are autonomous; 16.78% are local, and 11.75% are international. By Autonomous Communities, the Community of Madrid has 2219, followed by Catalonia (2013), Andalusia (1072), the Community of Valencia (665), and the Basque Country (489). If we look at the activity conducted by the

[18] The following communities have regulated foundations: Andalusia (Law 10/2005, of 31 May), Canary Islands (Law 2/1998, of 6 April), Cantabria (Law 6/2020, of 15 July), Castile and León (Law 13/2002, of 15 July), Catalonia (Law 5/2001, of 2 May), Community of Madrid (Law 1/1998, of 2 March), Community of Valencia (Law 8/1998, of 9 December), Basque Country (Law 12/1994, of 17 June), Galicia (Law 12/2006, of 1 December), La Rioja (Law 1/2007, of 12 February), Navarra (Law 13/2021, of 30 June), Spain (Law 1/2007, of 12 February).

foundations, 38.30% are for culture-recreation; 21.68% for education-research; 10.32% for the environment; 9.04% for social services; 7.29% for development-housing; 5.44% for health; 4.41% for international activities; 2.47% for business activities; and the remainder for religion (0.96%) and counselling (0.09%). Other interesting data refer to the status of the founding legal entities: 32.37% are public legal entities (General State Administration: 15.67%; Autonomous Communities: 42.27%; Local Entities: 31.01%) and 67.63% are private legal entities (Associations: 37%; Commercial Companies: 22.60%; Foundations: 15.65%; Savings Banks: 8.11%, and Church and religious entities: 7.29%).

3.4.1.3 Special Entities

Article 5 of the Law includes, among the social economy entities, the special entities created by specific regulations governed by the guiding principles of the social economy set out in Article 4. These entities include the Spanish National Organisation for the Blind (ONCE), a public law corporation of a social nature, regulated by Royal Decree 358/1991, of 15 March; or the Spanish Red Cross, regulated by Royal Decree 415/ of 1 March 1996, establishing the rules for the organisation of the Spanish Red Cross.

3.4.2 Entities Pursuing the Common Interest of Their Members

This category includes those entities that conduct an economic activity in the direct interest of their members. Within this category we can include associations, mutual societies, cooperatives, and other similar entities.

3.4.2.1 Associations Pursuing the Interest of Their Members

Associations, as we saw earlier, may be non-profit and may pursue general or particular interests, or both. It is not always easy to delimit the purposes of an association as strictly of general interest or of particular interest.

But in practice it is not difficult to find associations of consumers who develop common purchasing activities; craftsmen who associate to promote their activities and products; users of services who associate to obtain better prices or services. In their organisation and operation, these associations usually apply rules very similar to those of cooperatives (of consumers, craftsmen, users, etc.).

It is not surprising, therefore, that these associations, because of their mutualist aims, are integrated into the social economy, together with cooperatives and mutual societies. Moreover, they share many characteristics with the latter: no profit motive, open doors, democratic management, member participation in economic activity, etc.

3.4.2.2 Mutuals

Mutual insurance companies and mutual benefit societies are legal entities that conduct insurance and social welfare activities in the interest of their members (mutual members). The State has the power to issue basic insurance regulations. The basic regulation on insurance entities is contained in Law 20/2015 of 14 July on the regulation, supervision and solvency of insurance and reinsurance entities. Mutual benefit societies are also governed by RD. 1430/2002, of 27 December, which approves the Regulations on Mutual Benefit Societies. Some Autonomous Regions have assumed exclusive jurisdiction over mutual benefit societies and have passed laws to regulate them[19] (Catalonia, Valencia, Madrid, and the Basque Country).

Mutual insurance companies are defined in the Law as "not-for-profit commercial companies" whose purpose is to cover their members, whether individuals or legal entities, against insured risks by means of a fixed premium payable at the beginning of the risk. In the event of dissolution of the mutual and in the event of transformation, merger, and spin-off in which the entity resulting from the transformation or merger, or the beneficiary of the spin-off is a corporation, as well as in the event of global assignment of assets and liabilities, the current members and those who have been members in the last 5 years, or previously if the bylaws so provide, will receive at least half the value of the assets of the mutual (art. 41 LOSSEAR).

Mutual benefit societies are insurance entities that provide voluntary insurance as a complement to the compulsory social security system, through contributions from the mutual members or other entities or persons providing protection. In these entities, the condition of member-policyholder is inseparable from that of policyholder or insured, provided that the latter is the final payer of the premium. All mutual members have equal rights and obligations. Both mutuals are incorporated after their registration in the Commercial Register, at which time they acquire legal personality.

If we look at the principles that characterize social economy entities, all of them are present in both mutuals.

As regards the number of existing insurance entities, the 2020 report on the Insurance and Pension Funds sector published by the Directorate General of Insurance and Pension Funds of the Spanish Ministry of Economic Affairs and Digital Transition, showed that compared with 126 public limited liability companies, there are 29 mutual insurance companies and 44 mutual benefit societies. Mutual benefit societies mainly provide social welfare for employees and professionals.

[19] Catalonia (Law 9/2000, of 30 June), Community of Madrid (Law 10/2003, of 13 June), Community of Valencia (Law 7/2000, of 29 May), or the Basque Country (Law 5/2012, of 23 February).

3.4.2.3 Cooperatives

A cooperative is an entity constituted by persons who associate, on a free membership and voluntary deregistration basis, to conduct business activities aimed at satisfying their economic and social needs and aspirations, with a democratic structure and operation, in accordance with the principles formulated by the International Cooperative Alliance. These principles are: Voluntary and open membership; Democratic management by members; Economic participation of members; Autonomy and independence; Education, training, and information; Cooperation among cooperatives, and Interest in the community.

The Spanish Constitution of 1978 has had a major impact on the legislative development of cooperatives. On the one hand, Article 129 EC expressly refers to cooperatives and requires their promotion by means of appropriate legislation: "The public authorities shall promote the various forms of participation in business and shall encourage cooperative societies by means of appropriate legislation. They shall also establish the means to facilitate the access of workers to the ownership of the means of production". On the other hand, from the distribution of competences between the State and the Autonomous Regions, the regulation of cooperatives was assumed as an exclusive competence by all the Autonomous Regions. The State Law on Cooperatives (Law 27/1999, of 16 July 1999) applies to cooperative societies that conduct their economic activity with their members (cooperativized activity) in the territory of several Autonomous Regions, except when the main activity is conducted in one of them.

In addition to having various cooperative laws in the ACs,[20] there is also a specific regulation for European cooperatives domiciled in Spain (Council Regulation EC 1435/2003, of 22 July 2003 and Law 3/2011, of 4 March), and other regulations applicable to certain classes of cooperatives: credit (Law 13/89, of 26 May and RD. 84/93, of 22 January); insurance (Law 20/2015, 14 July LOSSEAR); or transport (Law 9/2013 LOTT), among others. Any lawful economic activity may be organised and developed through cooperative societies; these may also conduct cooperativized activities and services with non-member third parties when provided for in the bylaws, under the conditions and with the limitations established by law. Among others, the cooperative must distinguish the results obtained from the activity conducted in the interest of its members from the activity conducted in its own interest with third parties; and the former must always prevail.

[20] This is the case of: Andalusia (Law 14/2011, of 23 December), Aragon (Legislative Decree 2/2014, of 29 August); Asturias (Law 4/2010, of 29 June); Balearic Islands (Law 1/2003, of 20 March); Cantabria (Law 6/2013, of 6 November); Castilla-La Mancha (Law 11/2010, of 4 November); Castile and León (Law 4/2002, of 11 April); Catalonia (Law 12/2015, of 19 July); Community of Madrid (Law 4/1999, of 30 March); Community of Valencia (Law 2/2015, of 15 May); Basque Country (Law 11/2019, of 20 December); Extremadura (Law 9/2018, of 30 October); Galicia (Law 5/1998, of 18 December); La Rioja (Law 4/2001, of 2 July); Navarra (Law 14/2006, of 11 December); and Murcia (Law 8/2006, of 16 November).

The cooperative society is constituted by means of a Public deed and acquires legal personality when it is registered in the Register of Cooperatives.

In cooperatives, depending on the cooperative activity, both natural and legal persons, public or private, and communities of property may be members.

The members constitute or join the cooperative to satisfy a common need, through the development of a business activity whose main objective is to satisfy that need (employment, credit, housing, improvement of industrial or commercial exploitation, etc.). As a consequence, the member has the right and obligation to participate in such activity and to assume its consequences.

The cooperative is a democratically managed entity because all its members have the same right to vote, and all have the right to be elector and to be eligible for social positions.

Finally, it should be noted that the cooperative has a variable capital and non-distributable reserves, which facilitate open membership in the cooperative without jeopardising its equity stability. In turn, cooperatives must allocate part of their profits to the training and education of their members and workers in cooperative principles and values, to the dissemination of cooperativism, and to the promotion of their environment, among other purposes.

As for the number of cooperatives existing in Spain, according to the Social Economy Database of the Ministry of Labour and Social Economy as of June 30 2020, there are 18,035 cooperatives registered with the Social Security, of which 11,673 are in the General Social Security Regime and 6362 in the Self-Employed Regime. Of these entities, most are in Andalusia (3758); Catalonia (3063); Valencia (2180); the Basque Country (1618), and Murcia (1468). By classes of cooperatives there is no data for 2020, but there is data for 2018. In this year, of the cooperatives registered in the General SS Regime, the most numerous were worker cooperatives (6805); followed by agricultural cooperatives (3190), land exploitation cooperatives (479); professional services cooperatives (377); teaching cooperatives (291), and consumer cooperatives (276).

3.4.2.4 Related Entities

Some have a long tradition, such as the fishermen's guilds, and others are more recent, such as the labour companies, which have been incorporated into the social economy because they share many characteristics with the former: the members participate in the economic activity of the entity as workers or users of its services; they tend to have open doors and democratic management, and their main aim is not profit, but rather to offer the best service to their members, or the best working conditions.

Agricultural Processing Societies

Agricultural processing companies are civil companies; their regulation is the responsibility of the State, and they are governed by Royal Decree 1776/1981, of

3 August 1981. The purpose of these companies is the production, processing, and commercialisation of agricultural, livestock or forestry products, the improvement of the rural environment, the promotion and development of agriculture, and the provision of common services that serve that purpose. The partners are obliged to participate in the economic activity of the company; therefore, only persons holding the status of owner of an agricultural holding or agricultural worker, and legal entities pursuing agricultural purposes, may be partners in these companies.

The main characteristics of this type of company are that its members are liable for the company's debts on a subsidiary and unlimited basis, unless the articles of association limit such liability; that it can be set up as a private (not formal) document; and that it is registered in an administrative register of the department responsible for agricultural matters.

The operation of these companies tends to be democratic, each partner having one vote in the corporate bodies; but if the bylaws so provide, the vote may be proportional to the capital when the agreement to be adopted involves new economic obligations for the partners. This participation is also limited, since no partner may contribute more than one-third of the capital and, if there are partners who are legal entities, the total of their contributions to the capital may in no case reach 50%.

Agricultural processing companies are very similar in their purposes and characteristics to agricultural cooperatives.

According to data provided by the Ministry of Agriculture, Fisheries, and Food of the Government of Spain,[21] as of 31 December 2020, there were 12,221 agricultural processing companies in Spain, comprising 304,839 members, the majority of which are in the province of Valencia (979), followed by Coruña (542); Navarra (521), and Murcia (509).

Worker-Owned Companies Sociedades Laborales

Worker-owned companies are public limited companies and limited liability companies, in which certain characteristics concur: (a) the majority of their capital is owned by all the worker-members who provide personally and directly services for an indefinite period; (b) non-member workers cannot exceed a certain percentage; (c) the maximum capital that a partner can own is limited; (d) there are two types of shares depending on whether or not they are owned by workers; (e) workers have a preferential right of acquisition in the event of transfer of the shares ; and (f) they must set up a special reserve fund.

As they are commercial companies, their regulation is the exclusive competence of the State, but the Autonomous Regions have the competences of qualification and supervision. They are governed by Law 44/2015, of 14 October, and the Capital Companies Law 1/2010 applies on a supplementary basis.

[21] https://www.mapa.gob.es/es/alimentacion/temas/integracion-asociativa/informeanualsatano2020_tcm30-380032.pdf.

Worker-owned companies, as far as they make possible the participation of workers in the ownership of the means of production, are encouraged, as required by art. 129.2 of the Constitution, through a series of tax benefits and public policies.

Worker-owned companies are very similar in their aims and characteristics to worker cooperatives.

As regards the number of labour companies, according to the Social Economy Database of the Ministry of Labour and Social Economy as of June 30, 2020, there are 7801 labour companies registered with the Social Security,[22] of which 7024 are limited liability companies, and 777 are public limited companies. Of these, the majority are in Andalusia (1702), followed by the Community of Madrid (890), Castilla-La Mancha (691); Catalonia (628); the Community of Valencia (587), and the Basque Country (509). These types of entities are predominantly present in the service sector (64.9%), industry (19.2%), and construction (14.1%).

Fishermen's Guilds

The fishermen's guilds are public law corporations, non-profit, and representative of the economic interests of their members. They are governed by Law 3/2001, of 26 March 2001, on State Maritime Fishing, without prejudice to the competences assumed by some Autonomous Communities.[23]

The fishermen's guilds are subject to public law as regards their function of representation, advice and defense of the fishing sector, and consultation and collaboration bodies of the competent public administrations in fishing matters; and to private law as they develop economic activities, with the aim of improving the efficiency and profitability in the fishing activity of their members and of the community.

The guilds are made up of vessel owners and workers who conduct fishing activities. Membership is acquired by application for admission, and membership is terminated by resignation or cessation of professional activity. They are democratically managed.

The fishermen's guilds are very close in their aims and characteristics to the sea cooperatives.

According to data published by CEPES on its website[24] relating to 2019, there are 133 fishermen's guilds in Spain, most of which are in Galicia (48), followed by Catalonia and the Valencian Community (19 each) and Asturias and the Balearic Islands (16 each).

[22] https://www.mites.gob.es/ficheros/ministerio/sec_trabajo/autonomos/economia-soc/EconomiaSocial/estadisticas/SociedadesAltaSSocial/2020/2TRIMESTRE/Economia-Social-2do-trim-2020.pdf.

[23] Communities such as Andalusia (Decree 86/2004, of March 2); Catalonia (Law 22/2002, of 12 July), or Galicia (Law 9/1993, of 8 July) have regulated fishermen's guilds.

[24] https://www.cepes.es/social/estadisticas&t=cofradias.

3.4.3 Social Enterprises

The term "social enterprise" is used by Spanish authors with different meanings, and in no case has it been legally recognised. However, there is agreement in identifying as such those companies that are set up to create jobs for people with disabilities, and to favour the social insertion through work of people who are the most difficult to employ. The Report for the preparation of the law for the promotion of the social economy drafted by the group of experts included "social enterprises" as social economy entities, which would include insertion companies, special employment centres, and other entities with the same or similar purposes that could be integrated in the future.[25] Finally, it was not accepted to include the expression "social enterprise" in the law because it was not legally recognised at that time, nor is it currently; but the incorporation of insertion enterprises and special employment centres as social economy entities was accepted.

3.4.3.1 Social-Labour Insertion Companies

Insertion companies are commercial companies or cooperatives whose objective is to develop a business activity accompanied by social insertion actions, to enable the social and labour inclusion of excluded persons, for their subsequent placement in conventional companies or in self-employment projects.

Social insertion companies must also meet a series of requirements to obtain this qualification: be promoted and majority-owned by non-profit entities whose corporate purpose contemplates the social insertion of particularly disadvantaged persons; maintain a percentage of workers in the process of insertion of at least 30% during the first 3 years of activity, and of at least 50% of the total workforce thereafter; apply 80% of the profits to the improvement or expansion of their productive and insertion structures; and have the necessary means to comply with the commitments arising from the social-labour insertion pathways.

These companies produce goods and services for the market under the same conditions as other operators, but they do so with a particular social purpose: the incorporation into the normalized labour market of people in a situation of social disadvantage or exclusion.

The regulation of insertion companies is the responsibility of the State as regards labour matters and the responsibility of the Autonomous Communities as regards social assistance. All of them are subject to Law 44/2007, of 13 December 2007, for the Regulation of the Regime of Insertion Companies, and some are also subject to their respective Autonomous Community laws.[26]

---

[25] Monzón et al. (2010, pp. 79–81, 171).

[26] Insertion companies have been regulated by Andalusia (Decree 85/2003, of 1 April); Aragon (Decree 37/2006, of 7 February); Balearic Islands (Decree 60/2003, of 13 June); Canary Islands (Decree 137/2009, of 20 October); Catalonia (Law 27/2002, of 20 December); Castilla-La Mancha

They are instrumental entities, halfway between for-profit and non-profit entities, since, although they must be promoted and majority-owned by non-profit entities, if the insertion company has the legal form of a capital company, even if it can only partially distribute profits (20%), the reinvested profits will contribute to revaluing the value of the shares and participations of its partners.

3.4.3.2 Special Employment Centres

Special employment centres (CEE) are regulated by Royal Legislative Decree 1/2013 and are defined as companies integrated into the market, which aim to create paid employment for people with disabilities, and the provision of personal and social adjustment services that in each case are required, in order to facilitate their labour integration into the ordinary labour market.

To obtain the qualification as a special employment centre, the company must have a staff made up of at least 70% disabled workers, it must also have the necessary technical and support personnel required, and it must prove its business viability by means of the corresponding economic study.

Special employment centres can be public or private, profit, or non-profit. Their constitution can be promoted by public administrations directly or in collaboration with other bodies, or by any natural or legal person with the capacity to be an entrepreneur. As a result of this variety of purposes and interests, only the special employment centres of social initiative (CEEIS) are deemed to be included in the social economy.

The CEEIS have been defined in Law 9/2017, of 8 November, as those that are promoted and participated in more than 50 percent, directly or indirectly, by one or more entities, whether public or private, that are non-profit or that have their social character recognised in their statutes, whether they are associations, foundations, public law corporations, social initiative cooperatives or other entities of the social economy, as well as those whose ownership corresponds to commercial companies in which the majority of their capital stock is owned by any of the aforementioned entities, and provided that in all cases in their bylaws or social agreement they are obliged to reinvest all of their profits for the creation of employment opportunities for people with disabilities and the continuous improvement of their competitiveness and their social economy activity, having in any case the power to choose to reinvest them in the special employment centres itself or in other special employment centres of social initiative.

(Law 5/1995, of 23 March); Castile and Leon (Decree 34/2007, of 12 April); Community of Madrid (Decree 32/2003, of 12 March); Community of Valencia (Law 1/2007, of 5 February); Galicia (Law 9/1991, of 9 October); Murcia (Decree 109/2016, of 5 October); La Rioja (Law 7/2003, of 26 March); Navarra (Decree 130/1999, of 26 April), and Basque Country (Decree 182/2008, of 11 November).

3.5 Social Economy Representative Entities

Article 7 of the Social Economy Law regulates the organisation and representation of social economy entities, for the purpose of determining who may be considered intersectoral representative organisations at the state level and be able to participate in the institutional participation bodies of the General State Administration. In order to be a state-level intersectoral confederation, it is necessary to represent a high percentage of entities in most of the types of entities that form part of the social economy (art. 7), conditions that were only met by the Spanish Social Economy Business Confederation (CEPES). CEPES was incorporated in 1992. It currently brings together 43,192 companies associated with 29 organisations, representing cooperatives, labour companies, mutual societies, insertion companies, special employment centres, fishermen's guilds, associations in the disability sector, and solidarity economy entities.[27]

As representatives of the social economy, they participate in institutions such as the Spanish Economic[28] and Social Council 28 and the Council for the Promotion of the Social Economy. The former is an advisory body to the Government on socioeconomic and labour matters. The latter is an advisory and consultative body for activities related to the social economy. The Council for the Promotion of the Social Economy, together with its composition and functions, are regulated in art. 13 of the Law and in Royal Decree 219/2001, of 2 March.

The social economy entities in the Autonomous Communities have also organised themselves into structures similar to CEPES, such as CEPES-Andalusia, CEPES-Aragon and CEPES-Navarre.

3.6 Promotion of the Social Economy

Finally, Art. 8 of the Law recognises the promotion, encouragement and development of social economy entities and their representative organisations as a task of general interest, and orders the public authorities, within the scope of their respective competencies, to include, amongst other things, in the objectives of their policies for the promotion of the social economy, measures designed to remove obstacles to the start-up and development of economic activities by social economy entities; promote the principles and values of the social economy; promote training and professional retraining in the field of social economy entities and introduce references to the social economy in the curricula of the different educational stages; create an environment that favours the development of economic and social initiatives within the framework of the social economy; or encourage the development of the social economy in areas such as rural development, dependency, and social integration.

[27] https://www.cepes.es/principal/socios_miembros/4.

[28] http://www.ces.es/composicion.

Later, Law 31/2015 amended the Social Economy Law to incorporate promotion measures. However, these are not new measures, but rather existing measures that are now rearranged in the same legal text. These measures are currently found in articles 5.4, 9, 10, 11, and 12 of the Law. Article 5.4 qualifies insertion companies and special employment centres as entities providing Services of General Economic Interest; Article 9 regulates the incentives for the incorporation of workers as members of social economy entities (cooperatives and labour companies); Article 10 contemplates the capitalisation of workers'capital. Article 10 provides for the capitalisation of the unemployment benefit if the beneficiary becomes a worker-member of cooperatives and worker-owned companies; Art. 11 regulates the rebates on Social Security contributions for worker-members of cooperatives, and Art. 12 the single payment of the benefit for termination of activity, if the beneficiary proves that they are going to carry out a professional activity as a worker-member of a cooperative or worker-owned company. As can be seen, except for the first measure, the others are aimed at cooperatives and worker-owned companies.

In 2017, by agreement of the Council of Ministers of 29 December, the Spanish Social Economy Strategy 2017–2020 was approved, comprising 63 measures structured in 11 main areas aimed at favouring the creation and consolidation of Social Economy companies. The main areas refer to support for employment and entrepreneurship in the social economy: the promotion of the consolidation of these companies and their growth; the analysis of the legal framework and the elimination of barriers that prevent or limit their development; the promotion of the digital economy; the institutional participation of the social economy and its visualisation, as well as social responsibility, gender equality, social inclusion, and its participation in the design and implementation of the Agenda of the Sustainable Development Goals.

In addition to the above, there are several existing aids for insertion companies and special employment centres, both for hiring people for their insertion through work in this type of company, as well as for hiring support personnel, technical assistance, and final hiring by ordinary companies.

The legislation on public procurement recognises the possibility of reserving public contracts in favour of special employment centres and lately also of insertion companies. The recent Public Sector Contracts Law 9/2017, of 8 November, has limited to CEEIS the reservation of contracts that the previous legislation extended to all special employment centres. The new regulation was appealed by the National Confederation of CEE (CONACEE), and during its deliberations, the High Court of Justice of the Basque Country raised a preliminary question to the CJEU which was resolved in a judgment of 6 October 2021. The CJEU admitted the compatibility of the limitation established in the Spanish law with EU law but made it conditional on the respect of the principles of equal treatment and proportionality, which must be verified by the national judge. Subsequent to this judgment, the Court of Justice of Catalonia, in a judgment dated 16 February 2022, has validated the reservation of public tenders only for the CEEIS.

3.7 The Regulation of the Social Economy in the Spanish Autonomous Communities

Following the approval of the previous state law on social economy, other law proposals have been drafted in the ACs. The only one that has been approved for the time being is Law 6/2016, of 4 May, on the social economy of Galicia, but it is quite possible that throughout this year the social economy laws of Aragon and the Canary Islands, and the law on social and solidarity economy of Catalonia, will already see the light of day, as planned.

As regards the former, it can be said that it follows the wording of the state law fairly closely, but adopts some particular aspects, including the following:

(a) The Galician law applies to social economy entities whose domicile is in Galicia and which conduct their business and economic activity mainly in Galicia (art. 4).
(b) To the guiding principles of the social economy previously mentioned, it adds two more: "Commitment to the territory, facing depopulation and aging in the Galician countryside, injecting stability and future", and "Strengthening institutional and economic democracy" (art. 5 e and f).
(c) Regarding the social economy entities, it adds "the communities and commonwealths of neighbouring forests in common hand" (art. 6 i). The neighbouring common lands are indivisible, inalienable, imprescriptible, and unseizable assets, which will not be subject to any land tax, nor to any business quota of the Agrarian Social Security, and whose ownership corresponds, without assignment of quotas, to the neighbours who are members at any given time of the community group in question.[29]
(d) The advisory and consultative body for activities related to the social economy will be the Galician Social Economy Council, whose composition, functions and operation are regulated by law.
(e) The Eusumo Network is entrusted with the promotion of cooperativism and the social economy in Galicia.[30]

4 The Third Sector in Spain

As indicated above, there is no scientific or political consensus in Spain regarding the meaning of the term 'third sector'. Three visions of the third sector can be identified.

The first vision has identified the scope of the third sector with the social economy, in the sense of encompassing the set of entities "halfway between the

[29] Law 55/1980, of 11 November 1980, on neighbouring forests in common hand.

[30] http://www.eusumo.gal/.

State and for-profit companies" (Defourny and Monzón 1992).[31] The second vision, more restricted but more consolidated, especially socially and legally, is the one that identifies the third sector with non-profit organisations of civil society active in the care of vulnerable groups and social services. This vision identifies the third sector with the Third Social Sector. Finally, a third vision conceives third sector entities in multiple fields of activity, not only in the care of vulnerable social groups and social services, but also in areas such as culture, sports, the environment, or research and science, among others. This third vision of the third sector has been progressively consolidated since the last decade, having extended its social, media, political and scientific use,[32] with new terms such as Third Cultural Sector, Third Sports Sector, and Third Environmental Sector.[33]

This third perspective of the third sector is in line with the non-profit and voluntary organisations approach found in literature, especially American, whose main exponent is Lester Salamon,[34] who proposed a sectoral classification of third sector entities, the ICNPO—International Classification of Non-Profit Organisations[35]—from which the different 'third sectors'are discernible, not only the social action sector.

Once this contextualisation has been done, given that the regulation of the third sector in Spain has been limited to the social action sector, the legal analysis that we are going to conduct is that of the Third Social Sector in Spain.

4.1 Immediate Antecedents of the Third Sector Law

As we saw at the beginning, the expression third sector has appeared in legal texts in Spain from 2002 onwards, first in the preamble of the law on the tax regime for non-profit entities; in 2006, the third sector (or rather the third social sector) is

[31] This view is also found in Monzón et al. (2010) and in García-Delgado (2004).

[32] Cabra de Luna (1998); Chaves-Ávila and Zimmer (2017); Chaves Ávila and Monzón Campos (2020).

[33] The term third environmental sector is used in the field of ecology and environmental protection; there is an Observatory of the third environmental sector (http://afundacionesnaturaleza.org/recurso/), a Catalan Third Environmental Sector Bulletin; and some media, politicians, and administrations, also use the term (see the Ministry's Strategic Plan of Subsidies for the Ecological Transition and the Demographic Challenge (2019–2021). This sector is made up of non-profit legal entities that have among their purposes the protection of the environment, in general or in some of its elements in particular. The term third cultural sector is also used by the media; by the Ministry of Culture; the Basque Observatory of Culture, or the Government of Catalonia, which prepares statistics on the third cultural sector in Catalonia, which includes all associations that develop cultural and non-profit activities, and which are not part of the public sector. Finally, the term third sports sector is also used by the press and by public administrations when it comes to announcing aid for sport.

[34] Salamon and Anheier (1992a); Salamon et al. (2003).

[35] Salamon and Anheier (1992b).

defined in the Dependency Law, and finally, in 2015, the Third Sector of Social Action is regulated for the first time.

The Spanish Constitution of 1978 assigned competence in social assistance (art. 148.20) to the ACs. Since 1982, all the Autonomous Communities have regulated by law the social services and the collaboration of the social initiative in their provision. In determining what is known as social initiative entities, most of the laws coincide in indicating: foundations, associations, volunteer organisations, social initiative cooperatives or cooperatives classified as non-profit entities, and other non-profit entities that conduct social services activities as set out in their corporate purpose.[36]

The most immediate antecedents of the first law of the third sector are found in the creation, in 2012, of the Third Sector Platform, precisely when the Social Economy Law, passed in 2011, began to be developed.

The Third Sector Platform aims at, according to its statutes, the articulation of the most representative platforms and organisations of the Third Sector, in order to coordinate their activities and act with internal cohesion, common strategy, and real capacity for interlocution, influence, and co-responsibility.

To this end, seven organisations representing the social sector joined forces: the Platform for Volunteerism (PVE), the European Network to Combat Poverty and Social Exclusion in Spain (EAPN-ES), the Platform of Social Action NGOs (POAS), the Spanish Committee of Representatives of People with Disabilities (CERMI), the Spanish Red Cross, Caritas, and the National Organisation of the Blind (ONCE).[37]

The Third Sector Platform set out to promote the Third Sector Social Action Law and worked together with the Government of Spain in its preparation, as it acknowledges in its 2014 and 2015 Reports.

The statewide Third Sector Platform has been succeeded by various territorial platforms and later by a Territorial Coordination Committee for the debate and exchange of shared interests and good practices.

4.2 *Regulation of the Third Sector of Social Action*

The regulation of the Third Sector of Social Action at the state level is contemplated in Law 43/2015, of 9 October. This law is protected by the exclusive competence of the State to regulate the basic conditions that guarantee the equality of all Spaniards in the exercise of their rights and the fulfilment of their constitutional duties (second final provision). This has not prevented the Autonomous Regions, under other

[36] See, among others, the social services laws of the Community of Madrid (Law 11/2003, March 27); Catalonia (Law 12/2007, 11 October); Aragon (Law 5/2009, 30 June); Castile and Leon (Law 16/2010, 20 December); Andalusia (Law 9/2016, 27 December); Valencian Community (Law 3/2019, 18 February), or the Canary Islands (Law 16/2019, 2 May).

[37] http://www.plataformatercersector.es.

powers of their own (social assistance, foundations and associations, cooperatives, or community development), from also regulating the third social sector. This is the case of the Basque Country (Law 6/2016, of May 12); the Balearic Islands (Law 3/2018, of 29 May); Extremadura (Law 10/2018, of 22 November); Castilla-La Mancha (Law 1/2020, of 3 February), or Castile and León (Law 5/2021, of 14 September).

The purpose of the State Law 43/2015 is to regulate the entities of the third sector of social action, to strengthen their capacity as interlocutors before the General State Administration with respect to social public policies, and to define the measures of promotion that the public authorities may adopt for their benefit (art. 1). Its structure, which bears some resemblance to that of the social economy law, identifies who the entities of the third social action sector are, lists their guiding principles, regulates the participation of the sector's representatives in the institutional participation bodies and the measures for their promotion.

4.3 The Concept of the Third Social Sector and Its Guiding Principles

The State Law on the Third Sector does not define the Third Sector of Social Action, but rather the entities that make up this sector. Article 1 states that these are organisations of a private nature, arising from citizen or social initiative, under different modalities, that respond to criteria of solidarity and social participation, with purposes of general interest and not for profit, which promote the recognition and exercise of civil rights, as well as the economic, social, or cultural rights of persons and groups that suffer from conditions of vulnerability or are at risk of social exclusion. And in any case, it considers associations, foundations, as well as federations or associations that integrate them, as long as they comply with the provisions of this Law, to be entities of the Third Sector of Social Action. The law of Extremadura (art.2) and of Castile and León (art.2) express themselves in the same terms. The law of Castilla-La Mancha adds to the above, the special entities (Caritas, Spanish Red Cross, and ONCE) (art.2).

The law of the Basque Country (art. 3) adds associations and foundations, social initiative cooperatives, and any other legal entity that meets certain characteristics (voluntary action, part of civil society, private, participatory, and not-for-profit). This law considers as non-profit, the commercial companies that, by statutory provision, must reinvest their profits in the activities that constitute their purpose (art. 2.3b). The Balearic Islands law adds religious organisations to the above (art. 3).

The guiding principles that characterize the entities of the Third Sector of Social Action are: (a) To have their own legal personality; (b) To be of a private legal nature; (c) To be non-profit and altruistic in nature; (d) To guarantee democratic participation within them, in accordance with the provisions of the regulations applicable to the legal form they adopt; (e) To act in a transparent manner, both in the development of their corporate purpose and in the operation, management of their activities, and accountability; (f) To carry out their activities with full guarantees of autonomy in their management and decision making with respect to the General State Administration; (g) To contribute to making social cohesion effective, by means of citizen participation in social action, through volunteering; (h) To act in such a way as to effectively observe in its organisation, operation, and activities the principle of equal opportunities, equal treatment, and non-discrimination regardless of any personal or social circumstance, and with special attention to the principle of equality between women and men; and (i) To carry out objectives and activities of general interest (so defined in a regulation with the rank of law), and in any case, the following activities of social interest: attention to persons with comprehensive social and health care needs; attention to persons with educational or labour insertion needs, and the promotion of public safety and the prevention of delinquency.

To the above, several ACs add the principle of inter-cooperation and networking (Balearic Islands, Extremadura, and Castile and León).

4.4 *Third Social Sector Entities*

As we have seen in the previous section, the key elements that make it possible to identify third social sector entities in Spain are as follows: (1) they are private entities that arise from social initiative; (2) they have general interest purposes and are non-profit; (3) they respond to principles of solidarity and participation; (4) they focus their attention on defending the civil, social, economic, and cultural rights of certain groups of people (vulnerable or at risk of social exclusion).

As we have seen, for state law these characteristics seem to be present only in associations and foundations, but the Autonomous Regions have been opening up the scope of the third social sector by integrating other entities that also share the above features, such as social initiative cooperatives, special entities (Caritas, ONCE, and Spanish Red Cross), and other non-profit legal entities.

As can be seen, associations, foundations, cooperatives, and special entities are also present in the social economy and have been analysed in previous pages. However, it is worth making a brief reference to the social initiative cooperative, due to its particular nature, and to other entities that some regional laws include in the third sector, such as volunteer organisations and other non-profit legal entities.

4.4.1 Social Initiative Cooperatives

Social initiative cooperatives are included in the third social sector law of the Basque Country (art. 3.1) and the Balearic Islands, although the latter calls them "non-profit social action cooperatives" (art. 4). These entities are also incorporated in many of the social services laws as social initiative entities. This is the case of the Community of Madrid (art. 56); Catalonia (art. 69); Andalusia (art. 100), or the Community of Valencia (art. 85).

According to the State Law on Cooperatives 27/1999, of 16 July 1999, the first law in Spain to regulate social initiative cooperatives, these are non-profit cooperatives, regardless of their type, whose corporate purpose is either the provision of welfare services through the performance of health, educational, cultural, or other activities of a social nature, or the development of any economic activity whose purpose is the labour integration of persons suffering from any kind of social exclusion and, in general, the satisfaction of social needs not met by the market (art. 106.1). It is described in the same terms by the Basque Cooperatives Law 11/2019, of 20 December (art. 156.3). It is a very broad definition, as it does not specify who can be the recipients of these welfare services, nor what kind of social needs not met by the market can be satisfied.

The Balearic Cooperatives Law (Law 1/2003, 20 March) is a little more precise, and in its Article 138 it defines as social initiative cooperatives those that, without profit motive and regardless of their type, have as their corporate purpose the provision of services related to: Social services (Family; Childhood and Adolescence; Elderly people; People with disabilities; Women; Ethnic minorities and immigration; and Other groups or sectors in which situations of risk or social exclusion may manifest themselves); Health (alcoholics and drug addicts); Youth (youth protection); Education (special education) and other unmet social needs.

The reference that all these laws make to the "non-profit" cooperative merits an explanation. As we have said from the beginning, cooperatives as a mutual entity lack an objective profit motive, this means that it does not seek to obtain benefits in the economic activity developed with its members, and if it obtains profits, it must return the profits to its members, in addition to allocating a part to non-distributable reserves. Cooperative legislation referred to the non-profit nature of cooperatives until this reference disappeared from the law, although the regulation of cooperatives was not modified. That is, the profits (not the surpluses, since they belong to the members), as well as the patrimony at the dissolution of the cooperative remained non-distributable. From then on, cooperatives bidding for public contracts for the provision of social services could not so easily justify in their legislation the absence of profit motive. For this reason, and in order for them to be able to access the same aid and opportunities as other entities such as associations and foundations, the possibility of obtaining non-profit status was incorporated into the cooperative laws. When defining the requirements to be met by the cooperative in order to obtain such qualification, it was decided to opt for those that allowed foundations and public utility associations to benefit from the law on the tax regime for non-profit entities.

The regulation of the qualification as a non-profit entity, in the state law, is found in the first additional provision, according to which:

"Those that manage services of collective interest or of public ownership, as well as those that carry out economic activities that lead to the labour integration of persons suffering any kind of social exclusion, and in their Bylaws expressly state the following, may be qualified as non-profit cooperative societies:

(a) That the positive results produced in a financial year may not be distributed among its partners.
(b) The contributions of the members to the capital stock, both obligatory and voluntary, may not accrue interest at a rate higher than the legal interest rate, without prejudice to the possible updating of such contributions.
(c) The free nature of the performance of the offices of the Board of Directors, without prejudice to the appropriate financial compensation for the expenses incurred by the directors in the performance of their duties.
(d) The remuneration of the worker-members or, as the case may be, of the worker-members and employees may not exceed 150% of the remuneration which, depending on the activity and professional category, is established in the collective bargaining agreement applicable to salaried personnel in the sector.

This regulation is completed by the ninth additional provision, according to which the tax regime of cooperative societies classified as non-profit entities will be that established for other cooperatives in Law 20/1990, of 19 December 1990.

As we can see, the classification of a cooperative as a non-profit entity, distances it from the cooperative model where the collective interest of its members prevails and brings it closer to entities where the general interest prevails.

4.4.2 Volunteer Organisations

Volunteer organisations are not included in the laws analysed among the entities of the third social sector, but they are integrated through the Spanish Volunteer Platform (PVE) in the Third Sector Platform. In addition, all the laws on social services include these organisations among the social initiative entities, and one of the guiding principles of the third sector—as we have seen—is to contribute to making social cohesion effective through citizen participation in social action, by means of volunteering.

Volunteering entities are regulated in Law 45/2015, of 14 October 2015 on Volunteering, and are described as legal entities, legally constituted and non-profit, which are made up of volunteers and develop their activity, in whole or in part, through volunteering programmes designed and managed within the framework of activities of general interest that respect certain values and principles contemplated in the law (art. 5), and which are carried out in the field of social, development cooperation, environmental, cultural, sports, educational, socio-health, leisure and free time, community or civil protection volunteering (art. 13 and 6).

4.4.3 Other Non-Profit Legal Entities

The entities that form part of the third sector are basically the traditional non-profit entities (associations and foundations); special entities; social initiative cooperatives, and volunteer organisations.

In addition, both the law of the Balearic Islands and the law of the Basque Country incorporate other legal forms in the third sector, provided that they meet certain requirements.

The Balearic third sector law includes other legal forms in which the governing bodies are owned exclusively by organisations of the third social sector, or by public administrations up to a maximum of 50%, and which have been constituted to fulfil the social purpose of the latter. In this group, the Balearic Islands include social and labour insertion companies and certain special employment centres that meet certain conditions such as: non-profit and include in their staff 70% of people with disabilities and with greater support needs (people with physical or sensory disabilities to a degree equal to, or greater than, 65%, or people with cerebral palsy, mental illness, or intellectual disability to a degree equal to, or greater than, 33%), (art. 4).

The Basque law identifies third sector organisations with those of social initiative, which according to its art. 3 are: foundations, associations, social initiative cooperatives and any other entities, formally constituted and endowed with their own legal personality, that have certain characteristics: (a) that they have a social base made up, totally or partially, of volunteers; (b) that they are part of civil society; (c) that their bodies are not majority owned by for-profit companies or public institutions; (d) that do not pursue the distribution of economic benefits, and from whose legal figure derives the obligation to reinvest any profits; (e) that adopt forms of participation for decision-making, according to their legal form. Also forming part of the third sector in the Basque Country are those entities that, although they do not meet any of the above requirements, conduct activities in the field of social intervention, are majority owned (directly or indirectly) by organisations of the third social sector, have been set up to achieve their social objectives and maintain the non-profit nature of their activity (objective non-profit). And it adds: "in the case of commercial companies, the non-profit nature shall be understood as the statutory provision of the obligation to reinvest profits in the activities that constitute their corporate purpose." In particular, it goes on to say that special employment centres and social and labour insertion companies will be included in this area.

In short, the legal reference to other not-for-profit legal entities is once again specific to insertion companies and certain special employment centres, entities to which we referred earlier as part of the social economy.

4.5 Organisations Representing the Third Social Sector

The Third Sector Platform, as we have seen, was constituted in January 2012 by the seven most representative organisations in the social sphere at that time. As of today, the Platform is composed of twenty organisations and represents nearly 28,000 third sector entities, composed of 577,000 workers and 1.5 million volunteers.

These were joined later by collaborating entities and third sector platforms at regional level. There are currently 11 territorial entities in Andalusia, Extremadura, Aragon, Region of Murcia, Principality of Asturias, Community of Valencia, La

Rioja, Castilla-La Mancha, Community of Madrid, Canary Islands, and Castile and León. It also collaborates with the Taula d'Entitats del Tercer Sector Social de Catalunya and the Red del Tercer sector social de Euskadi (Sareen Sarea).

On 23 October 2019, the Territorial Coordination Committee was constituted, with the aim of creating an open, flexible space for debate and exchange of shared interests, to advance inter-territorial articulation and coordination, as well as providing a strong impetus for the cohesion of the sector. A further intention was to use the legislative and regulatory developments of the different Autonomous Regions as a reference and to exchange good practices among the different platforms and territorial roundtables.

The organisations that represent the majority of third sector social action entities are part of various institutional participation bodies such as the State Council of Non-Governmental Social Action Organisations or the Commission for Civil Dialogue with the Third Sector Platform, both regulated in the State Law. The third social sector laws also contemplate mixed participation bodies such as the Civil Dialogue Board or Commission of the Basque Country, the Balearic Islands, Extremadura, or Castile-La Mancha; the Economic and Social Council in the Basque Country or the Balearic Islands; or the Social Services Council of Castile and Leon.

4.6 Promotion of the Third Social Sector

The law of the third sector dedicates a chapter to the promotion of the entities of the third sector of social action of state scope, with numerous Measures of promotion (art. 6) and a Programme to boost the entities of the third sector of social action (art. 7).

Among the measures for the promotion of third sector entities, the following are mentioned: (a) Supporting and promoting the principles of the third sector of social action; (b) Encouraging the diversification of the sources of financing, especially by improving the regulations on patronage and promoting corporate social responsibility; (c) To guarantee the participation of the third sector of social action in the different social, employment, equality and inclusion policies designed in favour of vulnerable persons and groups and those at risk of social exclusion; (d) To recognise the entities of the third sector of social action, in accordance with the procedures to be established by regulation, as collaborating entities of the General State Administration; (e) To include in the study plans of the different educational stages, those contents and references to the third sector of social action necessary for its fair valuation as a means of participation of the citizenship and of the groups in which civil society is integrated; (f) To promote the entities of the third sector of social action as one of the relevant instruments to channel the effective exercise of the rights to social participation of the citizenship in an advanced democratic society, or (g) To strengthen and facilitate the initiatives of cooperation between companies and entities of the third sector of social action.

The Programme for the Promotion of the entities of the third social action sector includes certain promotion measures such as the promotion, dissemination and training of the third social action sector; support for the culture of volunteering, cooperation with public services; public financing of third sector social action entities, and access to financing through official credit institutions, or the strengthening of collaboration mechanisms with the Administration for the development of social inclusion programmes for people or vulnerable groups at risk of social exclusion and care for people with disabilities or in a situation of dependency, with special attention accorded to the use of agreements and arrangements.

It is not the purpose of this work to analyse all the programmed measures, but we do want to make express reference to some of them, such as corporate social responsibility, the status of collaborating entity with the Administration or the regulations on public procurement.

Corporate social responsibility has different approaches, one of them, the so-called solidarity responsibility of companies (García Nieto 2011), is characterised by the fact that the company has an interest in contributing to the resolution of social problems not necessarily connected with its organisation, but of general interest, and which it tends to address directly or by resorting to institutions such as patronage or the creation of foundations. Spanish legislation has regulated corporate social responsibility (Law No. 2/2011 of 4 March on Sustainable Economy, Art. 39; Law 15/2010 on CSR of Extremadura, and Law 18/2018, of 13 July, on the Promotion of Social Responsibility of the Valencian Community) and encourages it with various aids.[38]

The regulation of patronage in Spain is mainly fiscal. Law 49/2002 on the Tax Regime of Non-Profit Entities and its Regulations (Royal Decree 1270/2003) determine the entities benefiting from patronage, what type of donations are eligible for tax deduction, how these donations are valued to calculate the deduction, or the procedure to justify donations and deductible contributions.

The recognition of the status of entity collaborating with the Administration of third sector entities was introduced by Royal Decree-Law 7/2013, of 28 June. This law regulates the social interest programmes financed with 0.7% of the taxable base of Personal Income Tax. This percentage can be allocated by the taxpayer when filing their income tax return, to support the Church, to social purposes, or to both (allocating 1.4%). This law recognised in its explanatory memorandum that the legal recognition of the essential role that certain non-profit organisations and entities, have in responding to the increasingly pressing needs of society, collaborating directly with the public administrations, while at the same time guaranteeing the channelling of the public funds essential for them to fulfil and develop their own purposes, could not be delayed. This legal consideration as Third Sector entities collaborating with the public administrations is conferred to organisations of a private nature, arising from the citizens'initiative, non-profit and with purposes of general interest, whatever their legal form may be. These entities will receive the tax

[38] https://www.mites.gob.es/es/rse/ccaayrse/index.htm.

allocation for the performance of activities of general interest that the law considers to be of social interest. These activities are: (a) Attention to people with integral social and health care needs; (b) Attention to people with educational or labour insertion needs; (c) Promotion of public safety and crime prevention; (d) Environmental protection; (e) Development cooperation; and (f) Promotion and modernisation of the third sector of social action. This last interest has been incorporated by means of Royal Decree-Law 33/2020, of 3 November, and as we can see, it is not aimed at financing the actions developed by the third sector, but mainly at the maintenance of its structures. This regulation also approves a series of direct subsidies to a wide range of third sector entities to favour their liquidity needs, widely depleted by the exponential increase in social demands during the health emergency due to COVID-19.

Law 9/2017, of 8 November, on Public Sector Contracts (arts. 11.6 and 6.1) and the laws on social services allow public administrations to provide public services indirectly through agreements and concerts with private social initiative entities without being subject to the rules of public procurement.

In the latter case, preference is given to social initiative entities in the event of analogous conditions of efficiency, quality, and social profitability. Secondly, Law 9/2017 regulates the reservation of contracts in favour of insertion companies and special employment centres of social initiative (Additional Provision 4ª). Thirdly, it establishes a reservation of certain contracts for social, cultural and health services to certain organisations that meet each and every one of the following conditions: (a) That their objective is the performance of a public service mission linked to the provision of the services referred to in the first paragraph; (b) That the profits are reinvested for the purpose of achieving the organisation's objective; or in the event that profits are distributed or redistributed, the distribution or redistribution must be carried out in accordance with participation criteria; (c) The management or ownership structures of the organisation performing the contract are based on employee ownership, or on principles of participation, or require the active participation of employees, users or interested parties; (d) The contracting authority concerned has not awarded the organisation a contract for the services in question under this article in the preceding 3 years (Additional Provision 48th). As can be seen, the regulations on public procurement offer certain advantages to the social initiative entities that make up the third sector.

5 Convergences and Divergences Between the Social Economy and the Third Sector

As we have seen, the social economy and the third sector coexist in Spain, with their respective regulations, representative organisations, and promotion standards.

The term social economy identifies the business sector that lies between public companies and capitalist companies, and includes a plurality of legal entities, in which the profit motive is not relevant, because the main objective pursued by these entities is to meet the needs of their members, promote their interests or serve purposes of general interest.

The term third sector has been legally recognised to identify a part of the social economy, the so-called social action sector or social initiative entities which, until then, had been regulated mainly in the social services laws. This does not mean that the term third sector has no wider scope. For some years now, this term has been used to identify non-profit entities, usually associations, foundations and cooperatives that conduct their economic activity in the cultural, sports or environmental sectors, among others. But these have not yet received legal recognition as a third sector, unlike the social action sector.

The term third sector in Spain is therefore not equivalent to the term social economy, but rather to a part of it, the so-called non-market subsector of the social economy, whose main financing does not come from the sale of goods and services on the market but from the contributions of its own members, income, public aid, or donations. In this conception, third sector entities are conceived as part of the social economy.

The approval of the third social sector law in 2015 came in response to the recently approved social economy law in 2011. The latter includes in its scope all social initiative entities, but do not meet the expectations of the organisations representing them, who at the end of 2011 formed the Third Sector Platform. The main reasons that, in our opinion, could have justified this decision are: on the one hand, the legal configuration of the organisation representing the social economy, which, by requiring a more plural representation and not only of one sector of the social economy, did not make it possible for the organisations representing social initiative entities to take on the representation of the entire social economy; and on the other hand, because the public administration on which public policies and aid depend, is different. The Ministry of Employment is responsible for the social economy, while the Ministry of Social Services is responsible for social action and social services. This has not prevented the two representative structures from working together over the years to promote civil dialogue.

Focusing attention on the content of the laws, the structure of both is quite similar. After offering a concept of the social economy or third sector, their guiding principles are regulated, as well as some measures for promotion and the bodies in which they will participate. In this case, the third social sector law does not indicate how the most representative organisation of the third sector is to be determined but attributes this quality directly to the Third Sector Platform.

As regards the purpose pursued, third sector entities pursue objectives and conduct activities of general interest and in particular the following of social interest: attention to people in need of integral social and health care; educational or labour insertion and promotion of public safety and crime prevention. Social economy entities may pursue both the collective interest of their members and the general economic or social interest, or both.

Regarding the principles that characterise the social economy and the third sector, we can say that they coincide for the most part: solidarity, social cohesion, autonomous, transparent, democratic, participative management, equal opportunities and treatment, non-discrimination and equality between women and men, conducting activities of social interest, etc. The third sector law adds: non-profit and altruistic (art. 4 c); and the social economy law: applying the results to the economic activity (work or service provided by the members) and, where appropriate, to the social purpose of the entity (art. 4 b). As for the differences, the third sector law refers to volunteering, while the social economy law refers to the primacy of the person over capital, the commitment to local development, the insertion of people at risk of social exclusion, the generation of stable and quality employment, the reconciliation of personal, family and work life, sustainability, and independence from the public authorities.

In relation to the promotion measures, foundations and associations of general interest are the entities that enjoy the best tax advantages, benefits that do not reach other non-profit entities that pursue general interest purposes, such as social initiative cooperatives. All entities classified as non-profit entities can benefit from aid for the achievement of social interest purposes. Similarly, insertion companies and special employment centres, particularly if they are social initiative companies, enjoy various aids for the realisation of their social purposes, including the right to a reserved place in public procurement; however, they do not have tax advantages. The promotion of social economy entities pursuing the collective interest of their members is mainly focused on favouring the access of workers to the status of members of cooperatives and worker-owned companies, on promoting associations in the rural sector and on recognising certain tax advantages in favour of cooperatives.

Finally, as regards the representative organisation of the social economy sector and the third sector, the former has been integrated bottom-up through the association of grassroots entities in regional federations, and these in turn in other statewide federations, until CEPES was created. Most of the existing third social sector platforms have been formed from the territorial delegations of the large state-level organisations that formed the Third Sector Platform and those that have subsequently joined, in a reverse top-down process.

6 Conclusions

The social economy and the third sector are terms that, although initially used as equivalents, began to distance themselves from each other when they received legal recognition and promotion by the public administration.

The fact that the control and promotion of the social economy depends on the Ministry of Labour means that the promotion of the social economy is mainly oriented towards promoting self-employment and social insertion through employment, paying less attention to other sectors, whose promotion depends on other departments of the administration (financial sector, consumption, education, housing, agriculture, etc.).

The third sector began to develop in Spain with the creation of the Third Sector Platform, as a reaction to the model of representation of the social economy attributed to CEPES. This Platform is made up of entities representing social initiative entities and, despite its name, its actions have been aimed exclusively at the social services sector (Third Sector Social Action Law). Its control and promotion are the responsibility of the Department of Social Affairs. This attribution of powers also works against the development of other sectors of the third sector that are beginning to have a presence in society, because their promotion depends on other departments in which they do not yet have so much weight (culture, sports, environment, etc.).

This fragmentation of the control and promotion of social economy and third sector entities, resulting from the multiplicity of concurrent competencies, does not favour the development that they could have, if we consider the connection that exists between them both in terms of their purposes, their principles and the entities they integrate.

There is a lack of a public entity to ensure the recognition and promotion of the social economy (in a broad sense) and to do so in coordination with the various departments of the public administration. For this to be possible, greater integration between the representative structures of the third sector and the social economy at the State and Autonomous Community levels would also be desirable.

References

Acosta Gallo P (2019) Interés General. Eunomía, Revista en Cultura de la Legalidad 16:173–182

Álvarez de Mon S (ed) (1998) El Tercer Sector: retos y propuestas para el próximo milenio. Ministerio de Trabajo y Asuntos Sociales, Madrid

Ascarelli T (1964) Iniciación al estudio del Derecho mercantil (Introducción y traducción de Evelio Verdera y Tuells). Publicaciones del Real Colegio de España en Bolonia. Ed. Bosch, Barcelona

Barea J, Monzón JL (1994) Las cifras clave de la economía social en España. In: Ciriec-España, Revista de Economía Pública, Social y Cooperativa, 16 p 15

Barea J, Monzón JL (1995) Las cuentas satélites de la Economía Social en España: una primera aproximación. Ciriec-España, Valencia

Barea J, Monzón JL (2000) La economía social en España en el año 2000. Ciriec-España, Valencia

Cabra de Luna MA (1998) El Tercer Sector y las Fundaciones de España hacia el Nuevo Milenio: Enfoque económico, sociológico y jurídico. Fundación ONCE; Escuela Libre Editorial, Madrid

Cabra de Luna MA (1999) El tercer sector. In: Carpio M (ed) El sector no lucrativo en España. Pirámide, Madrid, pp 75–112

Chaves Ávila R, Monzón Campos JL (2020) Libro blanco de la economía social y del tercer sector de la Comunitat Valenciana. CIRIEC, Valencia

Chaves R (2017) Panorámica del tercer sector español. In: Chaves R, Zimmer A (eds) El tercer sector en España y en Europa. Crisis y resilencia. PUV, Universitat de Valéncia, Valencia

Chaves-Ávila R, Zimmer A (eds) (2017) El tercer sector en España y en Europa: Crisis y resilencia. Universitat de València, Valencia

De Lorenzo R, Cabra de Luna MA (1993) La constelación de las entidades no lucrativas: el tercer sector. In: El sector no lucrativo en España, Escuela Libre Editorial, Madrid

Defourny y Monzón, 1992

Fuentes Rey P (1996) Las organizaciones sociovoluntarias en el Tercer Sector. El Tercer Sector, Documentación Social 103:253–262
Fuster Asencio MC (2009) Razones que justifican una fiscalidad específica de las mutualidades de previsión social. Ciriec-España, Revista Jurídica de Economía Social y Cooperativa 20:149–182
García Nieto MT (2011) La regulación de la Responsabilidad Social Corporativa en España. Revista Internacional de Derecho de la Comunicación y de las Nuevas Tecnologías, 6
García-Delgado JL (ed) (2004). Las cuentas de la economía social. El tercer sector en España. Civitas, Madrid
Herrera M (1998) El Tercer Sector en los Sistemas de Bienestar. Tirant lo Blanc, Valencia
Monzón JL (1992) La Economía Social: Tercer Sector de un nuevo Escenario. In: Monzón JL, Defourny J (eds) Economía Social. Entre Economía Capitalista y Economía Pública. Ciriec, Valencia
Monzón JL, Calvo R, Chaves R, Fajardo G, Valdés Dal-Re F (2010) Informe para la elaboración de una Ley de Fomento de la Economía Social. Ministerio de Trabajo e Inmigración, Madrid
Salamon LM, Anheier HK (1992a) In search of the non-profit sector. I the question of definitions. Voluntas 3(2):125–151
Salamon LM, Anheier HK (1992b) In search of the non-profit sector II: the international classification of non-profit organisations. A framework for analysis. Voluntas 3(3):267–309
Salamon LM, Sokolowski SW, List R (2003) Global civil society: an overview. Center for civil society studies. Institute for Policy Studies, The Johns Hopkins University, Baltimore

Part II
European and Comparative Law of Third Sector Organizations

Chapter 11
Third Sector Organizations in a European and Comparative Legal Perspective

Antonio Fici

Contents

Abstract This chapter aims to analyze third sector law in a comparative perspective, on the basis of the existing legal framework in ten European countries, taking as a point of reference the Italian Code of 2017. Italy is the only country with a specific legislation on the "third sector". However, in the other European national legal systems, organizations equivalent to third sector organizations, or at least to a part of them, are recognized and regulated. The comparison between the Italian law of the

Antonio Fici is an Associate Professor of Private Law at the University of Rome "Tor Vergata" and Scientific Director of the Terzjus Foundation – Observatory on the Law of Third Sector, Philanthropy and Social Enterprise.

A. Fici (✉)
University of Rome Tor Vergata, Department of History, Cultural Heritage, Education and Society, Rome, Italy
e-mail: antonio.fici@uniroma2.it

A. Fici (ed.), *The Law of Third Sector Organizations in Europe*,
https://doi.org/10.1007/978-3-031-41744-3_11

third sector and the law of public benefit organizations and social enterprises, in force in other countries, shows the presence of many similarities. A common core of European third sector law can therefore be identified. On the other hand, as the chapter aims to demonstrate, the third sector is distinct from the social and solidarity economy sector as defined by national laws providing for it. The chapter also discusses EU law and policies on the organizations concerned and underlines the importance of EU legal intervention in this field.

1 In Search of the Third Sector

There is neither a universally recognized concept of "third sector", nor a general consensus definition of the organizations that compose this sector. Half a century has passed since Amitai Etzioni used this term for the first time to designate a class of organizations other than those that are "private" and "governmental",[1] and yet doubts and perplexities still persist in the relevant non-legal literature as to what the third sector is and what its constituent organizations exactly are. It has been recently reaffirmed, for example, that the term "actually denotes the sector of organizations that are neither public nor business, which means that it entails private organizations that are not-for-profit".[2] This "catch-all" definition[3] and the "acritical" approximation of the third sector to the non-profit organization area are no longer convincing and should be definitely surpassed. Nor is the idea acceptable that the extreme variety of the organizational forms that compose the presumed third sector should call into question the very existence of this sector. For several reasons, including their fundamental contribution to the common good, this group of organizations deserves specific recognition.

Indeed, one can certainly observe an evolution of the third sector theory, which is leading to a positive conceptualization of the organizations that are in-scope. These advances also regard the legal framework, whose contribution to the definition of the sector is essential. The time, therefore, seems ripe to attempt to state the specific identity of third sector organizations (TSOs), regardless of what their name and legal denomination might be depending on the country, to draw their distinction from other categories of organizations, notably non-profit organizations (NPOs), and to better understand their connections with contiguous categories of organizations, including social economy organizations (SEOs) and social enterprises.

[1] Cf. Etzioni (1973). Admittedly, the other "father" of the term "third sector" and precursor of the third sector theory is Theodore Levitt: see Levitt (1973).

[2] Cf. Gidron (2020), p. 1.

[3] Cf. Breen (2023).

As previously mentioned, the first use of the term "third sector" as a category of organizations is usually attributed to Etzioni.[4] This author conceived of the third sector as an alternative to the public and private sectors in best solving social issues. This "residual" approach[5] explains why only a "negative" definition of TSOs is found in Etzioni's seminal contribution. The third sector "is neither governmental nor private", he wrote. Significantly, in his analysis, the "private" sector is associated with the "profit motive", to the point that TSOs, which are "not-for-profit" entities, are also referred to as "public". However, TSOs are "public" but not "governmental"—as Etzioni points out—because their origin is exclusively or predominantly found in the private sphere, their governance structure is not "bureaucratic" and they are independent from the state.

The third sector, as outlined by Etzioni, is clearly different from the third sector as we currently conceive it in Europe, also in light of the existing legislation. For example, a public agency in charge of a service of general economic interest, like the U.S. Postal Service, was an example of a third sector organization in Etzioni's work. However, the idea of a sector distinct from the others, and therefore "third" in the sense of "diverse" (though not less important), has influenced the ensuing debate.[6] The term "third sector" has continued to be used, and eventually, 44 years after its introduction, even became a legal term: the relevant Italian law of 2017 is a "Third Sector Code" which recognizes and regulates "third sector organizations". The process of institutionalization of TSOs has thus reached its climax.

The not-for-profit nature of TSOs – meaning that TSOs, unlike organizations pertaining to the "private" or "market" sector, are not established to generate profits as they cannot distribute these profits to their owners and directors—has continued to be considered the main distinguishing feature of TSOs for a long time.

It is not a coincident that one subsequent famous attempt to provide a positive definition of TSOs on a cross-national basis was conducted under the label "non-profit sector" rather than "third sector".[7] The project leaders treated the two terms as if they were interchangeable. Emblematically, the first chapter of Salamon and Anheier's book of 1997 was entitled "In search of the nonprofit sector", while in the main text, the two authors maintained that the lack of a clear definition of "third sector" was the main factor behind the limited attention accorded to this sector and its insufficient recognition by the general public and the academic community.[8] To help solve this issue and thus favour the development of the third sector, the two

[4]As well as to Theodore Levitt: cf. Corry (2010), p. 13; Lorentzen (2010), p. 25. As Defourny (2013), p. 400, opportunely points out, the organizations included in the sector were already active in many areas of activity. Therefore, what was original is "the idea of bringing these entities all together and the theoretical basis on which this could be done".

[5]Cf. Corry (2010), p. 11; Gidron (2020), p. 1.

[6]Cf. Lundberg (1975); McGill and Wooten (1975).

[7]Namely, the "John Hopkins Comparative Nonprofit Sector Project".

[8]Salamon and Anheier (1997a), p. 3.

authors proposed the adoption of a "structural-operational definition", according to which TSOs, or rather NPOs, are entities:

- *organized*, that is, institutionalized to some extent;
- *private*, namely, separate from government, and therefore neither part of the governmental apparatus nor controlled by government;
- *non-profit-distributing*, namely, not returning any profits generated to their owners or directors, which implies that they do not exist primarily to generate profits;
- *self-governing*, meaning they have their own internal procedures for governance and are not controlled by outside entities; and
- *voluntary*, because they involve some meaningful degree of voluntary participation either in the actual conduct of the activities or in the management of their affairs.[9]

Indeed, this definition says little about the specific identity of TSOs and remains bent on affirming Etzioni's "negative" and "residual" conception, which constituted the first elaboration on the matter. Whilst it is clear what the sector is not, it remains unclear what the sector actually is and what organizations are included.

The profit non-distribution constraint remains the key element of the positive identification of TSOs, while the other elements lack an effective distinctive power. The fact of being "organized" is a somewhat tautological requirement if referred to "organizations" or "entities". The same is true of the "self-governing" requirement, because any organization, as such, has its own bodies and rules of governance. In addition to that, the fact of not being controlled by outside entities is not *per se* an element that prevents an organization from having its own bodies and procedures of governance. Moreover, this requirement might turn out to be unreasonably restrictive for TSOs, because it would prevent organizations that are subsidiaries of a parent TSO from formally qualifying as TSOs. Being "private" is a pure negative element, derived by contrast with the public (or rather, governmental) sector. The "voluntary" element is too loose to permit distinguishing TSOs from other organizations, notably NPOs.

In conclusion—notwithstanding the fundamental role played by the John Hopkins project in building a third sector theory—the definition of third sector provided within this Project does not make it possible to identify TSOs in positive terms. The only relevant element of this definition, namely, the not-for-profit nature of the organization, is, in turn, a "negative" element, because it only implies the non-distribution of profits, but does not focus on how profits must be used by the organization and for what purposes. Therefore, if this is the way in which an organization is identified as a TSO, even a non-profit association established by for-profit entities with the purpose of promoting their economic activities or profits would be a TSO, provided that no distribution of profits takes place. In principle, provided that no distribution of profits takes place, non-profit legal forms may

[9] Salamon and Anheier (1997b), p. 33 f.

indeed be used to satisfy private interests, including interests of a purely financial nature.

A different approach to the third sector was adopted, in reaction to the US-led approach as embodied in the John Hopkins project, by a group of European scholars at the beginning of the new Millennium. The specific features of this approach have been summarized on the basis of three parameters, which are "the type of organizations involved, the intermediary nature of the third sector within a 'welfare pluralism' or a plural economy, and a sociopolitical dimension that is as important as the economic dimension".[10]

The first parameter, namely, the type of organizations involved, is particularly worth mentioning here, also in light of the specific objectives of this chapter.

Indeed, following the "European approach", mutual business organizations, such as cooperatives and mutual aid societies, are included in the third sector notwithstanding the fact that they may distribute some profits to the members. The reason is that they are "social economy organizations" rather than "capitalistic organizations", and they have the objective of "generating collective wealth rather than a return on individual investment". A limited distribution of profits is therefore deemed compatible with the nature of a TSO, and may characterize a portion of the third sector, as long as aspects of sociality distinguish the organizations in question.[11]

This diverse, European, way of interpreting the third sector leads to a clear distinction between "third sector" and "non-profit sector". The two terms cannot be used interchangeably. The two sectors do not overlap. While profit non-distribution is essential to qualify TSOs in the US-led approach, to the point that TSOs are mostly referred to as NPOs, other factors become essential to this purpose in the European approach to the third sector.

A further step towards a positive identification and a better understating of the third sector has recently taken place.

A European research project, the "Third Sector Impact (TSI) Project", funded by the European Union, proposes a new and modern conceptualization of the third sector, with a view to providing a basis for systematic comparison among European countries and between them and other countries in other parts of the world, as well as to allow official statistical systems to generate reliable data on this sector on a regular basis. Indeed, the starting point of the analysis was that "the third sector in Europe lacks a clear identity and there is no clear-shared understanding across Europe and within the European Union regarding what exactly the third sector is and what its role is in the European public space".[12]

In the 2018 book that summarizes the project's findings,[13] Lester Salamon and Wojciech Sokolowski—in a chapter significatively entitled "Beyond Nonprofits: In

[10] Evers and Laville (2004), p. 11.

[11] Evers and Laville (2004), p. 13.

[12] Enjolras (2018), p. 4.

[13] Cf. Enjolras et al. (2018).

Search of the Third Sector"[14]—begin their essay by underlining that "existing diversity of views over whether something that could appropriately be called the 'third sector' actually exists in different parts of the world and, if so, what it contains", that "the 'third sector', and its various cognates [i.e., social economy, civil society and social entrepreneurship], is probably one of the most perplexing concepts in modern political and social discourse",[15] and that the same sector is identified using different terms, "including civil society sector, nonprofit sector, voluntary sector, charitable sector, third sector and, more recently, social economy, social enterprise and many more".[16]

Therefore, they propose to discuss a broader "third or social economy" (TSE) sector,[17] which embraces not only "classical" NPOs—namely, the organizations "governed by binding arrangements prohibiting distribution of any surplus, or profit, generated to their stakeholders or investors"[18]—but, more generally, all the organizations characterized by a "public purpose", that is, organizations "undertaken primarily to create public goods, something of value primarily to the broader community or to persons other than oneself or one's family, and not primarily for financial gain; exhibiting some element of solidarity with others".[19]

This leads the authors to consider the TSE sector composed not only of NPOs, but also mutuals, cooperatives and social enterprises, or rather some of them, precisely, those that are, by law or custom, "significantly limited" in the distribution of the surpluses generated by their activities.[20] This represents, in our opinion, significant progress relative to the previously commented "European approach" to the third sector, which viewed all cooperatives and mutual societies as components of the third sector.

The conclusion of the analysis is that, to be considered part of the TSE sector, entities must be:

---

[14] This chapter's title is significative especially if compared to the title of the Salamon and Anheier's book of 1997, previously mentioned in the main text, which was "In search of the nonprofit sector".

[15] Salamon and Sokolowski (2018), p. 10.

[16] Salamon and Sokolowski (2018), p. 11.

[17] Salamon and Sokolowski (2018), p. 15.

[18] Salamon and Sokolowski (2018), p. 18. These are the organizations covered covered by the well-known United Nations Handbook on Non-profit Institutions in the System of National Accounts of 2003.

[19] Salamon and Sokolowski (2018), p. 25. According to Defourny and Nyssens (2016), p. 1547: "The attempt made by Salamon and Sokolowski (2016) to propose an extended conception of the third sector, beyond typical non-profit institutions, represents a significant progress at various levels. Most importantly, it takes into account some rules and practices that are found in some cooperatives, mutuals and social enterprises. By doing so, the boundaries of the third sector are moved, thus allowing the inclusion not only of non-profit institutions but also of some social economy organizations as conceptualized in many countries, especially across Europe and Latin America".

[20] Salamon and Sokolowski (2018), p. 33.

- *Organizations*, whether formal or informal;
- *Private*;
- *Self-governed*;
- *Non-compulsory*; and.
- *Totally or significantly limited from distributing any surplus* they earn to investors, members or other stakeholders.[21]

To be properly understood and evaluated, these distinguishing features must be read in conjunction with the "operational terms" into which they are translated by the two authors.

Limiting ourselves to the last requirement, for it to be met, "organizations must be prohibited, either by law, internal governing rules, or by socially recognized custom from distributing either all or a significant share of the profits or surpluses generated by their productive activities to their directors, employees, members, investors or others".[22]

More precisely, the determination that an organization has a significant limitation on profit distribution is founded by the authors on the following four (cumulative) indicators[23]:

(a) explicit social mission ("to be considered in-scope of the TSE sector, an organization must be bound by law, articles of incorporation, other governing documents or settled custom to the pursuit of a social purpose");
(b) no distribution of more than 50% of surplus;
(c) capital lock (prohibition on the distribution of the retained surplus and any other assets owned by the organization to its owners, directors or other stakeholders, in the event of the organization's dissolution, sale or conversion to "for-profit" status);
(d) no distribution of surplus in proportion to capital invested or fees paid (which, however, "does not apply to payment of interest on invested capital so long as the interest does not exceed prevailing market rates or rates on government bonds").[24]

---

[21] Salamon and Sokolowski (2018), p. 33.

[22] Salamon and Sokolowski (2018), p. 36 f. The authors go on explaining that "this attribute distinguishes TSE sector organizations from corporations, which permit the distribution of surpluses generated to their owners or shareholders. TSE organizations may accumulate surplus in a given year, but that surplus or its significant share must be saved or plowed back into the basic mission of the agency and not distributed to the organizations'directors, members, founders or governing board. In this sense, TSE organizations may be profitmaking but unlike other businesses they are nonprofit-distributing, either entirely or to a significant degree".

[23] Salamon and Sokolowski (2018), p. 37 ff.

[24] Salamon and Sokolowski (2018), p. 39. According to Defourny and Nyssens (2016), p. 1550: "to reflect the 'public purpose' of TSE organizations by better combining key features from both the non-profit and the social economy approaches, we would therefore suggest to keep the authors'first three criteria and to transform the fourth one so as to avoid the above contradiction and to have four compulsory criteria that are easily observable characteristics: (i) Pursuing a legally binding social

The TSE sector, as delineated by Salamon and Sokolowski for the TSI project, is a fortunate non-legal attempt[25] to qualify the same category of organizations that in this volume we have sought to identify and discuss from a legal point of view, based on the existing legislation in some EU Member States.

The results we have reached are quite similar, although not identical, also because the legislation on TSOs is still at the first stage of its development. One similar aspect is certainly the centrality of the social (or "public") purpose in the identification of in-scope organizations and the less important and not determinant role played by the profit non-distribution requirement.[26]

2 The Italian Code as a Model for Third Sector Legislation

Of the ten EU Member States examined in this volume, Italy is the only one to have a general law on the third sector, namely, Legislative decree no. 117/2017 on the Code of the Third Sector (CTS), which must be read in conjunction with Legislative decree no 112/2017 on social enterprise.[27] In the other countries, "third sector" is not a legal term, although it is not unknown. It is frequently used in Germany; seldom in Denmark, where it is used interchangeably with terms like "social

---

mission; (ii) Operating under a 'asset lock'; (iii) Being prohibited from distributing more than 50% of profits; and (iv) Limiting by a clearly defined cap the interest that may be paid on capital shares".

[25] Following this study, the new United Nations' Handbook on Satellite Account on Non-profit of 2018, conceived of as an update of the well-known Handbook on Non-profit Institutions in the System of National Accounts of 2003, takes a broader approach and offers comprehensive methodological guidance for creating a coherent satellite account on what is called the third or social economy (TSE) sector, which embraces non-profit institutions and other "related institutions", including eligible cooperatives, mutual societies and social enterprises. Related institutions are different from non-profit institutions but, like the latters, chiefly serve social or public purposes and are not controlled by government. They take a variety of organizational forms, such as cooperatives, mutual societies, social enterprises and non-stock (or benefit) corporations. The related institutions that the 2018 Handbook recommends for inclusion in the TSE sector satellite account fall within the scope of the sector even if they distribute some profit to the units that establish, control or finance them, provided that such profit distribution is "significantly limited". That constraint is consistent with the principle that the primary purpose of the entities concerned is serving the public good and not generating income or profit for the units that establish, control or finance them. See United Nations (2018).

[26] On the importance of this shift of attention, from the non-profit purpose to the social or public purpose of TSOs, see Defourny and Nyssens (2016), p. 1551: "In our view, the 'public purpose' dimension, combined with relaxing the non-profit distribution constraint, represents an original and interesting avenue to enlarge the third sector conceptualization strictly based on non-profit institutions".

[27] To the author's best knowledge, this conclusion may be generalized. In the EU-27, only Italy has specific legislation on the third sector. However, in other countries, as we shall see, there are laws that may be attributed to the third sector legislation, and which are therefore relevant for the legal analysis of TSOs. Specific regulation on third sector entities is also found in Spain: see *infra* in the main text.

economy" or "voluntary sector", and in Poland, where it is used to refer to the legal category of "non-governmental organizations"; it is not commonly used in Belgium, France, Ireland and Portugal, where other terms are preferred, such as "social economy sector" or "voluntary or community sector". Admittedly, in Spain third sector organizations have also been legally recognized, but with limited regard to organizations active in the provision of services to vulnerable groups of people and people at risk of social exclusion (Law no. 43/2015 of 9 October, on "*Tercer Sector de Acción Social*"). Moreover, this law limits itself to identifying the category of TSOs of social action in order to give them institutional voice and state support.[28]

In light of its objectives, structure and contents, Italian third sector law is perfectly consistent with the "European" approach to the third sector last discussed in this chapter. For these reasons, Italian law clearly merits specific consideration in a European and comparative legal study on TSOs. It may serve as a model for third sector legislation. In this role, it does not necessarily have to be followed in all its details, but may provide useful guidelines for regulating TSOs or be treated as a benchmark for shaping TSO regulation. Italian law may also represent a point of reference for non-legal scholars wishing to compare their notion of the sector with a "certain" and "rigorous" definition as that provided by law.[29] In general, a law as the Italian law may offer a better understanding of the sector to all those who are interested in it and may significantly contribute to the development of the organizations that comprise the sector.

The importance of Italian third sector law is due to a series of factors.

First of all, the fact that TSOs have their own separate act—moreover entitled "Code of the Third Sector"—which identifies and regulates them for the implementation of principles of constitutional relevance (solidarity, substantial equality, subsidiarity),[30] explicitly referred to in the first article of the Code—is already particularly significant. In this way, dignity is given to TSOs, despite the "inconclusive" name[31] that they have maintained. This legislation contradicts the purely "residual" vision of TSOs, which has prevailed for decades in the history of ideas, based on the initial impulse of the North American doctrine, which we have referred to in this chapter. Notwithstanding their name, TSOs are not identified "by contrast" to the entities that form the "first" and the "second" sectors, but rather on the basis of their own rules and principles. The "third" nature of these entities is therefore solely the consequence of their being diverse from all the others (including NPOs),[32] or simply the cultural heritage of a theory that for decades has used this denomination to refer to these entities.[33]

---

[28] Cf. Fajardo-García (2023).

[29] Cf. Salamon and Anheier (1997b), p. 30, 35.

[30] Cf. Fici (2023c).

[31] Cf. Gidron (2020), p. 4.

[32] Cf. Fici (2023c).

[33] Indeed, previous Italian legislation on the sector (Legislative Decree no. 460/1997) employed a different denomination, that of "non-profit organizations of social utility" or ONLUS, but the

Secondly, wishing to consider TSOs as a unitary whole, Italian law has instituted a general legal category, that of third sector organizations, which did not previously exist. Italian law treats the various entities that compose the third sector as part of a single "family", while respecting, at the same time, the differences that characterize each type of TSO. Unity is achieved thanks to a precise legislative technique, which consists in considering that of "third sector" as a legal qualification (or status) that entities established in different legal forms and of a different nature can obtain if they meet some specific qualification requirements.[34] It thus happens that the Italian third sector can in principle house:

- both associations and foundations, and cooperatives and companies (the latter two only as social enterprises), which means that the access of an entity to the third sector is not dependent on the legal form and that having a specific legal form (e.g., that of an association or a foundation) does not per se entitle an entity to reach the third sector legal area, for which it is essential to hold the necessary legal requirements (the only exceptions are social cooperatives and mutual aid societies, because their particular laws already provide similar requirements for them)[35];
- both entities that, in a solidarity perspective, carry out activities in favor of third parties, such as voluntary associations, and entities that, in a mutualistic perspective, carry out activities in favor of their members, such as social promotion associations;
- both entities that carry out gratuitous activities, such as philanthropic foundations, and entities that carry out, even exclusively, entrepreneurial activities, such as social enterprises, and social cooperatives among them.

Thirdly, Italian law provides a precise definition of a TSO based on some specific requirements, and in this manner makes it possible to identify TSOs with precision and to distinguish them clearly from other classes of organizations, not only public and for-profit entities but also non-profit entities. Indeed, after the approval of the CTS, it is clear in Italy that third sector and non-profit sector are not the same (which also means that, as previously highlighted, an association or a foundation, which are essentially not-for-profit organizations according to Italian law, are not per se TSOs). There are more than 363,000 NPOs in Italy,[36] and approximately one-third are TSOs.[37] At the same time, as we will point out, the (full) prohibition on profit distribution does not characterize all TSOs, as there are some TSOs (i.e., social

independent Authority in charge of the supervision of these organizations was already called "Agency for the Third Sector".

[34] Cf. Fici (2023c).

[35] In the Spanish state law on TSOs of social action, only associations and foundations are mentioned as possible TSOs, but in some regional laws, social initiatives cooperatives and commercial companies are also eligible to acquire this legal status: cf. Fajardo-García (2023).

[36] According to the National Institute of Statistics, as of 31 December 2020.

[37] Our estimate based on the number of TSOs already present in the RUNTS and of those organizations whose registration is still pending.

enterprises in the company or the cooperative form) that may distribute some profits to their shareholders.

As regards the main requirements for an entity's qualification as a TSO, they concern the purpose pursued and the activity carried out. The status is attained only after registration in a special register for TSOs, named RUNTS (or in the case of social enterprises, in a special section of the Trade Register). However, TSOs must also observe specific rules on governance and transparency to maintain the status. Some entities, such as public administrations, political parties and trade unions ("excluded entities"), can never acquire the status of TSOs, nor can they direct or control a TSO (i.e., the directed or controlled organization could not acquire the status of TSO).[38]

TSOs must pursue purposes of "civic, solidaristic and social utility" and perform exclusively or at least prevalently one or more activities "of general interest" to be identified within a long list of general interest activities provided by law, including the provision of social services, health services, etc. (art. 5, para. 1, CTS).[39]

As already stated, while in principle TSOs must use their profits, and in general all their assets, only to pursue their institutional purposes, and consequently they can never (including at dissolution) distribute, neither directly nor indirectly, profits to their members, directors, workers, etc. (art. 8 CTS and art. 3 Legislative decree no. 112/2017), social enterprises, established in the form of a company or a cooperative, may distribute some profits to their shareholders. More precisely, these social enterprises are allowed to distribute no more than 50% of their annual profits to their shareholders, provided that each shareholder receives, on the shares held, no more than the maximum interest of postal bonds increased by 2.5 points (art. 3, para 3, lit. a, Legislative decree no. 112/2017).

Fourthly, Italian third sector organization law, unlike other countries'equivalent laws, not only identifies and promotes TSOs, but also extensively regulates TSOs, covering several aspects related to organizational law as well as to constitutional, labour, public procurement, tax and administrative law. TSOs are first located within the framework of the Italian Constitution and then identified and regulated in their governance structure and functioning, as well as in their relationships with volunteers and workers. The law regulates the registration procedures of TSOs and their supervision by specialized public offices. The law also provides for specific forms of relationship between public administrations and TSOs for co-programming, co-designing and co-performing activities of general interest (so called "shared administration" of articles 55–57 CTS),[40] which public administrations may opt for in lieu of ordinary public contracts. The law, finally, provides a specific tax regime for TSOs and various measures in their support (art. 79 ff. CTS and art. 18 Legislative decree no. 112/2017). Among these measures is the possibility for

[38] For greater details, cf. Fici (2023c).

[39] For greater details cf. Fici (2023c). Also in Spain, Law no. 43/2015 uses the term "general interest activities".

[40] Cf. Sacchetti and Salvatori (2023).

TSOs to receive tax-privileged donations (art. 83 CTS) and to be designated by individual tax-payers as recipients of 0.5% of the income tax due (legislative decree no. 111/2017).[41]

Finally, Italian law also clarifies the relationships between various actors usually mentioned in the discussion about the boundaries of the third sector and the entities that populate it. The general category of TSOs may embrace:

- associations and foundations that meet the relevant legal requirements;
- social enterprises, which are a particular typology of TSOs (approximately 20% of TSOs are social enterprises),[42] and may be incorporated as associations, foundations, companies or cooperatives[43];
- social cooperatives of Law no. 381/1991, which are social enterprises by law;
- mutual aid societies of Law no. 3818/1886, which are another particular typology of TSOs.

In conclusion, the 2017 Italian Third Sector Code is currently the most important example of TSO legislation in the EU. Not only does this legislation contain the term "third sector" in its name, but it also provides a detailed and systematic legal framework for TSOs. This Code can represent a model for other countries and legislators, and can be used as a benchmark to verify the existence of similar legislation in other countries. The Italian legal definition of TSO complies with the definition proposed by the researchers of the "Third Sector Impact" European project. Thanks to this legislation, the third sector definitively frees itself from the non-profit sector and the purely "residual" vision that characterized the first phase of its theoretical elaboration.[44] In this specific case, the law has played a key role in pursuing this significant result.

[41] Cf. Fici (2023c).

[42] Our estimate is based on the number of TSOs already present in the RUNTS and of those organizations whose registration is still pending.

[43] As already stated, companies and cooperatives may only acquire the status of social enterprises, which is a sub-status of the third sector. To acquire this status, companies and cooperatives must meet the legal requirements for the sub-status, which are similar to those generally valid for all TSOs. Not all companies and cooperatives are therefore TSOs.

[44] Clearly, this regulation would not satisfy those who, for several reasons, believe that the non-distribution contraint (or rather, the full asset-lock) should be the essential, but also the only element of a legislation trying to encourage the establishment and operations of socially oriented organizations, and therefore promote laws based on the asset-lock rather than the "worthy" purpose: see Möslein (2023). We do not believe that the asset-lock alone is sufficient to push organizations to pursue the public good.

3 In Search of Equivalent Regulations in Other EU Countries

As already stated, apart from Italy, there is no other country among those considered in this volume which has a general law on TSOs. This does not mean, however, that the same organizational reality, which is legally known as "third sector" in Italy, is not, fully, partially or differently, regulated in other countries, although using different terms.

In the following sections of this chapter, Italian law is used as a benchmark to identify and discuss national laws that substantially deal with TSOs, despite the fact that they do not refer to them specifically. As we shall see, regardless of the terminology, some of these laws only cover a portion of the whole third sector, and therefore have a more limited scope than Italian law, whereas others deal with a larger group of organizations, and therefore have a broader scope than the law on the third sector used as the standard for comparison. The extent of the regulation may also vary significantly depending on the jurisdiction, because some national laws have only few contents, for example they simply identify in-scope organizations and provide measures for their support, while others present broader contents.

3.1 Laws on Public Benefit Organizations

From a legislative point of view, in a comparative perspective, the category of entities most similar to Italian TSOs is that of public benefit organizations (PBOs), which is provided for, notwithstanding the variety of denominations, in almost all the MSs of the EU. In general, according to the relevant national laws, PBOs are not-for-profit organizations pursuing a public benefit purpose. They have several traits in common with Italian TSOs, although in comparison they can represent only a portion of the latter, as PBOs, unlike Italian TSOs, are fully non-profit. Although PBOs are non-profit organizations, they do not coincide with NPOs, because PBOs have a specific purpose and are subject to specific rules on the use of profits, their governance, accountability, etc.

As we shall see, the legislation regarding PBOs has many similarities with the Italian legislation on TSOs. In a comparative perspective, European PBOs (or equivalent organizations) have features in common with the category of organizations referred to by sect. 501(c)(3) of the US Internal Revenue Code.[45]

As is the case for the Italian "third sector organization", rather than being a particular legal type of organization, the term "public benefit organization" denotes a legal status that entities established in different legal forms, including the company form, may acquire. To hold the status, interested organizations must meet certain

[45] Cf. Brakman Reiser (2023).

legal requirements, relative to the purpose pursued, the activity carried out and the respect of some governance and transparency rules, and they must register in a special register. The public benefit purposes or activities are usually listed by law. PBOs are barred from distributing profits to their members, employees, directors or other board members, etc., and must use their assets exclusively in the pursuit of their public benefit purposes. This "asset-lock" is carefully regulated by the pertinent laws, which prohibit both direct and "indirect" distributions, as well as ex-post distributions in the event of the dissolution or conversion of the PBO or other extraordinary operations. The PBO status awards specific benefits to the organizations that possess it. In fact, it is created by law mainly to provide state promotion and support to organizations that contribute to the collective or general interest and the public good, and collaborate with the State in the provision of public benefit services. State promotion includes, among other things, tax breaks and the possibility to receive tax-deductible donations or other forms of private support. This may also explain why, in some European countries (just like in the US), the regulation of PBOs is found in tax laws. Finally, the status is usually protected by law (also to ensure that there is no abuse of state incentives) through the establishment of dedicated public bodies to supervise PBOs.

As previously stated, in spite of the inevitable differences in their general features and in the regulation of the subject matter, and notwithstanding the different terminology employed (public benefit organizations, non-governmental organizations, voluntary organizations, civil society organizations, non-profit organizations, charities, etc.), laws on PBOs are found in almost all the MSs of the EU. [46] Moreover, MSs are increasingly devoting attention to PBOs (or equivalent organizations, whatever their name might be). New laws on the public benefit status have been recently passed in some MSs, such as Greece and Portugal in 2021.[47] Previously abolished tax-privileged donations to PBOs have been recently reintroduced in Sweden.[48] In some countries, like for example Poland and Slovakia, the regulation of PBOs is more sophisticated than the regulation of NPOs, such as associations.[49] As we shall observe, recent events also indicate a growing interest among EU institutions in this category of organizations.[50]

With regard to the EU countries considered in this volume, we may focus our attention on Germany, Ireland and Poland, as they have the most developed PBO laws of all.[51] In particular, the 2009 Irish Act on "charities", as PBOs are named in

---

[46] Cf. Fici (2023b).

[47] Cf., in Greece, Law no. 4873/2021 on Civil Society Organizations; in Portugal, Public Benefit Status according to Law no. 36/2021 of 1 July, and Meira (2023).

[48] See Chap. 7, Sect. 3 ff., of Swedish Income Tax Act no. 1999:1229.

[49] See Slovakian Act no. 213/1997 on non-profit organizations. As for Poland, see Radwan et al. (2023).

[50] Cf. *infra* Sect. 4.

[51] As for the remaining countries, the equivalents to PBOs are in Italy the TSOs of Legislative decree no. 117/2017; in Belgium, the accredited organizations of art. 154/33 of the Income Tax Code of 1992; in the Netherlands, the organizations with the status of public benefit institutions

this country, can be taken as a reference model for legislation in this sector, just as the Italian law is for TSOs. The Polish law on the public benefit status shows very interesting features and has some specific measures in common with Italian law, as will be later highlighted. It is of a certain interest that these regulations are contained in acts of a different nature, namely, in a bespoke act in Ireland, in tax law in Germany, and in a separate act also dealing with non-governmental organizations (and volunteering) in Poland. Indeed, the source of the regulation may in some cases reveal the main (but of course, not the exclusive) intent of the national legislator in regulating PBOs, which, in Germany, is to provide tax incentives to meritorious organizations; in Poland, to identify organizations that can collaborate with the State and other public administrations in the provision of public benefit activities; and in Ireland, to offer a substantive legal framework for non-profit organizations that lack it.

3.1.1 Charity Status in Ireland

In Ireland, the conceptual distinction between NPOs and PBOs is clear, also thanks to the legislation in force. While NPOs are characterized by the sole fact of being "not-for-profit", PBOs are non-profit organizations meeting the legal requirements for registering as charities. Hence, "while not every non-profit will be a charity, every charity will be a non-profit".[52] There are more than 34,000 NPOs in Ireland, and approximately one-third are charities.[53] It is more or less the same proportion which currently exists between NPOs and TSOs in Italy.

The charity is not a legal form of an entity's incorporation but a legal status whose acquisition and maintenance are subject to the possession by the entity of specific legal requirements and its registration in a register held by the Charities Regulatory Authority (CRA), which is also the body responsible for the regulation and supervision of charities.

Like the TSO status in Italy, the charity status may be acquired by entities established in any legal form. All charitable trusts, bodies corporate and unincorporated bodies of persons that meet the requirements established by the Charities Act 2009 (CA) and are not "excluded bodies" may be registered as charities. The list of excluded bodies comprises political parties, trade unions or representative bodies of employers, and chambers of commerce, among others (sect. 2 CA).

(ANBIs); in Portugal, the organizations with the public benefit status of Law no. 36/2021, but also the "private institutions of social solidarity" of Decree-Law no. 119/1983; in Denmark, the organizations provided for in sect. 8A of Law no. 1735 of 17 August 2021; in Spain and France, a general law on public benefit organizations does not exist, but associations pursuing public benefit purposes may be recognized as such by law (see art. 32 ff. of French Law no. 1/2002 and art. 11 of French Law 1 July 1901) and foundations may only pursue such purposes.

[52] Breen (2023).

[53] Cf. Breen (2023).

Among the possible legal forms, the unincorporated association and the company limited by guarantee (CLG) are the most commonly used to establish a charitable entity.[54] A CLG is a company without share capital and therefore without shareholders in the strict sense. CLGs have legal personality (so that their members enjoy a limited liability) and may even be set up by only one person offering a guarantee of 1 EUR.

The status of charity is acquired by registration with the relevant Register maintained by the CRA (sect. 39(3) CA). Registration is possible only for organizations meeting the necessary legal requirements and which are therefore charitable organizations according to the Charities Act (sect. 39(8) CA). Only the registered charities are allowed to use this legal denomination (sect. 46(5) CA),[55] whilst non-registered entities would be guilty of an offence if they were to do so (sect. 46(2) CA).

Registered charities are required to promote a "charitable purpose only" (sect. 3(1) CA). The CA provides a list of charitable purposes, namely, (a) the prevention or relief of poverty or economic hardship; (b) the advancement of education; (c) the advancement of religion; and (d) any other purpose that is of benefit to the community (sect. 3(1) CA). The residual category under (d) includes 12 (sub-)purposes, such as, for example, the advancement of community welfare including the relief of those in need by reason of youth, age, ill-health, or disability; the advancement of community development, including rural or urban regeneration; the advancement of environmental sustainability; etc. (sect. 3(11) CA).

All charitable purposes must also be "of public benefit" (sect. 3(2) CA). This happens when the purpose is intended to benefit the public or a section of the public and when, in a case where it confers a benefit on a person other than in their capacity as a member of the public or a section of the public, any such benefit is reasonable in all of the circumstances, and is ancillary to, and necessary for, the furtherance of the public benefit (sect. 3(3) CA).

Charities do not face explicit restrictions regarding the activities that they may perform, which in principle may therefore be economic or not, provided they advance the charitable purpose. However, the economic nature of the activity may be relevant under tax law. To qualify for tax-exemption, profits must be applied solely to the purposes of the charity and in addition one of the two following conditions must be met:

---

[54] Cf. Breen (2023).

[55] In fact, registered charities are not only allowed, but are obliged to use the denomination of "charity". Sect. 46(7) CA stipulates: "A registered charitable organisation shall, in all public documents and such other publications as may be prescribed, including on television or the internet, state in legible characters (a) that it is a registered charitable organisation, and (b) provide such other information as may be prescribed, including the names of the charity trustees and the address of its principal office".

- either the trade is exercised in the course of the actual carrying out of a primary purpose of the charity (e.g., a hospital charging fees for the health care services provided), or
- the work in connection with the trade is mainly carried out by beneficiaries of the charity (sect. 208 Taxes Consolidation Act 1997).

"Economic activities that would not otherwise qualify may nonetheless fall under the trading exemption if they are ancillary to pursuing the charity's primary purpose. Examples include a theatre selling food and drink to its patrons, or a hospital selling papers, flowers, and toiletries to patients and visitors. The Revenue Commissioners make determinations on a case-by-case basis in these circumstances".[56]

A strict asset-lock applies to Irish charities, which makes them fully non-profits. A charity "is required to apply all of its property (both real and personal) in furtherance of that purpose" (sect. 2 CA). Assets may be used in the operation and maintenance of the body, including in remuneration and superannuation of staff members (sect. 2 CA), but this may be done only on the condition that remuneration be reasonable, ancillary and necessary pursuant to sect. 3(3) CA. Along the same lines, sect. 89(3) CA stipulates that "any sum or sums payable to a relevant person under an agreement shall not exceed what is reasonable and proportionate having regard to the service provided by the relevant person pursuant to the agreement", otherwise the agreement is null and void (sect. 89(11) CA). An asset-lock also applies at a charity's dissolution. The CA stipulates: "where a charitable organisation is dissolved, the property, or proceeds of the sale of the property, of the charitable organisation shall not be paid to any of the members of the charitable organisation without the consent of the Authority, notwithstanding any provision to the contrary contained in the constitution of the charitable organisation" (sect. 92 CA). However, "under the doctrine of cy près, as applied either by the CRA or upon application to the High Court, such property must be transferred to another charitable institution or institutions whose main objectives are similar to those of the dissolving body, or, failing that, to some other charitable body".[57] A clause to this effect in the charity's governing instrument is also required for tax exemption.[58]

In general, there is no detailed regulation in the CA of a charity's governance, which is in line with the fact that charities may have different legal forms. Thus, the governance of a charity mainly depends on the legal form of incorporation. The CA (as well as the applicable tax law) concentrates more on a charity's transparency and accounting, imposing upon a charity's trustees a wide number of related duties, including the submission of an annual report to the CRA,[59] rather than on its

[56] International Center for Not-for-profit Law (2020), p. 9.

[57] International Center for Not-for-profit Law (2020), p. 8; Cf. also Breen (2023).

[58] Cf. International Center for Not-for-profit Law (2020) and Breen and Smith (2019), chapter 10, for readers interested in the implications of economic activities of charities.

[59] Cf. O'Connor and McGrath (2020), p. 13; Breen (2023).

governance. The CRA partially compensates for this through its Code of governance.[60]

Some prescriptions are found in tax law in order for a charity to access tax breaks. A registered charity, regardless of its legal form, must have at least three "trustees" (a company's directors also fall within this notion) who are not related to each other and who are independent of one another.[61] Under tax law, directors are not allowed to receive any remuneration other than the refund of their expenses.[62]

The charitable status does not *per se* guarantee any tax benefit (sect. 7(1) CA). For that purpose, charities must register with the Revenue Commissioners in order to obtain the "charitable tax-exempt status" and be assigned a "CHY reference number", which indicates their eligibility for charitable tax exemption.[63] The Revenue Commissioners are not bound by the determinations of the CRA.

The income of tax-exempt charities is exempt from income tax (sect. 208 Taxes Consolidation Act 1997).

Charities are not *per se* exempt from VAT, but many activities that are VAT-exempt may be relevant for charities.[64] Tax-exempt charities are entitled to a refund of a proportion of their VAT costs under a VAT Compensation Refund Scheme introduced by the Minister for Finance in 2018.[65]

Donations are eligible for tax benefit only if their recipients are "designated charities", which requires, among other things, at least 2 years of tax-exempt status. The designation is valid for up to 5 years and, upon expiration, may be renewed.[66] Donations are eligible for tax benefit only if they exceed the minimum amount of 250 EUR per year and are within the limit of one million EUR per year. However, if there is a connection between the donor and the recipient charity (i.e., the donor is an employee or a member of the charity), tax relief is limited to 10% of the individual's total income per year.

Individual donors do not get tax benefits, but the recipient charity can claim a refund of tax paid on that donation. The relief is calculated by grossing up the donation at the specified rate, which is currently 31%. The amount of the refund cannot be more than the amount of tax paid by the donor for the same year.

---

[60] Cf. https://www.charitiesregulator.ie/media/4657/charities-governance-code-2022-final.pdf. On the governance of charities, cf. Breen and Smith (2019, Chap. 7.

[61] Cf. Breen (2020), p. 4 f.; O'Connor and McGrath (2020), p. 6.

[62] Cf. https://cof.org/sites/default/files/Common%20Requirements%20Charities%20Regulator%20Revenue.pdf.

[63] This number does not coincide with the number obtained by charities registering with the CRA: cf. International Center for Not-for-profit Law (2020), p. 7.

[64] E.g., the purchase of appliances for use by disabled persons: see International Center for Not-for-profit Law (2020), p. 15.

[65] Cf. International Center for Not-for-profit Law (2020), p. 15; O'Connor and McGrath (2020), p. 16; Breen (2023).

[66] Cf. International Center for Not-for-profit Law (2020), p. 13.

Corporate donors can claim a tax deduction as if the donation were a trading expense. Therefore, the relief corresponds to the corporation tax rate, which is currently 12.5%.

The CRA is the specific supervisor of Irish charities. Its general functions include ensuring and monitoring compliance by charitable organizations with the charity regulation (sect. 14(1)(g), CA). To this end, the CRA may appoint one or more persons "to investigate the affairs of a charitable organisation and to prepare a report thereon". These persons are referred to as "inspectors", and they have particularly incisive powers (sect. 64 CA). The CRA itself has specific powers of investigation and sanctioning (sections 68–69, 73 CA). The CRA can also apply to the High Court for the suspension or removal of any charity trustees or staff of a charity or prevent the sale of property as a result of misuse, misconduct or mismanagement.[67] Some decisions of the CRA can be appealed to a Charity Appeals Tribunal.[68]

3.1.2 Public Benefit Status in Germany

Unlike Ireland, where charities are the subject of a separate act, in Germany, the PBO status is provided for in the German Fiscal Code (AO) for tax purposes. The AO has an entire chapter dedicated to the "tax-privileged purposes", which is aimed at providing tax privileges to any legal person (a company, an association, a foundation, etc.)[69] that pursues directly and exclusively public benefit, charitable or religious purposes (sect. 51(1) AO).[70]

An organization serves a public benefit purpose "if its activity is dedicated to the altruistic advancement of the general public in material, spiritual or moral respects". Such an advancement does not subsist "if the group of persons benefiting from such advancement is circumscribed, for instance by membership of a family or the workforce of an enterprise, or can never be other than small as a result of its definition, especially in terms of geographical or professional attributes" (sect. 52(1) AO).

PBOs are thus identified by the fiscal German legislator on the basis of several requirements, regardless of the legal form of incorporation, which may even be that of a company.[71] All these requirements must be met by an organization to maintain the PBO status. Accordingly, the law stipulates that "the actual management of the organization shall be directed towards the exclusive and direct achievement of the

---

[67] Cf. O'Connor and McGrath (2020), p. 11.

[68] On the jurisdiction of this Tribunal, see Breen and Smith (2019), Chap. 6.

[69] Natural persons and partnerships without legal personality are not eligible for this status: cf. Von Hippel (2017), p. 393, fn. 40.

[70] All translations from German are official translations of the AO found on the website of the Ministry of Justice at https://www.gesetze-im-internet.de/englisch_ao/index.html.

[71] Public benefit limited liability companies are increasingly diffuse. They can use the abbreviation "gGmbH" instead of "GmbH", where the first "g" means "*gemeinnützig*" (public benefit).

tax-privileged purposes and shall conform to the provisions on the requirements for tax privileges contained in the statutes" (sect. 63(1) AO).

The first requirement regards the purpose that the organization shall pursue. According to sect. 52(2) AO, public benefit purposes are those included in a list of 25 items, including the advancement of science and research, religion, sport, protection of animals, etc. Moreover, other purposes not included in the (already rather) long list may be declared of public benefit by the fiscal competent authority if they satisfy the public benefit test in sect. 52(1) AO.

The second requirement regards the manner in which the advancement has to be provided, namely, altruistically (sect. 55 AO). The altruistic pursuit of a public benefit purpose presupposes that no economic, commercial or gainful purposes are served by the organization and, in particular, that the following conditions are met:

(1) the funds of the organization may be used only for the purposes set out in the statutes. Members or partners (members for the purposes of these provisions), as well as founders, donors and their heirs (in the case of foundations) may receive neither profit shares nor in their capacity as members any other allocations from the funds of the organization. The organization may use its funds neither for the direct nor for the indirect advancement or support of political parties;
(2) on termination of their membership or on dissolution or liquidation of the organization, members may not receive more than their paid-up capital shares and the fair market value of their contributions in kind;
(3) the organization may not provide a benefit for any person by means of expenditure unrelated to the purpose of the organization or disproportionately high remuneration;
(4) where the organization is dissolved or liquidated or where its former purpose ceases to apply, the assets of the organization in excess of the members'paid-up capital shares and the fair market value of their contributions in kind may be used only for tax-privileged purposes. This requirement can also be met if the assets are to be assigned to another tax-privileged organization or to a legal person under public law for tax-privileged purposes;
(5) subject to section 62 (which under certain conditions permits the allocation of funds to reserves), the organization shall in principle use its funds promptly for the tax-privileged purposes set out in its statutes. The use of funds for the acquisition or creation of assets serving the purposes set out in the statutes shall also constitute an appropriate use. Funds shall be deemed to have been used promptly where they are used for the tax-privileged purposes set out in the statutes by no later than two calendar or financial years following their accrual.

The third requirement is exclusivity, which is satisfied if the organization pursues only the public benefit purposes set out in its statutes (sect. 56 AO).

The fourth requirement is directness, which is met if the organization itself pursues the public benefit purposes (sect. 57 AO). In fact, however, there are several instances in which the requirement may be satisfied in an indirect manner. This happens, for example, when the organization acts through an auxiliary person or holds and manages shares in another tax-privileged organization (sect. 57(4) AO).

Sect. 58 AO lists a series of activities whose exercise does not negatively affect the PBO status. For example, the status would not be compromised by an organization assigning part of its funds, surpluses or gains to another tax-privileged organization or to a legal person under public law to be used for tax-privileged purposes (sect. 58(2) and (3) AO); by a foundation using a part not exceeding one third of its income for the appropriate upkeep of the donor and his or her near relatives, to maintain their graves and to honour their memory (sect. 58(6) AO); by an organization holding social events which are of secondary significance in comparison with its tax-privileged activities (sect. 58(7) AO); or by a sport association promoting paid, in addition to unpaid, sporting activities (sect. 58(8) AO); etc.

In a similar vein, sect. 62 AO allows a PBO to allocate all or part of its funds to reserves, within certain conditions and time limits (after a given period of time reserves must be dissolved and the funds used for pursuing the purposes) so as to prevent resources from being accumulated rather than used to reach the objectives of public benefit.

German PBOs may benefit from several tax exemptions.

They are exempt from corporate income tax (sect. 5(1), no. 9, Corporate Income Tax Act). The exemption applies to the income from the "ideal" sphere of a PBO (memberships fees; donations; etc.), from the "passive" management of its assets (e.g., bond interests), and from purpose-related economic activities.[72] In contrast, purpose-unrelated economic activities are subject to corporate income taxation if they generate total annual income including VAT that exceeds 35,000 EUR (sect. 64(3) AO).

Purpose-related economic activities are those activities that are directed towards achieving the public benefit purpose of a PBO as set out in its statutes, provided that this purpose can be achieved only by way of such activities, and these activities do not enter into competition with non-privileged activities of the same or similar type to a greater extent than necessary for achieving the public benefit purpose (sect. 65 AO). Moreover, there are some activities that are *per se* considered by law purpose-related, such as, for example, old people's homes, old people's residential and nursing homes, convalescent homes and services for the provision of meals (sect. 68 AO).[73]

Some public benefit activities are VAT exempt, including health-related, educational, cultural and scientific activities. If an economic activity is subject to VAT, PBOs apply a reduced VAT rate (7%) if the activity is purpose-related, while the ordinary VAT rate applies to their purpose-unrelated economic activities.[74]

---

[72] According to sect. 14 AO, "'Economic activity' shall mean an independent sustainable activity from which revenue or other economic benefits are derived and which comprises more than mere asset management. The intention to realise a profit shall not be required. As a rule, an activity shall be deemed to constitute asset management where assets are utilised, e.g., by investing capital assets to earn interest or by renting or leasing immovable property".

[73] Cf. Bishoff and Helm (2023), p. 142.

[74] Cf. Richter and Gollan (2020), p. 11; Bishoff and Helm (2023), p. 142.

Donations to public benefit organizations allow donors (both individuals and corporations) to obtain tax benefits. The donated amount may be deducted up to a certain extent, which is 20% of the total income for individual donors (sect. 10b (1) Income Tax Act) and 20% of the total income or 0.4% of the sum of gross revenues and salaries per year for corporate donors (sect. 9(1) n. 2, Corporate Income Tax Act).[75]

Since 2000, contributions to the endowment of foundations (including "non-independent foundations")[76] with the status of PBOs enjoy an additional tax relief. An individual donor (not a corporation) can deduct up to one million EUR from personal income tax over 10 years (sect. 10b(1a), Income Tax Act).[77]

3.1.3 Public Benefit Status in Poland

In Poland, a public benefit status is provided for by the Law of 24 April 2003. More precisely, this law first identifies (in its art. 3, para. 2) the category of "non-governmental organizations" (NGOs) and then establishes (in art. 20 ff.) the public benefit status, which may be obtained by NGOs and other organizations that carry out a public benefit activity to the benefit of society and meet other specific legal requirements related to governance, transparency and the use of profits and assets. The status is obtained upon the entity's registration in the National Court Register and lost upon cancellation from this register (art. 22 Law 24 April 2003). Polish PBOs receive significant benefits from this law and are considered fundamental partners of the public administration in the provision of public benefit activities. Indeed, cooperation between public administration and PBOs is one of the key features and objectives of this law. "Shared administration", which in Italy is only an option for public bodies, is compulsory in Poland pursuant to the provision in art. 5, para. 1, Law of 24 April 2003, according to which public administration authorities "must perform" public activities in cooperation with NGOs and other organizations eligible for the PBOs status.[78]

As regards the types of entities that may acquire the PBO status, substantially in line with Italian law on TSOs and other national laws on PBOs, including the previously examined German and Irish laws, Polish law makes the status of PBO available to all private not-for-profit entities, regardless of their legal form. Therefore, not only associations and foundations (i.e., NGOs), which are essentially non-profit according to their organic laws,[79] but also joint stock and limited liability companies may acquire the status of PBOs if they "do not operate for profit and

[75] Cf. Stanitzke (2020), p. 22; Bishoff and Helm, p. 143 ff.

[76] Non-independent foundations are in fact not legal persons but separate funds owned by individuals or legal entities.

[77] Cf. Von Hippel (2010), p. 210; Richter and Gollan (2020), p. 12.

[78] Cf. Radwan et al. (2023).

[79] Cf. Radwan et al. (2023).

allocate all of their profit to perform their statutory objectives, and they do not divide their profit between their members, shareholders, stockholders or employees" (art. 20, para. 1, and art. 3, para. 3, no. 4, Law of 24 April 2003). Religious entities may also obtain this status (art. 20, para. 1, and art. 3, para. 3, no. 1, Law of 24 April 2003). In contrast, there are some organizations that are by law ex ante "excluded" from this possibility, namely, all entities that form part of the public finance sector, political parties, trade unions, organizations of employers, and professional self-governing authorities. Significantly, social cooperatives of Law 27 April 2006 are also excluded. According to the law, they are allowed to perform public benefit activities but cannot acquire the status as PBOs, presumably because Polish social cooperatives are by law devoted to the work integration of disadvantaged people in business activities, rather than to the performance of public benefit activities.

The main legal condition for obtaining the status is performing public benefit activities. More precisely, an eligible organization may register as a PBO only if it shows that it has already carried out one or more public benefit activities for at least 2 years (art. 20, para. 1 and art. 22, para. 1, Law of 24 April 2003). These activities must be conducted "to the benefit of the entire society or of a specific group of individuals provided that such group can be distinguished from the society due to difficult living conditions or financial situation", and in any event not solely to the benefit of the members of the organization (art. 20, para. 1, no. 1, and art. 20, para. 2, Law of 24 April 2003). As happens in other jurisdictions, including those previously examined, Polish law lists the public benefit activities that PBOs must perform to retain the status. The list in art. 4, para. 1, of the Law, is very long and has been increased over time. It currently includes 40 activities, ranging from social assistance to supporting NGOs and other organizations that perform public benefit activities.

The law does not require that these public benefit activities be conducted for free and in a non-entrepreneurial way. Therefore, they may in principle even generate profits as long as profits are not distributed by the PBO and are reinvested in the latter's public benefit activities (art. 21, no. 2, Law 24 April 2003).[80] In contrast, as regards a PBO's activities which are not of public benefit, the rule is that PBOs "may pursue business activity solely as an activity auxiliary to public benefit work" and provided that income is allocated to the public benefit activities of the organization (art. 20, para. 1, no. 2 and 3, Law of 24 April 2003).

The other legal requirements for the maintenance of the status concern the entity's governance, transparency and the use of its profits and assets.

PBOs must have an internal supervisory body, which must be independent from the management body. The members of the supervisory body may be reimbursed for any reasonably incurred costs and can also be remunerated at a rate not exceeding the

[80] Specifically, art. 21, no. 2, is referred only to certain PBOs, namely religious entities and companies. It does not also address associations and foundations because these legal forms of organization are already non-profit on the basis of their particular laws. Of course, this rule does not allow an ordinary association—which, unlike a registered association, may not conduct business activities—to conduct public benefits activities that generate profits.

average monthly remuneration in the corporate sector announced for the previous year by the President of the Central Statistical Office (art. 20, para. 1, no. 4, Law of 24 April 2003). The members of the management body of a PBO must not have been convicted by virtue of a final court judgement for any crime involving intentional fault or for a tax offence (art. 20, para. 1, no. 5, Law of 24 April 2003).

To prevent "indirect" distributions of profits to the detriment of the public benefit purpose, the law prohibits PBOs from performing any act in which members, boards'members, employees, etc., might have a direct interest, such as, for example, granting loans or pledging the organisation's property to secure any financial liabilities of these people (art. 20, para. 1, no. 6, Law of 24 April 2003).

PBOs are also subject to specific reporting requirements. They must draft (in accordance with a detailed regulation from the competent minister) and publish an annual performance report describing their activities and an annual financial statement, and submit them to the competent minister (art. 23).

PBOs are subject to a specific form of public supervision aimed at verifying compliance with the requirements for qualification and the rules that apply to PBOs. The auditing procedure is carefully regulated by law and may culminate in the removal of the PBO from the relevant register, which implies the loss of the status and the obligation to devolve residual assets to other organizations with identical or similar statutory objectives (arts. 28–34 Law of 24 April 2003).

As is the case for Irish charities and German PBOs, as well as for Italian TSOs, Polish PBOs are granted several benefits by law. These benefits are not only those deriving from their being considered "natural" partners of the public administration in the performance of public benefit activities.

Art. 24 of Law of 24 April 2003 exempts PBOs from a number of taxes, including corporate income tax as long as the income is allocated to the performance of public benefit activities. Art. 26 of the same law prescribes that "public radio and television facilities shall provide public benefit organisations with free of charge broadcasting time to inform the general public of their activities, in conformity with the rules laid out in separate legal provisions". Art. 27 allows a personal income taxpayer to donate 1.5% of the tax to support personally selected PBOs, which is a promotional measure that we have already found in Italian law with regard to TSOs (where, however, it is limited to 0.5%).

Polish tax law gives incentives to donations. Both personal and corporate income tax payers can deduct from their taxable basis donations to PBOs and other organizations that conduct public benefit activities (as defined in the Law of 24 April 2003), within the limits of 6% of the taxable income for physical persons and 10% for corporations.[81]

The Polish legal framework regarding the third sector is richer and more articulated than those found in Germany and Ireland. In addition to NGOs and PBOs, the law also provides for social cooperatives, social enterprises and social economy entities. Unlike Italy, where the third sector explicitly includes social enterprises and

[81] Cf. International Center for Not-for-profit Law (2019), p. 9.

the category of social economy organizations does not exist, in Poland the relationships between NGOs, PBOs and social economic entities, such as social cooperatives and social enterprises, need to be properly understood. We will come back to this issue later in this chapter, after having introduced and discussed further elements of our analysis.

3.2 Laws on Social Enterprises

According to the Italian legislation, social enterprises form part of the third sector. More precisely, social enterprises represent the entrepreneurial subset of the Italian third sector, and contrary to other types of TSOs, they can also be incorporated (not only as associations and foundations, but also) as companies or cooperatives and may partially distribute profits to their shareholders. Evidently, these specificities have not been considered so relevant by the Italian legislator to exclude social enterprises from the third sector area, where they therefore co-exist with non-market organizations, such as voluntary organizations and philanthropic entities.[82] This may appear striking to all those—like American commentators—who observe this legislation from the point of view of a national law that identifies TSOs with charitable organizations,[83] but it is the result of a tailor-made regulation, capable of combining the pursuit of a charitable objective with business methods, which includes the legal provision of a complete or (at least) partial profit distribution constraint and a general lock on the organization's assets.

Technically speaking, in Italian law, "social enterprise" is a legal status of the third sector, available to organizations (established in any legal form) that meet certain requirements, which, in line with the general regulation of TSOs, concern the aim pursued (a civic, solidaristic and social utility purpose), the activity carried out (a general interest activity performed in an entrepreneurial way), governance (which must be inclusive) and transparency of the organization (including the obligation to draft and publish an annual social report). As previously underlined, companies and cooperatives which hold the Italian social enterprise status, may distribute part of their profits to their shareholders. In addition, Italian law also provides for "social cooperatives" in a separate act, Law no. 381/1991, which, as we shall see, can be considered the first ad hoc law on social enterprises in Europe. Italian social cooperatives are de jure social enterprises (and therefore they are de jure TSOs as well).

Admittedly, notwithstanding the initial impulse given by this country to the legal acknowledgement of this phenomenon, today social enterprise is not an Italian peculiarity, as it is now recognized and regulated in more than two-thirds of the EU Member States. With limited regard to the national jurisdictions examined in this

[82] Cf. Fici (2023c).

[83] Cf. Brakman Reiser (2023).

volume, the countries with specific laws on social enterprise, including social cooperatives, are—apart from Italy—Belgium, Denmark, France, Spain, Portugal and Poland, whereas in those that still lack an ad hoc legislation—namely, Germany, Ireland and the Netherlands—there are specific plans for their introduction.[84]

However, in these jurisdictions, the relationships between social enterprises and other categories of organizations, are not as clear as they are in Italy. For example, in some countries, such as Denmark and Spain, social enterprises seem to be kept separate from PBOs (or the equivalent national category, regardless of the name), mainly because social enterprises can distribute profits to their shareholders within certain limits, while PBOs are fully non-profit.[85] Yet, in Poland, the recent law of 2022 on the social economy, seems to allow an organization to have both the status of PBO and that of social enterprise, although it must be underlined that Polish social enterprises may not distribute profits to their shareholders (see art. 3, para. 1, and art. 9, para. 1, Law 5 August 2022). In the countries that have a general law on the social economy—namely, France, Portugal, Spain and most recently Poland—social enterprises are considered SEEs, whereas not all of them are always PBOs so, since it depends on whether the law subjects the qualification as an SEE to the carrying-out of economic activities. In Poland, for example, the definition of an SEE seems not to be contingent upon the performance of economic activities, whereas in France, Portugal and Spain the social (and solidarity) economy comprises only entities running an enterprise.

In this section, we will provide a general overview of social enterprise law in the EU Member States, focusing on the patterns of this legislation and its most recent trends. Readers can refer to other chapters of this volume if they wish to have more details on each national law on social enterprise.

3.2.1 Social Purpose Cooperatives

Italian Law no. 381 of 8 November 1991 on "social cooperatives" is widely recognized as the cornerstone of the legislation on social enterprise in Europe.[86] Indeed, this law has given rise to a wave of similar laws throughout Europe (and not only in Europe). In the EU alone, there are nine MSs that have specific laws on social

[84] Cf. Breen (2023); Möslein (2023); van der Sangen (2023).

[85] In contrast, in Poland, the recent law of 2022 on the social economy, seems to allow an organization to have both the status of PBO and that of social enterprise, but it must be underlined that Polish social enterprises are not authorized to distribute profits to their shareholders: see art. 3, para. 1, and art. 9, para. 1, Law of 5 August 2022.

[86] In this sense, cf., among others, Galera and Borzaga (2009); Defourny and Nyssens (2012), p. 3; Crama (2014), p. 17. However, although it cannot be denied that Italian Law no. 381/1991 initiated a process that involved several EU Member States and, therefore, had a strong cultural impact even outside the borders of its application, it must be acknowledged that the UK's Industrial and Provident Societies Act (IPSA) of 1965 already provided for the establishment of a "Community Benefit Society", that is, a society whose business "is being, or is intended to be, conducted for the benefit of the community" (see sect. 1(2)(b) IPSA 1965, and now sect. 2(2)(a)(ii) of the Co-operative and Community Benefit Societies Act of 2014).

cooperatives. Besides Italy, this group of MSs comprises Croatia,[87] Czech Republic,[88] France,[89] Greece,[90] Hungary,[91] Poland,[92] Portugal[93] and Spain.[94] Notwithstanding the commonalities, social cooperatives are differently denominated and regulated in each jurisdiction. In Hungary and Poland, only work integration social cooperatives are explicitly recognized by law. In other MSs, such as Germany, although they are not explicitly provided for by law, cooperatives with the substantial features of social cooperatives may however be established.[95] "Social purpose" cooperatives also exist in Belgium following the reform of organizational law which took place in 2019, but they are legally recognized in a different manner, as will be described later.

Italian social cooperatives are a sub-type of cooperatives with a particular function (different from that of "ordinary" cooperatives),[96] which is "to pursue the general interest of the community in the human promotion and social integration of citizens", either through the management of socio-health or educational services (social cooperatives of type A) or through the conduct of any business for the employment of disadvantaged persons (social cooperatives of type B or work integration social cooperatives), who must be at least 30% of the total workers of the social cooperative. Both types of social cooperatives may have volunteer members, but no more than 50% of total members. In "type B" social cooperatives, the disadvantaged persons must be members of the social cooperative if it is compatible with their state. Both types of social cooperatives may distribute profits to their members as dividends on the paid-up capital, but only up to a precise limit, which is

[87] Cf. art. 66 on social cooperatives (*socijalne zadruga*), of Law of 11 March 2011, no. 764, on cooperatives.

[88] Cf. sects. 758 ff., on social cooperative (*sociální družstvo*), of Law no. 90/2012 on commercial companies and cooperatives.

[89] Cf. art. 19-*quinquies* ff., on collective interest cooperative societies (*sociétés coopérative d'intérêt collectif*), of Law no. 47-1775 of 10 September 1947 on cooperatives.

[90] Cf. Laws no. 2716/1999 and no. 4019/2011 on social cooperatives (*Κοιωωνικοί Συνεταιρισμοί*).

[91] Cf. arts. 8, 10(4), 51(4), 59(3), 60(1), 68(2)(e), on social cooperatives (*szociális szövetkezetnek*), of Law no. X-2006 on cooperatives.

[92] Cf. Law of 27 April 2006 on social cooperatives (*spółdzielni´ socjalnà*).

[93] Cf. Law-Decree no. 7/98 of 15 January 1998 on social solidarity cooperatives (*cooperativas de solidariedade social*).

[94] Cf. art. 106, on social initiative cooperatives (*cooperativas de iniciativa social*), of Law no. 27/1999 of 16 July 1999 on cooperatives.

[95] Also due to the fact that German cooperatives may be established to pursue not only the economic interests, but also the "social and cultural interests" of their members (see art. 1, para. 1. of the German cooperative law of 1889 as amended in 2006).

[96] The "mutual purpose" (as referred to in some jurisdictions) that in general characterizes cooperatives is to act in the interest of the members as consumers/users, providers or workers of the cooperative enterprise. In contrast, social cooperatives pursue a "non-mutual" purpose, because they act primarily in the general interest of the community. A social cooperative's members, therefore, cooperate not to serve themselves (as is the case in ordinary cooperatives), but to serve others.

2.5 points more than the maximum interest of postal bonds (it is the same subjective limit that applies to Italian social enterprises, which, however, cannot distribute more than half of their annual profits).[97] Italian social cooperatives enjoy several tax-breaks and are recipients of various supporting measures provided by the State, in addition to those that they may receive in their quality as social enterprises and TSOs.[98]

The drivers of this form of legislation on social enterprise can be identified with the specific characteristics of the cooperative legal form of business organization. The Italian legislator, and the other national legislators following the Italian example, evidently considered the cooperative the most appropriate legal form to host social enterprises. Indeed, this was the legal form chosen in Italy by those who first set up social cooperatives even before the enactment of the relevant law of 1991.[99]

Firstly, cooperatives are recognized by the Italian Constitution, as well as by many other national Constitutions in Europe, as enterprises with a social function, which justifies the legislator's constitutional obligation to support them.[100] Therefore, nothing appeared more appropriate for those who wanted to establish a business enterprise with explicit social purposes, than to use this legal form to which the fundamental law of the State attributed a social function, providing for their promotion by the State.

Secondly, cooperatives have a governance structure that is immediately and straightforwardly consistent with the nature and purposes of a social enterprise. This is mainly due to the fact that, according to the applicable legislation, cooperatives are democratic organizations in which members of the assembly (the "supreme body" of a cooperative) each holds one vote regardless of the amount of capital held. Member-control and participation are additional principles normally enacted and promoted by the relevant cooperative laws (for example, mandating the presence of at least a majority of members in the board of directors). Other features, such as the "variable capital", the "variable number of members", and the "open door" principle, as well as the compulsory allocation of minimum percentages of profits to reserves that are indivisible among members, also contribute to this conclusion.[101]

---

[97] French law on SCICs also allows a limited distribution of profits to an SCIC's members (see art. 19 *nonies* Law no. 47-1775). On the other hand, such a possibility is not recognized to Polish, Portuguese and Spanish social cooperatives. In Portugal, social cooperatives are considered part of the non-market sector of the social economy and for this reason they are distinguished from social enterprises, which instead belong to the market sector: see Meira (2023). In Spain, social cooperatives are in some cases included within the third sector: see Fajardo-García (2023).

[98] As already stated in the main text, cooperatives are recognized by law as social enterprises and therefore as third sector organizations. See also Fici (2022).

[99] Cf. Consorzio Gino Mattarelli (1988).

[100] The list of countries is very long: It includes Italy, Spain, Portugal and many others. See, also for further references, Fici (2015) and Douvitsa (2022).

[101] Cf. van der Sangen (2023) for additional arguments in favour of the cooperative model for social enterprise.

The above leads to a preference for the social enterprise in the cooperative form which is found even in countries, like Italy, that adhere to the model of legislation on social enterprise described in the next sub-section of this chapter, and in which, therefore, social enterprises may assume different legal forms, not only the cooperative form. Indeed, in these jurisdictions, social cooperatives receive better legal treatment (under tax law, for example) than social enterprises established in other legal forms.[102]

The preference for the cooperative form of social enterprise is yet more evident in the case of Belgium, which has moved from a model of social enterprise legislation based on the company form to one based on the cooperative form.[103] In this country, the law previously provided for a specific form of company with a social purpose, or rather for a specific label that could be attached to any form of company meeting the necessary legal requirements (*société à finalité sociale* or SFS). After the reform in 2019 that led to the adoption of the Code of Companies and Associations (which in reality also regulates other forms, including foundations), the SFS was repealed, and it is now provided that only cooperatives may be accredited as social enterprises. Cooperatives will qualify for this status if their "main objective is not to provide their shareholders with an economic or social advantage, in order to satisfy their professional or private needs", but "to generate a positive societal impact for the human being, the environment or the society" (art. 8:5).[104]

Therefore, "social enterprises as social cooperatives" characterizes the first generation of laws on social enterprise in the MSs of the EU. The Belgian and Italian examples show that MSs continue to express a positive attitude towards the cooperative form of social enterprise.

By way of contrast, in the first two decades of specific legislation on social enterprise in the EU, national legislators very rarely adopted social enterprise solutions focused on the company form.

A "social purpose" company, as a sub-type or modified type of company with a particular function (not to distribute profits to shareholders or to maximize their value, but to pursue the general interest, the interest of the community, or, if one prefers, the "social value"),[105] existed only in Belgium before the reform of 2019. Of course, before Brexit, the British "community interest company" or CIC was the most prominent example of this type of legislation at the EU level, also in virtue of

[102] Another significant example of this being the case is to be found in Portugal, where social insertion enterprises, which are considered social enterprises, may take the form of a cooperative, an association or a foundation, but not that of a company: cf. Meira (2023).

[103] Cf. Culot and Defer (2023).

[104] Translation by Author. The French original text is the following: their "*but principal ne consiste pas à procurer à ses actionnaires un avantage économique ou social, pour la satisfaction de leurs besoins professionnels ou privés*", but "*de générer un impact sociétal positif pour l'homme, l'environnement ou la société*".

[105] Cf. Liptrap (2020), p. 15.

the huge success of this form of social enterprise,[106] even greater than that of the first form to appear in Europe, namely, the Italian social cooperative.[107] In the Netherlands, in 2021, the Ministry of Economic Affairs launched a proposal to introduce a limited liability company with a social objective, which attracted criticism from commentators questioning why other legal forms, including cooperatives, were to be excluded from the status.[108]

The limited use, if not non-use, of the company form for social enterprises by MSs in the first phase of the legislation on social enterprise was not only due to the ample diffusion of the cooperative model but also to the concerns surrounding this alternative. Companies are normally used for making and distributing profits to their shareholders and have a governance structure based on the capital, with the unlimited possibility for a single member, even profit-oriented, to control the enterprise. This increases the risk of a social enterprise adopting a company form deviating from its social purposes. In other words, the risks of abuses were considered to be greater with the company form than with others, notably the cooperative form.

This preoccupation emerges from the relevant legislation. In Belgium, where social enterprises in the form of companies were permitted before the reform of 2019, in a social purpose company no shareholder could have more than one-tenth of the votes in the shareholders'general meeting.[109] This line of thought permeates other legislation as well. In Italy, for example, companies with the status of social enterprises may not be formed by a single member who is an individual or a for-profit legal entity, nor may a social enterprise company be subject to the dominant influence (by way of majority shareholding or other means) of a for-profit legal entity.[110] In Slovenia, for-profit companies may establish social enterprises only in order to create new jobs for redundant workers, but not with the exclusive aim of transferring their businesses or assets to the social enterprise.[111]

[106] 26,000 CICs as of 31 March 2022, according to the Regulator of Community Interest Companies Annual Report 2021/2022. On this specific subject, cf. Liptrap (2021a).

[107] The current number of active Italian social cooperatives ranges between 15,000 and 17,000.

[108] Cf. van der Sangen (2023).

[109] Cf. repealed art. 661, para. 1, no. 4, of the Belgian Company Code. This maximum percentage was even lower (i.e., equal to one-twentieth), if the shareholder were a '*membre du personnel engagé par la société*' (staff member employed by the company). Cf. also art. 23 of Slovenian Law no. 20/2011, which imposes on social enterprises the obligation to treat members equally in decision-making processes and, in particular, prescribes a single vote for all members, regardless of the particular law of the entity's incorporation.

[110] Cf. art. 4, para. 3, Italian Legislative Decree no. 112/2017, as well as art. 7, para. 2, of the same act. The solution found in Spanish Law no. 44/2007 is even stricter, given that only not-for-profit entities, associations and foundations may promote the establishment of integration enterprises (see articles 5, lit. a) and 6).

[111] Cf. art. 9, para. 1, of Slovenian Law no. 20/2011. In addition, it is worth mentioning that the second paragraph of the same article of this national law suggests that an entity may not acquire the social enterprise qualification if it is subject to the dominant influence of one or more for-profit companies.

However, it is worth highlighting that in some countries, like previously examined Germany and Ireland, the company form is widely used to obtain the public-benefit or charitable status. Although not formally recognized as such, these public benefit companies fit neatly into the concept of social enterprise. They are *de facto* social enterprises, even though their qualification as PBOs prevents them from distributing any profit to their shareholders.[112]

Indeed, with a proper regulation that seeks to reduce the risk of abuse, mandates and safeguards the primacy of the social purpose (which may imply specific rules on the nature and composition of shareholding, on the use of profits and on governance), even the company form may be usefully employed to shape a social enterprise.

The social enterprise in the company form may also have some comparative advantages over cooperative alternatives. Among other things, a social enterprise taking a company form may in principle attract more risk capital and finance when necessary for certain business operations, may be used to arrange relationships for which the democratic structure of a cooperative would be unfit, and may be employed by other non-profit organizations to conduct an entrepreneurial activity separately.

3.2.2 Social Enterprise Status

The enactment of original laws on social enterprise, first in Finland in 2003 and then in Italy in 2006,[113] together with certain initiatives from the EU institutions in this field (which will be discussed later in this chapter), triggered a new wave of national social enterprise laws in Europe. These laws share common features and are based on a specific concept of social enterprise inspired by the work of the European Commission in this area. This new trend is on-going. After Cyprus in 2020 and Malta in 2022, the last Member State that has followed this model of legislation is Poland, where the status of social enterprise is now provided for in the law of social economy of August 2022.

These second-generation laws on social enterprise were even adopted by MSs, like France, Italy and Slovakia, which already had social enterprise laws based on the cooperative model previously examined in this chapter. Thus, now there are some MSs that have more than one law addressing social enterprise. This evolution is also influencing the debate in those MSs, like Ireland and the Netherlands, which continue to lack specific legislation on this subject.[114]

---

[112] The possibility to use any legal form, including the company form, to set up and operate a *de facto* social enterprise, which may additionally have the status of charity (or PBO), may justify the lack of a tailored legal form for social enterprises in these countries, although its introduction, as pointed out in the main text, is under discussion.

[113] The first Italian law on social enterprise was Legislative decree no. 155/2006, now repealed by Legislative Decree no. 112/2017, which provides the new regulation.

[114] Cf. Lalor and Doyle (2021); Breen (2023); van der Sangen (2023).

The main characteristic of these second-generation national laws is that they consider the social enterprise as a legal status based on some requirements related to the purpose pursued (a social purpose, a general interest or public benefit purpose, etc.), the activity carried out (an enterprise of social utility or of general interest, as well the work integration of disadvantaged people[115]) and the governance (which must be democratic or inclusive) and transparency of the organization (including the obligation to draft and publish a social report). The legal form of incorporation of the entity is in principle not relevant for the acquisition of the status, so that these laws allow associations, foundations, companies and cooperatives all to qualify as "social enterprises". The exclusive social mission does not prevent social enterprises from being able to distribute part of their profits to their shareholders (as is the case in Belgium, Denmark and Italy, among others), although in some jurisdictions, like Poland, a full prohibition regarding profit distribution exists.

Furthermore, an organization does not incorporate as a social enterprise but acquires this status by its own decision, if and when it can meet the necessary legal requirements. Accordingly, an organization may lose the status of social enterprise while remaining legally organized if it chooses to do so or fails to maintain the legal requirements for social enterprise qualification. The legal status is supervised, and enforcement ensured, by public authorities, which de-qualify an entity when they find irregularities and these irregularities are not resolved. Upon de-qualification, an organization has to disinterestedly devolve its assets, or rather, either all its assets or only those accumulated after registration, depending on the national law.

The impact of this status-based model of legislation on national laws has been so strong that, in some countries, it was applied even to a specific legal form. Rather than providing for the establishment of a social cooperative as a sub-type of cooperative and of a social purpose company as a sub-type of company, Belgium and Latvia introduced an accreditation system limited to a single type of entity. In Belgium, only a cooperative may qualify as a social enterprise.[116] In Latvia, only a limited liability company may so qualify.[117] There are also MSs, such as Luxembourg and Malta, that limit the status to some legal forms, such as companies and cooperatives.[118] But the majority of MSs, as noted earlier, make the social enterprise

[115]Disadvantaged people must be a minimum of 30% of total workers in a social enterprise according to the Italian law of 2017 and now also to the Polish social enterprise regulation of 2022.

[116]Cf. art. 8:5 of the Code of companies and associations of 2019 and Culot and Defer (2023).

[117]Cf. Social Enterprise Law of 12 October 2017.

[118]Cf. Luxembourg Law of 12 December 2016 on social impact societies and art. 3 of Maltese Social Enterprise Act IX of 2022, which restricts the status of social enterprises to companies, partnerships and cooperatives. Along similar lines, the qualification as an "integration enterprise" according to Spanish Law no. 44/2007 is limited to those enterprises with the legal form of a commercial company (*sociedad mercantil*) or a cooperative (*sociedad cooperative*) (art. 4, para. 1).

legal status or qualification available to any organization regardless of the legal form.[119]

This model of legislation on social enterprise has been widely praised. It has been recommended by legal scholars[120] and was bolstered by the European Parliament's Resolution of 5 July 2018.[121] This document called on the European Commission to introduce at Union level a "European Social Economy Label" to be awarded to enterprises complying with certain criteria but incorporated in any form available in the legislation of the MSs and the EU. [122]

A number of advantages may be attributed to this status-based model of social enterprise legislation in comparison to models based on specific legal forms. The first advantage is practical. A status-based model permits existing organizations to become social enterprises without having to re-incorporate using alternative forms and permits existing social enterprises to shed this qualification without having to dissolve, convert, or re-incorporate. By reducing the cost of classification as a social enterprise, the status-based model thereby facilitate access to (and exit from) the social enterprise domain.[123]

Rather than imposing a specific legal form for said purpose, the status-based model of social enterprise legislation[124] also promotes pluralism of organizational forms, through a multiplication of the options available to those who wish to create a social enterprise. The most suitable legal form for running a social enterprise may vary according to the circumstances and the nature of a particular business or the legal and cultural background found in a given country. Permitting entities adopting various organizational forms to access the social enterprise status recognizes these specific needs and contexts. This openness particularly favours associations and foundations, whose capacity to run a business has not been addressed by many MSs or at the EU level. It also legitimates the social enterprises taking company forms, which, as explained above, may present particular advantages under some

[119] As clearly stated in art. 1, para. 1, of Italian Legislative Decree no. 112/2017 on social enterprise, which reads: "all private entities, including those established in the forms of the fifth Book of the Civil Code, may acquire the qualification of social enterprise". The legal forms of the fifth Book are companies and cooperatives. See also Bulgarian Law no. 240/2018 on social and solidarity enterprises; Danish Law no. 711 of 25 June 2014 on registered social enterprises; Finnish Law no. 711 of 25 June 2014 on registered social enterprises; art. L3332-17-1 of the French Labour Code on the solidarity enterprise of social utility; Greek Law no. 4430/2016 on the social and solidarity economy; Lithuanian Law no. IX-2251 of 1 June 2004; Art. 8 ff. of Romanian Law no. 219/2015 of 23 July 2015 on the social economy; Slovakian Law no. 112/2018 of 13 March 2018 on social economy and social enterprises; Slovenian Law no. 20 of 2011 on social entrepreneurship; Spanish Law no. 44/2007 of 13 December 2007, on integration enterprises, and art. 43 ff. of Spanish Royal Legislative decree no. 1/2013 of 29 November 2013, on special employment centres.

[120] Cf., in particular, Sørensen and Neville (2014) and Lavišius et al. (2020).

[121] Available at https://eur-lex.europa.eu/legal-content/EN/TXT/PDF/?uri=CELEX:52018IP0317&rid=4. This resolution was based on the final recommendations provided in Fici (2017).

[122] Cf. Vargas Vasserot (2021) and Liptrap (2021b).

[123] Cf. Sørensen and Neville (2014), p. 284.

[124] In Cafaggi and Iamiceli (2009) this model of legislation is referred to as the "open-form" model.

circumstances. Of equal importance, this model of legislation allows legislators to organize and combine the legal requirements for qualification in different ways depending on the legal form of incorporation of the social enterprise, thereby making the qualification as social enterprise more flexible.[125]

A status-based model can resolve the dilemma between the company form and the cooperative form, which the other model of social enterprise legislation inevitably poses,[126] while still imposing consistent and exacting demands. Imposing robust requirements on all social enterprises (or rather, on all organizations that wish to qualify as social enterprises), independently from their legal form of incorporation ensures that all social enterprises share a common identity.[127] Finally, under this model of legislation, imposing sanctions may be simpler for the public authority in charge of the enforcement of the social enterprise qualification (and less onerous for the same organization). In circumstances of noncompliance, it can suffice to revoke the qualification (or threaten to revoke it if irregularities are not removed), rather than requiring the legal entity to dissolve or convert to another form.[128]

3.3 *Laws on the Social Economy*

The "social and solidarity economy" (SSE) is at the centre of a growing institutional interest. First the European Commission in December 2021,[129] soon after the International Labour Organization and the OECD in June 2022,[130] and finally the

[125] For example, the democratic and participatory character of a social enterprise in the cooperative form permits relaxation of the profit non-distribution requirement, while the non-democratic character of a social enterprise in the company form imposes rigidity as regards profit distribution, as well as specific measures to ensure stakeholders'involvement.

[126] This does not mean, however, that the social enterprise in the company form does not also require specific rules under this model of legislation, in order to make it (more) consistent with a social enterprise's identity, as we have clarified *supra* in the main text.

[127] Moreover, nothing prevents legislators from providing different treatment for social enterprises established in different forms; for example, to favour, under tax law or policy measures, a social enterprise in the cooperative form, in consideration of its democratic nature as compared to a social enterprise in the company form.

[128] Cf. Sørensen and Neville (201), p. 284 f.

[129] EC's Communication of December 2021 entitled "Building an economy that works for people: an action plan for the social economy", available at file:///Users/antoniofici/Downloads/Building%20an%20economy%20that%20works%20for%20people%20-%20an%20action%20plan%20for%20the%20social%20economy%20(3).pdf and cf. *infra* Sect. 4.

[130] See, respectively, ILO Resolution of 10 June 2022 concerning "decent work and the social solidarity economy", available at https://www.ilo.org/wcmsp5/groups/public/%2D%2D-ed_norm/%2D%2D-relconf/documents/meetingdocument/wcms_848633.pdf, and OECD Recommendation of 10 June 2022 on "the social and solidarity economy and social innovation", available at https://legalinstruments.oecd.org/en/instruments/OECD-LEGAL-0472%20.

United Nations in April 2023,[131] adopted strategies, recommendations and resolutions on the social and solidarity economy, highlighting its essential role for economy and society and encouraging all their addressees to promote it with various measures, including an enabling legal framework.

Although using different words, these acts substantially agree on the concept of SSE and the types of organizations that compose this sector.

According to the definition in the ILO Resolution of 2022, also referred to by the UN Resolution of 2023, "the SSE encompasses enterprises, organizations and other entities that are engaged in economic, social, and environmental activities to serve the collective and/or general interest, which are based on the principles of voluntary cooperation and mutual aid, democratic and/or participatory governance, autonomy and independence, and the primacy of people and social purpose over capital in the distribution and use of surpluses and/or profits as well as assets. SSE entities aspire to long-term viability and sustainability, and to the transition from the informal to the formal economy and operate in all sectors of the economy. They put into practice a set of values which are intrinsic to their functioning and consistent with care for people and planet, equality and fairness, interdependence, self-governance, transparency and accountability, and the attainment of decent work and livelihoods. According to national circumstances, the SSE includes cooperatives, associations, mutual societies, foundations, social enterprises, self-help groups and other entities operating in accordance with the values and principles of the SSE".

In a similar vein, in the OECD document of 2022, the SSE "is made up of a set of organisations such as associations, cooperatives, mutual organisations, foundations, and, more recently, social enterprises. In some cases, community-based, grassroots and spontaneous initiatives are part of the social economy in addition to non-profit organisations, the latter group often being referred to as the solidarity economy. The activity of these entities is typically driven by societal objectives, values of solidarity, the primacy of people over capital and, in most cases, by democratic and participative governance".

Both definitions have their roots in the definition formulated by the European Commission in the pertinent communication of December 2021.

According to the EC, the social economy "covers entities sharing the following main common principles and features: the primacy of people as well as social and/or environmental purpose over profit, the reinvestment of most of the profits and surpluses to carry out activities in the interest of members/users ('collective interest') or society at large ('general interest') and democratic and/or participatory governance".

The EC goes on clarifying that "traditionally, the term social economy refers to four main types of entities providing goods and services to their members or society at large: cooperatives, mutual benefit societies, associations (including charities), and foundations".

---

[131] See UN Resolution on "promoting the social and solidarity economy for sustainable development", available at https://unsse.org/wp-content/uploads/2023/04/A-77-L60.pdf.

The EC also includes social enterprises, and work integration social enterprises among them, in the social economy. According to the EC, "social enterprises operate by providing goods and services for the market in an entrepreneurial and often innovative fashion, having social and/or environmental objectives as the reason for their commercial activity. Profits are mainly reinvested with a view to achieving their societal objective. Their method of organisation and ownership also follow democratic or participatory principles or focus on social progress. Social enterprises adopt a variety of legal forms depending on the national context".

The EC finally points out that terms such as "social economy enterprises", "social and solidarity enterprises" and "third sector" are also used by some stakeholders, countries and international organisations to refer to social economy entities.

Notwithstanding their undoubtable importance, all these definitions are very general and based on different criteria, such as the way in which the entities operate (primacy of people over profit, etc.), the legal form (association, cooperative, etc.), and the possess of a legal status (social enterprise). What is not clear is how they combine with each other. Does, for example, the legal form prevail over the operational principles and values, so that associations, foundations and cooperatives are in any event to be considered SEEs regardless of their missions and the manner in which they concretely operate? The relationship between the recognition of an entity as an SEE and the performance of economic/entrepreneurial activities is also unclear. Are therefore only entities running economic activities to be included in the SSE? Or also pure voluntary and philanthropic entities?

These doubts do not favour an analysis of the SSE from the point of view and in the perspective of the third sector and its regulation.

On the other hand, the social economy is recognized by ad hoc laws in some national jurisdictions, including France, Poland, Portugal and Spain, among the countries covered by this volume.

Moving from these laws, we will therefore try to clarify the legal relationships between social economy entities and third sector organizations, including public benefit organizations and social enterprises.

3.3.1 Spanish Law No. 5/2011 on Social Economy

Spanish Law no. 5/2011 is the first law on social economy in Europe, thus testifying to the attention paid by this country to the concept of social economy and the leading role played by it in the diffusion and promotion of this concept.

This Law does not purport to regulate the entities of the social economy in detail, but only to recognize them as a unitary category of organizations based on common characteristics, as well as to support them in various ways (art. 1).[132] Among other things, Law no. 5/2011 considers the promotion of SEEs as a general interest task (art. 8, para. 1) and creates the "Council for the Promotion of the Social Economy" as

[132] Cf. Fajardo-García (2023).

an advisory body composed of representatives of the State and the autonomous regions and of representatives of the SEEs and their umbrella organizations.

The social economy is defined in art. 2 as the complex of economic and entrepreneurial activities performed by the entities of the social economy in the collective interest of their members and/or in the general economic or social interest.

As regards the identification of SEEs, the Spanish Law uses two separate criteria, which are the legal form of the entity and the manner in which the entities operate. More precisely, some entities, such as cooperatives, mutual societies, foundations and associations that carry out economic activities, as well as social-labour insertion companies and special employment centres (which in Spain are considered social enterprises), are recognized as SEEs by art. 5, para. 1. In contrast, other entities may be so qualified only if they act in conformity with certain principles laid down in art. 4 and are included in a catalogue of entities (art. 5, para. 2).[133] The "guiding principles"[134] in art. 4 of the Law concern.

(a) the primacy of people and of the social purpose over capital, which has implications on the decision-making process of the organization (which must be transparent, democratic and inclusive, based on the members'contribution to the entity's activity and not on their capital contribution);
(b) the allocation of profits according to members' participation in the entity's activity (as workers or providers) or to the entity's social purpose;
(c) the promotion of solidarity to reach particular objectives (such as local development, social cohesion, etc.);
(d) independence from public authorities.

The social economy, as delineated by the Spanish law of 2011, clearly does not correspond to the third sector emerging from Italian law and the comparative legal analysis conducted within this chapter. Nor is it possible to conclude that the Spanish legal concept of social economy comprises that of the third sector, and that TSOs are a species of SEEs. The two concepts are distinct and the two categories of organizations not overlapping, being characterized differently by law. The main divergences are evident.

First, as a consequence of the manner in which in-scope organizations are identified, the two sectors inevitably refer to different sets of organizations. In third sector law, in-scope organizations are usually not identified on the basis of the legal form per se, but on other requirements, whereas in the Spanish law on social economy there are some legal forms that are included in the sector by definition (provided that they carry out entrepreneurial activities), such as, for example, cooperatives and associations, regardless of the real purpose that they pursue and the activity that they carry out (which depend on their own organizational law, which

[133] This catalogue has not yet been created, so that at present this second group of SEEs does not exist: cf. Fajardo-García (2023).

[134] On the principles and values that characterize the social and solidarity economy, see, in a comparative perspective, Hiez (2021), p. 50 ff.

both cooperatives and associations must of course conform to). Applying this criterion, for example, a large cooperative bank and an association providing lobbying services to certain companies, are SEEs. In contrast, they would not be TSOs, because cooperatives and associations are not per se TSOs, as they must meet the requirements for qualification as any other type of entity.

The above, however, does not imply that some categories of organizations cannot in principle belong to both sectors. For example, social enterprises, as we have identified them in this chapter, and social initiative cooperatives are part of both the Spanish social economy sector and the third sector, as construed in a comparative perspective in this chapter.[135]

Second, Spanish SEEs are identified by law as entities that conduct economic/entrepreneurial activities, which means that entities delivering services without consideration or not entirely remunerated by the price paid in exchange for them (such as, for example, a philanthropic foundation or an association of volunteers) cannot fall within the social economy. In contrast, the third sector, as we have understood it, includes both commercial and non-commercial organizations (and the same happens in Spain, where the third sector includes associations, foundations and social initiative cooperatives, even if they do not carry out entrepreneurial activities).

Third, there is no correspondence between the principles according to which SEEs are identified by law and the legal requirements for an entity's qualification as TSO. The former are mostly mutually-oriented, showing the influence of the Spanish cooperative movement in the elaboration of the social economy law, whereas the latter are of a different nature and mostly solidarity oriented. On the other hand, Spanish law excludes the possibility of profit distribution according to the capital, whilst in TSO law social enterprises are entitled to do so even though within precise limits.

Last but not least, in general (and unless otherwise provided by law) a company could never acquire the status of SEE (even if set up completely not-for-profit). Indeed, the company is not a legal form included among those listed in art. 5, para. 1, and would not satisfy many of the guiding principles formulated in art. 4 of the Law. In contrast, companies are permitted to acquire the status of PBO or that of social enterprise in the countries that have specific laws on these subjects.

3.3.2 Portuguese Framework Law No. 30/2013 on Social Economy

The Portuguese Law no. 30/2013 was the second law on the social economy to be introduced in Europe. It was strongly influenced by the Spanish Law of 2011, with

[135] Of course, if one adopts a different concept of third sector, one may draw different conclusions. For example, the Spanish third sector of social action, as delineated by Spanish Law no. 43/2015, does not comprise social enterprises: cf. Fajardo-García (2023).

which it shares objectives, structures and almost all aspects of regulation, beginning with the definitions.

In the definition of social economy (art. 2, para. 1), the reference to "socio-economic" (rather than "economic") activities stands out, as well as the idea that pursuing the interests of the members is a way to reach the general interest of society (art. 2, para. 2). No concrete consequences, however, are derived from this wording.

The double criterion of identification of SEEs is also present in the Portuguese Law. Hence, there are SEEs by legal form (foundations, cooperatives, etc.) or by legal status (private social solidarity institutions) and SEEs that act pursuant to certain guiding principles (arts. 4 and 5). Two differences are however relevant. The first is the specification regarding associations, because only those associations "that, with altruistic purposes, act in the cultural, recreational, sports and local development fields" are considered SEEs, thus preventing the qualification as SEEs of associations pursuing pure private interests. The second is the different formulation of some principles. For example, one principle is the democratic control of an entity's internal bodies by the members. Another principle is the obligation to allocate profits to the pursuit of the SEÈs aims, but without prejudice to the specific manner of profit distribution typical of the nature or the structure of each SEE.

The conclusions we have reached relative to Spanish law may therefore be proposed again here, although the different wording of Portuguese Law no. 30/2013 may allow partially different outcomes, for example with regard to the possibility for a company to qualify as an SEE, which some Portuguese legal scholars indeed admit.[136]

3.3.3 French Law No. 2014-856 on Social and Solidarity Economy

France has been a pioneer in the development of the concept of "social and solidarity economy",[137] which in this country has a long history, since its roots go back to the nineteenth century, and a significant weight in terms of number of entities involved, GDP and jobs.[138]

The social and solidarity economy and the SEEs—which in France are more precisely referred to as "enterprises of the social and solidarity economy"—have been recognized by Law no. 2014-856, which has played an important role in the development of the sector, although the visibility of these enterprises still remains limited as compared to that of private for-profit organizations.[139]

As in the case of Spanish and Portuguese laws on the subject, French Law no. 2014-856 defines the social and solidarity economy (described as "an entrepreneurial and economic development mode, suitable for all areas of economic

---

[136] Cf. Meira (2023).

[137] Cf. Hiez (2021), p. 25 f.

[138] Cf. Magnier (2023).

[139] Cf. Magnier (2023).

activity") and SEEs on the basis of two alternative criteria: the entity's legal form and certain founding principles or values, which in the law are treated as legal requirements for obtaining a status.

Some legal forms, namely cooperatives, mutual societies, associations and foundations, are automatically recognized by law as SEEs (art. 1-II, no. 1, Law no. 2014-856).

On the other hand, private legal entities established in other legal forms may be recognized as SEEs only if they meet all the requirements in art. 1 of the Law. They must therefore

(1) have a purpose other than the sole sharing of profits;
(2) have a democratic governance, not exclusively determined by the financial contribution of their participants; and.
(3) be managed in accordance with the following principles: a) profits are mainly used for the maintenance and development of the activity; b) compulsory reserves are not distributed unless the statutes provide otherwise and, in any event, only up to certain limits fixed by the law; residual assets at dissolution are disinterestedly devolved to other social and solidarity economy enterprises (art. 1-I Law no. 2014-856).

Unlike the other previously examined national laws on the social economy, French law allows even a commercial company to acquire the social and solidarity economy status. However, to obtain this qualification, a commercial company must meet two further conditions (art. 1-II, no. 2, Law no. 2014-856), which are the pursuit of a social utility[140] and the respect of some management principles.[141]

In addition, to qualify as enterprises of the social and solidarity economy, commercial companies must be registered in the trade and companies register with

[140] Pursuant to art. 2 Law no. 2014-856, this requirement is satisfied if one of the following conditions is met:

(1) the company aims to provide support to people in fragile conditions, including employees, users, customers, members or beneficiaries of the same company;
(2) its objective is to contribute to the preservation and development of the social or the territorial cohesion;
(3) its objective is to contribute to the education of citizens, in order to reduce social and cultural inequalities, in particular between women and men;
(4) the company aims to contribute to sustainable development, energy transition, cultural promotion or international solidarity.

[141] According to art. 1-II, no. 2, lit. c), Law no. 2014–856, these principles are:

- at least 20% of the annual profits are allocated to a compulsory reserve denominated "development fund" until the total amount of all reserves reaches a certain percentage (as defined by the Minister in charge of the social and solidarity economy) of the amount of the share capital;
- at least 50% of the annual profits are carried forward or allocated to mandatory reserves;
- the share capital is not reduced for reasons other than losses and the necessity to continue the activity.

the mention of this status, which also requires that their statutes have the minimum contents provided for by decree (art. 1-III and 1-IV Law no. 2014-856).[142]

The qualification as an SEE in conformity with the aforementioned legal provisions is also necessary for an entity to acquire the status of social enterprise, or rather of "social enterprise of social utility" (or "ESUS" as mostly used in France), which art. 11 of Law no. 2014-856 has introduced into art. L3332-7-1 of the French Labour Code.

Accreditation as an ESUS is reserved for social and solidarity economy enterprises that satisfy the following cumulative conditions:

(1) they mainly aim at pursuing one of the social utility objects mentioned in art. 2 of Law no. 2014-856;
(2) the costs incurred in the fulfilment of the social utility objects have a significant impact on their balance sheet;
(3) in the remunerations of workers, a certain maximum salary gap (as determined by law) is not exceeded;
(4) the enterprise's securities, if any, are not exchanged on a market of financial instruments;
(5) the object of social utility is mentioned in the statutes.

A special regime applies to certain subjects, among which associations and foundations of public utility are included: they only need to meet the conditions mentioned above in (3) and (4).

The French social economy, as delineated by the law of 2014, has certainly more traits in common with the third sector (as we have identified it) than the Portuguese and the Spanish social economy, as identified by the respective national laws. In particular, the inclusion of companies within the admissible legal forms and the compatibility of a limited distribution of profits with the possession of the status must be underlined.

On the other hand, the French social economy, unlike the third sector, consists only of "enterprises" and is based on the legal form of the entity's incorporation, so that there are some entities that are by law SEEs—such as cooperatives and associations—which would not necessarily fit into the third sector.

Therefore, the conclusions are the same as those previously drawn. The social economy and the third sector, as well as SEEs and TSOs, are, according to their

[142] Decree no. 2015-858 of 13 July 2015 requires that the statutes of such companies:

(1) define the company's purpose in accordance with art. 2 of Law no. 2014-856;
(2) contain provisions ensuring their democratic governance, in keeping with the requirement in art. 1-I, no. 2), of Law no. 2014-856;
(3) establish that profits are allocated in accordance with the requirement in art. 1-I, no. 3), lit. a), of Law no. 2014-856;
(4) establish that compulsory reserves are indivisible and non-distributable in accordance with art. 1-I, no. 3), lit. b), of Law no. 2014-856;
(5) contain provisions that implement the principles of management laid down in art. 1-II, no. 2), lit. c), of Law no. 2014-856.

constitutive laws, different organizational realities. Moreover, they cannot be placed in relation of genus to species, because due to the different internal composition, neither of the two categories could absorb the other. In brief, the social economy would not comprise the non-entrepreneurial third sector, while the third sector would not comprise all cooperatives, associations and foundations that are recognized as SSEs.

3.3.4 Polish Social Economy Act of 5 August 2022

We have already highlighted the complexity of the Polish legal framework as regards the topics of our current analysis. In this jurisdiction, complexity has been further augmented by the recent enactment of a law on the social economy, which however is of particular interest to us because of its different approach to the social economy as compared to the previously examined, and certainly better known, national laws.

The Polish Law of 5 August 2022 first defines the social economy as "the activity of social economy entities for the benefit of the local community in the field of social and vocational reintegration, creating jobs for persons at risk of social exclusion, and providing social services, carried out in the form of economic activity, public benefit activity and other gainful activity" (art. 2, no. 1), and then identifies SSEs by making reference to some legal forms and statuses. Contrary to other national laws, no guiding or operational principles for SEEs are laid down.

More precisely, Polish law considers as SSEs, among others, social cooperatives, worker cooperatives, agricultural production cooperatives as well as all those entities that may acquire the status of PBOs, namely, NGOs (a category which includes associations and foundations) and the other entities listed in art. 3, para. 3, Law of 14 April 2003, among which are non-profit companies.[143]

It is not clear whether the same entity may hold both statuses, namely, that of PBO and that of SEE. It is equally unclear whether the qualification as SEEs is reserved for entities that perform commercial activities in exchange for a consideration or rather is also open to entities that act mainly or exclusively for free.

The Polish Law of 5 August 2022 also institutes the new status of "social enterprise", providing that this status may be held by an SEE that performs remunerated activities in the field of public benefit works (as defined by Law of 14 April 2003) or other remunerated activities in the area of social services or for the work integration of certain disadvantaged people. The social enterprise status would end up coinciding with the social economy entity status if the latter also had to be tied to the performance of remunerated activities. Therefore, to be logically distinct from the social enterprise status, the SEE status should not require the performance of remunerated activities.

[143] Cf. Radwan et al. (2023).

In any event, what is worth highlighting with regard to the new Polish regulation on social economy is that, if it is interpreted in the way we propose, then it is more inclusive than the national laws on social economy previously examined. Indeed, the Polish social economy encompasses both non-market and market organizations, and social enterprises among them. It would be very similar, though still not identical, to the Italian third sector as delineated by the Code of 2017.

4 Third Sector Organizations in EU Law and Policies

TSOs are not regulated at the EU level, nor have TSOs as such, as a class of organizations, been considered by EU institutions in policy documents and programmes. This does not mean, however, that the EU has never manifested any interest in the organizations that compose the third sector. Rather, the opposite is true. However, the interest of the EU institutions in these entities has fluctuated and has intensified only in recent years due to the serious economic, social and health crises that have hit Europe. Moreover, the focus has varied over time, showing an uncertain and changing trajectory, prone to current fashions or the influences of stakeholder groups. Thus, as we shall see, whilst initially the Union focused on certain legal forms of non-profit organizations (associations, foundations and mutual societies), it later devoted its attention to social enterprise. Today, the subject of the social economy has gained centrality. At the same time, the matter of the legal forms of the non-profit sector, notably associations, is recovering space. In this section we will present and discuss these various stages, by analysing the main documents on which they are based. To address the subject, however, it is appropriate to begin with an analysis of the patterns and objectives of EU law's approach to private entities and organizational forms.

In the Treaty on the European Union (TEU), the only reference to private organizational forms is in art. 11, which obliges the institutions of the EU to give citizens and their "representative associations" the possibility to express their opinions in all areas of Union action, as well as to maintain an open, transparent and regular dialogue with these associations and civil society. Whilst it is significant that the TEU refers to "associations" in close relationship to "citizens"'and "civil society", it does not seem that the TEU intends here to refer to a precise legal form, that of the association, and in any event the provision is not relevant for our specific purposes, because art. 11 does not regulate associations (nor does it confer enforceable rights upon them), but rather the activity of the EU institutions (which are obligated to establish a dialogue with civil society).

As regards EU primary legislation, of utmost importance in our area of law is art. 54 of the Treaty on the Functioning of the European Union (TFEU), where specific types of private organizations are mentioned, namely, companies, cooperative societies and "non-profit-making" private legal persons. The function of this provision is to specify the scope of freedom of establishment within the EU, with particular regard to the freedom "to set up and manage undertakings".

More precisely:

- art. 49(1) TFEU prohibits restrictions on the freedom of establishment of nationals of a Member State in the territory of another Member State;
- prohibited restrictions—according to art. 49(2)—are also those relative to the establishment and management of "companies or firms";
- art. 54(1) specifies that "companies or firms formed in accordance with the law of a Member State and having their registered office, central administration or principal place of business within the Union shall [. . .] be treated in the same way as natural persons who are nationals of Member States", and therefore enjoy the same freedom of establishment as the citizens of the EU; and
- art. 54(2) clarifies what "companies" are for the said purposes, namely, "companies or firms constituted under civil or commercial law, including cooperative societies, and other legal persons governed by public or private law, save for those which are non-profit-making".

With the aim of safeguarding and ensuring the effectiveness of this particular aspect of the freedom of establishment, these provisions of the TFEU have stimulated the development of an EU organizational law.

More exactly, what happened is that—having freedom of establishment as its main objective and favoured by the EU institutions'focus on the internal market and its inherent virtues—a set of EU rules on companies (and cooperatives) was produced over several decades, starting from the 1960s.[144] This corpus of law comprises both EU regulations and directives[145] with different objects and purposes, including harmonization and uniformization of certain aspects of national company laws,[146] which have been considered necessary to ensure and promote freedom of establishment, as well as the creation of supranational legal forms, which have been provided to EU citizens and organizations as optional and additional types of entities,[147] which are pan-European (albeit not fully so)[148] and equipped with full mobility

[144] Following the "General Programme for the abolition of restrictions on freedom of establishment", adopted by the Council of the European Economic Community (as the European Union, comprising only six Member States, was named at the time) on 18 December 1961, in 1968 the First Council Directive 68/151/EEC on company law was approved.

[145] Among the legal acts of the EU, a regulation has general application, is binding in its entirety and directly applicable in all Member States, whereas a directive is binding, as to the result to be achieved, upon each Member State to which it is addressed, but leaves to the national authorities the choice of form and methods (art. 288 TFEU).

[146] More precisely, (public and private) limited liability company laws.

[147] "Optional" and "additional" in relation to their national law equivalents. This is why the European Company (as well as the European Cooperative Society) is also understood as the "28th type" of (public limited-liability) company available in the EU. In fact, equivalence is not full, because the European Company (as well as the European Cooperative Society) requires a supranational element to be established (indeed, easy to be met). See art. 2, Reg. 2157/2001, and art. 2, Reg. 1435/2003.

[148] "Not fully" because European Companies (and European Cooperative Societies, to an even greater extent) are also regulated by the national law of the Member State in which the European

across the EU. [149] These European legal forms are the European Economic Interest Grouping (EEIG),[150] the European Company (*Societas Europaea* or SE)[151] and the European Cooperative Society (*Societas Cooperativa Europaea* or SCE).[152]

European company law[153] does not comprise only statutory law but also includes the case law of the Court of Justice of the European Union (CJEU), which has significantly contributed to its formation, notably by clarifying the contents and limits of a company's freedom of establishment.[154]

In contrast, NPOs, such as associations, foundations and mutual societies, have not received the same degree of consideration from the EU legislator. No harmonization or uniformization measures have addressed non-profit organization law.[155] No European legal forms for NPOs exist. As regards harmonization and uniformization of national laws, this is mainly due to insufficient knowledge of non-profit organizations[156] and the misleading reference to "non-profit-making" legal entities in art. 54(2).[157] The different cultural and historical roots of national NPO laws, and their resulting variety, have also contributed to this result.

Company (or the European Cooperative Society) has its registered office. See art. 9, Reg. 2157/2001, and art. 8, Reg. 1435/2003.

[149] European Companies and European Cooperative Societies are required to establish their registered offices in the same Member State as their head offices (see art. 7, Reg. 2157/2001, and art. 6, Reg. 1435/2003), but their registered office may freely be transferred to another Member State (see art. 8(1), Reg. 2157/2001, and art. 7(1), Reg. 1435/2003). This means that the legal entity continues in the Member State of arrival, no winding-up takes place and there is no need to re-incorporate the legal entity in the country of destination.

[150] Council Regulation no. 2137/1985 of 25 July 1985, available at https://eur-lex.europa.eu/legal-content/EN/TXT/PDF/?uri=CELEX:31985R2137&from=EN.

[151] Council Regulation no. 2157/2001 of 8 October 2001, supplemented by Council Directive 2001/86/EC of 8 October 2001 with regard to the involvement of employees, available at https://eur-lex.europa.eu/legal-content/EN/TXT/PDF/?uri=CELEX:02001R2157-20130701&from=EN.

[152] Council Regulation no. 1435/2003 of 22 July 2003, supplemented by Council Directive 2003/72/EC of 22 July 2003 with regard to the involvement of employees, available at https://eur-lex.europa.eu/legal-content/EN/TXT/PDF/?uri=CELEX:02003R1435-20030821&from=EN.

[153] For a very useful introduction to the subject, see De Luca (2021).

[154] This long list of judgements includes, at least, *Daily Mail* (C-81/87), *Centros* (C-212/97), *Überseering* (C-208/00), *Inspire Art* (C-167/01), *Sevic* (C-411/03), *Cartesio* (C-210/06), *Vale* (C-378/10), and *Polbud* (C-106/16).

[155] A recommendation, which is however a non-binding legal instrument of the EU (see art. 288 TFEU), was issued in 2007 with regard to non-governmental organizations or NGOs. A European Convention on the Recognition of the Legal Personality of International NGOs was introduced in 1986, although it was ratified by only eight Member States of the EU.

[156] It is still not always clear, for example, that the non-profit character refers to the purpose of the entity, moreover in a purely negative way (as a profit non-distribution constraint), and not to the activity of the entity. Therefore, NPOs may, in principle, conduct commercial activities that generate profits (provided profits are not distributed but are reinvested in the activity).

[157] A global and systematic interpretation of EU law does not allow for the conclusion that art. 54(2) TFEU refers to non-profit organizations, because it is a principle of EU law that undertakings which carry out economic activities must be treated equally whatever their legal form, including a non-profit form (cf. *Höfner and Elser* (C-41/90), para. 21; *Poucet and Pistre* (C-159/91 and

As regards supranational legal forms, the absence of EU non-profit legal forms is mainly due to a lack of political consensus. Indeed, the creation of supranational legal forms for NPOs by means of EU regulations equivalent to those establishing the European Company and the European Cooperative Society has been under discussion for several years. The first official proposal on the European Association dates back to 1991[158]; a proposal for a European Foundation was formulated in 2012[159]; the first proposal on mutual societies was made in 1992 and a subsequent draft proposal on the same subject was discussed later.[160] However, despite the considerable efforts of the EU institutions and the pressure applied by the stakeholders, all these proposals have been unsuccessful.

Following a resolution of the EP in February 2022,[161] the debate about the introduction of a European statute for associations and NPOs has now re-started. In September 2023, a proposal for an EU directive on a European Cross-Border Association was issued by the European Commission.[162] The new political climate, of which the Commission's "Action Plan on the Social Economy" of 2021 (and the

---

160/91), para. 17; *Fédération Française des Sociétés d'Assurance and others* (C-244/94), para. 22; *Albany* (C-67/96), para. 85, and a number of following decisions). Therefore, art. 54(2) should properly refer to gratuitous, non-economic activities and to entities that exclusively perform these kinds of activities. NPOs are not per se organizations that may only conduct non-economic activities. This is clear not only under national laws but also under EU law, as shown by the fact that NPOs are potential VAT payers (although art. 132(1)(l)(m), Directive no. 112/2006, provides for some exceptions). Under EU public procurement law, NPOs are explicitly considered "undertakings that carry out economic activities" (see, among many others, *Pavlov* (C-180/98 to 184/98), *Ambulanz Glöckner* (C-475/99); *Conisma* (C-305/08) and *Parsec* (C-219/19).

[158] An EU statute on associations was first recommended in Nicole Fontaine's "Report on Non-Profit Making Associations in the European Community" of 8 January 1997, followed in the same year by a Resolution of the EP. The first official proposal was presented by the European Commission on 18 December 1991. A second amended proposal was put forward in 1993. It attracted criticism by some MSs, notably Germany, Denmark and the United Kingdom. The proposal was officially withdrawn by the European Commission in 2005. After public protest against this decision, both the EESC in 2006 and the EP in 2011 pushed for the adoption of a European statute for associations. The withdrawal in 2015 of the proposed European Foundation statute led the EC to maintain that the endorsement of such an initiative by the Council seemed unlikely at that time. The EESC has revisited this point, once again calling upon the Commission to take actions in this regard.

[159] The European Commission officially withdrew the proposal for a European Foundation statute in 2015 after eight MSs (Austria, Denmark, Estonia, Germany, the Netherlands, Portugal, Slovakia and the UK) rejected it.

[160] The first proposal was officially withdrawn in 2006. Activities on the subject resumed in 2010. Two studies on mutuals were then commissioned. The European Commission launched a public consultation in 2013. Since then, there has been no news on the EC website. AMICE – the association of mutual insurers and insurance cooperatives in Europe – refers on its website to a draft regulation sent to inter-services consultation in April 2014.

[161] Cf. European Parliament resolution of 17 February 2022 with recommendations to the Commission on a statute for European cross-border associations and non-profit organisations (2020/2026(INL)) https://www.europarl.europa.eu/doceo/document/TA-9-2022-0044_EN.pdf.

[162] Available at https://ec.europa.eu/commission/presscorner/detail/en/ip_23_4242

ensuing proposed Recommendation of June 2023)[163] is a clear manifestation, might on this occasion yield a different result. This would put NPOs on an equal footing with companies (and cooperatives) and finally terminate an unreasonable disparity of treatment which has lasted for several years, to the benefit of both the European internal market (also because NPOs undertaking commercial activities, due to their non-profit orientation, may solve several market failures[164]) and European civil society at large (which may find in NPOs the legal forms suitable for carrying-out activities of general interest).

In the absence of EU secondary legislation on NPOs, the CJEU has played a significant role in their favour. The CJEU has elaborated a non-discrimination principle under tax law, which may be usefully employed when equal treatment of NPOs relative to companies and cooperatives is more generally under discussion. More precisely, the CJEU has ruled that foreign PBOs[165] may not be discriminated against in favour of national PBOs to which the former are "comparable".[166] For

[163] Available at https://ec.europa.eu/commission/presscorner/detail/en/ip_23_3188

[164] Reference must be made here to the work of Prof. Henry Hansmann, beginning with Hansmann (1980).

[165] On this category of organizations, as distinct from simple NPOs, cf. *supra* Sect. 3.1.

[166] The list of relevant judgments includes at least the following:

- *Laboratoires Fournier* (C-39/04): Article 49 TEC precludes legislation of a Member State which restricts the benefit of a tax credit for research only to research carried out in that Member State.
- *Centro di musicologia Walter Stauffer* (C-386/04): Article 73b of the EC Treaty, in conjunction with Article 73d of the EC Treaty, must be interpreted as precluding a Member State which exempts from corporation tax rental income received in its territory by charitable foundations which, in principle, have unlimited tax liability if they are established in that Member State, from refusing to grant the same exemption in respect of similar income to a charitable foundation established under private law solely on the ground that, as it is established in another Member State, that foundation has only limited tax liability in its territory.
- *Hein Persche* (C-318/07): Where a taxpayer claims, in a Member State, the deduction for tax purposes of gifts to bodies established and recognised as charitable in another Member State, such gifts come within the compass of the provisions of the EC Treaty relating to the free movement of capital, even if they are made in kind in the form of everyday consumer goods. Article 56 TEC precludes legislation of a Member State by virtue of which, as regards gifts made to bodies recognised as having charitable status, the benefit of a deduction for tax purposes is allowed only in respect of gifts made to bodies established in that Member State, without any possibility for the taxpayer to show that a gift made to a body established in another Member State satisfies the requirements imposed by that legislation for the grant of such a benefit.
- *Missionswerk* (C-25/10) Article 63 TFEU precludes legislation of a Member State which reserves application of succession duties at the reduced rate to non-profit-making bodies which have their centre of operations in that Member State or in the Member State in which, at the time of death, the deceased actually resided or had his place of work, or in which he had previously actually resided or had his place of work.
- *European Commission v Austria* (C-10/10): By authorising the deduction from tax of gifts to research and teaching institutions exclusively where those institutions are established in Austria, the Republic of Austria has failed to fulfil its obligations under Article 56 TEC. As a sign of the increased attention of the EU institutions towards non-profit organizations, and public benefit

example, donations to foreign PBOs must be granted in a given jurisdiction the same tax privileges as donations to national PBOs to the extent that foreign organizations are "comparable" to national organizations.

This brief analysis suffices to demonstrate that current EU law is not favourable to TSOs (which are mainly set up as associations and foundations) and social enterprises among them (which in some countries are mainly incorporated as associations). Only TSOs (notably social enterprises) established in the form of a company or a cooperative may take advantage of the existing EU legal framework on companies and cooperatives, both for their incorporation (in principle, nothing prevents a social enterprise from being incorporated, for example, as a European company rather than a national company) and for carrying-out cross-border operations (e.g., a cross-border conversion).

In conclusion, NPOs and "unconventional" forms of enterprise, such as social enterprises, have not attracted the EU legislator's attention for many years. The focus of European integration was on the internal market and those that were seen as its "traditional" actors, namely, for-profit companies. European directives and regulations favoured the development of an enabling legal framework limited to companies (and cooperatives), which includes optional European forms, such as the European Company (and the European Cooperative Society), and rules allowing and simplifying the cross-border activity and mobility of national companies (and cooperatives). In contrast, NPOs could not count on equivalent European forms, nor on secondary legislation, promoting their cross-border activity and mobility across the EU. In this last regard, only some important CJEU's judgements have supported NPOs by trying to resolve issues related to national tax law barriers to their cross-border operations.

Only since the crisis of 2008, when complements to the "Welfare State" needed to be identified, has the interest of EU institutions in "alternative" models of enterprise, not based on profit maximization but on other values, increased. Social enterprises thus became the focus of specific EU documents and policies, beginning with the European Commission's Communication no. 682 of 25 October 2011 entitled "Social Business Initiative Creating a favourable climate for social enterprises, key stakeholders in the social economy and innovation" (SBI).[167]

Based on the assumption that social enterprises generate several positive socio-economic effects, the SBI contemplated a series of key actions in their favour,[168] some of them related to "improving the legal environment" for social enterprises. More precisely, key action no. 9 of the SBI included: launching a proposal for simplification of the existing regulation on the European Cooperative Society

associations among the, the EC has recently published a staff working document on this topic: the document is available at https://ec.europa.eu/social/main.jsp?langId=en&catId=89&furtherNews=yes&newsId=10117

[167] https://eur-lex.europa.eu/LexUriServ/LexUriServ.do?uri=COM:2011:0682:FIN:EN:PDF.

[168] Cf. Haarich et al. (2021).

(in order to make it more independent from national laws and easier for its potential adoption by social cooperatives); making a proposal for the introduction of a European Foundation Statute (along the same lines as those on the European Company and the European cooperative Society); and conducting a study on the situation of mutual societies in all Member States.[169]

None of those specific actions was eventually taken; however, by providing a definition of social enterprise, the Commission's Communication on the SBI has significantly promoted and influenced the legislation on social enterprises in the EU Member States.[170] Following its publication, several MSs adopted specific laws on SEs in which the social enterprise was regulated according to the definition contained in the SBI. This has also led, as we have previously highlighted in this chapter,[171] to the development of a particular model of legislation on social enterprise, namely, laws in which social enterprise is not conceived of as a particular type (or sub-type) of a legal entity, namely as a specific legal form of an entity's incorporation, but rather as a particular legal "status" (or "qualification", "accreditation", "label", etc.) that entities meeting certain requirements may acquire, regardless of their legal form of organization (association, foundation, company or cooperative).

The SBI Communication was strongly influenced by the EMES Research Network's approach to social enterprises. EMES has adopted the position that social enterprises should not be precisely defined, but identified through substantial criteria (or indicators) related to three different dimensions: the entrepreneurial dimension (social enterprises are at least prevalently engaged in commercial activities), the social dimension (social enterprises prioritize a social purpose), and the organizational dimension (social enterprises have a democratic or inclusive governance, which ensures the involvement of their different stakeholders).[172] Following this theoretical approach, and also with the aim of respecting national diversity, the SBI Communication defined a social enterprise as

---

[169] Curiously, no specific action on the regulation of social enterprises at the EU level was envisaged in the SBI. It is also curious that, in this regard, the SBI did not refer to associations and the European Statute thereof.

[170] In fact, not only the definition per se, but also subsequent actions based on that, such as the mapping study on social enterprise in Europe, contributed to this result. Cf. European Commission (2020). On this point, see also Fici (2020) and Fici (2023a).

[171] Cf. *supra* Sect. 3.2.2.

[172] More precisely, these indicators are: (1) economic and entrepreneurial dimensions of social enterprises, which comprises: (a) a continuous activity of producing goods and/or selling services; (b) a significant level of economic risk; (c) a minimum amount of paid work; (2) social dimensions of social enterprises, which comprises: (d) an explicit aim to benefit the community; (e) an initiative launched by a group of citizens or civil society organisations; (f) a limited profit distribution; (3) participatory governance of social enterprises, which comprises: (g) a high degree of autonomy; (h) a decision-making power not based on capital ownership; (i) a participatory nature, which involves various parties affected by the activity. Cf. Defourny and Nyssens (2012). EMES is a non-profit association incorporated under Belgian law, composed of research centres and individual researchers. Its conception of social enterprise has been reshaped over time. Cf., initially, Defourny (2001).

> an operator in the social economy whose main objective is to have a social impact rather than make a profit for their owners or shareholders. It operates by providing goods and services for the market in an entrepreneurial and innovative fashion and uses its profits primarily to achieve social objectives. It is managed in an open and responsible manner and, in particular, involve employees, consumers and stakeholders affected by its commercial activities.[173]

It clearly emerges from this definition that social enterprise is not considered here as a specific legal form but as a general concept.

The SBI's operational definition was subsequently employed by the EU legislator in regulations providing for specific funding, namely, the "EaSI"[174] and the "EuSEF"[175] Regulations (see articles 2(1) and 3(1)(d), respectively).

---

[173]Cf. COM(2011) 682 final, of 25 October 2011, p 2. The EC goes on to specify the types of business covered by the term "social enterprise", namely:

- those for which the social or societal objective of the common good is the reason for the commercial activity, often in the form of a high level of social innovation,
- those where profits are mainly reinvested with a view to achieving this social objective,
- and where the method of organisation or ownership system reflects their mission, using democratic or participatory principles or focusing on social justice.

Thus:

- businesses providing social services and/or goods and services to vulnerable persons (access to housing, health care, assistance for elderly or disabled persons, inclusion of vulnerable groups, child care, access to employment and training, dependency management, etc.); and/or
- businesses with a method of production of goods or services with a social objective (social and professional integration via access to employment for people disadvantaged in particular by insufficient qualifications or social or professional problems leading to exclusion and marginalisation) but whose activity may be outside the realm of the provision of social goods or services.

[174]"EaSI" stands for "European Union Programme for Employment and Social Innovation". The programme ran from 1 January 2014 to 31 December 2020, with the aim "to contribute to the implementation of Europe 2020, including its headline targets, Integrated Guidelines and flagship initiatives, by providing financial support for the Union's objectives in terms of promoting a high level of quality and sustainable employment, guaranteeing adequate and decent social protection, combating social exclusion and poverty and improving working conditions" (art. 1, Reg. no. 1296/2013).

[175]"EuSEF" stands for "European social entrepreneurship funds". The Regulation "lays down uniform requirements and conditions for managers of collective investment undertakings that wish to use the designation 'EuSEF' in relation to the marketing of qualifying social entrepreneurship funds in the Union, thereby contributing to the smooth functioning of the internal market. It also lays down uniform rules for the marketing of qualifying social entrepreneurship funds to eligible investors across the Union, for the portfolio composition of qualifying social entrepreneurship funds, for the eligible investment instruments and techniques to be used by qualifying social entrepreneurship funds as well as for the organisation, conduct and transparency of managers that market qualifying social entrepreneurship funds across the Union" (art. 1, Reg. no. 346/2013).

These regulations were later replaced by Regulation no. 1057/2021 establishing the European Social Fund Plus (ESF+),[176] where the definition of a social enterprise is found in art. 2(1) n. 13, which reads: "'Social enterprise' means an undertaking, regardless of its legal form, including social economy enterprises, or a natural person which:

(a) in accordance with its articles of association, statutes or with any other legal document that may result in liability under the rules of the Member State where a social enterprise is located, has the achievement of measurable, positive social impacts, which may include environmental impacts, as its primary social objective rather than the generation of profit for other purposes, and which provides services or goods that generate a social return or employs methods of production of goods or services that embody social objectives;
(b) uses its profits first and foremost to achieve its primary social objective, and has predefined procedures and rules that ensure that the distribution of profits does not undermine the primary social objective;
(c) is managed in an entrepreneurial, participatory, accountable and transparent manner, in particular by involving workers, customers and stakeholders on whom its business activities have an impact".

This new definition is substantially in line with the one contained in the repealed regulations, except for the (surprising) reference to "natural persons"[177] as possible social entrepreneurs, and to "social economy enterprises", which is a more general category of organizations that ultimately, as we shall soon observe, have become the new focus of EU policies.

Notwithstanding its importance for the development of social enterprises, the decennial programme foreseen in the SBI has not led, at the Union level, to any change of the legal environment regarding social enterprises (apart from the regulations providing for funding measures), and this in spite of the fact that the European Parliament in 2018 explicitly called for its introduction.[178] Apart from some specific provisions on social enterprises in EU public procurement law,[179] positive effects were produced only at the national level, as many MSs, encouraged by the Commission's actions, adopted specific laws on social enterprises. Inspired by the concept of social enterprise found in the SBI, these national laws conceived of

[176] https://eur-lex.europa.eu/legal-content/EN/TXT/PDF/?uri=CELEX:32021R1057&from=IT.

[177] Only in a few jurisdictions of the EU, do legislators even allow an individual entrepreneur to acquire the qualification of social enterprise. This happens in Finland, where Law no. 1351/2003 allows the registration as social enterprises of all traders, including individuals, registered under sect. 3 of Law no. 129/1979, and in Slovakia, where art. 50b, para. 1, of Law no. 5/2004, refers, in defining a social enterprise, to both legal and physical persons. The same occurs in Slovakian Law no. 112/2018, with regard to the definition of the subjects of the social economy, among which are social enterprises.

[178] Cf. *supra* Sect. 3.2.2.

[179] Cf. recital no. 36 and articles 20 of Directive no. 2014/24/EU of the European Parliament and of the Council of 26 February 2014, on public procurement and repealing Directive 2004/18/EC.

"social enterprise" as a legal status open to entities established in different legal forms and meeting the necessary requirements for qualification. This model of legislation has spread over Europe and offers many potential benefits, as previously highlighted in this chapter.

After 10 years of work on social enterprise, the focus has now shifted to the social economy, which represents, at the Union level, the most recent theoretical development and the new frontier of the EU institutions'actions in the area of our interest.[180]

In December 2021, the European Commission launched a new decennial programme, which this time does not directly address social enterprises, but instead the "social economy". The "Action Plan on the Social Economy" has a larger scope and a more comprehensive and ambitious objective than the SBI, because it aims to build a different economy that works for people. After having highlighted the benefits of the social economy (in terms of quality job creation, contribution to the green and digital transitions, complementing welfare state systems, implementing the United Nations'Sustainable Development Goals at the Union and global levels, etc.), the Communication identifies its addressees, namely the "social economy entities". The influence of the existing national legislation on social economy is evident. According to the Commission, SEEs share some common principles and features, which are:

- the primacy of people as well as social and/or environmental purpose over profit,
- the reinvestment of most of the profits and surpluses to carry out activities in the interest of members/users ('collective interest') or society at large ('general interest'), and
- democratic and/ or participatory governance.

The Commission goes on to explain that "traditionally, the term social economy refers to four main types of entities providing goods and services to their members or society at large: cooperatives, mutual benefit societies, associations (including charities), and foundations. They are private entities, independent of public authorities and with specific legal forms".

The Commission does mention "social enterprises" as part of the social economy and explains that "social enterprises operate by providing goods and services for the market in an entrepreneurial and often innovative fashion, having social and/or environmental objectives as the reason for their commercial activity. Profits are mainly reinvested with a view to achieving their societal objective. Their method of organisation and ownership also follow democratic or participatory principles or focus on social progress. Social enterprises adopt a variety of legal forms depending on the national context".

The Action Plan of 2021 aspires to create the right framework, including a legal one, for the social economy to thrive, to open up opportunities for social economy entities to develop, and to enhance recognition of the social economy and its potential. Many actions are foreseen to fulfil these general objectives. Unfortunately, as regards the legal framework of social economic entities, the Action Plan does not

[180] Admittedly, the subject of social economy was first put forward by the European Parliament in its Resolution of 19 February 2009.

identify the creation of EU legal forms or statuses or harmonization or uniformization measures necessary to ensure the development of social enterprises at the Union level as action items. The only legal instrument foreseen is a Recommendation to MSs to better adapt policy and legal frameworks to the needs of social economy entities. As already stated, in June 2023, the Commission adopted an official proposal for a Recommendation on developing social economy framework conditions.

The Action Plan made reference to a forthcoming EP initiative on associations and non-profit organizations. Indeed, as already mentioned in this chapter, in February 2022, after the adoption of the Action Plan by the EC, the EP finalized a resolution with recommendations to the Commission about the adoption of a European Regulation establishing the European Association (along the same lines as the existing EU legal forms of the European Company and the European Cooperative Society, previously mentioned in this paper) and of a European Directive on common minimum standards for non-profit organizations.[181] Following this initiative, the Commission has just launched, as already stated, a proposal for a directive on a European Cross-Border Association (ECBA).[182]

The choice of the Commission to shift attention from social enterprises to social economy entities presents the classical risk of all very large and ambitious projects: to remain "on paper", without producing any concrete result. Indeed, whilst the difficulties in treating the legal aspects of social enterprises at the Union level were already great, it will be yet more complex to deal with the even wider and more diversified universe of "social economy entities". There is already complexity regarding a preliminary issue, namely, the identification of these organizations. Not surprisingly, in the Action Plan of 2021, the Commission fluctuates between various identification criteria. It refers both to precise legal forms (associations, foundations, cooperatives, etc.) and to legal statuses identified on the basis of substantive requirements that the entities must meet (primacy of people, reinvestment of profits, etc.). How to combine the two criteria remains to be understood. Furthermore, in the background there are also the principles common to social economy entities and it is not clear what role they can play, whether that of delimiting the scope of the social economy or of extending it beyond the legal forms and legal statuses explicitly mentioned in the Action Plan. Apparently, the Action Plan, unlike most national laws on the same subject, does not limit the social economy to enterprises but considers this sector also open to entities which do not run a business. Indeed, the Action Plan literally refers to "entities" and not to "enterprises", but the

[181] Both proposed instruments deal with the public benefit status as a legal status available to associations and other non-profit organizations (see art. 20 of the proposed Council Regulation on the European Association and art. 14 of the proposed Directive on common minimum standards for NPOs). The public benefit status as delineated by the EP in these proposals is similar to the national public benefit statuses that we have previously examined in this chapter.

[182] The Commission's proposal does not address public benefit organizations, which are not even mentioned.

conceptualization of the social economy at the national level (where the social economy is composed only of enterprises) could end up prevailing.

In conclusion, the same perplexities that we have already highlighted in the discussion about national laws on the social economy are re-proposed at the Union level.

The hope is that this enlarged focus on the social economy will not disorient the Commission and that the Commission will be able to resume the path interrupted several times and put forward concrete proposals to address TSOs and social enterprises among them. These include the introduction of EU legal forms for non-profit organizations (the European Association, the European Foundation and the European Mutual Society), as well as of an EU legal label for third sector organizations (or at least for public benefit organizations).

5 Concluding Remarks

Taking advantage of the national contributions to the first part of this volume, in this comparative chapter we have presented and discussed four categories of organizations, namely, non-profit organizations, third sector organizations, public benefit organizations, social enterprises and social economy entities. The main objective of the analysis has been to read the legislation concerning these groups of legal entities from the point of view of the concept of the third sector which, at the European level, has emerged from the "Third Sector Impact Project" and finds its legislative roots in the Italian Code of 2017.

TSOs and NPOs are two distinct categories of organizations. While NPOs are characterized by the profit non-distribution constraint, this requirement is not essential for the qualification of TSOs. Indeed, TSOs have other distinguishing features, first of all a social (or general interest) purpose, which they pursue in a particular way, abiding by legal requirements regarding transparency, governance and the use of assets. Furthermore, some TSOs may distribute profits within certain limits set by law.

In light of these characteristics, it is not surprising that TSOs are seen by law as promoters of the public good and natural candidates for undertaking special relationships with public administrations interested in the general interest of their citizens. It is also not surprising that TSOs are recipients of public support in many ways, including a beneficial tax treatment. States are increasingly promoting organizations that are socially oriented rather than organizations that are simply non-profit. And these types of organizations are also the most suitable forms for citizens wishing to pursue the common good in a subsidiarity perspective, in which the performance of general interest activities is not only a task for public administrations but also an area of civic engagement.

Among the national jurisdictions covered by this volume (and more generally in Europe), Italy is the only one to have a specific regulation on TSOs. It is a comprehensive and organic law which considers TSOs as a whole and identifies them with precision, thus contributing to their distinction from other categories of organizations. Therefore, the Italian Law of 2017 may be chosen as a model for comparison and as a basis for building a common third sector law in Europe. It provides a conceptual apparatus useful for both law-makers and scholars. It may serve as a guide for all those who are interested in the third sector, not only for legal reasons.

However, Italian law is not isolated in the European scenario. The same objectives and substance of Italian third sector law pervade other national laws which (only) formally are not third sector laws.

Indeed, striking similarities exist between the Italian TSO law and the laws on PBOs present in many European countries, including those examined in this volume. PBOs are qualified and regulated substantially in the same way as TSOs, as confirmed by the analysis of German, Irish and Polish laws, among others. Like TSOs, PBOs may have any legal form (including the company form), must carry out certain public benefit activities in the general interest, are subject to specific governance and transparency requirements to ensure consistency with their social purpose, may benefit from tax breaks, tax-privileged donations, and other promotional measures, are supervised by public authorities to verify the respect of the rules that shape their nature and action. However, unlike TSOs, PBOs are totally non-profit, and this is the main element of distinction between the two categories of organizations, because a limited distribution of profits is permitted to (some) TSOs.

Traces of third sector law are also found in those jurisdictions that specifically recognize and regulate social enterprises (including social cooperatives), since social enterprises (and social cooperatives among them) are part of the third sector as conceptualized in the "Third Sector Impact Project" and as delineated by the Italian Code of 2017. More precisely, social enterprises represent the entrepreneurial subsector of the third sector, and may also be established as companies or cooperatives in which a limited distribution of profits to the shareholders (or members, as they are usually referred to in cooperative law) is allowed. Therefore, the third sector is populated not only by traditional non-profit organizations, such as associations and foundations, but also by companies and cooperatives, and may host not only fully non-profit organizations but also organizations that are only limitedly so.

In jurisdictions (like Poland) in which, albeit in separate acts, both PBOs and social enterprises are regulated, a legislation on TSOs may be considered to substantially exist, as it does in Italy, notwithstanding the lack of a sole law that explicitly refers to the "third sector". As regards the legislation on third sector, Italy is not, therefore, an isolated case in Europe, although its legislation has singular features, which currently cannot be found in any other jurisdiction.

EU law and institutions could play a significant role in developing coherent legal frameworks for TSOs in MSs. Unfortunately, however, so far EU action has been limited to the promotion of some entities attributable to the third sector, mainly social enterprises. Little has been done regarding the EU legal framework in this area. Unlike companies and cooperatives, NPOs, like associations, foundations and mutual societies, cannot rely on supranational legislation allowing them to incorporate under EU law rather than national law or to effectively exercise the right of establishment throughout the EU (through cross-border conversions and other operations). No EU statute on social enterprise has been passed, despite requests made by EU bodies such as the European Parliament and the European Economic and Social Committee.

Some signs of change now appear to be afoot. In February 2022, the European Parliament gave new impetus to the European Association Statute, which moreover includes a regulation of the public benefit status. Following that, a proposal on the European Cross-Border Association was adopted by the European Commission in September 2023, which however does not deal with the public benefit status. In December 2021, the Commission launched a new plan for the promotion of social economy entities, which, as explained in this chapter, is a different category of organizations to that of TSOs. Within this plan, no actions are currently envisaged regarding the introduction of EU regulations concerning SEEs or some forms of them, for example social enterprises, although in June 2023 the Commission adopted a proposal for a recommendation on the development of the framework conditions, including the legal framework, for the social economy. This new category of the social economy is likely to create confusion, as it includes completely different entities, such as a large cooperative bank and a small voluntary organization. No one doubts that promoting the social economy is important for Europe, its institutions and its citizens. However, a less ambitious objective, such as giving greater legal substance at EU level to a sector that is certainly more widespread and homogenous at national level, such as the third sector, would perhaps have been more easily achievable.

References

Brakman Reiser D (2023) European law of third sector organizations from the US standpoint. In: Fici A (ed) The law of third sector organizations in Europe: foundations, trends and prospects. Springer (this volume)

Bishoff C. and Helm T. (2023), Philanthropy and Charitable Giving: Taxation of Public Benefit Organizations in Germany. Betriebs-Berater, (3): 138 ff.

Breen OB (2020) Ireland. Country profile. In: Legal environment for philanthropy in Europe. https://philea.eu/wp-content/uploads/2021/12/Ireland_2020LegalEnvironmentPhilanthropy.pdf

Breen OB (2023) Third sector Organisations in Ireland: assembling the regulatory jigsaw pieces of an evolving, if fragmented, sector. In: Fici A (ed) The law of third sector organizations in Europe: foundations, trends and prospects. Springer (this volume)

Breen OB and Smith PA (2019), Law of Charities in Ireland. Bloomsbury Professional, Dublin

Cafaggi F, Iamiceli P (2009) New frontiers in the legal structure and legislation of social enterprises in Europe: a comparative analysis. In: Noya A (ed) The changing boundaries of social enterprises. OECD, Paris

Consorzio Gino Mattarelli (1988) Le cooperative di solidarietà sociale. Forlì

Corry O (2010) Defining and theorizing the third sector. In: Taylor R (ed) Third sector research. Springer, New York, p 11 ff

Crama M (2014) Entreprises sociales. Comparaison des formes juridiques européennes, asiatiques et américaines. Think Tank européen Pour la Solidarité – PLS. https://www.pourlasolidarite.eu/

sites/default/files/publications/files/2014_06_entreprises_sociales_comparaisons_juridiques.pdf
Culot H, Defer J (2023) The third sector in Belgium. In: Fici A (ed) The law of third sector organizations in Europe: foundations, trends and prospects. Springer (this volume)
De Luca N (2021) European company law, 2nd edn. Cambridge University Press, Cambridge
Defourny J (2001) From third sector to social enterprise. In: Borzaga C, Defourny J (eds) The emergence of social enterprise. Routledge, London, p 1 ff
Defourny J (2013) Third sector. In: Bruni L, Zamagni S (eds) Handbook on the economics of reciprocity and social enterprise. Edward Elgar, Cheltenham-Northampton, p 400 ff
Defourny J, Nyssens M (2012) The EMES approach of social Enterprise in a Comparative Perspective. EMES Working Papers Series no. 12/03. https://emes.net/content/uploads/publications/EMES-WP-12-03_Defourny-Nyssens.pdf
Defourny J, Nyssens M (2016) How to bring the centres of gravity of the non-profit sector and the social economy closer to each other? Voluntas 27:1547 ff
Douvitsa I (2022) National constitutions and cooperatives: an overview. In: Tadjudje W and Douvitsa I (eds.) Perspectives on cooperative law. Festschrifts in honour of Professor Hagen Henry. Springer, Singapore, p 57 ff
Enjolras B (2018) Introduction. In: Enjolras et al (eds) The third sector as a renewable resource for Europe. Concepts, impacts, challenges and opportunities. Palgrave Macmillan, Cham, p 1 ff
Enjolras B et al (2018) The third sector as a renewable resource for Europe. Concepts, impacts, challenges and opportunities. Palgrave Macmillan, Cham
Etzioni A (1973) The third sector and domestic missions. Public Adm Rev 33(4):314 ff
European Commission (2020) Social enterprises and their ecosystems in Europe. Comparative synthesis report. European Union, Luxembourg
Evers A, Laville J-L (2004) Defining the third sector in Europe. In: Evers A, Laville J-L (eds) The third sector in Europe. Edward Elgar, Cheltenham-Northampton, p 11 ff
Fajardo-García G (2023) Social economy and third sector in Spanish law. Convergences and divergences. In: Fici A (ed) The law of third sector organizations in Europe: foundations, trends and prospects. Springer (this volume)
Fici A (2015) La función social de las cooperativas: notas de derecho comparado. Revesco 117: 77 ff
Fici A (2017) A European statute for social and solidarity-based Enterprise. European Union, Brussels. https://www.europarl.europa.eu/RegData/etudes/STUD/2017/583123/IPOL_STU%282017%29583123_EN.pdf
Fici A (2020) Social Enterprise Laws in Europe after the 2011 "Social Business Initiative". A Comparative Analysis from the Perspective of Worker and Social Cooperatives. CECOP, Brussels. https://cecop.coop/uploads/file/bzuQI79nF5yrrwoDvUNUg47Ro7iaHA6wAxsvK9yo.pdf
Fici A (2022) Social enterprises and social cooperatives in the new Italian legal framework for third sector organizations. In: Tadjudje W, Douvitsa I (eds) Perspectives on cooperative law. Festschrifts in honour of Professor Hagen Henry. Springer, Singapore, p 77 ff
Fici A (2023a) Models and trends of social Enterprise regulation in the European Union. In: Peter H et al (eds.) The international handbook of social Enterprise law benefit corporations and other purpose-driven companies. Springer, Cham, p 153 ff
Fici A (2023b) Public benefit status and CMD systems for associations and non-Profit organisations in the EU. European Union, Brussels
Fici A (2023c) The new Italian code of the third sector. Essence and principles of a historic legislative reform. In: Fici A (ed) The law of third sector organizations in Europe: foundations, trends and prospects. Springer (this volume)
Galera G, Borzaga C (2009) Social enterprise. An international overview of its conceptual evolution and legal implementation. Soc Enterp J 5:210 ff
Gidron B (2020) Third sector. In: List RA et al (eds) International encyclopedia of civil society. Springer, Cham

Haarich S et al (2021) Impact of the European Commission's social business initiative (SBI) and its follow-up actions. Study for DG Employment, Social Affairs and Inclusion. European Commission, European Union, Luxembourg
Hansmann H (1980) The role of nonprofit enterprise. Yale Law J 89(5):835 ff
Hiez D (2021) Guide to the writing of law for the social and solidarity economy. SSE International Forum, Les Rencontres du Mont-Blanc
International Center for Not-for-Profit Law (2019) Nonprofit law in Poland. https://base.socioeco.org/docs/poland-201910.pdf
International Center for Not-for-Profit Law (2020) Nonprofit Law in Ireland. https://cof.org/sites/default/files/documents/files/Ireland/ireland-county-note-022020.pdf
Lalor T, Doyle G (2021) Research on legal forms for social enterprises. Government of Ireland, Dublin
Lavišius T et al (2020) Social entrepreneurship in the Baltic and Nordic countries. Would the variety of existing legal forms do more for the impact on sustainable development? Entrep Sustain Iss 8(1):276 ff
Levitt T (1973) The third sector: new tactics for a responsive society. Amacom Press, New York
Liptrap JS (2020) The social Enterprise company in Europe: policy, theory and isomorphism. Legal studies research paper series no. 5, University of Cambridge
Liptrap JS (2021a) British social enterprise law J Corp Law Stud 21(2):595 ff
Liptrap J S (2021b) Social enterprise company in EU organisational law? Cambridge yearbook of European Leg Stud 23:193 ff
Lorentzen H (2010) Sector labels. In: Taylor R (ed) Third sector research. Springer, New York, p 21 ff
Lundberg CC (1975) Organization change in the third sector. Public Adm Rev 35(5):472 ff
Magnier V (2023) Economie Sociale et Solidaire in the middle of the ford. In: Fici A (ed) The law of third sector organizations in Europe: foundations, trends and prospects. Springer (this volume)
McGill ME, Wooten LM (1975) Management in the third sector. Public Adm Rev 35(5):444 ff
Meira D (2023) The legal regime of the social economy sector in Portugal. In: Fici A (ed) The law of third sector organizations in Europe: foundations, trends and prospects. Springer (this volume)
Möslein F (2023) Law in transitions: reforming the legal framework of the third sector in Germany. In: Fici A (ed) The law of third sector organizations in Europe: foundations, trends and prospects. Springer (this volume)
O'Connor JC, McGrath H (2020) Charitable organisations in Ireland: overview. file:///Users/antoniofici/Downloads/Charitable%20organisations%20in%20Ireland%20overview%20(1).pdf
Radwan A et al (2023) Third sector in the third republic: an overview of the law and practice in Poland
Richter A, Gollan AK (2020) Charitable organizations in Germany: overview. In: Charty Global Guide, Country Q&A. https://uk.practicallaw.thomsonreuters.com/3-632-5987?transitionType=Default&contextData=(sc.Default)&firstPage=true
Sacchetti S, Salvatori G (2023) "Shared Administration" as a New Relationship between the Public Sector and the Social Economy. Euricse Working Paper no. 126/2023
Salamon LM, Anheier HK (1997a) Introduction: in search of the nonprofit sector. In: Salamon LM, Anheier HK (eds) Defining the nonprofit sector: a cross-national analysis. Manchester University Press, Manchester, p 1 ff
Salamon LM, Anheier HK (1997b) Toward a common definition. In: Salamon LM, Anheier HK (eds) Defining the nonprofit sector: a cross-national analysis. Manchester University Press, Manchester, p 29 ff
Salamon LM, Sokolowski W (2018) Beyond nonprofits: in search of the third sector. In: Enjolras et al (eds) The third sector as a renewable resource for Europe. Concepts, impacts, challenges and opportunities. Palgrave Macmillan, Cham, p 7 ff

Sørensen KE (2023) The diversity of third sector organisations in Denmark. In: Fici A (ed) The law of third sector organizations in Europe: foundations, trends and prospects. Springer (this volume)

Sørensen KE, Neville M (2014) Social enterprises: how should company law balance flexibility and credibility? Eur Bus Org Law Rev 15(2):267 ff

Stanitzke A (2020) Germany. Country Profile. In: Legal Environment for Philanthropy in Europe. https://www.transnationalgiving.eu/wp-content/uploads/2022/09/Germany_2020 LegalEnvironmentPhilanthropy.pdf

United Nations (2018) Satellite Account on Non-profit and Related Institutions and Volunteer Work. United Nations, New York. https://unstats.un.org/unsd/nationalaccount/docs/UN_TSE_HB_FNL_web.pdf

van der Sangen GJH (2023) The legal infrastructure of the third sector and the social economy in The Netherlands. In: Fici A (ed) The law of third sector organizations in Europe: foundations, trends and prospects. Springer (this volume)

Vargas Vasserot C (2021) Las empresas sociales. Regulación en derecho comparado y propuestas *de lege ferenda* para España. Revista del Ministerio de trabajo y economía social 150:63 ff

von Hippel T (2010) Nonprofit organizations in Germany. In: Hopt K J and von Hippel T (eds.) Comparative corporate governance of non-profit organizations. Cambridge University Press, Cambridge, p 197 ff

von Hippel T (2017) Legal aspects of civil society organizations and their relation with government: Germany. In: van der Ploeg et al (eds) Civil society in Europe. Minimum norms and optimum conditions of its regulation. Cambridge University Press, Cambridge, p 384 ff

Chapter 12
The Taxation of Social Economy Entities in the Perspective of EU Law

Gabriele Sepio

Contents

Abstract The EU institutions promote the development and growth of the social economy, based on the awareness of the role this sector can play as a key factor for social cohesion and the consolidation of social rights, but also to boost the economic growth of the Union. At the same time, the regulatory barriers to a coordinated framework are clear, given (*inter alia*) the multiplicity of sectoral policies that have a sweeping effect across the social economy. This paper takes a close look at two of these sector-wide areas: taxation and competition. The necessary balancing act

---

G. Sepio (✉)
E-Ius Law Firm, Rome, Italy

General Secretary, Terzjus Foundation, Rome, Italy

Tax Law Professor, Università Pontificia Salesiana, Rome, Italy
e-mail: gabriele.sepio@e-ius.it

A. Fici (ed.), *The Law of Third Sector Organizations in Europe*,
https://doi.org/10.1007/978-3-031-41744-3_12

between providing financial support to non-market organisations of the social economy and prohibiting market-distorting national subsidies prompts the search for forms of tax harmonisation, with reference both to general tax regimes and to more *ad hoc* measures relevant in the individual Member States or with cross-border effects.

1 Introduction: The European Debate on the Taxation of Social Economy Entities and the Link with State Aid Rules

Ever since the first European policies aimed at institutional recognition of the social economy were launched in the 1980s, it has always been clear that there were essentially two problems to be addressed in the European legal system. Firstly, the conceptual definition of the field of social economy and the multiplicity of related terms (third sector, non-profit activities, social and solidarity economy, economy for the common good, etc.). Secondly, the inadequacy of the legal basis, starting with the fundamental texts of the European Union (the Treaty of Rome and the Treaty of Maastricht), which lack any explicit reference to the social economy.

These two problems are still very much relevant today.

Focusing, in particular, on the latter issue, successive attempts to solve the lack of a common legal basis have met with little success, a fact that clearly emerges if we compare one of the first positions adopted by the European Commission on the matter with the latest communication published by the same institution.

Indeed, the debate that began in the 1980s on the need for European policies in support of the social economy culminated, in 1989, with the important communication presented by the Commission to the Council entitled "*Businesses in the social economy sector – Europe's frontier-free market*" [SEC(89) 2187 final]. Back then, the need to create a European legal basis in the form of a statute for cooperatives, associations and mutual societies was already clear.

The same issue is still relevant today in the latest act issued by the Commission on this matter, in the Communication of 9 December 2021 on "*... an action plan for the social economy*" (COM(2021) 778 final) – hereinafter the "*Action Plan 2021-30*", which aims to support the development of the social economy through a series of initiatives to be implemented in the period 2021–2030.[1]

Although the Commission considers the development of coherent legal frameworks for the social economy as essential, it explicitly states in the *Action Plan 2021-30* that the pursuit of this goal is no easy task. The most critical aspects are not

[1] For his comments, see Athanasopoulou and Klein (2022), p. 48 ff.

limited to the different types of actors in the social economy, but also include the intersectoral nature of this area.

In fact, the social economy features numerous horizontal sector policies, such as fiscal and social policies, public procurement, competition, labour market, education, skills and training, care services, including healthcare, support for small and medium-sized enterprises (SMEs), and the circular economy.

In this regard, we should focus on two of these policies which horizontally affect the social economy sector: taxation and competition rules related to the provision of fiscal incentives and advantage measures.

With regard to taxation, in the *Action Plan 2021-30* the Commission considers taxation as important for the development of the social economy. It is noted how few countries have developed a specific and coherent tax framework for social enterprises. Many offer incentives ranging from corporate tax exemptions on retained earnings to exemptions or reduced VAT rates, from reduced or subsidised social insurance costs to tax reductions for private and institutional donors. However, access to these incentives can be complex and the different actions are not always adequately coordinated.

Likewise, with regard to the rules of competition, the Commission recognises that public financial support plays an important role in enabling the start-up and development of social economy actors. On the other hand, financial support, also through favourable tax regimes, has to be balanced with the principle of fair competition in order to avoid distortions in the European single market. This is the purpose of controlling state aid. This is why, in the *Action Plan 2021-30*, the Commission calls on public authorities and beneficiaries to make the most of existing State aid opportunities, highlighting the fact that national public authorities often unnecessarily limit the amount of aid granted to social enterprises to the general *de minimis* threshold of EUR 200,000, over a period of 3 years, without considering the opportunities arising, for example, from the Services of General Economic Interest (SGEI) framework.

Faced with this rapidly emerging scenario of uneven legal frameworks within the EU and the difficulty of adopting common provisions, in view of the numerous implications they would have, the Commission has proposed a number of initiatives in the *Action Plan 2021-30,* such as the organisation of seminars and workshops on—*inter alia*—State subsidies and taxation, as well as the publication of guidelines on the relevant fiscal frameworks for social economy actors, based on the analysis and input provided by Member State authorities and stakeholders. In implementing such initiatives, the Commission announced its intention to present a proposal for a recommendation to the Council on the development of framework conditions for the social economy, in order to enable policy makers to better adapt legal frameworks and policies to the needs of social economy actors, as well as to make recommendations for specific policies on—*inter alia*—State subsidies and taxation.

While welcoming the ever-increasing attention paid by the European institutions to the subject of the social economy, a few remarks should nevertheless be made on this point.

First of all, with respect to the social economy ecosystem, the Commission seems to offload onto the shoulders of the individual Member States the burden of defining a more coherent legal framework, leaving to itself the promotion of simple *soft-law* initiatives, recommendations, with a purely informative value. However, in order to overcome the regulatory barriers to a coordinated reference framework on the matter—which, as noted, constitutes a critical issue that has emerged since the very beginning of the debate—a more incisive intervention by the Commission, clearly within the limits of the division of matters of EU competence, would be needed.

In this respect, the comments made by the European Economic and Social Committee (EESC), in its opinion of 18 May 2022 entitled "*Action Plan for the Social Economy*" (INT/972), in which it commented on the Commission's *Action Plan 2021-30,* appear particularly pertinent. In this opinion, the EESC encouraged the Commission to pay specific attention to the taxation of social economy entities[2] as part of the ongoing legislative initiative to harmonise corporate taxation.[3]

Equally interesting and deserving of support is the EESC's call, again addressed to the Commission, for regulatory intervention to clarify the access requirements and the amount of state aid available to social economy entities, particularly in the SGEI sector.

---

[2]Among the semantic difficulties in the nomenclature of the social economy is the problem concerning the correct identification and delimitation of "social economy entities or organisations".

On this issue, the "*operational definition of the social economy*" drawn up by the EESC in its opinion of 18 May 2022, cited in the text, appears entirely acceptable, in the following terms: *"The set of private, formally-organised enterprises, with autonomy of decision and freedom of membership, created to meet their members'needs through the market by producing goods and providing services, insurance and finance, where decision-making and any distribution of profits or surpluses among the members are not directly linked to the capital or fees contributed by each member, each of whom has one vote, or at all events are decided through democratic, participatory processes. The social economy also includes private, formally-organised entities with autonomy of decision and freedom of membership that produce non-market services for households and whose surpluses, if any, cannot be appropriated by the economic agents that create, control or finance them".*

It follows from the above definition that the social economy can be divided into two sub-sectors, one market-based, or entrepreneurial, and the other non-market-based. The non-market sub-sector, again in the EESC's view, includes organisations that, in addition to sharing the characteristics common to all social economy entities, are: *(i)* non-profit in the strict sense of the term (prohibition on non-distribution of profits or operating surpluses) and *(ii)* produce goods and services that cannot be sold, as they are provided free of charge or at economically insignificant prices.

This paper focuses on the tax implications of entities operating in the non-market subsector of the social economy; therefore, the term "*non-market organisations of the social economy*" will be used in the text to identify these entities.

[3]The reference is to the initiative called *Business in Europe: Framework for Income Taxation* (BEFIT), through which the Commission intends to propose a directive, by the third quarter of 2023, on a common set of rules allowing EU companies to calculate a common tax base with a formula-based allocation of profits between EU Member States. The BEFIT is not the Commission's first attempt, being the latest initiative to propose EU-wide harmonisation of corporate taxation rules to the Member States.

Secondly, when thinking about the tax profiles of the social economy, the focus seems to be on single and isolated facilitation measures adopted by Member States in favour of *non-market organisations of the social economy* (see footnote 2). On the other hand, a broader vision does not seem to emerge in the debate capable of envisaging the possibility of establishing an organic system of taxation for *non-market organisations of the social economy*, with an *ad hoc* tax treatment for direct taxation purposes.

Thirdly and lastly, the two fields of taxation and competition (with the implications on the state aid side), although constantly referred to in the debate as "horizontal" regulations that intersect with the "vertical" regulation of the social economy, do not seem to have ever been linked in any way. In other words, the question of how an *ad hoc* tax regime envisaged specifically for *non-market organisations of the social economy*, constituting in itself a form of support in favour of a specific category of actors, fits in with the rules of state aid, does not seem to have been examined in any depth.[4]

Based on this foreword, we can outline an analysis, which will be elaborated on in the following paragraphs, where possible forms of harmonisation with EU law of national tax measures on social economy can be explored, looking at the national regulatory models (with a special focus on the Italian legislation), reasoning both in terms of the established law (so-call *de iure condito*) and in term of the law being established (so-call *de iure condendo*), and tackling cases with an impact exclusively at the domestic level or also at the cross-border level.

To this end, we will first of all examine a case of harmonisation based on the compatibility with State aid rules of a specific treatment in favour of *non-market organisations of the social economy,* adopted within a general organic framework, modelled on the Italian tax regime for Third Sector entities.[5] This will be discussed in Sect. 2 below.

This will be followed by several concrete cases of tax harmonisation, taken from Italian domestic law, of purely domestic (Sect. 3) and cross-border relevance (Sect. 4).

[4] A hint, indeed, can be found in the EESC opinion mentioned several times in the text, where it is stated: *"A specific tax treatment for social economy enterprises and entities exists in most of the EU countries (see CIRIEC/EESC, 2012). Opponents of this specific treatment have long argued that it could be considered unequal treatment that constitutes unlawful state aid in contravention of the free competition rules. In 2011, the Court of Justice of the European Union ruled that the specific tax treatment is justified because social economy entities (cooperatives in the case before it) are different in nature to for-profit companies. Rigorous conceptualisation and legal recognition of social economy entities is needed to highlight the significant differences between the different forms of enterprise"*.

[5] Italian lawmakers, as part of the overall reform of the Third Sector approved by Legislative Decree No. 117 of 3 July 2017, have set up a specific tax regime for third sector entities, with a dedicated section of the measure, which contains provisions on income tax, indirect taxes and local taxes.

2 Fiscal Harmonisation of General Tax Regimes in Favour of Social Economy Entities with Respect to State Aid Rules

Article 107(1) of the TFEU defines State aid as aid granted by a Member State or through State resources in any form whatsoever which distorts or threatens to distort competition by favouring certain enterprises or the production of certain goods, insofar as it affects trade between Member States.

The requirements of the notion of State aid are, therefore, the existence of an enterprise; the State origin of the aid, in terms of both the responsibility of the State for introducing the measure and its financing through State resources; the granting of an advantage; the selectivity of the measure; the impact of the aid on competition and trade between Member States.[6]

As already set out in the previous paragraph, we can focus on a case of reasoning based on compatibility with European rules on State aid as consisting not of particular favourable measures for non-profit entities but of an overall tax regime that provides for a generally favourable treatment of the activities of such entities, for the purpose of direct taxation (the "*postulated general system of taxation*"). The reference model is, as mentioned previously, the tax regime established by Italian lawmakers in favour of third sector entities (see also footnote 5).

In outlining the fundamental requirements of State aid, within the above-mentioned framework, it primarily ensues that even a fiscal measure envisaged by a State in favour of a specific group of subjects can, in principle, constitute State aid.[7]

Indeed, the transfer of state resources underlying this aid can also take any form, such as direct grants, loans, guarantees, direct investments in the capital of enterprises, as well as benefits in kind. Moreover, there doesn't even have to be an effective transfer of funds, because a waiver of the resources that would otherwise have had to be paid into the state coffers is sufficient.[8] This is the case with tax benefits. In the case law of the European Court of Justice there is the well-established principle that the forfeiture of tax revenues in itself, as a result of reductions or exemptions granted by the Member State, fulfils the criterion of "State resources" referred to in Article 107(1) of the Treaty.[9]

Another precondition, which often recurs in the present case, is granting an economic advantage arising from the *postulated general system of taxation*, given

---

[6]The reconstruction, in terms of the abstract case, of the constituent requirements of the notion of State aid carried out in the text takes account of the Commission's guidelines on the subject, summarised in the "*Communication on the notion of State aid as referred to in Article 107(1) of the Treaty on the Functioning of the European Union*" (2016/C 262/01).

[7]For a general overview of the impact of the state aid rules on the national tax system and its function in implementing social market economy principles, see Miceli (2021), p. 17 ff.

[8]See on this point CJEU, 16 May 2000, *France/Ladbroke Racing Ltd and Commission,* C-83/98, paras. 48–51.

[9]In this sense CJEU, 5 March 1994, *Banco Exterior de España,* C-387/92, paragraph 14.

the broad interpretation of the notion of "advantage", which can possibly include any intervention that alleviates the economic burden on the beneficiary enterprise. Such a notion can certainly include a state intervention in the form of tax relief, i.e. a reduction of the amount of tax normally paid by enterprises.

Finally, when the State grants a fiscal advantage to an enterprise from its own resources, relieving it of expenses which it would otherwise have to incur in its normal course of business, there is normally a distortion of competition, as such capable of affecting trade between Member States. Therefore, the further prerequisites of the (potential) impact of aid on competition and trade between Member States, for the purpose of identifying State aid, are considered to be fulfilled in this case.

While all the criteria examined so far can be viewed as self-explanatory, the key elements with the greatest implications for the *postulated general system of taxation* are (i) the nature of the beneficiaries as enterprises, and (ii) the selective nature of the aid, which is capable of favouring certain enterprises to the detriment of others that find themselves in a similar situation.

2.1 Defining the Concept of "Enterprise"

State aid rules only apply if the beneficiary of a measure is an "enterprise".

According to the established case law of the European Court of Justice,[10] EU law has embraced a "substantive" and "functional" definition of "enterprise", by virtue of which any entity engaged in an economic activity is an enterprise, regardless of its legal status and how it is financed, which means that the application of the State aid rules does not depend on whether the entity has been set up to make a profit or not. Indeed, non-profit organisations may also offer goods and services on the market and, as such, be regarded as beneficiaries of State aid.

Therefore, the Euro-unitarian rationale is based on the distinction between economic and non-economic activities rather than between profit-making and non-profit-making entities. On this point, the European Court of Justice already mentioned in the footnote has consistently held that any activity consisting in offering goods and services on a marketplace constitutes an economic activity.

It therefore becomes necessary to verify whether or not there is a "market" for a given service within the individual Member State.

As clarified by the guidelines of the Commission and the rulings of the European Court of Justice,[11] this question essentially depends on the manner in which certain services are organised in the relevant Member State, i.e. whether the individual State considers the provision of a certain service as being open to competition from a

[10] See CJEU,12 September 2000, *Pavlov and Others*, Joined Cases C-180/98 to C-184/98; 10 January 2006, *Cassa di Risparmio di Firenze SpA and Others*, C-222/04; 27 June 2017, *Congregación de Escuelas Pías Provincia Betania*, C-74/16.

[11] See CJEU, 17 February 1993, *Poucet and Pistre*, Joined Cases C-159/91 and C-160/91.

number of economic operators or, alternatively, as forming part of its institutional purpose to be universally provided to all citizens.

The issue is of core importance for certain "typical" sectors of the social economy, such as social services, health care, education and research activities, which are frequently subject to state control and financing. When this is the case, we can rule out the economic nature of these activities.[12]

A second profile, which is important as a further criterion for distinguishing between economic and non-economic activities, consists in the circumstance that services are provided for remuneration, i.e. against payment of good and valuable consideration for the service received.[13]

Systematically linking the two above-mentioned profiles (public control and financing of the service, on the one hand, and the non-remunerative nature of the contributions received, on the other), it follows that where *non-market organisations of the social economy* engage in activities subject to state control—typically, activities in the fields of social security, health care, education and research—and lacking the payment of consideration, then the activities at issue are of a non-economic nature.

This is the case when the competent public authorities entrust public services to be provided by *non-market organisations of the social economy* on the basis of an accreditation, a contract or an agreement, in a perspective of a "strict" form of subsidiarity[14] and, in return, the engaged organisations undertake to carry out these activities in compliance with the same principles of solidarity, universality and non-discrimination that inform the public sector.

Any cost-sharing schemes, which require the beneficiaries of the services to share in the costs (in the form of prescription charges or public-school fees) are not of the essence when the charges levied are purely token and have no relation to the actual cost of the service.

Another case characterised by the lack of a true market approach includes all activities of a purely social nature, which, for example are not paid for or are based on the principle of solidarity, such as charitable activities or those that promote human, civil and social rights, non-violence, civil protection and international cooperation. These are non-economic activities by virtue of their very "nature" (so to speak).

---

[12] These are the sectors given as examples of non-economic activities by the European Commission in the aforementioned Communication on the concept of State aid (2016/C 262/01).

[13] See CJEU, 11 September 2007, *Schwarz and –GootjesSchwarz*, C76/05 – and the case law cited therein.

[14] On the possibility for the State to "delegate", also to private-sector entities, the performance of activities that are inherently part of the prerogatives of public authorities, the Commission has clarified that, in the case of activities for which a State has decided not to introduce market mechanisms "*it is irrelevant whether the State is acting directly through a body forming part of the State administration or by way of a separate body on which it has conferred special or exclusive rights*" (cf. Commission Staff Working Document of 29 April 2013 on "*Guide to the application of the European Union rules on state aid, public procurement and the internal market to services of general economic interest, and in particular to social services of general interest*").

This analysis of the nature of the activities carried out by an organisation, for the purpose of defining its nature as an "enterprise", however, does not automatically lead to the conclusion that all activities which qualify as "economic" should be considered, for that reason alone, to be relevant for the purpose of envisaging State aid.

In fact, this line of reasoning can be further developed on the basis of the SGEI framework.

As also noted by the European Commission, and as mentioned above, the SGEI framework is constantly mentioned as an opportunity for Member States to grant aid to social economy organisations in compliance with State aid rules.

According to the definitions set out in the Commission Communication of 20 December 2011, COM(2011) 900, with the title "*A Quality Framework for Services of General Interest in Europe*", SGEI—services of general economic interest—are commercial services of general economic utility subject to public-service obligations, which would not be carried out by the market if there were no state incentives (or would be carried out under different conditions, in terms of their quality, safety, affordability, equal treatment or universal access). Providers are therefore required to comply with and abide by public service obligations, on the basis of an engagement and a criterion of general interest, which ensures that the service is provided under conditions that enable it to fulfil its tasks.

SGEI are subject to the application of EU State aid rules, with specific reference to compensation granted for the fulfilment of public service obligations.

More specifically, following the 2011 reform, the Commission adopted a new SGEI-related State aid package, in which it clarified the conditions under which compensation constitutes State aid, as well as the conditions under which State aid can be considered compatible with the TFEU. In this regard, four different hypotheses can—in essence—be envisaged, as follows:

(i) Public service compensation that meets the 4 cumulative conditions developed in the judgment of 24 July 2003, *Altmark,* C-280/00[15] does not constitute state aid within the meaning of Article 107 TFEU;

[15] In the *Altmark* judgment cited above, the European Court of Justice ruled that public service compensation does not constitute state aid, provided that the following four criteria are cumulatively met:

the recipient service provider must have actually been engaged to provide public services and be required to fulfil clearly defined public service obligations;
the method for calculating the compensation must be objective, transparent and set out in advance;
the compensation cannot exceed the relevant costs incurred in providing the public service obligations, taking into account the relevant receipts and a reasonable profit; and
lastly, where the provider of the public services is not chosen through a public procurement procedure, which would allow for the selection of the tenderer capable of providing those services at the least cost to the community, the level of compensation must be calculated based on an analysis of the costs incurred by an average well-run and adequately equipped enterprise operating in the relevant sector.

(ii) Public service compensation falling within the scope of Commission Regulation (EU) No. 360/2012 of 25 April 2012 on the *de minimis* aid regime for SGEI (which sets a ceiling of EUR 500,000, over three financial years) does not constitute State aid within the meaning of Article 107 TFEU;
(iii) public service compensation constituting State aid, because it does not fall under (i) and (ii), may be declared compatible with the internal market pursuant to Article 106(2) TFEU[16] and on the basis of the comparability conditions developed by the Commission[17]; in this case, compensation is not subject to the prior information requirement under Article 108(3) TFEU;
(iv) other public service compensation constituting State aid is subject to the prior information requirement of Article 108(3) TFEU.

Based on this legal framework, we can verify the compatibility with the notion of State aid of those services entrusted by a Member State to *non-market organisations of the social economy* for discharging services in the public interest. Compliance with the legal requirements, beginning with the provision of economic compensation to the entrusted entity covering the costs arising from the fulfilment of the public service obligations and recognising a reasonable profit, renders the aid measure envisaged by the individual State irrelevant for the purpose of the State aid rules, despite the economic nature of the activity entrusted to the entity.

That said, it must be added, however, that the SGEI guidelines do not cover all the possible types of tax measures in favour of *non-market organisations of the social economy*, starting from the case postulated herein, concerning the provision of a general tax regime that recognises *ad hoc* treatment of general interest activities for the purpose of direct taxation. In fact, it is one thing to grant aid in the form of economic compensation, in the terms indicated above, for the entrustment of a service in the public interest and quite another to grant a specific group of entities

---

[16] Article 106(2) TFEU: "*Undertakings entrusted with the operation of services of general economic interest or having the character of a revenue-producing monopoly shall be subject to the rules contained in the Treaties, in particular to the rules on competition, in so far as the application of such rules does not obstruct the performance, in law or in fact, of the particular tasks assigned to them. The development of trade must not be affected to such an extent as would be contrary to the interests of the Union*".

[17] Pursuant to Commission Decision C(2011) 9380 of 20 December 2011 on the application of Article 106(2) TFEU to State aid in the form of public service compensation granted to undertakings entrusted with providing services of general economic interest, the conditions for the compatibility of such State aid are as follows

an act of entrustment, not exceeding a term of 10 years, specifying the content and duration of the public service obligations, the undertaking and, where applicable, the territory concerned, the nature of any exclusive or special rights granted to the undertaking, the parameters for calculating, controlling and reviewing the compensation and the arrangements for avoiding and recovering any overcompensation, and including a reference to the said Decision;

the compensation shall not exceed what is necessary to cover the net cost incurred in discharging the public service obligations and a reasonable profit; for this purpose, all costs and revenues must be calculated;

the control of overcompensation by the public authorities of the Member States.

a differentiated tax regime directly linked to the peculiar subjective *status* they hold. This case does not appear to fall in its entirety within the narrower confines of the concept of SGEI.

2.2 Defining the Concept of "Selectivity"

If, therefore, a given economic activity carried out by a *non-market organisation of the social economy* fails to fulfil the requirements of the SGEI legislation, the relevant tax regime would not necessarily qualify as State aid. A final key requirement, that of "selectivity", must be verified in order to bring the measure within the fold, so to speak, of this concept.

Not all measures favouring economic operators fall within the concept of State aid, but only those that selectively grant an advantage to certain undertakings or categories of undertakings or to certain economic sectors.

The very concept of selectivity underlies the discriminatory effect of the aid. It is not sufficient for a given state measure to simply benefit a certain group of actors, it must also give rise to discriminatory treatment between undertakings, i.e. in the presence of other market actors which find themselves in similar (factual and legal) circumstances as the beneficiaries of the aid. Only in this case does the aid become a potentially distortive factor of competition. Hence the need for an analysis of comparability.

Under the *postulated general system of taxation*, this examination should compare *non-market organisations of the social economy* benefiting from the general tax system to commercial enterprises.

This examination can be based on the precedent, set by the European Court of Justice in its judgment of 8 September 2011, *Paint Graphos*, Joined Cases C-78/08 to C-80/08, which ruled in respect of the Italian tax regime of exemption from corporate income tax of income earned by cooperative companies.[18]

The Court ruled, on that occasion, that in view of the specific characteristics of cooperative societies, which conform to particular operating principles, this type of company could not be considered to be in a comparable factual and legal situation to commercial companies. Consequently, it ruled that the favourable tax treatment reserved by Italian law for cooperative societies could not automatically be considered prohibited State aid, due to the specific requirements that distinguish social cooperatives from other economic operators subject to the ordinary tax regime.[19]

---

[18] *The Paint Graphos* judgment is consistently cited in subsequent case law, which has reaffirmed the legitimacy of the tax regime specific to cooperative societies (Judgment 16 July 2020, *OC and Others,* C-686/18) and, on a more general level, the justification of an "*a priori selective tax regime*" (Judgment 19 December 2018, *Finanzamt B*, C-374/17).

[19] For an in-depth discussion of the ruling, see Fici (2011), p. 33.

The jurisprudential precedent is of great interest, not only because of the principle itself, but also for the circumstance that the *status* of the *non-market organisation of the social economy* more conspicuously differs from the regime of commercial enterprises than that of cooperative societies, which, after all, still carry out entrepreneurial activities.

Therefore, it is worthwhile to list the specificities of *non-market organisations of the social economy*, in order to determine the elements that clearly differentiate them from commercial enterprises. In this regard, reference can be made to the indications developed by the EESC in the said opinion of 18 May 2022 (already mentioned in footnote 2), which provided a description of non-market social economy organisations. More specifically, these are organisations, mainly associations and foundations, with a formal organisation, characterised by decision-making autonomy and freedom of membership, which are considered to be producers of non-commercial goods, in the sense that they provide most of their goods or services free of charge or at economically insignificant prices, and whose possible operating surplus cannot be distributed to the economic entities that created, control or finance them. Their main resources, again in the view of the EESC, in addition to those coming from the sale of occasional goods and services, come from voluntary contributions in cash or in kind, payments made by public administrations and capital income.

If we view the organisational profiles of this type of entity in a systematic perspective, we can clearly see that they have a subjective *status* that differs from that of commercial enterprises, which undoubtedly operate on a different market and both objectively and subjectively pursue a profit-making purpose.[20]

Lacking a similar factual and legal situation, with respect to business-minded entities operating in the market,[21] the measures in favour of *non-market organisations of the social economy* could not be considered as being "selective" in nature, since they would actually apply to "all" undertakings[22]—and not just to "certain" ones (as required by Art. 107(1), cited above)—belonging to the same uniform category (the non-market sub-sector of the social economy), without any discriminatory distinction.

In any event, even if the specific characteristics of the *non-market organisations of the social economy* do not exclude the selectivity of the measure and, therefore,

[20] The profit-making form presupposes not only the earning of a profit (objective profile) but also the subsequent distribution of the profit among the members of the organisation (subjective profile).

[21] It has already been observed that the business model is not incompatible with the social economy and the socially useful purposes pursued therein. Consequently, the most authentic distinction that comes to mind for a correct examination of comparability is not so much between entities operating within or outside the social economy but between entrepreneurial (social economy) and non-entrepreneurial organisations.

[22] In the European Union sense (see § Sect. 2.1).

the existence of State aid, they would nevertheless be relevant for the purposes of the compatibility analysis of the aid.

It can be argued, in fact, that state intervention by means of an *ad hoc* tax regime is necessary and proportionate to favour the financing of activities with a significant social impact, carried out by non-profit (subjective) entities and aimed at achieving general interest objectives, which, without the envisaged subsidies, could not otherwise be adequately carried out, compared to the purpose of the law.

The bottom line, therefore, is that the specific subjective *status* of the entities operating in the social economy (for a non-commercial purpose), while considered irrelevant in terms of (the exclusion of) the said requirements of State aid, especially with regard to the criterion of selectivity, should at least be considered relevant from the point of view of compatibility with State aid. In particular, an aid regime, as envisaged here, could be considered compatible with the internal market under Article 107(3)(c) TFEU, which recognises the legitimacy of *"aid to facilitate the development of certain economic activities ….. where such aid does not adversely affect trading conditions to an extent contrary to the common interest"*.

It is our opinion that the *postulated general system of taxation* may be included within such a regulatory framework, by virtue of the purposes it pursues of facilitating the development of general interest activities based on solidarity and social utility, in light of the social value of associative and volunteer activities and the culture and practice of giving.[23]

3 Tax Harmonisation at National Level: Case Studies of EU-Compatible National Measures

In this paragraph, we will focus on a range of tax measures aimed at favouring *non-market organisations of the social economy*, taken from the Italian legislative experience, which have had to face up to Euro-unitarian rules to ensure their compatibility.

To this end, we will review two rather illustrative cases concerning, respectively: (i) exemption from municipal property tax for properties used by non-commercial entities and used exclusively for welfare, social security, health, educational, accommodation, cultural, recreational, sporting activities, as well as religious and worship activities; and (ii) exemption from VAT of teaching courses held by amateur sports associations.

[23] In this sense, the general principles expressed by the Italian national legislation on the Third Sector (Article 2, Legislative Decree No 117 of 3 July 2017).

3.1 Profiles of Compatibility with EU Law of Property Tax (ICI) Exemption for Properties Used by Non-commercial Entities

In 1992, Italy introduced a municipal property tax, called "*Imposta Comunale sugli Immobili*" (ICI) levied on all natural and legal persons possessing immovable property (by way of ownership, usufruct, use, habitation or emphyteusis).[24]

The national legislation provided for a peculiar tax exemption regime. In particular, properties used by non-commercial entities, and used exclusively for welfare, social security, health, educational, accommodation, cultural, recreational and sports activities, as well as religious and worship activities, were made exempt from the tax.

The exemption applied if two cumulative conditions were met:

(i) if the property was used by non-commercial entities, i.e. by entities other than companies whose exclusive or core purpose is not to engage in activities of a commercial nature;
(ii) if the property was used exclusively for the performance of the activities specifically listed.

Pursuant to Article 108(2) TFEU, the Commission initiated a formal investigation procedure concerning the relief measure at issue, as it appeared to meet the conditions to qualify as State aid. The procedure, initiated in 2006, ended only in 2012, after an intervention by Italian lawmakers, who, in 2012, reformed the rules governing property taxation by introducing a new property tax called "*Imposta Municipale Urbana*" (IMU).

But let's start from the beginning.

The main doubts that prompted the Commission to initiate a formal investigation centred on the nature of the activities covered by the exemption (welfare, social security, health, educational, accommodation, cultural, recreational and sports activities, as well as religious and worship activities). Under the law, in order to be exempted, the activities at issue could also be of a commercial nature, provided they were not of an "*exclusively*" commercial nature.[25]

In other words, non-commercial entities were exempt from the property tax, even when the activities they carried were of a partially economic nature.

The Commission noted that, for example, in the case of healthcare activities, non-commercial entities could be exempted simply by entering into a partnership agreement with a public authority. The same applied to educational activities, whereby the educational establishment at issue was required to meet specific teaching standards, accommodate handicapped pupils, apply collective bargaining rules and ensure non-discrimination of pupils. These conditions obviously did not

[24] The national regulatory reference here is Legislative Decree No 504 of 30 December 1992.

[25] Indeed, Article 39 of Decree-Law No 223 of 4 July 2006, converted by Law No 248 of 4 August 2006, clarified that exemption from ICI property tax for non-commercial entities applied to activities deserving protection that were *"not exclusively of a commercial nature"*.

exclude—*per se*—the economic nature of the activities concerned, within the meaning of Euro-unitarian law.

As already pointed out above (see Sect. 2.1), the decisive element for distinguishing an economic from a non-economic activity, according to the European regulatory framework, is whether or not there is a market in which the relevant entity can offer its goods and services. However, a market can be found even in the health and education sectors, which means that a non-commercial entity, even a non-profit-making organisation pursuing a civic and social purpose, can effectively engage in economic activities, for example, by requiring the payment of a fee for the services it provides.

Pending the conclusion of the procedure initiated by the Commission, the Italian lawmakers subsequently replaced the ICI property tax with a new property tax called IMU, bringing forward to 2012 the entry into force of this new tax, originally scheduled to start on 1 January 2014.

The new tax featured a number of changes, compared to the previous ICI property tax, regarding the taxation of property owned or used by non-commercial entities, with the innovative approach of restricting exemption to a list of specified activities carried out by non-commercial entities in a non-commercial manner.

In the event that a same property was used for both commercial and non-commercial activities, specific rules were introduced to allow the proportional payment of the property tax, aimed at restricting exemption from the tax only to the part of the property effectively and exclusively used for non-commercial activities.

Moreover, the Italian lawmakers also approved a regulation containing general and sectoral requirements, to determine the cases in which the relevant activities were carried out in a non-commercial manner.[26]

This regulation, which is still in force today, was clearly aimed at adapting Italian law to EU law, providing for additional and more restrictive requirements than those previously applied. Continuing in the example used above, relative to social and health care activities, besides the requirement for a partnership agreement with the State, or other public administration bodies, the new regulation also requires that the activities accredited for performance by the non-commercial entity should be carried out in a complementary or supplementary manner, with respect to the public service, and that the relevant services be provided to users free of charge or under a cost-sharing scheme, to cover the costs of the universal service. Where the social and health care activities have not been accredited with the public service, they can be exempted from the property tax only if they are provided free of charge or against payment of a token amount. With regard to educational activities, the relevant regulation provides that they should be considered as carried out in a non-commercial manner if, in addition to fulfilling the conditions already provided

[26]Ministry of Economy and Finance Decree No. 200 of 19 November 2012.

for under the previous legislation, the activities are equal to public education and are carried out free of charge, or against payment of a token amount, covering only a fraction of the actual cost of the service.

The change of course is clear and convinced the European Commission to close its formal investigation, qualifying the ICI property tax exemption (under the previous legislation) as State aid that was incompatible with the internal market and, at the same time, excluding the current IMU property tax exemption from the scope of the State aid rules (see the Commission's decision of 19 December 2012).

3.2 *Profiles of Compatibility with EU Law of the VAT Exemption for Tuition by Amateur Sports Associations*

Article 132(1) of Directive No 2006/112/EC of 28 November 2006 lists among the activities that Member States may exempt from the payment of VAT, under point (i) *"the provision of children's or young people's education, school or university education, vocational training or retraining, including the supply of services and of goods closely related thereto, by bodies governed by public law having such as their aim or by other organisations recognised by the Member State concerned as having similar objects"*. The following point (j) of the same article provides that *"tuition given privately by teachers and covering school or university education"* is also exempt from VAT.

In the Italian legal system, the two aforementioned provisions have been implemented into Article 10(1)(20) of Presidential Decree No. 633/1972, establishing the exemption of *"educational services for children and young people and educational services of all kinds, including for training, updating, requalification and vocational retraining provided by establishments or schools recognised by public administrations and by third sector entities of a non-commercial nature"*.

With regard to the latter provision, the question arose as to its applicability to tuition by amateur sports clubs.

While in the past Italian administrative practice had applied VAT exemption for services provided by ski or tennis schools for non-professional purposes,[27] the most recent documents issued by the Italian tax authorities had, instead, ruled out the applicability of the said Article 10. The Administration notes, in particular, that

[27] See Ministerial Resolutions No. 361426/1978; No. 551/1993.

exemption is subject to the fulfilment of two conditions, one objective and the other subjective, insofar as the services:

(a) are educational in nature, for children and young people, including training, refresher, requalification and vocational retraining activities (objective requirement);
(b) are provided by establishments or schools recognised by public administrations or non-commercial entities (subjective requirement).

In particular, attention is drawn to the objective requirement of the provision, where the expression "*school or university education*", for VAT purposes, must refer, as the Court of Justice of the European Union also ruled in its judgment of 21 October 2021 in Case C-373/19, to *"an integrated system for the transfer of knowledge and skills covering a wide and diversified set of subjects, and to the furthering and development of that knowledge and those skills by the pupils and students"*.

Indeed, this ruling, which stemmed from the German tax authorities'refusal to grant VAT exemption to a Munich school offering swimming tuition, the Court of Justice held that this sports tuition, while of undoubted importance and in the general interest, nevertheless constitutes specialised tuition, which does not amount, in itself, to the transfer of knowledge and skills covering a wide and diversified set of subjects, which is characteristic of school or university education.

It is clear that the interpretation of the Italian tax authorities, which goes beyond the literal wording of the national law provision (the said Article 10), conforms to the Euro-unitarian source, as interpreted by the EU Court of Justice.

In truth, at the national level, the said Article 10 recognises the VAT exemption regime for educational services "*of all kinds*", an expression which, *ex se,* allows for the inclusion of sports tuition as well. However, the obligation to comply with EU law, especially in a harmonised matter such as VAT, in conjunction with the extra-judicial effectiveness of the rulings made by the European Court of Justice in preliminary rulings,[28] leads to forms of tax harmonisation also at the level of interpretation by the national tax authorities, if necessary by bending the literal wording of the domestic provision.

Lastly, it should be noted that sports tuition services may, in abstract, be included among the exempt services, within the meaning of Article 132(m) of Directive 2006/112/EC, which includes *"certain services closely linked to sport or physical education by non-profit-making organisations to persons taking part in sport or physical education"*.

This provision, however, which provides for a favourable regime limited to *non-profit-making* entities, has not been specifically transposed into the Italian legal system.

[28] See CJEU, 3 February 1977, *Benedetti v. Munari F.lli sas,* C-52/76; 5 March 1986, *Wünsche Handelgesellschaft Gmbh& Co. v. Federal Republic of Germany*, C-69/85.

4 Cross-Border Tax Harmonisation: Taxation of Cross-Border Donations

4.1 Foreword: General Overview of Cross-Border Philanthropy in the EU

Donations and, in particular, donations of a cross-border nature, i.e. donations involving non-resident donors or non-profit beneficiary entities, have been highly debated with respect to possible forms of harmonisation of EU law with national tax measures, as noted, inter alia, by the European Foundation Centre (EFC) in "Policy and Programmes Boosting cross-border philantrophy in europe towards a tax-effective enviroment" and by Lideikyte-Huber in "Foundations in Europe from a tax perspective – Observations and trends. Comparative Highlights of Foundation Laws, Donors and Foundations Networks in Europe". These are by their very nature "cross-border" cases that are becoming increasingly important in the current framework of philanthropy, according to the released data,[29] which boasts more than 147,000 non-profit organisations in Europe with a cumulative annual expenditure of almost 60 billion euros and with a workforce that accounts for about 13% of the total workforce in Europe.

In this regard, digitalisation and the development of an increasingly interconnected system have contributed to redefining the perimeter of the potential pool of non-profit entities. In fact, we are witnessing a growing development of organisational models in the social economy through entities carrying out general interest activities and whose operations cross the national borders, in pursuit of their solidarity-based aims, e.g., Non-Governmental Organisations (NGOs) operating in the field development cooperation in low-income foreign countries. Today, the topics of interest for philanthropy are increasingly becoming transnational and cross-border since the major issues of public interest (e.g., educational poverty, climate change and health risks) transcend national borders. Therefore, these organisations are becoming more and more internationally mobile.

Non-profit organisations undoubtedly play a role in many areas of the social economy, which is traditionally regarded in Europe as a way of making up for the failure of the state and the market. During the COVID epidemic, the social economy got to play a major role demonstrating its ability to contribute to economic development and job creation, particularly for more vulnerable people. Despite its proven relevance—as noted in the study prepared, in April 2021, by the European Parliament's research unit[30]—an increasing number of non-profit organisations are

---

[29] Data compiled by the Donors and Foundations Networks in Europe (DAFNE) and analysed by the US Foundation CentER in 2016. See OJEU, *Opinion of the European Economic and Social Committee on "European philanthropy: an untapped potential"*, exploratory opinion requested by the Romanian Presidency (2019/C 240/06).

[30] "A statute for European cross-border associations and non-profit organisations" commissioned by the European Parliament's Policy Department for Citizens'Rights and Constitutional Affairs – Directorate-General for Internal Policies 693.439-May 2021.

nevertheless facing civil, fiscal and administrative obstacles when they look to develop their activities across borders.

Several factors have to be taken into account. First of all, philanthropic flows are protected by the freedoms enshrined in the European Treaties. The rights set out in the Charter of Fundamental Rights of the European Union, and in particular the right of association, make sure that citizens have the freedom to create and organise entities that can carry out public benefit and philanthropic activities. They therefore promote the values of the European Union set out in Article 2 of the EU Treaty, including respect for human dignity, the rule of law and human rights. However, it should also be considered that, as highlighted in the previous paragraphs, these non-profit organisations still lack an EU-wide specific *ad hoc* regulation, unlike other types of legal entities (such as, for instance, joint stock companies, cooperative societies and the European Economic Interest Groupings), despite not being alien to EU law, as confirmed by the fact that the Treaty on European Union recognises their fundamental role for the institutions (Article 11(2) TEU).

Secondly, on an objective level, there is a lack of consistent definitions at EU level, as well as inconsistent approaches by the various EU Member States, regarding the application of tax exemptions to cross-border donations. The philanthropic activities carried out across borders by non-profit organisations, in fact, find no place within the tax framework at both EU and national level. Until the jurisprudential developments of the EU Court of Justice, in terms of taxation, the traditional approach has always envisaged the exclusion of preferential tax measures in favour of non-resident donors or in support of non-domestic non-profit entities. In other words, EU Member States have continued to apply their domestic regulations excluding from the scope of application public benefit organisations or donor entities on account of the different EU State in which they are established. As a result, even though these entities operate in many areas of general interest, such as education, culture, healthcare and humanitarian assistance, and have comparable requirements to organisations established in other EU Member States, to date non-profit entities are not beneficiaries of the opportunities offered by the EU single market.

Evidence of this lies in the fact that the different national legislative systems and legal traditions of the Member States have adopted different approaches to the definition or recognition of non-profit organisations, as well as to the definition, recognition and granting of public benefit status. Moreover, the difficulty in achieving a harmonised system for non-profit organisations carrying out their institutional activities in the Union is also linked to the fragmented legislative framework, in which it has been estimated that there are more than 50 different regulations governing the establishment and operation of the entities. However, it should be pointed out that openings on this point have come about thanks to the jurisprudential developments of the Court of Justice of the European Union (hereinafter also only "CJEU") which, as we shall see, has provided clear legal principles for building a system that overcomes the critical issues resulting from the fragmentary nature of the legislation and avoids any form of discrimination based on the place of establishment of the non-profit organisation.

4.2 The Jurisprudential Developments of the CJEU. From the Stauffer and Persche Judgments to the Principle of Fiscal Comparability

An important contribution to overcoming the fragmented system of taxation has come from the developments of the Court of Justice of the European Union. In particular, in its judgment in the *Persche* case (C-318/07),[31] the Court posed important questions on the relationship between the fiscal treatment of subsidised donations and the charitable purposes of the beneficiary entity.

This is not the first case in which the taxation of non-profit organisations has come under the lens of the CJEU. Previously, in its judgment in the *Stauffer* case,[32] the Court ruled against the German tax legislation for exempting from the payment of corporation tax the rental income received in Germany by charitable foundations established in Germany. However, it excluded the recognition of the same tax relief in respect of another foundation, on the assumption that the latter is established and recognised as a non-profit entity in another EU Member State.

In the judgment at issue, the Court provides clear indications on two important issues concerning the taxation of non-profit entities. Firstly, it confirmed that the EU principle of free movement of capital and, therefore, the fundamental economic freedoms provided for by EU law also apply to entities other than corporations. In essence, non-profit entities are placed on the same footing as companies and, like the latter, are essential players in the EU market and enjoy the fundamental economic freedoms when they carry out cross-border activities in the EU. Secondly, the Court specified that the application of tax exemption regimes, provided for in an EU Member State only in respect of organisations recognised in that State and not also to foreign-based organisations, constitutes an obstacle to the principle of the free movement of capital, as well as a case of discrimination. That is to say, measures imposed by an EU Member State which treat cross-border movements less favourably than domestic movements and which, as a result, are likely to dissuade residents from making capital movements in other Member States constitute a restriction on the movement of capital, which is prohibited by EU law. The principle expressed by the Court is clear: where an entity that is recognised as being of public benefit in one Member State also fulfils the conditions laid down for that purpose by the legislation of another Member State and has as its objective the promotion of identical public interests, that entity cannot be denied the right to equal (fiscal) treatment merely because it is not established in the territory.

In line with this jurisprudential orientation is the *Persche* ruling, where the Court of Justice had the opportunity to extend the line of reasoning previously anticipated

[31] See CJEU, judgment of 27 January 2009, Case C-318/07, Persche v Finanzamt Lüdenscheid.

[32] See CJEU, judgment of 14 September 2006, Case C-386/04, Centro di Musicologia Walter Stauffer.

in the *Stauffer* ruling, by taking a definitive position on the issue of tax comparability between domestic and foreign entities.

The Court has in fact ruled on the applicability of the German tax relief system to donations made to non-profit organisations established in Germany. This also applies—as in case at issue—if the non-profit organisation receiving the donation is located in another EU Member State (e.g. Portugal). On this point, the Court held that the recognition of relief, under the national legislation, only to entities established in the country, prevents the free movement of capital, in so far as it is not possible to prove that a donation made to an entity established in another Member State satisfies the requirements of that legislation for granting the benefit. In simpler terms, although each Member State, under its own legislation, may treat recognised bodies of general interest established in its territory differently from those established in other Member States, this is permissible in so far as the latter pursue objectives that differ from those laid down in its own legislation. Indeed, EU law does not require Member States to ensure that foreign entities that qualify as general interest entities in their country of origin automatically enjoy the same recognition in the other States as well. It goes without saying, however, that where an entity recognised as being of public benefit in a Member State also fulfils the conditions laid down for that purpose by the legislation of another Member State, and has the purpose of promoting identical public interests—to the extent that, in principle at least, it may be recognised as being of public benefit in that State—then the authorities of the latter State shall not deny that entity the right to equal treatment, solely on the ground that it is not established on their country.

In this sense, the less favourable treatment of cross-border donations cannot be justified—in the view of the CJEU and the Advocate General—by the need to ensure the effectiveness of fiscal controls. Without prejudice to the Member State's duty to carry out the necessary checks to establish whether a non-profit-making entity meets the conditions laid down by national law for access to specific advantageous tax regimes, the fact that such checks are harder to perform, in the case of entities established in another EU Member State *"constitutes a disadvantage of a purely administrative nature which is not sufficient to justify a refusal on the part of the authorities of the State concerned to grant such a foundation the same tax exemptions as are granted to a foundation of the same kind, which, in principle, has unlimited tax liability in that State"*.[33]

Ultimately, the principles expressed in the *Stauffer* and *Persche* judgments had the merit of overcoming the traditional approach in favour of the recognition of a truly harmonised tax system, with regard to cross-border donations, taking an unequivocal position on the issue of tax comparability. That is to say, by admitting the application of tax benefits under national law to both domestic and foreign organisations, thus recognising the application of the free movement of capital while guaranteeing the principle of non-discrimination.

[33] Opinion of Advocate General Mengozzi of 14 October 2008, see para. 80. Case C-318/07.

4.3 Tax Harmonisation: National and EU Outlook

Within the regulatory and case law framework outlined so far, steps towards the recognition of the principle of fiscal comparability have also been taken at national level.

This is the case, for example, of the clarifications provided by the Italian Revenue Agency[34] which, in response to an appeal, allowed a foreign-based non-profit entity to benefit from the favourable tax regime provided by the reform of the Third Sector, as per Article 83 of Legislative Decree no. 117/2017 (Third Sector Code) on the subject of donations. This, however, was made subject to the condition that the said entity was registered in accordance with Italian law. Overall, therefore, it is recognised that an entity residing abroad is allowed to apply for tax relief in Italy to the extent that it is recognised as a "non-profit organisation of social utility" (Onlus) under Italian legislation, by having registered with and being listed in the relevant Register (*Anagrafe*) (which, once the system is fully operational, will be replaced by the so-called *Registro unico nazionale del Terzo Settore*—Single National Register of the Third Sector).

In short, foreign-based non-profit organisations are not excluded from entitlement to tax benefits in Italy, provided, however, that the State is able to carry out fiscal checks for establishing their eligibility for the status of non-profit organisation, under national law, to which the said benefits are linked.

In any case, the obligation to enrol with an Italian register is an administrative requirement that, although not in conflict with European economic freedoms insofar as it is justified by the need for fiscal control, generates still an obvious procedural "burden" for the interested entities. Despite the critical issues observed herein, it is our opinion that the practical intervention provided by the Italian Internal Revenue Service should be welcomed, since—in light of the aforementioned CJEU rulings—it extends the scope of application of the national tax regimes also to foreign-based non-profit entities precisely because of the principle of comparability.

However, in order to ensure the effective harmonisation of the national measures with EU law, it would be necessary to outline a more efficient system aimed at ensuring the legal and practical application of the free movement of capital combined with the principle of non-discrimination. This is to ensure (and not deter) the effective realisation of cross-border philanthropic activities by non-profit organisations. In other words, it would be necessary to achieve an "EU-wide" legal recognition of Third Sector entities and to introduce adequate regulations. One proposal, in this regard, could be to establish, at EU level, a set of standards for qualifying compliance of non-profit organisations, on the basis of certain unfailing objective requirements. For example, the prohibition to distribute profit, performing activities in clearly specified sectors of general interest, or registration with a public cross-border register. These aspects are also consistent with the proposal for a Council

[34] Reply to the appeal made to the Internal Revenue Service, 16 June 2021, No. 406.

Regulation on the Statute for a European Foundation.[35] The proposal, in particular, concerns the possibility of setting up a new "supranational" legal entity that would complement the legal forms already existing in the EU Member States and that, in compliance with national and local legislation, would operate across the EU and, in terms of taxation, would be on the same footing as national public benefit entities. The bylaws should contain minimum mandatory requirements for the recognition of the organisation as a European Foundation and, therefore, set up a management structure comparable in all Member States.

On this point, the legislative innovations introduced in Italy with the reform of the Third Sector—initiated pursuant to Delegated Law No. 106/2016—the establishment of a single register in which all entities wishing to acquire the status, at national level, of "Third Sector entity" are required to enrol, could represent the benchmark to achieve a harmonised framework of non-profit entities operating within the EU. More specifically, the provision of a "supranational" legal entity operating at EU level and in accordance with minimum standards shared by all Member States and registered with a "*Single European Register of Third Sector Entities*" could help to strengthen social and legal cohesion. This is also with a view to encouraging the cross-border channelling of funds for public benefit purposes, also from a fiscal perspective.

On the other hand, the incentive for cross-border philanthropy could also be pursued through international tax agreements.[36] Precursors in this sense are the double taxation treaties signed by the US with Germany and the Netherlands which, on closer inspection, contain specific clauses providing for mutual recognition of certain categories of non-profit entities. In particular, according to these agreements, an entity resident in one of the two States (US/Germany or the Netherlands) that operates in specific sectors of general interest (religion, charity, science, education or other public benefit purpose) may enjoy tax exemption also in the other State to the extent that *(i)* in the State of origin it would enjoy similar benefits in pursuit of the same public interest purposes; *(ii)* in that other State it would enjoy the exemption regime in relation to income generated for activities carried out.

In conclusion, the legal framework is crucial to create a suitable environment for the success of the social economy at both national and EU level. In this sense, the proposals outlined here would lead to a system that facilitates cross-border activities and cooperation between non-profit organisations within the European Union and thus contribute to the strengthening of these actors in the social economy landscape.

---

[35] Proposal for a Council Regulation on the Statute for a European Foundation (FE) (COM(2012) 0035-2012/0022(APP).

[36] Agreement between the United States of America and the Federal Republic of Germany for the Avoidance of Double Taxation and the Prevention of Fiscal Evasion with Respect to Taxes on Income and on Capital and Certain Other Taxes, August 29, 1989, art. 27; Agreement between the United States of America and the Kingdom of the Netherlands for the Avoidance of Double Taxation and the Prevention of Fiscal Evasion with Respect to Taxes on Income, December 18, 1992, art. 36.

References

Athanasopoulou A, Klein P (2022) L'economia sociale nel panorama europeo [The social economy in the European landscape]. Impresa Sociale 1:48 ff

European Foundation Centre (EFC) Policy and Programmes (2017) Boosting cross-border philantrophy in europe towards a tax-effective enviroment. pp 4–14

Fici A (2011) L'identità delle società cooperative nella decisione della Corte di giustizia UE in tema di aiuti di Stato. Enti non profit 12:33

Lideikyte Huber G (2021) Foundations in Europe from a tax perspective – Observations and trends. Comparative Highlights of Foundation Laws, Donors and Foundations Networks in Europe AISBL (Dafne) and European Foundation Centre AISBL (EFC) pp 24–25

Miceli R (2021) La funzione degli aiuti di Stato europei nella fiscalità del XXI secolo. Studi Tributari Europei 11:17 ff

Chapter 13
European Law of Third Sector Organizations from the US Standpoint

Dana Brakman Reiser

Contents

Abstract This chapter takes stock of the European law of third sector organizations described in this volume, using US law as a point of departure. Its comparison focuses on one particularly striking distinction between the two sets of jurisdictions. European nations have begun experimenting with distribution-constrained forms and designations for social enterprise, while the US has not. None of the many specialized forms for social enterprise developed by US states, nor B Corp certification, provides for any constraints on distribution of their profits or assets. This

D. Brakman Reiser (✉)
Brooklyn Law School, Brooklyn, NY, USA
e-mail: dana.brakman@brooklaw.edu

A. Fici (ed.), *The Law of Third Sector Organizations in Europe*,
https://doi.org/10.1007/978-3-031-41744-3_13

failure to contemplate distribution-constrained options contributes to the lack of inclusion of social enterprises within a broad third sector legal category in the US, and its comparative lack of tax and other financial supports for social enterprises thus far.

1 Introduction

When taking in this volume's descriptions of the European law of third sector organizations from a US standpoint, the most striking point of departure is the inclusion of social enterprises within its coverage. Many organizations in the US, as in Europe, combine a social mission with revenue generation using business methods. The growth of US social enterprise in recent decades is much remarked and examined. Yet, American social enterprises, and particularly those organized using specialized legal forms developed for them, would not fall within the idea of a "third sector" identified with charitable organizations.[1]

This difference can be explained by US law's lack of organizational forms or designations that combine a for-profit orientation with partial or complete constraints on distribution of profits or assets.[2] In contrast, several of Europe's diverse jurisdictions have created designations or legal forms for social enterprises including restraints on distribution of profits or assets. Eligibility for the Danish registered social enterprise (RSE) designation is conditioned on limiting dividends to shareholders or owners.[3] The Italian third sector organization (TSO) status requires comprehensive asset-locking, preserving the residual assets of registered entities for social purposes even after they terminate TSO status.[4] France has legislatively defined its *Economie sociale et solidaire* to exclude entities with a profit making purpose and imposes at least partial distribution constraints even on commercial companies within its scope.[5] Specialized cooperative forms adapted for social enterprise like social cooperatives in Poland, social solidarity cooperatives in Portugal and nonprofit cooperatives in Spain are likewise subject to distribution constraints.[6] Although not detailed in a chapter in the current volume, the community interest company (CIC) available in England and Wales offers another example.

[1] Gidron (2010).

[2] This Chapter will use the terms such as "asset-locked" and "asset-constrained" or "distribution-constrained" interchangeably, to refer broadly to legal constraints imposed on distribution of an entity's midstream or residual assets.

[3] Sørensen (Chap. 2, this volume).

[4] Fici (Chap. 6, this volume).

[5] Magnier (Chap. 3, this volume).

[6] Radwan, Mazgaj, Żak (Chap. 8, this volume); Meira (Chap. 9, this volume); Fajardo-García (Chap. 10, this volume).

Adopters of the CIC form may issue only limited dividends and all residual assets of are irrevocably dedicated to the benefit of the community.[7]

Of course, distribution-constrained forms or designations for social enterprises are not yet found in every European jurisdiction. Ireland has no designation or organizational form with this feature[8] and Germany and the Netherlands are only now considering proposals to provide one.[9] Even in European jurisdictions with such offerings, they may not be available regardless of organizational form. For example, in Belgium post-2019, only cooperatives can qualify as "social enterprises" characterized by an asset lock.[10] While not available universally, distribution-constrained social enterprise forms and designations are a familiar feature in European law and appear poised to become even more widely available under the influence of the new EU Social Economy Action Plan.[11]

In contrast, despite significant adoption of social enterprise forms by US state legislatures over the last decade, none of these more than 30 enactments contains an asset lock or distribution constraint of any kind.[12] In this context, no legal category combining social enterprises and traditional nonprofits—whether that category might be dubbed the "third sector," a "social" or "social solidarity economy," or any other similar term—has become prevalent and vanishingly few government incentives or supports for social enterprises have materialized. US state and federal governments have shown no appetite to provide social enterprises with tax and other financial benefits or procurement preferences. This insight begs the question whether US law would become more encouraging to social enterprise were a distribution-constrained social enterprise form or designation to be introduced.

This Chapter will explore the similarities and differences between US and European jurisdictions'regulation of nonprofit organizations and social enterprises. Section 2 will introduce the types of organizational forms and designations that have traditionally been available to such entities under US law. Section 3 will introduce the variety of specialized forms and designations that US states have developed for for-profit social enterprises in recent years. Section 4 will demonstrate that financial incentives and other supports offered to US entities engaged in social missions are available almost exclusively to nonprofit, tax-exempt, distribution-constrained organizations. Section 5 will highlight the growing availability of distribution-constrained forms and designations for social enterprise in Europe as critical to understanding the many legal innovations, financial incentives, and other supports for social enterprises in Europe that remain unavailable in the United States. Section 6 will propose Europe's experimentation and success with

[7] CIC Regulator (2016).

[8] Breen (Chap. 5, this volume).

[9] Möslein (Chap. 4, this volume); van der Sangen (Chap. 7, this volume).

[10] Culot and Defer (Chap. 1, this volume).

[11] European Commission (2021).

[12] Brakman Reiser and Dean (2017).

distribution-constrained social enterprises recommends the development of such options under US law and will briefly conclude.

2 Traditional Organizational Forms and Designations Under US Law

Organizations pursuing a social mission may adapt any of three types of organizational form under US law: a nonprofit form, a traditional for-profit form, or a specialized social enterprise form. US nonprofit organizations are regulated in important ways by two legal regimes. The organizational forms on offer are determined by state law. Specifically, nonprofits may take the form of nonprofit corporations or unincorporated associations or may organize as charitable trusts. For those nonprofit organizations which are exempt from federal income taxation under I.R.C. § 501(c)(3) and seek to maintain this status, federal tax law will also play a key role.

Many US for-profit firms and their founders desire to pursue social goals that might place them within a European conception of the third sector. Traditional for-profit forms offer such entities considerable latitude to engage in these dual goals. In addition, the last decade has seen significant uptake by state legislatures of new legal forms specifically designed for for-profit social enterprises. Regardless of whether they are organized along traditional lines or using one of these new forms, the B Corp designation is also available to US companies seeking to broadcast their dual missions. To allow for comparison with European jurisdictions, this Part will provide a brief introduction to each of these offerings.

2.1 *Nonprofit Organizational Forms*

Each US state has the authority to vary the nonprofit organizational forms it offers and the governance requirements each form imposes individually. Still, the law across states is sufficiently similar to be described together—and compared as such with European approaches. The nondistribution constraint universally applies to prohibit distribution of profits to individuals or entities maintaining control positions within US charitable nonprofits.[13] This asset-locking restriction precludes social enterprises seeking equity investment from utilizing nonprofit organizational forms. For those social enterprises capitalized by donations, governmental support, earned revenues, or a combination of those sources, however, nonprofit organization remains an attractive option.

[13] Hansmann (1980).

Each state permits nonprofits to take corporate or unincorporated forms or to operate as charitable trusts.[14] Most formally organized nonprofits are nonprofit corporations,[15] created by the public act of filing articles of incorporation with a single state's Secretary of State. Bylaws will describe the operations of the entity, which will be managed by a group of individuals often denominated the board of directors.[16] These directors are fiduciaries bound by duties of care and loyalty, as are any officers they appoint.[17] States typically invest their attorneys general with authority to take enforcement action against violations.[18] Directors of a nonprofit corporations are usually self-perpetuating, meaning they may nominate and elect their own successors.[19] It is possible instead for a nonprofit to empower a membership constituency to elect directors, but few do. [20]

Many significant US nonprofits are organized as charitable trusts, which are created by their founders and require no state filing.[21] A charitable trust must have one or more charitable trustee fiduciaries,[22] though founders are permitted considerable flexibility in arranging trust governance as they see fit. Although unincorporated nonprofit associations are also easy to form and are quite numerous, they are rarely entities of considerable size.[23] Unincorporated association members typically do not benefit from limited liability, so the form predominantly suits quite small organizations and those early on in their organizational journey. Often, those that succeed will ultimately adopt a corporate or trust approach.

US nonprofits frequently engage in business or commercial activities, either as part of their charitable work or to generate revenue to fund that work. State nonprofit corporate law often explicitly authorizes these endeavors[24] and charitable trust law also provides trustees a wide berth for their activities in service of charitable

---

[14] Phelan (2000).

[15] *Id.*

[16] Fremont-Smith (2004).

[17] *See, e.g.*, Revised Model Nonprofit Corp. Act (b) (1987) [hereinafter RMNCA]. This version of the RMNCA was adopted by nearly half of US states, and thus will be cited for purposes of illustration.

[18] Fremont-Smith (2004).

[19] *Id.*

[20] Brakman Reiser (2003).

[21] Fremont-Smith (2004).

[22] Brody (2005); Uniform Trust Code § 703 (2020) [hereinafter UTC] Versions of the Uniform Trust Code has been adopted by 36 states and will be referenced as illustrative.

[23] Phelan (2000).

[24] *See, e.g.*, RMNCA (1987) §§ 3.01(a), 3.02(16-d) (1987) (setting the default purpose of nonprofit corporations as "[to] engag[e] in any lawful activity" and empowering them "to carry on a business").

purposes.[25] But state organizational law is rarely the primary regulation of concern for US nonprofits.

2.1.1 US Federal Tax Law as Nonprofit Regulator

Those US nonprofits desiring federal tax benefits for themselves or their donors must comply with federal tax law requirements. Statutorily, to qualify for tax-exemption as a charitable nonprofit, organizations must meet three core elements found in Internal Revenue Code section 501(c)(3). An entity must be:

- "organized and operated exclusively for religious, charitable, scientific, testing for public safety, literary, or educational purposes, or to foster national or international amateur sports competition (but only if no part of its activities involve the provision of athletic facilities or equipment), or for the prevention of cruelty to children or animals;"
- "no part of the net earnings [may] inure[s] to the benefit of any private shareholder or individual;" and
- "no substantial part of the activities [] is carrying on propaganda, or otherwise attempting, to influence legislation (except as otherwise provided in subsection (h)), and [the entity] does not participate in, or intervene in (including the publishing or distributing of statements), any political campaign on behalf of (or in opposition to) any candidate for public office."[26]

Broadly similar requirements apply for donors'contributions to such organizations to qualify as tax-deductible.[27]

The tripartite statutory regime ensures that tax-exempt charities will primarily pursue broadly defined prosocial purposes and largely eschew political activities. Most importantly for present purposes, however, its prohibition on distributing profits to private individuals or entities imposes a complete asset lock. As under state law, social enterprises capitalized by equity investment simply will not qualify. If a tax-exempt entity makes profit distributions to parties with influence within the organization, hefty penalties will apply and the ultimate punishment—loss of exemption—is also available.[28] If substantial, even distributions to unrelated parties can have these disastrous results as well.

Moreover, federal regulations provide that even organizations that maintain this asset lock may be ineligible for exemption if found to be overly commercial. The law

[25] Uniform Trust Code § 404 (2020) (requiring charitable trusts to pursue purposes that are "lawful, not contrary to public policy, and possible to achieve" and noting an intention to encourage third parties to engage in commercial transactions with trustees).

[26] I.R.C. § 501(c)(3).

[27] I.R.C. § 170(c)(2).

[28] I.R.C. §§ 4941, 4958.

centers in particular on commercial activity unrelated to the nonprofit's charitable mission.

> An organization may meet the requirements of section 501(c)(3) although it operates a trade or business as a substantial part of its activities, *if the operation of such trade or business is in furtherance of the organization's exempt purpose or purposes and if the organization is not organized or operated for the primary purpose of carrying on an unrelated trade or business.*[29]

Commercial activities tightly connected to charitable purposes, such as those of a traditional sheltered workshop, pose little risk. Determining where the line between acceptable and unacceptable levels of commerciality lies has long been notoriously hazy, however.[30] It can prove vexing for social enterprises that achieve great success, operate in a manner indistinguishable from purely for-profit competitors, or that pursue purely commercial activities to fund their social missions rather than closely integrating these two functions.[31] As such, social enterprises that operate indistinguishably from commercial firms other than using sustainable or socially-valuable practices or donating substantial portions of their revenues or profits to charity generally fail to qualify for tax-exemption.

The unrelated business income tax (UBIT) creates additional obstacles, even for asset locked social enterprises that remain sufficiently non-commercial for entity-level exemption. Under it, any income earned from active conduct of unrelated businesses will not qualify for tax-exemption anyway.[32] Instead, ordinary tax rates apply to

> any trade or business the conduct of which is not substantially related (aside from the need of such organization for income or funds or the use it makes of the profits derived) to the exercise or performance by such organization of its charitable, educational, or other purpose or function constituting the basis for its exemption.[33]

Passive income like dividends, rents, and royalties escapes UBIT,[34] but the regime means a tax-exempt entity that conducts an unrelated business to earn revenues to support itself will be excluded from this important means of government support.

A final distinction is critical to understanding federal tax law's influence on nonprofit organizations in the US. Every entity qualifying for tax exemption under Section 501(c)(3) is further categorized as either a "public charity" or a "private foundation."[35] These categories bear some resemblance to the association and foundation forms of organization found in European law, but they are far from

---

[29] Treas. Reg. § 1.501(c)(3)-1(e)(1) (emphasis added).

[30] Colombo (2002, 2007).

[31] Brakman Reiser (2010); Brody (2008); Colombo (2007).

[32] I.R.C. § 511.

[33] I.R.C. § 513(a).

[34] I.R.C. § 511(b).

[35] I.R.C. § 509; see generally Fremont-Smith (2004).

identical.[36] Public charities are characterized by a broad set of financial supporters, significant revenues derived from a wide group of consumers rather than investment income, or a very close relationship with another public charity.[37] They are not, however, required to have a membership or general assembly. Like many European foundations, typical US private foundations are supported by contributions from a single individual, family, corporation, or other small group and passive income earned from investments. Private foundations in the US, however, face targeted tax regulation.[38] Federal tax law compels private foundations to distribute at least 5% of their assets per year and imposes a series of excise tax penalties on private foundation transactions with insiders and donors, substantial investment stakes in individual businesses, speculative investing practices, political activities, and other conduct deemed incompatible with their exempt purposes.[39] Private foundation investment income is also subject to a small tax (currently 1.39%, though it has fluctuated over time)[40] and private foundation donors receive less generous tax benefits than their public charity counterparts.[41] Private foundations are also subject to heightened transparency obligations compared not only to taxable entities, but also to public charities.[42] For social enterprises funded by a single individual or small cadre of donors, the potential benefits of tax-exemption may be outweighed by the accompanying regulatory load of private foundation status.

The line between nonprofit and for-profit organizational forms is policed by a combination of state organizational law and federal tax law and its demarcation remains stark. Nonprofits are asset-locked. Tax-exempt nonprofits are asset-locked, must not skew toward the overly commercial, and are tax-exempt on their passive and related active income. If they are deemed private foundations, even this tax-exemption is further reduced, and additional regulation applies. For many organizations pursuing social missions, these regulatory costs will exceed the potential benefits, and for-profit forms take on greater appeal.

2.2 *Traditional For-Profit Organizational Forms*

For-profit organizational forms are also creatures of US state, rather than federal law. The various states, however, offer large and generally similar menus of incorporated

---

[36] Brakman Reiser and Miller (2017).

[37] I.R.C. § 509.

[38] Brakman Reiser (2020); Fremont-Smith (2004).

[39] I.R.C. §§ 4940-4941, 4943-45.

[40] I.R.C. § 4940(a).

[41] *See, e.g.*, I.R.C. § 170(b) (imposing greater limitations on the deductiblity of private foundation contributions than those made to public charities).

[42] *See, e.g.*, I.R.C. § 6104 (requiring public disclosure of foundation donors, but not donors to other exempt entities).

and unincorporated forms from which founders of social enterprises may choose. All these forms contemplate distribution of profits to owners, but few patently exclude formation in pursuit of a social mission. The general partnership's definition of "an association of two or more persons to carry on as co-owners a business for profit" comes perhaps closest.[43] In contrast, most speak of the permissible purposes of a business entity broadly, as do corporate statutes authorizing the "conduct or promot [ion of] any lawful business or purposes."[44] The contract-based limited liability company (LLC) form promises even greater flexibility.[45]

Positions vary on the degree to which an ordinary corporation will be inhospitable to a dual profit-making and social missions under US law. Shareholder primacy purists argue sacrificing value for owners in service of other constituencies violates the core tenets of the for-profit form,[46] and can find some solace in Delaware jurisprudence, particularly cases involving corporate takeover defenses.[47] Stakeholder theorists argue instead that US corporate directors need not prioritize shareholder value.[48] The capacious discretion afforded corporate leaders under the business judgment rule[49] and 30+ state constituency statutes specifically granting directors this latitude bolster their position.[50] In at least some circumstances, furthering employee, customer or even environmental interests can be harmonized with profit making, but statutory and even case law offers surprisingly little guidance in cases when the choice is stark.

For the run of mostly small social enterprises funded by like-minded investors, the risk of challenge to decisions disfavoring shareholder return is low. Such firms can also employ an LLC structure rather than incorporating.[51] Including their dual goals in an operating agreement binding all parties should avoid the issue. Cooperative forms can be employed in a similar fashion.[52] But for those social enterprises with visions of mass scale and even public investors, incorporation—and often Delaware incorporation—remains the gold standard. In that limited but much-discussed legal and market context, the norm of shareholder primacy remains difficult to fully dislodge.

---

[43] Revised Uniform Partnership Act (1997) §101(6).

[44] Del. Gen. Corp. Law §101(b).

[45] Ribstein and Keatinge (2021).

[46] *See, e.g.*, Strine (2015); Strine (2012); Friedman (1970); Berle (1931); *see also* Wells (2002) (collecting sources).

[47] *See, e.g.*, eBay Domestic Holdings, Inc. v. Newmark, 16 A.3d 1, 34 (Del. Ch. 2010); Revlon Inc. v. MacAndrews & Forbes Holdings, Inc., 506 A.2d 173, 182 (Del. 1986).

[48] *See, e.g.*, Stout (2012); Elhauge (2005); Dodd (1932).

[49] Elhauge (2005).

[50] Tyler (2010); Fairfax (2002).

[51] Brakman Reiser and Dean (2017).

[52] Autry and Hall (2009).

3 Specialized Forms and Designations for Social Enterprise

It is in an effort to resolve this concern that state legislatures have enacted variations on the traditional for-profit organizational forms designed for social enterprise for over a decade.[53] The earliest entry, the low-profit limited liability company (L3C) first offered in Vermont in 2008[54] has now been eclipsed by two incorporated alternatives.[55] The benefit corporation form is today available in over thirty US jurisdictions, and was pioneered by B Lab, which also offers the B Corp designation to US for-profit firms of all types. Delaware, a pivotal jurisdiction in US corporate law, has developed its own specialized "public benefit corporation" form as well.

3.1 Benefit Corporations

Although each of the dozens of state statutes authorizing benefit corporations contains slight variations, again the similarities suffice to permit a general discussion.[56] These benefit corporation enabling statutes vary four key features of traditional corporate law: corporate purpose, fiduciary conduct, shareholder voting, and disclosure.[57] Notably, none imposes a full or partial asset lock or a limitation on distributions of any kind.

[53] Details on state adoptions are available through a continuously updated web resource tracking and linking individual states'benefit corporation statutes. Social Enterprise Law Tracker (2022).

[54] 11 V.S.A. § 3001(27). The L3C used the US limited liability company form as a starting point, with relatively few changes. As such, L3C founders could adopt the form by simply filing articles of organization with the sectretary of state and had broad discretion to design the entity's governace, financing, and operations by contractual operating agreement. Almost all of the variations L3C statutes put in place are drawn from the federal tax law concept of a "program-related investment." This is a category of expenditure private foundations may treat as they would a charitable grant. Madoff (2020). The only additional variation provides that if an L3C "at any time ceases to satisfy any one of the [statute's purpose] requirements, it shall immediately cease to be a low– profit limited liability company, but . . . will continue to exist as a limited liability company." 11 V.S.A. § 3001 (27)(D). This change is automatic and requires no regulatory or other notice or approval. After Vermont first adopted L3C enabling legislation, a few other states quickly followed, but adoptions stalled in 2011 with fewer than 10 and one state repealed its enabling statute. Tyler et al. (2015). Although data is scarce, utilization of the L3C form by operating entities appears to remain low. Intersector Partners (2022) (tallying 2134 active L3Cs).

[55] Individual US states have also experimented with a handful of state-specific forms. *See, e.g.*, Cal. Corp. Code § 3500 et seq. (2015) (California Social Purpose Corporation); Del. Code Ann. tit. 6, §§ 18-1201 to –1208 (2018) (Delaware Public Benefit LLC); Md. Code Ann., Corps. & Ass'ns §§ 11–4A– 1201 to 11– 4A– 1208, 11– 1– 502, 5– 6C– 03 (2013) (Maryland Benefit LLC); Ore. Rev. Stat. §§ 60.750 to.770 (2014) (Oregon Benefit LLC); Wash. Rev. Code § 23B.25.005 et seq. (2013) (Washington Social Purpose Corporation).

[56] Brakman Reiser and Dean (2017).

[57] The similarities are largely traceable to the Model Benefit Corporation Act endorsed by B Lab, which served as a resource for state legislatures. Model Benefit Corporation Act, available in Clark

Benefit corporation statutes require adopting entities to have a "purpose of creating general public benefit."[58] General public benefit is defined to mean "[a] material positive impact on society and the environment, taken as a whole, *assessed against a third-party standard*, from the business and operations of a benefit corporation."[59] This invocation of a third-party standard *does not* mandate certification by any third party. Rather, founders incorporating a benefit corporation must only self-assess their organizations against such a standard and find themselves in compliance. They need not obtain confirmation of that fact from the third party creator of the standard they employ. Benefit corporation statutes also do not identify specific third-party standards to be employed for these purposes; any comprehensive and credible standard articulated by a transparent and independent entity will suffice.[60]

This variation on traditional corporate purposes also establishes no prioritization or hierarchy. Benefit corporation statutes conclusively deem adopting entities'pursuit of public benefits to be "in the best interests of the benefit corporation,"[61] resolving any lingering concerns about an entity's proper objectives. A dual mission including the generation of social good is not only permitted but required. Yet, the other half of this mission—generating profits for owners—is likewise acceptable. Either goal may eclipse the other in individual corporate decisions or overall corporate strategy.

Benefit corporation statutes' fiduciary provisions are likewise broadly discretionary. In addition to the standard duties of care and loyalty imposed on traditional corporate fiduciaries, benefit corporation directors must consider the effects of their decisions on a broad group of stakeholders. For example, the California and New York statutes both require directors to consider the interests of shareholders, "employees and workforce of the benefit corporation and its subsidiaries and suppliers," customers "as beneficiaries of the general or specific public benefit purposes of the benefit corporation," "community and societal considerations, including those of any community in which offices or facilities of the benefit corporation or its subsidiaries or suppliers are located," "the local and global environment, the short-term and long-term interests of the benefit corporation, including benefits [of remaining independent]," and the benefit corporation's ability

---

and Vranka (2013) app.; *see also* McDonnell (2016) (describing B Lab's advocacy efforts around benefit corporations). As B Lab no longer broadly distributes this document, exemplary references from California and New York are provided below.

[58] Cal. Corp. Code. § 14610(a); N.Y. Bus. Corp. L. § 1706(a). Benefit corporations may also identify "specific public benefits" they will pursue in their articles of incorporation. Cal. Corp. Code. § 14610(b); N.Y. Bus. Corp. L. § 1706(b).

[59] Cal. Corp. Code. § 14601(c); N.Y. Bus. Corp. L. § 1702(b).

[60] Cal. Corp. Code. § 14601(g); N.Y. Bus. Corp. L. § 1702(g).

[61] Cal. Corp. Code. § 14610(c); N.Y. Bus. Corp. L. § 1706(c).

"to accomplish its general, and any specific, public benefit purpose."[62] Directors may also consider any "other pertinent factors" or the interests of anyone else they deem appropriate.[63]

Benefit corporation statutes in different states offer varying enforcement regimes for this obligation of consideration. Many include a "benefit enforcement proceeding" in which directors, shareholders (who typically must meet ownership thresholds), and stakeholders (only if identified by an individual benefit corporation in its charter) may raise claims the firm has failed to pursue public benefit.[64] If successful, a court may issue injunctive relief. Most pair this new enforcement route, however, with elimination of monetary liability. Directors are not personally liable neither for "failure of the benefit corporation to create general public benefit or specific public benefit."[65]

The shift here from traditional corporate law is, importantly, purely one of process. Benefit corporation boards must take the interests of nonshareholder constituencies into consideration, which may lead them to prioritize their concerns, or may not. The likelihood of successful challenge is minimal, as no consideration is made primary or paramount,[66] and even success promises injunctive relief alone. Unlike in many European social cooperatives and other social enterprises, the US benefit corporation imposes no overriding social orientation.

Benefit corporation statutes shift not only corporate purposes and norms of fiduciary conduct, but also shareholder voting. Again, however, the differences sound in degree, not in kind. As in other US corporate forms, shareholders elect benefit corporation boards of directors and must approve fundamental corporate transactions like merger and dissolution. Unique to benefit corporations, however, is a requirement that shareholders approve charter amendments or transactions that adopt or eliminate benefit corporation status. Generally, the statutes require supermajority approval for such actions.[67]

The potency of these shareholder gatekeeping powers will turn on the identity, sophistication, and distribution of shareholders. It will provide little counterweight to management in a benefit corporation with a large constituency of widely dispersed small shareholder owners, but a more serious disciplinary force if a few sophisticated or highly committed shareholders hold significant stakes. Importantly, however, only the interests of shareholders, and not of other stakeholders, will be felt through these processes. Successful recent efforts to elect climate advocates to the

[62] Cal. Corp. Code. § 14620(b); N.Y. Bus. Corp. L. § 1707(a)(1). Cal. Corp. Code. § 14610(c); N.Y. Bus. Corp. L. § 1706(c). This list of stakeholders whose interests directors should consider mirrors lists found in many states'constituency statutes.

[63] Cal. Corp. Code. § 14620(c); N.Y. Bus. Corp. L. § 1707(a)(2).

[64] *See, e.g.*, Cal. Corp. Code. § 14623; *see also* Model Benefit Corporation Legislation § 305.

[65] Cal. Corp. Code. § 14620(f); *see also* Model Benefit Corporation Legislation § 301(c); McDonnell (2014).

[66] Cal. Corp. Code. § 14620(d); N.Y. Bus. Corp. L. § 1707(a)(3).

[67] *See, e.g.*, Cal. Corp. Code. §§ 14601(d); 14610 (requiring 2/3 majority approval); N.Y. Bus. Corp. L. §§ 1702(d), 1705 (requiring ¾ majority approval).

ExxonMobil board of directors vividly demonstrates that shareholders with strong views and the money and influence to advocate for them can use voting rights to pursue a vision of a sustainable corporation.[68] But not all benefit corporations will be (or remain) capitalized by shareholders who see value—financial or otherwise—in public benefit enhancing decisions. For those shareholders who do not, support for director candidates or transactions that trade public benefit for shareholder value will be easy to generate, and other voices are excluded from the voting process.

The final shift worked by benefit corporation statutes involves disclosure. Benefit corporation must annually prepare a "benefit report," distribute it to shareholders, and make it available to the public.[69] These reports provide a narrative description of the firm's progress toward its public benefit goals, again self-assessed against a third-party standard. In some states, the benefit report must also be filed with the secretary of state,[70] but almost none impose penalties for failure to comply with these disclosure obligations.[71] Unsurprisingly in this environment, compliance is dismal. Several studies have found fewer than 10% of benefit corporations produce the required reports.[72]

3.2 *Delaware Public Benefit Corporations*

In the United States, the tiny state of Delaware has outsized influence on corporate law, especially for large and publicly traded companies. The Delaware Secretary of State receives articles of incorporation for tens of thousands of companies per year, and more than two-thirds of Fortune 500 firms are incorporated there.[73] When the state adopted its specialized social enterprise form in 2013, it commanded attention.[74]

The Delaware "public benefit corporation" (or PBC) too uses the traditional for-profit corporation as a foundation and adjusts its treatment of corporate purpose, fiduciary conduct, shareholder voting, and disclosure, but imposes no asset lock. Delaware PBCs are "intended to produce a public benefit or public benefits and to

[68] Exxon Mobil (2021).

[69] Cal. Corp. Code. § 14630; N.Y. Bus. Corp. L. § 1708.

[70] *See, e.g.*, N.Y. Bus. Corp. L. § 1708(d).

[71] Outlier Minnesota does authorize revocation of benefit corporation status from firms that fail to file required reports, Minn. Stat. § 304A.301 (2015), and has been found to have exceptionally high rates of compliance, Verheyden (2018) (reporting a 100% compliance rate in Minnesota while other states'rates were far lower).

[72] Verheyden (2018) (reporting compliance rates in Delaware (8%), Colorado (11%), Oregon (14%)); Berrey (reporting 6% compliance in a national study); Murray (2015) (reporting 8% compliance).

[73] Delaware Division of Corporations (2020).

[74] Del. Code Ann. tit. 8 §§ 361-68 (2013); *see generally* Plerhoples (2014) (describing the state's adoption of the PBC form and its early reception).

operate in a responsible and sustainable manner" alongside profit for owners.[75] At its inception each PBC must identify one or more specific public benefits it will pursue in its charter.

> 'Public benefit' means a positive effect (or reduction of negative effects) on 1 or more categories of persons, entities, communities or interests (other than stockholders in their capacities as stockholders) including, but not limited to, effects of an artistic, charitable, cultural, economic, educational, environmental, literary, medical, religious, scientific or technological nature.[76]

Adopting firms must be managed in a way that balances this public benefit with shareholder value and "the best interests of those materially affected by the corporation's conduct."[77]

The variations Delaware PBC law applies to fiduciary standards also depart somewhat from the benefit corporation approach, but similarly provide substantial discretion and liability protection. Directors of Delaware PBCs are also instructed to "balance" the financial interests of shareholders, the interests of other stakeholders impacted by the firm's conduct, and the public benefit the firm identifies in its charter.[78] This obligation is satisfied if a "director's decision is both informed and disinterested and not such that no person of ordinary, sound judgment would approve."[79]

The PBC statute's provisions on shareholder voting and disclosure and reinforce the salience of shareholder interests in the form. While originally the legislation required shareholder supermajority approval for any charter amendment or transaction that would change or remove a PBC's public benefit commitments, amendments in the ensuing years reduced the level of consensus required for such actions to a simple majority.[80] Disclosure requirements mandate reports on the company's public benefit every two years, but only require them to be shared with shareholders, not the public.[81] Use of a third-party standard as a point of reference for these reports is optional.

[75] Del. Code Ann. tit. 8 § 362(a).

[76] *Id.* § 362(b).

[77] *Id.* § 362(a).

[78] *Id.* § 365.

[79] *Id.* § 362(a).

[80] *Compare* 79 Del. Laws 122 (2013) (requiring 90% of shareholders to vote for adoption of public benefit status and two-thirds to vote to terminate it) *with* 79 Del. Laws 122 (2015) (allowing two thirds of shareholders to approve creation of public benefit corporation) *and* 82 Del. Laws 256 (2020) (allowing a simple majority of shareholders to adopt or remove public benefit status).

[81] Del. Code Ann. tit. 8, § 366(c).

3.3 *B Corp Designation*

In addition to these state law organizational forms, for-profit social enterprises in the US may also obtain B Corp status. This private certification is offered by B Lab: a nonprofit, tax-exempt organization that describes its goal as "transforming the global economy to benefit all people, communities, and the planet."[82] B Lab licenses the B Corp mark to companies that meet its governance and operational standards.[83] Again, no asset lock applies. To qualify, applicants must take legal steps necessary to adopt a stakeholder focused model of governance. This may be achieved by utilizing particular legal forms the like benefit corporations or the Delaware PBC but can also be accomplished through individualized changes to an entity's governing documents.[84] To become a B Corp, firms must also accept the enhanced transparency that will come with information about the company appearing on B Lab's website. Last, but certainly not least, successful applicants must score at least 80 points on the B Impact Assessment (BIA) (out of a possible 200).[85] Several versions of the BIA exist, designed to appropriately gauge the environmental and social commitments of firms of various sizes, and the assessment offers questions relevant for firms operating in myriad industries and geographies. Successful firms can license the Certified B Corp mark and many display it on their websites, other promotional materials, and products.

B Lab also offers certification to non-US firms, including in several European jurisdictions as described elsewhere in this volume, as part of its global network footprint.[86] Its website points to operations in 80 countries to date.[87] These offerings are critically distinct from the government sponsored social enterprise designations that are available in some European jurisdictions, in both their provenance and their substance. Examples like the Danish RSE and Italian TSO are labels granted and overseen by government bodies, while B Corp status—whether in the US or elsewhere across the globe—is a purely private certification. These government designations and statuses also require a partial or complete asset lock; B Corp designation does not.

3.4 *Potential Unrealized*

Despite the widespread adoption of specialized social enterprise legal forms by legislatures in states across the US, uptake by operating social enterprises has been

[82] About B Lab (2022).

[83] About B Corp Certification (2022).

[84] *Id.*

[85] *Id.*

[86] B Lab, Our European Network (2022).

[87] B Lab Homepage (2022).

slow. Although collecting data from secretary of state offices nationwide is a difficult task, initial studies have identified quite limited use of these legal forms. A 2018 study reported only 7704 benefit corporations (including Delaware PBCs) had formed in the entire United States to that point.[88] An earlier study found just 4500 organizations had adopted either these or any other specialized form designed for social enterprise since the first L3C enabling statute was enacted in 2008.[89] B Lab boasts just 5181 companies certified as of June 2022 globally, "more than 1700" are in the US firms and Canada.[90]

Over the past few years, a few firms formed as Delaware PBCs or holding B Corp certification have debuted on the US public markets. Laureate Education, a for-profit higher education company organized as a Delaware PBC, was the first to do so in a 2017 offering.[91] A handful more followed with traditional IPOs in 2020 and 2021: insurance start-up Lemonade; pasture-raised egg brand Vital Farms; online learning platform Coursera; sustainable shoe B Corp Allbirds; and biotech Zymergen.[92] Joining the trend for IPOs run through special purpose acquisition companies, agritech B Corp AppHarvest and satellite imaging PBC PlanetLabs became public in 2021 utilizing SPAC transactions.[93] Sustainable Development Acquisition I Corp. was also organized as a Delaware PBC SPAC firm, for the explicit purpose of "acquiring a business addressing global challenges identified by the UN Sustainable Development Goals."[94] This uptick in IPOs coincided with Delaware's removal of the supermajority requirement to terminate PBC status,[95] and only underscores the lack of asset constraints present in US social enterprise forms and designations.

The modest uptake figures could be read to suggest there is little demand for the types of specialized forms US law provides; alternatively, the numbers could reflect instead gradual and growing acceptance of a novel legal concept. Whether this question is ultimately resolved by significant use of US specialized forms or designations for social enterprise or whether they remain niche legal products, they reflect a quite different view of the possible contours of a social enterprise than is true in Europe. Neither US legal forms for social enterprise nor the B Corp designation requires adopting firms to prioritize social mission. Their fiduciaries are left without direct guidance regarding how to behave when profit and mission point in opposite directions but restricting enforcers to shareholders and eliminating personal liability for failures to pursue mission makes profit maximization the safest course. US legal forms and the B Corp designation also do not require a participatory governance approach reaching beyond shareholders. Perhaps most critically, none

---

[88] Berrey (2018).

[89] Murray (2016); *see also* Cooney et al (finding about 2000 benefit corporations and L3Cs in 2014).

[90] B Lab US & Canada (2022); BLab Homepage (2022).

[91] Stone (2021).

[92] Stone (2021); de León (2021); Levy (2021).

[93] Powell (2021); Clough (2021).

[94] B Sustainable Development Acquisition I Corp. (2022); Westaway (2021).

[95] Littenberg et al. (2020).

imposes or even offers either any type of asset lock. Only nonprofit organizations are subject to a nondistribution constraint under US law. The midstream earnings and residual assets of US benefit corporations, PBCs, and B Corps may be distributed at any time, and in any amounts, to their investors.

4 Only Nonprofit Organizations Qualify for US Financial Incentives Based on "Third Sector" Participation

Despite the great surge of innovation on the border between commerce and charity, the nondistribution constraint and asset locking of any kind maintain a clear line between the two spheres under US law. Only nonprofits are asset-constrained and there are no exceptions. For-profit forms, on the other hand, even those using new forms designed for social enterprise, include no such feature. This helps explain why financial incentives or other supports available for third sector organizations in the US are almost exclusively confined to those operating within its nonprofit sphere. Nonprofit firms may qualify for numerous federal and state tax and other advantages. But none of these benefits are available to traditional for-profit entities, benefit corporations, Delaware PBCs or B Corps, and targeted incentives and supports for social enterprises taking on specialized forms or obtaining these designations remain extremely rare.

4.1 Federal Income Tax Exemption for Nonprofits

Charitable nonprofits can be advantaged under the US federal tax system in two distinct ways. First, their income will largely, if not entirely, avoid taxation. As noted earlier, those nonprofit, tax-exempt entities deemed to be private foundations must pay a very small tax on their investment income.[96] For both private foundations and public charities, non-passive income from businesses unrelated to their charitable purposes will be taxed at ordinary rates.[97] But nonprofits can otherwise operate free of federal income tax.[98] For-profit firms, whether or not they are organized as benefit corporations or Delaware PBCs, and whether or not they are certified B Corps, are entirely excluded from this benefit. Their income will be subject to federal tax as would any other for-profit business.

[96] I.R.C. § 4940.

[97] I.R.C. § 511.

[98] I.R.C. § 501(c)(3).

4.2 Federal Tax Benefits for Nonprofit Donors

The second key advantage is tax benefits for donors. Donors to Section 501(c)(3) tax-exempt organizations may reduce their adjusted gross income by the amount of their contributions in determining their income tax liability.[99] The amount of these deductions will vary depending on the recipient organization's status as a public charity or private foundation and the type of asset contributed. Donations made in cash by individual donors to public charities may be deducted up to 60 percent of an individual taxpayer's adjusted gross income; a lower 30 percent ceiling applies to cash donations to private foundations.[100] When donors contribute appreciated property, both lower percentage caps and rules that reduce the amount of the deduction's value—as compared to the same gift to a public charity—apply.[101] Federal estate and gift tax law provides even more generous benefits; contributions to both public charities and private foundations qualify for unlimited deductions under both regimes.[102]

In sharp contrast, while there are myriad tax breaks and benefits available to for-profit firms on various bases, no federal tax provision entitles investors in or donors to benefit corporations, Delaware PBCs, or B Corps to deduct their contributions to such firms by virtue of their organizational form or certification. Indeed, even efforts to persuade Congress to designate L3Cs as appropriate recipients of foundation "program related investments" failed to succeed.[103] Such an action would only have allowed foundations to count investments in L3Cs toward their required annual distributions and would not have bestowed any tax benefits directly upon social enterprises adopting a specialized for-profit form. Yet they went nowhere.

4.3 Other Government Benefits for Nonprofits

In the US, government entities at various levels also offer additional financial benefits to nonprofits only. Important among these governmental supports under federal law are authorization to issue tax-exempt debt as part of financing efforts for

[99] I.R.C. § 170(c).

[100] I.R.C. § 170(b).

[101] *Id.*

[102] I.R.C. §§ 2055, 2522.

[103] Philanthropic Facilitation Act, H.R. 2832, 113th Cong. (2013); Philanthropic Facilitation Act, H.R. 3420, 112th Cong. (2011); *see also* Brakman Reiser and Dean (2017) (describing this failed effort and noting that the Internal Revenue Service likewise has not issued a ruling taking this position).

some capital projects[104] and discounted postal rates for certain mailings.[105] The state unemployment insurance tax system allows nonprofits to reimburse only their own former employees who file unemployment claims, rather than contributing to the statewide pool as do other types of employers.[106] Social enterprises organized using traditional business forms or as benefit corporations or Delaware PBCs will not qualify for the benefits of any of these programs. Neither will firms that earn B Corp designation.

State property tax laws also offer nonprofit exemptions that vary in how closely they align with the federal rules for income tax exemption.[107] These regimes are often based on state constitutional language exempting charitable property,[108] but frequently are applied only to property solely used for charitable purposes. States and localities have challenged the scope of exemption on this basis, even for seemingly quintessential charitable property owners like hospitals.[109] State sales tax exemptions are similarly limited. Whether social enterprises organized as non-profits will run afoul of these limitations will depend on their business models. But those organized as traditional for-profits, using specialized forms, obtaining B Corp status need not even apply.

4.4 A Dearth of Incentives or Supports for For-Profit Social Enterprises

Local governments have engaged in isolated experiments to provide financial benefits to social enterprises adopting specialized forms or earning B Corp designation. Philadelphia created a tax credit for sustainable businesses in which B Corp certification serves as one component necessary for applicants to qualify.[110] The benefit was quite small—a maximum $4000 credit per year was made available for 50 firms for tax years 2017–2018 and 75 firms for tax years 2019–2022. Los Angeles County includes "certified social enterprise" on its list of preferred vendors for procurement efforts.[111] To be eligible, firms must be either certified B Corps or incorporated under one of California's specialized forms for social enterprises. These rare examples are not yet indicative of a groundswell of interest in designing governmental financial supports for social enterprises in the US.

---

[104] I.R.C. § 145.

[105] U.S. Postal Service Publication 417, https://pe.usps.com/cpim/ftp/pubs/pub417/pub417.pdf.

[106] I.R.C. § 3309.

[107] Brody (2002).

[108] Gallagher (2002).

[109] Brody (2007); Gallagher (2002).

[110] City of Philadelphia (2023).

[111] Los Angeles County Consumer & Business Affairs (2022).

5 Potential Explanations for US/European Divergences

There are surely countless factors explaining divergences between US and European law of the third sector. While not uniform across all European jurisdictions, the prevalence of asset locked business forms for social enterprise in Europe holds significant explanatory power. This key distinction has empowered many European jurisdictions to begin to speak coherently of a third sector encompassing both nonprofits and social enterprises, to regulate this sector holistically, and to offer incentives and supports to it in a way that the US has not. Experimentation with a US form for social enterprise containing a partial or complete asset lock, whether modelled on one of the many European examples detailed in this volume or designed specifically to align with US organizational law, would likely spur developments in each of these directions.

5.1 Why Distribution-Constraints Matter

Distribution constraints matter because they enable those outside the firm to trust its commitments to social purposes.[112] A nonproft can ensure donors, grantmakers, beneficiaries, and community supporters that its profits and assets will be solely devoted to its charitable mission. Social enterprises adopting traditional US business forms, specialized ones like the benefit corporation or Delaware PBC, or obtaining B Corp status cannot offer the same assurances of their social commitment. Any and all of their profits and assets may be distributed to owners, rather than used to pursue the social missions they claim. Indeed, they cannot even point to a prioritization mandate to place their firms'social goals ahead of profit.[113] Distribution constraints—certainly when complete but even if partial—enforce a commitment, at least at some level, to prioritization of social mission over the interests of owners or others in control of a firm. These features backstops the prioritization of social mission also common in many European legal forms and designations for social enterprise.

Distribution constraints also differentiate European social enterprises that operate under them from their ordinary business counterparts. Traditional businesses too, after all, serve social goals. They employ workers, produce vital goods and services, enable communications and so much more. US law expressly authorizes corporate charity[114] and corporate social responsibility programs are ubiquitous,[115] though corporate law could do more to encourage them to consider the needs of non-investor stakeholders in their conduct of operations. For a business to be

---

[112] Hansmann (1980).

[113] Brakman Reiser and Dean (2017).

[114] Pearce (2016); Stevelman Kahn (1997).

[115] Business Roundtable (2021); Fairfax (2007); Vogel (2005).

regulated, labelled, or subsidized based upon its social mission, however, requires a greater level of commitment. By tying some or all the entity's profits or assets irrevocably to social good generation, distribution constraints secure this commitment. Without such constraints, US benefit corporations, Delaware PBCs, and B Corps may portray themselves as different, more socially conscious, more public-spirited, but it is only their intentions that hold them to their word.

5.2 Distribution Constraints and Regulation

Of course, cultural differences too likely contribute to the greater willingness of European jurisdictions to develop regulatory structures for a third sector encompassing both nonprofits and social enterprises. American political culture, especially currently, is filled with calls for small government and reducing regulation. Political actors in European jurisdictions, along with their constituencies, may well be more amenable to regulation in general than their US counterparts. A greater openness to regulation would obviously ease the path to creating and empowering social enterprise regulation.

The multilevel nature of US nonprofit regulation also adds confounding issues of federalism to the project of third sector regulation. State laws experimenting in this fashion could create a patchwork of innovation. But they could just as easily drive a race to the bottom with greenwashing firms seeking out jurisdictional homes that impose the fewest restrictions, sowing confusion and the potential for reputational harm. Europe, though, offers exemplars for successful innovation in the context of multiple levels of government regulation. The experience of Spain and its autonomous regions, many of whom enacted their own social sector laws following national adoption of the Third Social Action Sector Law, is illustrative.[116] The coverage of these laws, again, can be found to converge around entities that prioritize social mission, through both asset locking and Spain's pre-existing cooperative law.

While constructing the third sector as a legal category in the US would require surmounting strong anti-regulatory sentiments and coordinating across levels of government, the lack of US social enterprise forms or designations including distribution constraints has made these challenges even more difficult. Absent asset-locking or dividend caps, the boundaries of a broad third sector classification blur in ways that would frustrate efficient regulatory execution. Without a clear prioritization of social mission over profit for owners, accountability mandates become slippery and transparency requirements lose coherence.

[116] Fajardo-García (Chap. 10, this volume).

5.3 Distribution Constraints and Public Benefits

Perhaps most troubling, without distribution constraints to dissuade would-be greenwashers, incentives designed for social enterprises would be vulnerable to abuse. If a mere social orientation or desire to do good draws an entity into the third sector category, any business that portrays itself as a virtuous corporate citizen would seem to qualify. If tax benefits or government preferences were available for those that do, every business would be encouraged to try.

The United States can boast one of the largest nonprofit sectors in the world and one of its most charitable populations.[117] This tremendous strength has been supported by generous tax and other benefits for more than a century. Along with the exemption from federal income tax for organizations and income, gift, and estate tax deductions for supporters come access to a host of other financial benefits offered by federal, state, and local government programs. Yet there has been virtually no interest expanding these financial benefits to social enterprises. None of the specialized forms designed by dozens of state legislatures to house social enterprises contemplate access to state level tax or procurement preferences. The only benefits as yet available are isolated at the local and operate on quite a small scale.[118] The federal government's frosty reaction to the L3C—which did not even seek financial benefits for itself—only underscores the improbability of expanding tax benefits beyond the traditional nonprofit sector on the national level.

Of course, expanding tax benefits for any purpose is a difficult prospect in US at the present moment. The current era of enormous budget deficits, rising inflation, and political polarization is a particularly unlikely time for such measures to succeed. But specialized forms for social enterprises began to be available in the US over a decade ago and this type of expansion never appeared to be on the table. And for good reason. Benefit corporations, Delaware PBCs, and B Corps can all choose to use their profits to pursue social good—or to enrich their shareholders. Tax or other government financial benefits conditioned only on adopting one of these forms would be an invitation to abuse.

6 Conclusion

The prevalence of asset-constrained social enterprises is not the only important difference between the law of the third sector in Europe and that found in the United States. Many European jurisdictions have profound and longstanding experience with the cooperative form, which has deeply influenced the development of their third sector regulation. Nonprofit entities in Europe too possess important legal differences from those in the US, such as the deeper commitment to participatory

[117] Independent Sector (2022); World Giving Index (2018).

[118] City of Philadelphia (2023); Los Angeles County Consumer & Business Affairs (2022).

governance found in much of its law of associations. It is also admittedly reductive to speak of a unitary European law of the third sector, especially in a volume such as this one chronicling the tremendous variation and innovation in individual European nations.

Yet, the dichotomy between the European openness and the US disinclination to asset-locked forms and designations for social enterprises remains arresting. Asset-constrained entity choices or designations for social enterprises aid European nations that offer them to recognize, regulate, and privilege these organizations alongside nonprofit entities with similar missions. Tax benefits, procurement preferences, data collection, and countless other efforts to encourage the social economy become easier and less prone to exploitation. With nothing to constrain ordinary, profit-first firms with finance-first investors from claiming the mantle of US social enterprise forms and designations, a broad third sector regulatory or benefit scheme would be at best inapt. At worst, it would embolden greenwashing and fraud.

Identifying asset constraints as a key aspect of the European third sector can be instructive to US audiences. The many state laboratories of innovation where specialized forms for social enterprise have been developed thus far remain capable of revising their offerings to include asset-locked options. The experiences of European jurisdictions provide a surfeit of examples, and more appear on the way. Commentators and critics of US forms and designations, including this author, have also recommended improvements that would improve enforcement of their social mission commitments,[119] including asset constraints.[120]

There is no shortage of possibilities. Each would bring along with its distribution constraining mechanism the ability to enforce a commitment to prioritization of social mission. This, in turn, would both enable social enterprises to brand themselves as meaningfully different from other for-profit firms and allow regulators to treat them—and benefit them—as an authentic part of the third sector.

References

11 V.S.A. § 3001(27)
79 Del. Laws 122 (2013)
79 Del. Laws 122 (2015)
82 Del. Laws 256 (2020)
Autry CT, Hall RF (2009) The law of cooperatives. American Bar Association, Chicago, IL
B Lab, About B Corp Certification. https://www.bcorporation.net/en-us/certification
B Lab, About B Lab. https://www.bcorporation.net/en-us/movement/about-b-lab
B Lab, Homepage. https://www.bcorporation.net/en-us/
B Lab, Our European Network. https://bcorporation.eu/about/our-european-network/
B Lab US & Canada, More Than 1,700 B Corps in the U.S. & Canada., https://usca.bcorporation.net/?_ga=2.257161035.1359220607.1656366320-1446593623.1652363761

[119] *See, e.g.*, Winston (2018); Tyler et al. (2015).

[120] Brakman Reiser and Dean (2017); Murray and Hwang (2011).

Berle AA (1931) Corporate powers as powers in trust. Harv Law Rev 44:1049–1074
Berrey E (2018) Social enterprise law in action: organizational characteristics of U.S. benefit corporations. Transactions: the tenn. J Bus Law 20:21–114
Brakman Reiser D (2003) Dismembering civil society: the social cost of internally undemocratic nonprofits. Or Law Rev 82:829–900
Brakman Reiser D (2010) Charity Law's Essentials. Notre Dame. L. Rev. 86: 1–64
Brakman Reiser D (2020) Foundation regulation in our age of impact. Pittsburgh Tax Rev 17:357–385
Brakman Reiser D, Dean SA (2017) Social enterprise law: trust, public benefit, and capital markets. Oxford University Press, New York
Brakman Reiser D, Miller S (2017) Foundation law in the united states. Stärkung des Stiftungswesens: 27–45
Brody E (2002) Property-tax exemption for charities. The Urban Institute Press, Washington, D.C.
Brody E (2005) Charity governance: what's trust law got to do with it? Chi-Kent Law Rev 80:641–687
Brody E (2007) The states' growing use of a Quid-Pro-Quo rationale for the charity property-tax exemption. Exempt Org Tax Rev 56:269–288
Brody E (2008) Business activities of nonprofit organizations: legal boundary problems in non-profits & business. In: Cordes JJ, Steurle CE (eds) The Urban Institute Press, Washington D.C., pp 83–128
Business Roundtable (2021). Statement on the Purpose of a Corporation. https://system.businessroundtable.org/app/uploads/sites/5/2021/02/BRT-Statement-on-the-Purpose-of-a-Corporation-Feburary-2021-compressed.pdf
Cal. Corp. Code §§ 3500, 5410, 14601(c), 14601(d), 14601(g), 14610, 14610(a), 14610(b), 14610(c), 14620(b), 14620(c), 14620(d), 14620(f), 14623, 14630
City of Philadelphia (2023) Payments, Assistance and Taxes: Sustainable Business Tax Credit. https://www.phila.gov/services/payments-assistance-taxes/tax-credits/sustainable-business-tax-credit/
Clark WH, Vranka L (2013) White paper: the need and rationale for the benefit corporation: why it is the legal form that best addresses the needs of social entrepreneurs, investors, and, ultimately. The Public. https://drive.google.com/file/d/1QyMrBS9_6fC9guMYotZ5DElsTxuD16K9/view
Clough R (2021) Planet labs has roller-coaster debut after blank-check deal. Bloomberg. https://www.bloomberg.com/news/articles/2021-12-08/planet-labs-has-roller-coaster-debut-after-blank-check-deal
Colombo JD (2002) Commercial activity and charitable tax exemption. William Mary Law Rev 44:487–567
Colombo JD (2007) Reforming internal revenue code provisions on commercial activities by charities. Fordham Law Rev 76:667–691
Cooney K, Koushyar J, Lee M, Murray JH (2014) Benefit corporation and L3C adoption: a survey. Stanford Social Innovation Review. http://ssir.org/articles/entry/benefit_corporation_and_l3c_adoption_a_survey
de León R (2021) Coursera Closes Up 36%, Topping $5.9 Billion Market Cap in Wall Street Debut. CNBC. https://www.cnbc.com/2021/03/31/coursera-ipo-cour-begins-trading-on-the-nyse.html
Del. Code Ann. Tit. 6, §§ 18-1201 to –1208 (2018), ? 8 §§ 361-68, 362(a), 362(b), 366(c) (2013)
Del. Gen. Corp. Law §101(b)
Delaware Division of Corporations (2020) 2020 Annual Report Statistics. https://corpfiles.delaware.gov/Annual-Reports/Division-of-Corporations-2020-Annual-Report.pdf
Dodd EM (1932) For whom are corporate managers trustees? Harv Law Rev 45:1145–1163
eBay Domestic Holdings, Inc. v. Newmark, 16 A.3d 1, 34 (Del. Ch. 2010)
Elhauge E (2005) Sacrificing corporate profits in the public interest. N Y Univ Law Rev 80:733–869
European Commission (2021) Social Economy Action Plan (2021). https://ec.europa.eu/social/main.jsp?catId=1537&langId=en

ExxonMobil, Press Release (2021) ExxonMobil updates preliminary results on election of directors. https://corporate.exxonmobil.com/News/Newsroom/News-releases/2021/0602_ExxonMobil-updates-preliminary-results-on-election-of-directors
Fairfax LM (2002) Doing well while doing good: reassessing the scope of directors' fiduciary obligations in for-profit corporations with non-shareholder beneficiaries. Wash Lee Law Rev 59:409–474
Fairfax LM (2007) Easier said than done? A corporate law theory for actualizing social responsibility rhetoric. Fla Law Rev 59:771–828
Fremont-Smith MR (2004) Governing nonprofit organizations. Belknap Press of Harvard University Press, Cambridge, MA
Friedman M (1970) The social responsibility of business is to increase its profits. New York Times Magazine 33
Gallagher J (2002) The legal structure of property-tax exemption. In: Brody E (ed) Property-tax exemption for charities. The Urban Institute Press, Washington D.C.
Gidron B (2010) In: Anheier HK, Toepler S (eds) "Third Sector" in international encyclopedia of civil society. Springer, New York, pp 1550–1553. https://doi.org/10.1007/978-0-387-93996-4_48
Grunin Center for Law and Social Entrepreneurship at NYU School of Law. Social Enterprise Law Tracker, https://socentlawtracker.org/#/map
Hansmann HB (1980) The role of nonprofit enterprise. Yale Law J 89:835–901
Harvard Law School Forum on Corporate Governance. Littenberg MR, Oldshue EJ, Pifer BN (2020) Delaware Public Benefit Corporations – Recent Developments. https://corpgov.law.harvard.edu/2020/08/31/delaware-public-benefit-corporations-recent-developments/
I.R.C. §§ 145, 170(b), 170(c), 170(c)(2), 501(c)(3), 509, 511, 511(b), 513(a), 2055, 2522, 3309, 4940, 4940(a), 4941, 4943-45, 4958, 6104
Independent Sector (2022) The Charitable Sector. https://independentsector.org/about/the-charitable-sector/#:~:text=The%20nonprofit%20sector%20%E2%80%93%2010%20percent,U.S.%2C%20behind%20retail%20and%20manufacturing
Intersector Partners (2022) What is an L3C? https://www.intersectorl3c.com/l3c
Kahn FS (1997) Pandora's box: managerial discretion and the problem of corporate philanthropy. UCLA Law Rev 44:579–676
Levy A (2021) Synthetic biology company Zymergen Plunges 68% after saying product revenue will be "Immaterial" in 2022, Removing CEO. CNBC. https://www.cnbc.com/2021/08/03/zymergen-zy-plunges-68percent-on-forecast-for-immaterial-revenue-in-2022.html
Los Angeles County Consumer & Business Affairs (2022). https://dcba.lacounty.gov/social-enterprise/
Littenberg MR (2020) Delaware Public Benefit Corporations—Recent Developments. Harvard Law School Forum on Corporate Governance. https://corpgov.law.harvard.edu/2020/08/31/delaware-public-benefit-corporations-recentdevelopments/
Madoff R (2020) The five percent fig leaf. Pittsburgh Tax Rev 17:341–355
McDonnell B (2014) Committing to do good and doing well: fiduciary duty in benefit corporations. Fordham J Corp Finance Law 20:19–72
McDonnell B (2016) Benefit corporations and strategic action fields (or the existential failing of delaware). Seattle Univ Law Rev 39:263–290
Md. Code Ann., Corps. & Ass'ns §§ 11–4A–1201 to 11–4A–1208, 11–1–502, 5–6C–03 (2013)
Minn. Stat. § 304A.301 (2015)
Model Benefit Corporation Legislation §§ 301(c), 305
Murray JH (2015) An early report on benefit reports. West Virginia Law Rev 118:25–57
Murray JH (2016) The social enterprise law market. Maryland Law Rev 75:541–589
Murray JH, Hwang E (2011) Purpose with profit: governance, enforcement, capital-raising and capital-locking in low profit limited liability companies. Univ Miami Law Rev 66:1–52
N.Y. Bus. Corp. L. §§ 1702(b), 1702(d), 1702(g), 1705, 1706(a), 1706(b), 1706(c), 1707(a)(1), 1707(a)(2), 1707(a)(3), 1708, 1708(d)

Ore. Rev. Stat. §§ 60.750 to.770 (2014)
Pearce JA (2016) The rights of shareholders in authorizing corporate philanthropy. Vill Law Rev 60:251–282
Phelan ME (2000) Nonprofit enterprises: corporations, trusts and associations. West Group, Minneapolis, MN § 1:03
Philanthropic Facilitation Act, H.R. 2832, 113th Cong. (2013)
Philanthropic Facilitation Act, H.R. 3420, 112th Cong. (2011)
Plerhoples AE (2014) Delaware public benefit corporations 90 days out: who's opting in? U.C. Davis Law Rev 14:247–280
Powell J (2021) AppHarvest's SPAC Forecasts Go Splat. Financial Times. https://www.ft.com/content/52b775ce-54bc-4111-85b9-e3c3f29c3ebf
Revised Model Nonprofit Corp. Act (1987) §§ 3.01(a), 3.02(16-d), 8.01(b) http://www.muridae.com/nporegulation/documents/model_npo_corp_act.html
Revised Uniform Partnership Act (1997) §101(6)
Revlon Inc. v. MacAndrews & Forbes Holdings, Inc., 506 A.2d 173, 182 (Del. 1986)
Ribstein LE, Keatinge RR (2021) Ribstein & Keatinge on Limited Liability Companies § 4.13 Thomson Reuters, Eagan, MN
Stone BD (2021) Public benefit corporations are going public. Natl Law Rev. https://www.natlawreview.com/article/public-benefit-corporations-are-going-public
Stout LA (2012) The shareholder value myth: how putting shareholders first harms investors, corporations, and the public. Berrett-Koehler, Oakland, CA
Strine L (2012) Our continuing struggle with the idea that for-profit corporations seek profit. Wake Forest Law Rev 47:135–172
Strine L (2015) The dangers of Denial: the need for a clear-eyed understanding of the power and accountability structure established by the delaware general corporation law. Wake Forest Law Rev 50:761–801
Sustainable Development Acquisition I Corp. (2022). https://www.waterfoodenergyspac.com/
Treas. Reg. § 1.501(c)(3)-1(e)(1) (emphasis added)
Tyler J (2010) Negating the legal problem of having "two masters": a framework for L3C fiduciary duties and accountability. Vermont Law Rev 35:117–161
Tyler J, Absher E, Garman K & Luppino A (2015) Producing better mileage: advancing the design and usefulness of hybrid vehicles for social business ventures. Quinnipiac Law Rev 33:235–337
Uniform Trust Code §§ 404, 703 (2020)
U.S. Postal Service Publication 417 (2017). https://pe.usps.com/cpim/ftp/pubs/pub417/pub417.pdf
UK Office of the Regulator of Community Interest Companies (2016) Information and Guidance Notes Chapter Six: The Asset Lock. https://assets.publishing.service.gov.uk/government/uploads/system/uploads/attachment_data/file/605418/14-1089-community-interest-companies-chapter-6-the-asset-lock.pdf
Verheyden M (2018) Public reporting by benefit corporations: importance, compliance, and recommendations. Hast Bus Law J 14:37–106
Vogel D (2005) The market for virtue: the potential and limits of corporate social responsibility. Brookings Institution Press, Washington, D.C.
Wash. Rev. Code § 23B.25.005 et seq. (2013)
Wells H (2002) The cycles of corporate social responsibility: an historical retrospective for the twenty-first century. Univ Kansas Law Rev 51:77–140
Westaway K (2021) The First Public Benefit Corporation SPAC. Forbes. https://www.forbes.com/sites/kylewestaway/2021/02/11/the-first-public-benefit-corporation-spac/?sh=1bb5fff2518d
Winston E (2018) Benefit corporations and the separation of benefit and control. Cardozo Law Rev 39:1783–1841
World Giving Index 2018. CAF World Giving Index 2018. www.cafonline.org/docs/default-source/about-us-publications/caf_wgi2018_report_webnopw_2379a_261018.pdf)

MIX
Papier aus verantwortungsvollen Quellen
Paper from responsible sources
FSC® C105338

If you have any concerns about our products,
you can contact us on
ProductSafety@springernature.com

In case Publisher is established outside the EU,
the EU authorized representative is:
Springer Nature Customer Service Center GmbH
Europaplatz 3, 69115 Heidelberg, Germany

Printed by Libri Plureos GmbH
in Hamburg, Germany